SEPARATE PEOPLES, ONE LAND

SEPARATE PEOPLES,

ONE LAND

The Minds
of Cherokees,
Blacks, and Whites
on the
Tennessee Frontier

CYNTHIA CUMFER

The University of
North Carolina Press
Chapel Hill

© 2007 The University of North Carolina Press
All rights reserved
Designed by Jacquline Johnson
Set in Minion
by Keystone Typesetting, Inc.
Manufactured in the United States of America

The paper in this book meets the guidelines for
permanence and durability of the Committee on
Production Guidelines for Book Longevity of the
Council on Library Resources.

Library of Congress Cataloging-in-Publication Data
Cumfer, Cynthia.
Separate peoples, one land : the minds of Cherokees, Blacks, and Whites on the Tennessee frontier /
Cynthia Cumfer.
p. cm.
Includes bibliographical references and index.
ISBN 978-0-8078-3151-9 (cloth: alk. paper)
ISBN 978-0-8078-5844-8 (pbk.: alk. paper)
1. Tennessee—Race relations—History—18th century. 2. Tennessee—Race relations—History—19th
century. 3. Frontier and pioneer life—Tennessee. 4. Acculturation—Tennessee—History.
5. Nationalism—Tennessee—History. 6. Cherokee Indians—Tennessee—History. 7. Slaves—
Tennessee—History. 8. Free African Americans—Tennessee—History. 9. Whites—Tennessee—
History. 10. European Americans—Tennessee—History. I. Title.
F445.A1C86 2007
305.8009768′09033—dc22
2007015298

Portions of this work appeared earlier,
in somewhat different form, as
"Local Origins of National Indian Policy:
Cherokee and Tennessean Ideas about
Sovereignty and Nationhood, 1790–1811,"
Journal of the Early Republic 23 (Spring 2003):
21–46, © 2003 Society for Historians of the
Early Republic, and are reprinted here with
permission of the Universiy of Pennsylvania Press.

cloth   11 10 09 08 07   5 4 3 2 1
paper   11 10 09 08 07   5 4 3 2 1

To
VALERIE LYON

CONTENTS

ILLUSTRATION AND MAPS

ACKNOWLEDGMENTS

The Buddhist philosopher Thich Nhat Hanh illustrates the interdependent nature of reality by considering the table. The table, he explains, can only exist because the entire non-table world—the forest, the carpenter, the carpenter's ancestors, the iron ore of the nails, the sun and rain, and all other aspects of the universe—made it possible. He could have been talking about the production of a book. It is a pleasure to be able to thank some of the people who have been most instrumental in creating this book.

One true reward I reaped in writing this book has been the discovery of how helpful the academic community can be. Joyce Appleby, Stephen Aron, and Andrew Cayton read entire drafts of this manuscript and offered invaluable comments and wonderful support. They are the sun and rain for this book. Many other scholars read parts of this manuscript, directed me to sources, or contributed ideas. For these courtesies I thank Eric Altice, Robert Baker, Tom Belt, Greg Beyrer, Ruth Bloch, Seth Cotlar, Ellen DuBois, Laura Edwards, Lisa Ford, Chris Gantner, Tim Garrison, Tom Hatley, Lanita Jacobs-Huey, Tony Iaccarino, Kenneth Karst, Naomi Lamoreaux, Muriel McClendon, Sandy Moats, Eric Monkkonen, Melissa Meyers, David Nichols, Richard Nisbett, Nathaniel Sheidley, Nancy Shoemaker, Wendy St. Jean, Brenda Stevenson, Amy Sturgis, Greg Vanderbilt, and Kariann Yokota. Dan Opatoshu, I appreciate the timely advice on Eighty Ways to Cure Writer's Block. Reed College offered me the opportunity to deepen my thinking by teaching courses in my field. I also benefited greatly from comments on my conference papers at the American Historical Association, the Organization of American Historians, the Western Historical Association, the Society for Historians of the Early American Republic, and the American Society of Legal Historians. For their generous financial support, I am indebted to the Reed College Professors' Summer Research Fund, the National Society Daughters of Colonial Wars, and the Institute for Humane Studies.

My journey into Tennessee history brought me to some truly wonderful archivists and librarians. I spent months bothering the saints at the Tennessee

State Library and Archives, a very special facility. A big thank you to Marilyn Hughes, Susan Gordon, Julia Rather, little Justice (who I never met but heard a lot about), Delmar Dorr, Darla Brock, Vince McGrath, Karina McDaniel, and the rest of the staff who made my time in Nashville so productive and even fun. I want to thank the archivists and librarians at the Chattanooga/Hamilton County Library, the Davidson County Archives, the Huntington Library, the Knox County Archives, the Library of Congress, the McClung Library, the National Archives, the Newberry Library, the Southern Baptist Historical Library and Archives, the Sumner County Archives, the University of California at Los Angeles, the University of Tennessee Special Collections, the White County Archives, and the Wilson County Archives. Thank you also to the librarian at Tennessee Tech in Cookeville, Tennessee. I didn't find any material useful to my research, but I loved the story about white patrons searching for Cherokee ancestors ("but not just any Cherokee, they want Cherokee chiefs").

I gratefully acknowledge the kindness of William Dollarhide and William Thorndale for their kind permission to adapt their map of Tennessee in 1810 published in *Map Guide to the U.S. Federal Census, 1790–1920* (1987). Portions of chapters 2 and 3 appeared originally in the *Journal of the Early Republic* and are included here with permission of the publisher. I also want to thank Mark Simpson-Vos and Ron Maner, my terrific editors at the University of North Carolina Press.

I have had tremendous support from my family and friends in undertaking this project. For their patience and attention to the ramblings of a preoccupied scholar, as well as many favors along the way, I thank my longtime friends Kathleen Herron, Kay Sohl, Lynn Travis, and Barbara Willer. My biggest debt is to my family. A special thanks to my father, Don Cumfer, for a large lump of intellectual curiosity and the self-confidence to pursue it, and to my mother, Wincy Cumfer, for amazing organizational skills, a sense of humor to keep the trip lively, and the heart to look for the human in old records. To my goddaughter, Kiera Bethwiller, kudos for asking if historians made more money than lawyers, for tolerating my absences, and for your own terrific brand of humor. To my partner, Valerie Lyon, my most heartfelt thank you for urging me on; for picking up the pieces I dropped along the way; for over 100 trips to the airport; for explaining, when the Oxford English Dictionary could not, what John Sevier meant by "bilins," and for your love.

NOTE ON CHEROKEE NAMES

I use Cherokee names where known in the text. Many of the sources use the anglicized names, so I provide them here for convenience. Many Cherokee people had more than one Cherokee or English name during their lives. To avoid confusion, I use only one name although I list here some of the more commonly known second names. In cases where the Cherokee name was virtually always used, I do not list it here. In some places in the text, I use the English name because I do not know the Cherokee name.

Atawgwatihih	The Glass
Attakullakulla	Little Carpenter
Chulcoah	Creek Linguister, The Boot
Chuquilatague	Doublehead
Enola	Black Fox
Iyahuwagiatsutsa	Pumpkin Boy
Kanorcortuker	Standing Turkey
Kenneteag	Little Turkey
Kunoskeskie	John Watts
Nan-ye-hi	Nancy Ward
Nentooyah	Bloody Fellow
Oconostota	Great Warrior
Ocunna	The Badger
Onitositah (also, Kay etaeh)	Old Tassel, Corn Tassel
Ookoousdi	Little Owl
Oostope'teh	Mankiller from Highwassee
Oskuah	Abraham
Ostenaco	Judd's Friend
Savanukeh	The Raven
Scolacutta	Hanging Maw
Selukuki Wohellengh	Turtle at Home

Sequuanysho	John Walker
Talotiskee	Nettle Carrier
Toowayelloh	Bold Hunter
Tsi-yugunsini (also, Chincanacina)	Dragging Canoe
Tuskegateehee	Longfellow
Uwenahi	Dick Justice

While I was engaged in this project, I was introduced to a chemist who inquired politely about the subject of my research. I gave him the ten-second version—that I was working on an intellectual history of Tennessee from 1768 through 1810. He looked surprised and said, "I didn't know they had an intellectual history." "Well," I answered, "they were people. Everybody thinks."

Over the past two decades, scholars have addressed in part the sentiments my chemist acquaintance expressed. Intellectual historians of the backcountry and of the early West have studied rebellions, republican political ideas and culture, and attitudes about race and ethnicity. Little else, though, is known about the minds of the trans-Appalachian black and white men and women in the early republic, yet the transmontane West was the site of the development of ideas about diplomatic relationships with indigenous peoples, property rights and allocations, and civilization that gained international currency.[1] Although the Cherokees are an important exception, most scholars who are concerned with the cognitive worlds of Native Americans in the colonial and early national period study the northern Indians.[2] Very few writers examine the mental worlds of each of the major groups that interacted in a borderland setting. In this book, I explore both the articulated ideas and the cultural logic of the Cherokee, black, and white peoples who met in the eastern and middle Tennessee regions from the time of permanent white settlement in 1768 until 1810. These groups came together because of two massive movements of people initiated by Europeans—settlers seeking land as part of the great land rush of 1650 to 1900 and slaves exported from Africa to cultivate the lands appropriated during colonization. I chose this time because I am interested in the ideas generated in frontier regions during and in the generation after the American Revolution. By 1810, the Cherokees had unified against further land cessions, heralding a realignment in Cherokee and settler relations, and the population explosion in the African American and Euro-American communities closed the frontier in most of eastern and middle Tennessee. I selected this venue because Tennessee has not received the attention from historians that it deserves.

Tennessee is well positioned for study as a frontier meeting site for indigenous peoples, slaves, and Euro-American land hunters, yet it occupies a somewhat obscure place in American history. During the Civil War, this border state sided with the Confederacy but split violently over secession. Conquered early by Grant, it was spared the dramatic battle scenes that entrenched Georgia, South Carolina, and Virginia in southern mythology. This anonymity is particularly unfortunate for students of the early national period. Although the removal of the southeastern indigenous peoples is often associated with Georgia, the Tennessee region was the northern home to many Cherokees who were removed in the 1830s under the aegis of Tennessean Andrew Jackson. The thinking developed in Tennessee during the earlier period informed local Cherokee leaders Sequoyah, the creator of the Cherokee syllabary, and John Ross, principal chief of the Cherokees after the adoption of their Constitution in 1828 and a strong opponent of removal. Meanwhile, Tennessee served as a gateway to the West and a source of ideas for expansionist-minded emigrants. Many easterners poured through the Cumberland Gap, lived in Tennessee, then moved on to Mississippi, Missouri, Texas, and other points west. William C. C. Claiborne, governor of the Mississippi Territory, began his political career in the post-Revolutionary years in Tennessee, as did Thomas Hart Benton, later senator from Missouri. Sam Houston was a congressman and governor of Tennessee before he was elected president of Texas. Tennessee's mediating location may explain why it alone among southern states nurtured three future presidents—the expansionists Andrew Jackson and James Polk, and the populist Andrew Johnson— during the early republic and antebellum years.[3]

By focusing on Tennessee during this turbulent period, I can explore in depth the ideologies of the three communities brought together by the land rush and how contact and revolutionary and postcolonial ideas transformed their concepts and assumptions. I argue that the two sovereign peoples that met in the Tennessee region from 1768 through 1810 brought dissimilar intellectual approaches to diplomacy and each of the three communities had different ideologies about social organization.[4] The Cherokees structured international relations and domestic arrangements based on ideas about balance and harmony. White settlers crafted their foreign and internal affairs by relying on concepts about civilization. A people without sovereignty, African Americans did not participate in diplomacy but most arrived with an understanding of social arrangements structured around paternalism. The movement by settlers into the Tennessee region in violation of the British Proclamation of 1763 presaged the American Revolution in which thirteen of the British colonies rejected their colonial status. The forces unleashed by these changes and others required the Cherokees and land hunters to reassess their beliefs and cultural logic about how to make foreign connections and how to reconcile localism with authority in the national political body. All three groups reenvisioned social, governmental, and material relations.

Now colonizers, the westering people became embroiled in what ultimately became an expansionist nationalization project—one in which settlers gradually accepted federal authority but defined a strong state role in the new American nation that was growing beyond its thirteen founding states. Tennesseans constructed this aggressive civilized nationalism by inflecting European notions about civilization as a progressive stage of societal development with local beliefs that stressed earned rather than inherited or natural entitlements, consent in communal and political affairs, social compacts, and private property rights. Because this middle-ground contact occurred on Cherokee territory, the Cherokees responded by engaging in efforts to retain ancestral lands and by participating more actively in the international economy. Like the settlers, the Cherokees acceded to a federal relationship but, rather than seek incorporation into a federal system with limited powers, they desired federal protection while retaining their sovereignty. They created a defensive nationalization project—one that empowered a National Council in conjunction with the older chiefs and the Women's Council, rather than local chiefs who consulted all the people, to act for the Cherokee people in order to protect Cherokee lands and sovereignty. This reconceptualization of the national political sphere relied on a philosophy of balance and harmony that invoked older Cherokee values about communal ownership of land, a political role for women, and consensus decision making and newer ideas about the incorporation of outsiders into Cherokee society, representative democracy, and the maintenance of international equilibrium through economic independence. Excluded from the nationalization process, slaves revived and modified African and American ideas about community and patronage to maneuver in this volatile terrain. Free blacks tied norms about sponsorship to beliefs about entitlement, fashioning an African American concept of freedom that was both individual and communal.

The study of frontier regions offers intellectual and cultural historians a special opportunity to investigate the creation and transformation of ideologies. Ideas and societal premises are particularly likely to be revealed in a setting in which diverse peoples come together for the first time. Cultural dissonance induces participants to articulate their thinking and stimulates contrasts in behavior that point to implicit cultural norms. Sustained contact between people of different cultures also creates a site of difference where values are negotiated, and it inevitably produces changes in the cognitive worlds of those in each society.[5] Scholars from a variety of fields—frontier and western, Native American, transatlantic, postcolonial, and intellectual and cultural history—contribute to the study of ideologies in the potent cauldron of borderland encounters.

Focusing on the interactions between various peoples who come together on a common ground, frontier and western historians have developed several interpretive frameworks to understand the meeting of cultures that takes place in borderland locations. Frederick Jackson Turner's influential 1893 thesis located in the frontier setting important impulses feeding democracy, an interpretation that nurtured a picture of American exceptionalism. He regarded American history as a regenerative process—the advance of the frontier westward in repetitive stages by white men bringing civilization with an American accent. Herbert Bolton in the early twentieth century recast the frontier interactions in Florida and along the Mexican boundary as a border-lands experience—an analysis that recognized the importance of the Spanish to the history of the United States—although Turner's thesis remained more influential. In the 1980s, many frontier and western historians reinterpreted the West as a meeting place for diverse cultures. Some reassessed their under-standing of what constituted the West by recognizing the trans-Appalachian region in the early republic as the West. The best work now treats the West as both a place and a process, integrating the histories of the inhabitants at contact with westering peoples while recognizing the dynamics involved in European colonialism and American expansionism.[6]

Virtually all borderland meetings in the United States involved interac-tions between Native Americans and newcomers. Early scholars narrated an account in which westering peoples believed in the superiority of Anglo-Saxon civilization, classified Native Americans as savages, and sought to exterminate them or expected their demise with the advance of civilization. Recent scholarship centers on ethnic and racial identities and cultural inter-mingling and has explored the diverse experiences of Spanish, French, Brit-ish, and American interactions with indigenous peoples.[7] Less interrogated has been the related but distinct question of how local white frontier people constructed their relationship to their indigenous neighbors as a polity rather than how they conceived of them racially.[8] Scholars have also paid virtually no attention to how settlers' ideas about indigenous people and about civilization informed the newcomers' thinking about their own communities, government, and economic relations.

Responding to historians who wrote about contact primarily from the European or American viewpoint, Native American historians have pressed for interpretations of the encounter between Europeans and Americans and indigenous peoples that include Native American perspectives.[9] One area of study benefiting from this reassessment is the field of international relations. Challenging older accounts that assumed a quick conquest, writers have produced some excellent studies on the ideas and cultural practices fashioned by indigenous peoples in order to conduct diplomacy. Most describe a philosophy of international affairs in which the first peoples constructed a clan-like kinship with each other and with Europeans through carefully observed protocols.[10] Based largely on studies of peoples north of the Ohio River, these scholars generally concur that the expansion of settlement by Americans after the Revolution upset the middle ground that permitted Native Americans and Europeans to realize their goals through a process of creative misunderstandings negotiated by relatively equal parties. Historians conclude that the numerically and technologically superior whites largely imposed their own agendas onto these native populations after 1790.[11] The middle-ground thesis has great explanatory power but some limitations. Middle-ground contacts did not really take place in geographical areas between Native American and European territories but occurred on Native American grounds. This meant that Native American populations, environments, economies, and social and political structures were impacted by contact far more intensely than were European and American environments and societies.[12]

While a growing number of studies explore the logic of traditional Native American diplomacy, important areas remain largely unexamined. Very little work has been done on the ways that American contact transformed the conceptual foundation of customary Indian practices and on the impact that indigenous ideas had on American thought about the relationship between the parties.[13] Historians have credited native women who married government officials and traders with a diplomatic role, but writers generally neglect the more direct involvement of women and their ideas in constituting diplomatic kinships. With the exception of important research on nativist movements, the authors tend to assume a uniformity of tribal views and neglect dissenting voices within the tribes about how to fashion and respond to the westering "other."[14]

As frontier, western, and Native American historians reassessed their terrain and its inhabitants, historians of immigration, slavery, and the Revolutionary period recast the framework for their fields by locating their subjects in a transatlantic world, a perspective that highlights the significance of European colonialism to the study of early America.[15] Frontier and Native American historians have joined this effort, recognizing that the cis-Mississippi frontier was deeply enmeshed with Europe. These writers show how European traders and diplomats intermarried and traded with the various native peoples in the Midwest region. A few frontier and slavery scholars have studied the role of African slavery in the West during this period. Most studies that place the West in the transatlantic world are economic or social histories, not studies of the ideologies of western inhabitants.[16] More recently, scholars have expanded the reach of frontier studies by locating them in an international context, studying similarities and variations during colonizing processes around the world. These studies challenge the Turnerian notion of American exceptionalism by showing the commonalities among Neo-European settler colonies in their attitudes and policies toward native people, land acquisition, expansionism, and market relations. Transnational comparisons also draw our attention to the important intellectual role that concepts about civilization played in the colonizing enterprise, as European imperialists contended that colonization benefited indigenous people in many settings around the world because it civilized them.[17]

In a related area of study, historians have articulated the dual position of the United States as a confederation of colonies that became a colonizer, directing attention to postcolonial theory. Like scholars who compare frontier experiences during colonization across national boundaries, many postcolonial theorists describe common themes of postcolonial societies but are more likely than comparative frontier historians to emphasize the importance of local processes and locally imagined national identities. These scholars stress that an identity like "American-ness" is constantly negotiated. Postcolonialists have also theorized beyond the notions of assimilation and agency utilized by western and Native American historians to articulate the concept of hybridity, the in-between spaces produced in the articulation of cultural differences in which people may utilize elements of both societies to create new values and practices. Some postcolonialists describe the reinvention of cultural materials that can occur in the meeting of cultures as transculturation. Others theorize about retraditionalization, a framing that encourages historians to notice traditional values that survive cultural mixing or that signal disentanglement from rather than engagement with colonial structures. Although postcolonialists developed the classifications of hybridity, transculturation, and retraditionalization, these constructions are usefully applied to cultural contact in colonizing as well as postcolonial settings. Early American historians have only recently begun the work of placing the early republic in a postcolonial context and have devoted very little attention to western regions.[18]

Scholars studying the cultural premises and ideas of groups that meet in frontier encounters must articulate the tacit logic as well as the spoken ideas of the borderland inhabitants. To do so, they draw on insights that cultural historians have brought to intellectual history.[19] The strongest cross-disciplinary influences on intellectual history came from theorists in linguistics and in cultural anthropology. Studies in linguistics disclose the polysemic nature of texts—the realization that texts contain multiple potential meanings and tensions. A related insight has been the poststructuralist insistence that readers import their own cultural framework onto their interpretation of a text. Consequently, historians cannot assume that an author conveys an idea in a communication that is passively received by the reader. An important unintended consequence of the study of ideologies has been the recognition of unintended consequences, as producers of ideas do not always anticipate correctly the outcomes and interpretations of their theories.[20]

Meanwhile, borrowing from cultural anthropologists, the scholars-formerly-known-as-intellectual-historians[21] have recognized that each human society embeds its cognitive universe in cultural practices. By cracking the cultural code, scholars can uncover the meanings that inform these mental worlds. Because cultural logic is often unconscious or only partly understood, writers using this approach to cultural studies rely heavily on social history to study behavior, which offers clues to the tacit premises that undergird human actions. This microstudy of culture offers a view of the epistemological process at its source. By studying knowledge as it is produced and inscribed, historians view the mutually reinforcing and transforming dynamics of historical events and the creation of beliefs.[22] All of this complexity makes cultural history a messy business.

My study of Tennessee embraces the synthetic approach of frontier and western historians by viewing Tennessee as a place inhabited by Native Americans while recognizing the expansionist ideology of the white settlers and the marginalized position of slaves. In presenting the Cherokee perspective, I discuss the Cherokee understanding of diplomacy, including the critical ideas advanced by women and dissenters that transformed the tenets of international kinships. I further describe the ways in which Cherokee ideas about community, politics, and the economy changed as a defensive response to colonizing contact, resulting in the creation of a nation. By examining the constructions by local whites about their own and Cherokee polities, I uncover a critical linkage between the white imagination of a civilized American nationhood and the degradation of Cherokee sovereignty, as settlers defined an expansionist nationalism. I then explore how the philosophical underpinnings of the logic about savagery and civilization that supported the white views of indigenous peoples and nationhood also informed the settlers' perceptions of their own society, government, and material relations. My study is strongly informed by the transatlantic viewpoint—the Cherokees used their ties to the international economy to rework their understanding of balance, African Americans relied on African ideas about patronage, and white westering people drew on a variety of European intellectual traditions to interpret their frontier experiences. I point to the similarities and differences between the ideas and logic of the borderland inhabitants of Tennessee and those of frontier residents in other countries and argue that local land hunters and first peoples actively shaped ideologies that informed the ideas and policies of later British settler colonies in India, South Africa, Australia, New Zealand, and Canada. The postcolonial understanding of the United States as a group of colonies in the process of becoming an expansionist colonizer explains in part the instability of the frontier understanding of nationhood; offers the concepts of hybridity, transculturation, and retraditionalization for understanding the Cherokees' reinvention of their society in response to American efforts at colonization; and locates the settlers and the United States as early advocates using the doctrine of civilization to justify the colonization of the first peoples.

The Tennessee region has been inhabited by humans for more than ten thousand years. The Overhill Cherokees probably moved across the Appalachian Mountains into the Tennessee Valley in the seventeenth century, leaving the Cherokees of the Carolinas in order to settle in territory available because of the breakup of the Mississippian chiefdoms. The Overhill Cherokees became the primary inhabitants of the Tennessee Valley region, with some Chickasaws, with whom the Cherokees clashed at times, residing in the west. The Creeks lived to the southwest of the Cherokee lands and were enemies of the Cherokees until 1755. Smaller groups of indigenous peoples lived or hunted in the region.[23]

During the period from the seventeenth until the twentieth century, Europe colonized much of the world. The Spanish, Portuguese, Dutch, Russian, and later the French governments exercised considerable bureaucratic control over land distribution in their colonies, generally conveying large grants to favored proprietors. Smaller settlers challenged these systems but with less success than in the more permissive British structure. British settlement colonies appropriated at least 1.5 to 2 billion acres of the world's most arable lands in the Americas, South Africa, Australia, and New Zealand. While the Crown bestowed large grants to important men, England did not exercise a strong hand over the settlement of its colonies, allowing servants and poorer land hunters an opportunity to acquire property.[24]

A number of England's eighteenth-century colonies were located on the Atlantic seaboard of the Americas, with western boundaries stretching to the sea, while France established colonies and traded along the Mississippi River and competed with the Spanish in the Gulf region. The area that is currently Tennessee was, to the British, part of the western lands of their North Carolina colony. During the early eighteenth century, traders from a variety of European countries—primarily England, Scotland, and France—and from the British American colonies moved into the Overhill villages. In 1768 the first permanent white settlers—many of them Scottish, Irish, English, and German—crossed the Appalachians with their slaves in violation of the British Proclamation of 1763 that prohibited settlement west of the mountains. They established farms on Cherokee lands that they thought were part of Virginia's grant. Far removed from Virginia, they largely governed themselves. The Cherokees responded ambivalently, welcoming the trade but objecting to hunting and the growing encroachment on Cherokee territory. In 1775 Richard Henderson, a North Carolina judge and speculator, held a treaty in his private capacity at which he claimed to purchase about one-half of the Cherokee hunting grounds in much of present-day Kentucky and northern Tennessee. The Cherokees asserted that they had been defrauded.

With the American Revolution in 1776, the former colonies became independent states and the frontier people discovered that they were in North Carolina's claim. As the colonies separated from Great Britain, Tsi-yugunsini and a group of angry warriors attacked the settlements against the wishes of many of the chiefs and women, who looked to the British for a resolution to the problem. Militias from Virginia, North and South Carolina, and Georgia responded by destroying many of the Cherokee towns. At the peace conference in July 1777, North Carolina commissioners pressured the chiefs attending the talks to cede land to North Carolina without compensation, a concession that resulted in increased migration of settlers and hostilities between the parties. Native American conflicts were not the only violence. Patriots excluded loyalists, some of whom moved to Cherokee villages, and confiscated their slaves. During the 1780s, the Upper Towns, closest to the settlers, struggled to maintain peace, to trade with the westering people, and to protect their lands from encroachers. The Cherokee dissenters, who came to be known as Chickamaugans, eventually separated from the Upper Towns and maintained separate villages, first along Chickamauga Creek and later further south and west in an area called the Lower Towns. They established significant ties with Native Americans in the Ohio region and in the Southeast. Allied at times with the Creeks, the Chickamaugans attacked the settlements but focused much of their energies on profitable participation in the international economy.

In 1780 land hunters led by John Donelson followed the Tennessee River to middle Tennessee about 150 miles west of the original towns and established a second group of settlements on Cherokee hunting grounds in the Cumberland area, centered around what is now Nashville. The Chickamaugans mounted frequent assaults on these farms. The next year, General Nathanael Greene, commander of the Continental army in the South, made peace with the Upper Town Cherokees but the confederated government did not have the ability to enforce the treaty. At the end of the Revolution in 1783, North Carolina unilaterally issued land grants on Upper Town lands. Dissatisfied that North Carolina did not open more land offices, many of the eastern settlers, led by prominent farmer, speculator, and militia leader John Sevier, separated from North Carolina and established the new state of Franklin in late 1784. Opposed by North Carolina, the Franklinites engaged in occasional armed battles with the antistate faction from 1786 to 1788, after which the state of Franklin collapsed. The United States treated a second time with the Cherokees at Hopewell, South Carolina, in 1785, but the treaty was protested by North Carolina and ignored by the settlers, creating more hostilities. In 1788 the Upper and Lower Towns united in war when Sevier's militia massacred several of the Upper Town peace chiefs under a flag of truce. Congress. interceded to calm tensions. During this period, some of the settlers, including Sevier and recent immigrant Andrew Jackson, flirted with offering allegiance to Spain, which then controlled New Orleans and the Mississippi River, in order to secure a market for their goods and to gain assistance against the Indians.

North Carolina ceded its lands in the Tennessee region to the United States in 1789, and Congress organized the region into the Southwest Territory in 1790. Under the Indian policy of the new United States, the federal government sought to enter into treaties with Native Americans to obtain peace and land cessions and to encourage Indians to become civilized. At that time, the Cherokee population numbered about 10,000, the white population about 32,000 and the black inhabitants about 3,800, most of whom were enslaved. The United States and the Cherokees signed a treaty at Holston in 1791, but because many Cherokees contested the treaty terms claimed by the United States, hostilities continued until 1794. With federal control, new immigrants came from states all along the Atlantic seaboard. The tremendous white population expansion after 1790 and the defeat of their northern Indian allies in 1794 persuaded the Chickamaugans to agree to a permanent peace. By 1795, when the Pinckney Treaty secured the right to navigate the Mississippi, there were almost 67,000 white and 10,500 black inhabitants. These population numbers sufficed to secure statehood in 1796.

After peace in 1795, the Cherokees were internally divided and the federal Indian agents exploited the factionalism to pressure and bribe individual chiefs to make a number of land sales. The agents also made efforts to civilize the Cherokees. Meanwhile, settlers and Cherokees, the latter often using equipment furnished by the civilization program, began raising cotton, a very profitable crop. The Louisiana Purchase in 1803 excited Tennesseans by opening up the West. In 1805 the United States bribed several Cherokee spokesmen to sign a treaty for Cherokee lands between the eastern part of the state and the Cumberland region. This cession extended white control from the eastern border to west of Nashville. The southern and western region of the state remained Indian land. The Cherokee nation united in 1809 and 1810 under leaders who refused to sell or accept bribes to part with more territory. The region's population grew exponentially, reaching approximately 262,000 white and 46,000 black inhabitants in the state of Tennessee and 12,500 Cherokees on Cherokee lands in 1810.

A project that describes the changing ideologies of three cultures in one book requires some restrictions and explanations. Although I have invoked the metaphor of a meeting ground, I have refined my study by leaving out certain groups. The Tennessee region supported a variety of peoples and nations during the period from 1768 through 1810. The largest group of native inhabitants was the Cherokees. Some of the Chickasaw people also lived in the area that is now western Tennessee. The Creeks, Shawnees, and Choctaws hunted on lands in the Tennessee area as did many other smaller groups of indigenous peoples. In order to keep this study manageable, I focus on the Cherokees because they were the Native American people with the largest

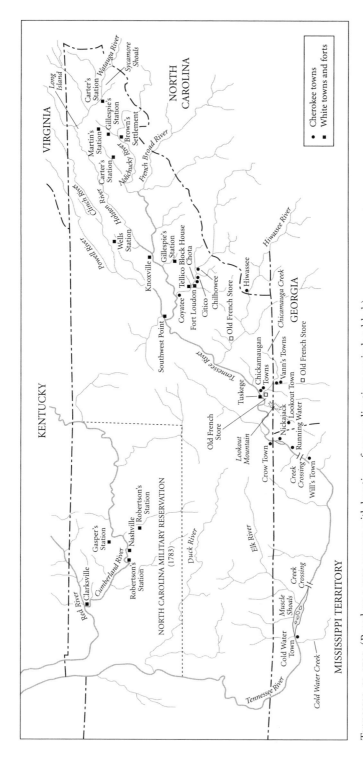

Tennessee, ca. 1799. (Based on a 1799 survey, with locations from earlier time periods added.)

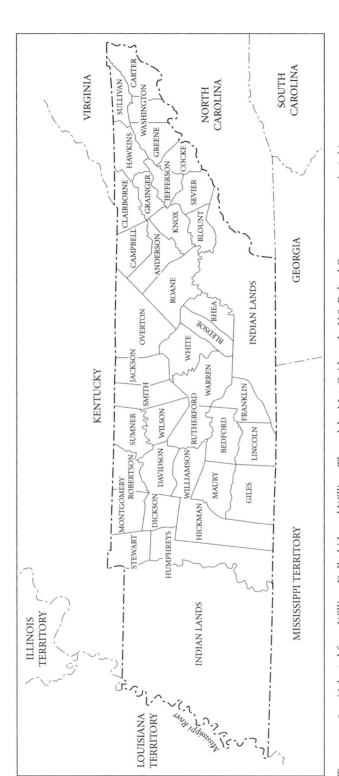

Tennessee, 1810. (Adapted from William Dollarhide and William Thorndale, *Map Guide to the U.S. Fedreal Census, 1790–1920* [1987].)

resident population in Tennessee and the one with the most extensive inter-action with newcomers. In addition to the first inhabitants and the colonial peoples who moved westward in 1768, the English, French, and Spanish all exerted influence in the area. Although these European powers informed Native American thinking at some points, I study the ideas of the black and white borderers who persisted in the region after 1800 rather than those of European governmental officials and traders.

There are limits to writing history without hypertext and without over-lapping transparencies. By opting to draw the borders consonant with the boundaries of present-day Tennessee, I chose to consider a territory defined by British colonialists and later American expansionist politicians, rather than domains recognized by Native Americans or other European powers. This has the disadvantage of dividing the Cherokee people, since only the Overhill towns resided within these boundaries, and of redefining their expe-rience along lines that are artificial to them. On the other hand, the United States government ultimately came to exercise sovereignty over the region and its efforts to control the territory now known as Tennessee spurred much of the intellectual and cultural change described in this book.

The question of borders requires a further explanation, because I refer to Tennessee as both a frontier and a borderland. Historians distinguish be-tween the terms "frontier," "borderlands," and "bordered lands," though without complete agreement on their meaning. Many see frontiers as cultural meeting grounds in which no one culture is dominant, creating some mixing and accommodation between diverse peoples. Borderlands are places where autonomous peoples of different cultures are bound together by the presence of more than one imperial power, allowing indigenous inhabitants to play them off against each other. When one imperial power successfully imposes boundaries, borderlands become bordered lands.[25] During the period of early settlement, Tennessee exhibited characteristics of both a frontier and a borderland, as the relative power that different European nations exerted in the region waxed and waned. This instability makes a definitive designation like frontier or borderland problematic. By statehood in 1796, the region was a bordered land but even this classification is ambiguous, since both Native Americans and Tennesseans claimed and attained land possessed by the other after that date. Because of these ambivalences and because the westering people often referred to themselves as "frontier people," even in periods that historians might consider them to be residents of a borderland, I use the designations of frontier and borderlands interchangeably. I speak of "closing the frontier" in 1810 to signal that very little land in middle or eastern Tennessee was available to the landless without purchase, changing significantly who was drawn to the region.

I have organized my argument about how the parties crafted their ideologies by dividing my study into two parts. In part I, I examine the ideas and assumptions underlying the construction of the connection between the Cherokees and the westering peoples. Because black newcomers had no separate sovereignty and virtually no voice in native relations, this section is largely biracial rather than triracial. When two distinct societies claim and reside in the same territory, issues about possession, separation, and commingling inevitably arise. Treaty negotiations are the sites at which parties molded much of their relationship with the other as a political unit. In order to get as close as possible to the words of the Cherokees on this subject, I use as my principal primary sources the extensive negotiations carried on by the Cherokees over Tennessee territory from 1768 until 1810. This prolonged series of negotiations produced hundreds of pages of documentation.[26] In many cases, a transcriber recorded lengthy talks by Cherokee speakers during conferences that often lasted weeks. In addition, the Cherokees conferred frequently between treaties with government commissioners and other agents, and many of these communications have been preserved.[27]

I consider the construction by Cherokees and whites of their ideas about each other as political communities in three chronological periods in part I. Chapter 1 explores the era from first permanent white settlement in 1768 until the war of 1788. During this period, the peace faction of the upper Cherokee towns responded to the newcomers from a cosmology in which foreign parties established a kinship from which flowed mutual obligations. When land concessions failed to assure peace and trade, these men and women incorporated new notions of justice, renewal of commitments, and equality of the parties into their framing of connection, doctrines that placed responsibilities on their diplomatic kin to provide for and to protect the lands of the weaker Cherokees. Meanwhile, the westering people understood connection with other societies through a European vocabulary of nationhood, one in which international relationships were formed through contractual treaties between nations from which emanated rights and duties. The European law of nations did not extend the right to territorial integrity to nations that claimed large tracts of land for nonagricultural uses. Although considerable numbers of westering men advanced a policy of extermination of the indigenous peoples, peace-minded frontier people challenged this view by using treaties to forge a relationship with their imagined Cherokee nation and by making local efforts to civilize the Cherokees.

In chapter 2, I examine the reformulation of the thinking of both the Cherokees and frontier people from 1776 until statehood in 1796. In 1776 a critical minority of the Cherokees, the Chickamaugans, rejected the Upper Town construction of white society as the stronger diplomatic kin and inserted their more aggressive ideas into the peace process, grafting onto the traditional diplomatic kinship more robust notions of equality and justice. In 1791 a coalition of Chickamaugan and Upper Town women and men obtained an explicit recognition of equality and an implicit commitment to the permanency of the Cherokee nation from the United States. During the same period, local white men responded to the federal government's pressure to restrain their attacks on the Indians by recasting the Cherokees as a savage or uncivilized nation in contrast to their own more advanced civilized nation.

One area that has been largely neglected by historians is the triangular relationship crafted between the first peoples, the westward-moving settlers, and the federal government in the early national period, a connection considered in chapter 3. After peace in 1795, Cherokee statesmen and stateswomen refrained from warfare and, in return, expected their federal father to regenerate the commitments between the parties, to protect the Cherokees from the encroachments and violence of the local settlers, to provide assistance in time of need, to recognize the Cherokees as equal to white inhabitants, and to grant the Cherokees autonomy in their political affairs. Operating from its own ideological perspective, the United States agreed that it assumed a protective relationship and that it would provide aid but transformed an early commitment to equality into a paternalistic relationship of guardian and ward. With statehood in 1796, Tennessee leaders formulated and embarked on a vigorous state role in Indian affairs under a theory of nationhood in which states retained strong local control. Treating the first people as liminal figures, they denigrated the status of the Cherokees from an uncivilized nation with a country to that of tenants at will with, at best, extinguishable claims to land and urged the federal government to remove the indigenous people in order to accelerate the civilization of the region. The ideas of the Cherokees and the local whites about the protective relationship, civilization, nationhood, and sovereignty that developed in this period informed the thinking of United States' Supreme Court Justice John Marshall and President Andrew Jackson during the removal debates several decades later. Marshall's doctrines influenced the ideologies of governments and settlers in British colonies throughout the world.

The multiethnic convergence in the Tennessee Valley affected more than the conceptualization of international relations by the Cherokees and the newcomers. The meeting of the Cherokee, black, and white peoples also informed the ideologies of the inhabitants of each society about their internal affairs. In the five chapters of part II, I examine the ideas and cultural logic of the inhabitants of Tennessee around three important intracommunal relations of power—society and family, government, and the economy. I focus on the Cherokees in chapter 4, African Americans in chapter 5, and European Americans in chapters 6 through 8. In contrast to the integrated approach I adopt in part I, I study the three groups separately in order to consider the complexity of the ideological transformations in each society and in order to construct a more coherent narrative about the worldviews of the three peoples.

Chapter 4 describes the new identity formulated by the Cherokee people after contact with the frontier people. After the Cherokees abandoned warfare, both Upper and Lower Town men and women reframed their concept of their social structure to absorb growing numbers of useful non-Cherokee residents—black, white, and red—who remained outside the clan system. To maintain peace and to preserve their lands, many Cherokees fashioned a stronger national government that included important functions previously exercised by the clans and moved away from the localism of past decision making. The Cherokees viewed balance in economic relations as crucial for their independence and bolstered their autonomy by utilizing international trade and annuity payments from the federal government to create an independent economy.

Chapter 5 considers the cognitive worlds of black Tennesseans. As in Africa, many transmontane African Americans operated from a cultural logic that placed relationality and sponsorship at the heart of their views about sociability, governance, and economic relations. In contrast to the Cherokees and settlers, enslaved African Americans were not engaged in a nationalization project. Consequently, they focused on constructing a community with each other and occasionally with free blacks. Moving away from the paternalism of Virginia and North Carolina, they crafted patronage ties with white men and women that allowed them a limited voice, particularly in churches and in the economy. A tiny fraction of the population, free blacks combined their African understanding of personal bonds with an American belief in political and economic entitlements similar to that of white Tennesseans.

Because settlers formed the largest and most powerful population in the region after 1790, I give them the most attention. World historians describe a wide variety of civilizations envisioned by societies across place and time. Frontier people whose families emigrated from Europe as part of the great land rush located their intellectual touchstone in the eighteenth-century European concept of civilization. The precepts that constituted their ideology of civilization were particularly potent because this cognitive system integrated domestic and international beliefs, creating a more totalizing worldview. Tennesseans generally imagined an oppositional identity to native peoples and slaves rather than the hybridity described by postcolonialists in some other settings.[28] In contrast to settlers in other British colonies whose values centered on improvement, trans-Appalachian settlers sought happiness, a condition that they believed was best produced by the civilized life.[29] The relative freedom from authority and the dangers in the frontier setting encouraged westering men and women to reimagine familial, communal, religious, political, and economic connections as chosen, not ascribed, and to favor achievement over birthright. They embraced beliefs in consensual relationships over customary marital and political arrangements, human agency and merit over hereditary or monarchical authority or natural rights, and happiness and prosperity as an outcome of civilization. Their orientation toward human agency released tremendous energies but existed uneasily with conflicting Enlightenment ideas about natural rights and Christian views of morality. I study the development of ideas about civilization among whites in chapters 6 through 8 on social relations, governance, and the economy.

Very little is known about the ideas and assumptions of backcountry people about family and society, the subject of chapter 6. Most white women and many men believed strongly in the importance of family and community—sources of happiness that they contrasted to the isolated lives of "wandering savages"—and they supported voluntary over customary social arrangements. Women rooted their home life and developed their ideas about sociability in the larger world of extended family and neighbors, whereas men constructed their notions about community in the wider society, particularly in voluntary associations. This robust social life was an important marker, for white Tennesseans, of civilization.

Historians have neglected an important tension in the political philosophies of Americans in the post-Revolutionary period—the ambiguity within Lockean liberal theory between natural rights and rights arising from the social compact, an ambivalence explored in chapter 7. In contrast to accounts that suggest that they were isolated and nonpolitical, ordinary white Tennessee men engaged in a vibrant participatory political culture based on their belief in an explicit social contract. At the same time, they sought to construct a civilized polis by contrasting their government to neighboring "savage" societies—communities in which Indians did not aim to secure their property or rights—and by tying government to notions of prosperity heavily dependent on slave labor. In constructing an advanced society, white men believed that the concepts of consent and merit that empowered them supported a model of civilization that disenfranchised others.

Ideas about civilization, human achievement, and consensual relationships collided as white westerners fashioned economic relations—the focus of chapter 8. Both men and women embraced an understanding of civilization that linked it to prosperity and prosperity to happiness. Their economic system exalted farming and commerce instead of their picture of an Indian economy supported by savage hunters. The kingpin of prosperity was their belief in private property, the construct that encouraged men and women to be industrious and that stimulated population growth; however, leading and ordinary men and women disagreed about how to convert land into private ownership, which natural resources should remain public, whether human beings should be property, and whether individuals should aggregate large property holdings. As the period of land appropriation from the Cherokees by bribery ended, Tennesseans had not settled their ideological differences about how to create and share wealth.

The meeting of the indigenous Cherokees and the black and white newcomers on Tennessee land thus brought together and transformed the cosmologies of separate peoples. In 1768 African Americans and white land hunters moved onto a land possessed by the Cherokees. As a result of their meeting, four decades later the Cherokees unified in 1810 with a recrafted national identity based on balance, African Americans negotiated within an intricate network of social bonds and sponsors, and white Tennesseans promoted an expansionistic but limited nationalism as they refined their understanding of civilization. This book explores the imaginative worlds that they constructed during the frontier and borderland years in the trans-Appalachian Southwest.

PART ONE

Diplomatic Relations

CHAPTER ONE

Kinship and Nationhood

The Construction of
Relationship between Cherokees
and Settlers, 1768–1788

Harbingers of spring in 1775, Onitositah and John Sevier smoked the peace pipe together to open the negotiations that culminated in the Treaty of Sycamore Shoals. Both men were poised to assume greater leadership in their communities. Onitositah was a councillor to Oconostota, one of the principal chiefs at the treaty. John Sevier was present as a representative of the settlers. Two years later, Onitositah attended the April and July peace conferences at Long Island in Overhill country as the principal peace chief. Meanwhile, Sevier led the local militia into Cherokee country, pursuing a scorched earth policy that left many Cherokee men, women, and children dead or starving. Onitositah devoted the next decade to promoting a Cherokee style of diplomacy, while Sevier, later governor of the state of Franklin and six times governor of Tennessee, gained popularity among the settlers for his military exploits against the Cherokees.[1]

The peace chief and war chief met again at peace talks in 1781. Addressing the younger Sevier as his "elder brother," Onitositah put aside any sentiments he might have had about Sevier's several invasions of Cherokee country. Instead, Onitositah expressed his hope that Sevier's heart would be good and peaceable. Onitositah was joined by Nan-ye-hi, who urged peace on her "sons" of both races. John Sevier assured the Cherokees that he was pleased with "you and your nation."[2]

The manner in which Onitositah and Nan-ye-hi fashioned their relationships to John Sevier, as elder brother and son, was a Cherokee construction. Native American historians have explored the use of kinship metaphors and treaty protocols by eastern woodland Indians in the contact period but have generally failed to examine how the concepts changed over time and have largely neglected women's role in diplomacy.[3] During the two decades after permanent white settlement, Cherokee peacemakers sought to bring all participants to a peaceful state of mind by putting past misdeeds behind them, establishing a present relationship, and creating an intent to continue peace in the future. As with most Native Americans, peace chiefs imagined that they would establish diplomatic relations with the settlers by fashioning them as fathers, elder brothers, and brothers, a metaphor of intercommunal kinship that assumed a reciprocity of obligations between the members. As the Cherokees increasingly ceded lands to the frontier people who failed to reciprocate this imagined kinship on Cherokee terms, the Cherokees began to emphasize the connection between reciprocity and justice to protect their lands. A special note in the diplomatic voice, Cherokee women drew on their matriarchal authority to declare themselves the mothers of Cherokee and white men. As such, they sought to preserve Cherokee territory by restoring balance in two domains—they pressed for peace in the face of male warfare, and they urged recognition of the common humanity and equality of the two peoples. By 1788 many Cherokees considered these intellectual approaches inadequate, undermined by violence and land losses.

John Sevier's reply to the diplomats and their "nation" was a European response. Scholars have documented European theories about nationhood, race, and savagery but, except for beliefs about the right to vacant land, have done much less to explore how local colonists understood indigenous sovereignty.[4] In the European imagination, governments characterized other political sovereignties as nations but challenged a nation's right to occupy large tracts of land that it did not cultivate. Following this logic, early pioneers to the Tennessee region maintained political separation from the southeastern Indians by invoking the doctrine of nationhood but contested the rights of Native American nations to sovereignty over their soil. In the vocabulary of nationhood, states connected with each other through treaties —a relationship maintained by carefully defined contractual rights and duties and not by kinship obligations. In fashioning a relationship with the Cherokees, peaceful factions of frontier people recognized the Cherokees as a nation and contested the policies of extermination of the more violent segment of the community. After some of the Cherokees supported the British in the Revolution, veterans coming to Tennessee and other landholders clamored for the right to Cherokee lands by conquest. Despite considerable pressure for the extermination of the indigenous peoples, Cherokee resistance and the actions of white settlers who sought coexistence overrode these voices.

The primary inhabitants of the Tennessee Valley during the seventeenth and eighteenth centuries were people of Iroquoian descent, who identified themselves as the Ani-Yun Wiya, the Real People. The Ani-Yun Wiya, called Cherokee or cave people by the Iroquois, lived in four clusters of towns at the beginning of the eighteenth century—the Lower Towns, located in present-day South Carolina, the Middle Towns and Valley Towns in North Carolina, and the Overhill Towns, located in what is now eastern Tennessee. As the century progressed, white settlements pushed these towns west. The Overhill Towns, situated west of the Appalachians, were removed from early colonial settlements but engaged in considerable trade with South Carolina beginning in the late seventeenth century and with Virginia after 1730.[5]

Traditional Cherokee cosmology located the source of its norms and behavior in a spirit world, whose principles aimed toward harmony. Harmony was attained by a balance of opposite forces, such as war and peace, men and women, and plants and animals. The Cherokee worldview emphasized boundaries and the autonomy and equality of moieties, rather than hierarchies. Great power resided in the supernatural world and could be accessed by crossing boundaries and by dreams and conjurers. Witches and evil spirits could also tap into spiritual power to cause sickness and death. The corn mother, Selu, and the hunter, Kana'ti, were the first people.[6]

Kinship was the nucleus of Cherokee society, which was structured around seven clans. The primary identity of each Cherokee was the clan of his or her mother. The father was not related to his children, and the mother's male kin, usually her oldest brother, instructed the children, took responsibility for them on the mother's death, and usually formed the closest male parental relationship with them. Individuals without clan ties, whether they lived in Cherokee villages or were members of other nations, were considered strangers. Clan ties affected virtually all arrangements in Cherokee society, including marriage, politics, and social practices. One of its significant concerns was the stilling of crying blood. In Cherokee metaphysics, the spirit of one person killed by another, whether accidentally or intentionally, could not move into the spiritual universe until the kinsmen of the deceased balanced his or her death by killing the murderer, or a clan relative of that person. The Cherokees occasionally recognized exceptions to this rule by permitting sanctuary in a beloved town or by acts of forgiveness or substitution in which the murderer's clan offered a prisoner or a payment for the life taken.[7]

Spiritual and communal principles dictated the material relations of the Cherokees. The Cherokees believed that a supernatural being gave them their lands. They were attached to the lands because their ancestors were buried there and the spirits of the dead lingered in some localities. They owned their land in common, with occupants having rights to tenure. Women did most of the farming and child-rearing while men hunted. Personal property was individually owned, but a strong ethic of reciprocity required that those who had goods shared with those who did not. With the growth in trade in the last half of the century, some individuals increasingly owned more property than others.[8]

The Cherokees had weak and amorphous notions of personal power but did believe that power could be acquired and lost and that each person possessed power in differing degrees. The Ani-Yun Wiya highly valued independence and disapproved of compulsion. Although women and men had some separate areas of authority, they generally shared governance, with the women presenting their views through a representative of the Women's Council. Each person had a voice in decision making, with decisions made by consensus. From early childhood, they sought to nurture an autonomous will in all individuals. The Cherokees did not try to resolve controversies but to avoid them, and dissidents unable to persuade the majority typically withdrew.[9] Prior to 1753, most governance was local, taking place in the towns. National councils of all Cherokee people met only in emergencies. Everyone could speak at council, and decisions made in national councils were not binding on the towns. From 1753 until 1776, Chota emerged as a mother city with the authority to conduct diplomacy and regulate trade, but all other decisions continued to be made at the town level. The English made efforts to organize the Cherokees politically, designating a national chief, a practice continued by the Americans. These chiefs also governed by influence, not compulsion, though over the course of the eighteenth century the growing importance of war and their access to treaty goods enhanced their power.[10]

Because clanship was central to the Cherokee understanding of social and political relations, the Cherokees conducted diplomatic relations by establishing kinship connections with non-Cherokee people. Like many Native American peoples, the Cherokees pursued kinship diplomacy through two venues. One was to incorporate foreigners into Cherokee society through marriage and adoption. In the Cherokee matriarchal society, women conducted much of this diplomacy. Women commonly integrated traders and diplomats into tribal life and into the clan system by marrying them. The husband then became a relation of his wife's clan, giving him important connections and protections. As was true in other native communities, a woman also tapped into a source of power when she crossed a boundary to form a sexual relationship with a non-Cherokee male. By midcentury, men and women considered women's alliances with merchants to have significance comparable to that of heroic war deeds. Women extolled their accomplishments in obtaining goods from traders whom they loved in the same councils in which warriors boasted of their exploits. Women also chose whether to adopt prisoners or to torture captives for revenge.[11]

To establish a diplomatic connection with peoples who remained outside the clan structure, the Cherokees reconstituted the foreign community as kin. The Delaware, for example, were their grandfathers. The English were their fathers, elder brothers, and brothers. Constructing international relations in this way meant that the conduct of foreign affairs centered on relationship and mutuality, with each party having obligations specified by their relationship. If one party disturbed the balance of reciprocity by acting contrary to the expectations of their kinship duties, those actions destroyed harmony and led to war. Because the Cherokees abhorred compulsion, peacemaking centered on good talks and rituals to bring all to the common mind of peace. From this perspective, the parties were careful to avoid blaming each other. The atmosphere, not any agreements reached, was central. Such alliances were fragile, and the parties maintained their relationship over time by conferences and frequent visits to each other.[12]

By midcentury if not before, peace diplomacy included women, who advanced their own diplomatic concerns rooted in their roles as mothers. Women acted in international affairs on their own initiative but primarily through the Women's Council, composed of the most influential women in the nation. The British insistence on negotiating with men and the growing centralization of national councils that excluded women who could not travel easily restricted but did not eliminate women's involvement in the peace process. From 1755 until at least 1819, the Women's Council was headed by Nan-ye-hi, a Beloved Woman and a member of the Wolf Clan, the most prestigious of the clans. Nan-ye-hi had important diplomatic clan connections through her mother, whose brothers included major peace chiefs Attakullakulla and Willinawaw.[13]

In defiance of the English Proclamation of 1763 that forbade trans-Appalachian settlement, Virginians and North Carolinians began migrating to the region now known as Tennessee in 1768. Cherokee leaders, including the primary chiefs Oconostota and Attakullakulla and the Women's Council headed by Nan-ye-hi, were concerned about encroachments from the beginning, but they tolerated some settlement, primarily because they desired easier access to trade. The pioneer communities presented a challenge for the Cherokees. In the past, merchants lived in the Cherokee villages, subject to Cherokee law and customs, but the new traders now lived in white communities. Acting in their private capacity, the traders responded to Cherokee uneasiness by offering financial compensation for the presence of the settlements. In accepting these payments, the Cherokees realized that they were not dealing with the British authorities, whom they saw as having the power to purchase property and to set boundary lines. They understood the offer of the merchants for goods in exchange for the presence of the settlements from the perspective of Cherokee law that included a concept of land usage in which Cherokees allowed friends to live on their lands as a courtesy. The Cherokees believed that the payments that businessmen offered were funds to cover game that their hunting destroyed, not money to purchase property rights. The white bargainers encouraged this understanding by describing the arrangements in which the Cherokees signed deeds as temporary leases. In fact, the traders deliberately misled the Cherokees. For instance, one merchant, Jacob Brown, held his treaty with about 100 Cherokees and an interpreter on John McDowell's property with McDowell furnishing the food and goods. Although Brown characterized the transaction as a lease with the Cherokees, he had a secret agreement with McDowell to give him two tracts of land in payment, showing that Brown intended to claim ownership of the property.[14]

During the early period of intermixture, the Cherokees cast the settlers as their brothers—a designation that assumed equivalent strength and resources. However, this kinship had clear boundaries. In 1774 Oconostota insisted that the borderers observe the line drawn between the Cherokees and settlers in the 1770 Virginia treaty.[15] As a result of growing tension, North Carolina judge Richard Henderson faced an unsympathetic audience when he sought to obtain a huge grant of land from the Cherokees in a private purchase at the Treaty of Sycamore Springs in 1775. Henderson claimed that he purchased about one-half of the Cherokee hunting grounds, constituting most of present-day Kentucky and northern Tennessee and a path through the Cumberland Gap to allow access to this vast territory. The Cherokees denied selling their hunting grounds and contended that the goods they received were payment for the game that the travelers destroyed and for a small parcel of land on the Kentucky River, not purchase money for the sale of half of their lands. Along with the chiefs, the women almost certainly did not support a land cession. Oconostota's wife became very uneasy when a trader told her that the chiefs had signed a deed for the lands, and she went to talk to the chiefs about it.[16]

During the year after the conference, the pioneers made it clear that they interpreted the deeds as a land grant and new land hunters flooded into the region. In response to this cataclysmic loss, Tsi-yugunsini, a young Cherokee warrior, led many of the young men to war in 1776, an action opposed by the Women's Council and many peace chiefs, who accepted the assurances of the British Indian agent that Britain would handle the problem. Warned by Nan-ye-hi, many settlers fled but the Cherokee dissidents were successful in killing some frontier people and forcing others off their lands. In response, the militias of Virginia, North Carolina, South Carolina, and Georgia invaded Cherokee country, killing many people, burning houses, and destroying crops. Some of the nation met at Long Island on the Holston River with commissioners from North Carolina and Virginia to agree to peace in 1777. Tsi-yugunsini and many of his warriors objected and gradually withdrew from the nation, first to towns on the Chickamauga Creek, giving rise to their characterization as Chickamaugans, and later to towns near the bend of the Tennessee River, creating settlements that became known as the Lower Towns. During the American Revolution, they allied with the British and later established connections with the Spanish.[17] The Chickamaugans became the major dissenting voices to the peace faction of the Upper Towns.

Many Cherokee men and women refused to abandon their ancestral land to incoming whites and declined to join Tsi-yugunsini and the Chickamaugans. Aware by 1777 that England could not control its colonists, the residents of the Upper Towns sought a kinship with state and later federal officials who could manage the land hunters in order to preserve Cherokee lands and permit good trade relations. At the peace conferences in 1777, Onitositah and Savanukeh, the nephew of the aging Oconostota, conducted negotiations for the Cherokees. North Carolina demanded and received a land cession without compensation as a condition for peace. Unaware that North Carolina would insist on a land cession, Nan-ye-hi and the Women's Council did not attend the conferences, although some women did. Antagonized by North Carolina's arrogant actions, Savanukeh declared himself done with the Big Knives and allied with the British and Chickamaugans in 1780. After Savanukeh's defection, Onitositah, joined later by Scolacutta, continued as the primary peace chief of the Upper Towns until his murder in 1788. Upon Attakullakulla's death about 1778, Nan-ye-hi became the most prominent diplomat in the Wolf clan.[18]

After 1776, male and female diplomats at the numerous peace talks initially conducted diplomacy by following the traditional Cherokee understanding of peace as a state of mind. In common with other eastern woodland peoples, the Cherokees believed that the parties could engage in rituals and reasoned discussion to further accord only after each individual became committed personally to peace. Because peacemaking was a time-consuming endeavor, the Upper Town statesmen resisted white demands to rush a conference agenda to consider issues of land cession or to link peace with setting boundary lines. Creating a peaceful state of mind involved a three-pronged process —a preliminary clearing of past transgressions, the establishment of a relationship rooted in the present moment, and a resolution of intent to hold that relationship into the future.[19]

Prior to the meeting at treaty grounds, those Cherokees inclined toward peace persuaded other Cherokees of its desirability, frequently described as "making the path clear." Cherokee diplomats continued this process during treaty negotiations in order to establish a peaceable frame of mind for Cherokees and white negotiators and audience members. Making the way clear included an intention to put past misdeeds out of mind.[20]

Once "the way was made clear," the parties were ready to "take hold of each other" to establish a contemporaneous connection. Scholars frequently overlook the literal sense of these expressions. Large numbers of Cherokee women, men, and children attended all the treaties. During a period in which the entire scattered Cherokee nation probably numbered about 10,000 people with the Overhill people a few thousand of that number, there were 1,200 Cherokees at Henderson's Purchase at the Overhill hunting grounds at Sycamore Shoals in 1775; 400 Cherokees in addition to the warriors at the 1777 Treaty of Long Island in Overhill country; 600 at the 1781 peace talks on Long Island; and 918 Cherokees at the 1785 Treaty of Hopewell in South Carolina. As Savanukeh explained, the chiefs brought many of their people to hear the good talks.[21]

During the evenings and on days when there were no treaty talks, Cherokees and whites attending the conferences took each other "by the hand" by eating, drinking, dancing, and engaging in games and races. The socialization was rarely free of tension. There were episodes of violence at many of the treaties, and at some conferences troops guarded the Indian encampments. Nonetheless, because commissioners and Cherokees took days and sometimes weeks to convene, fraternization was often extensive. For example, at the Treaty of Long Island at Holston in the summer of 1777, the Cherokees began arriving on June 28 and held preliminary talks on July 13. During the intervening two weeks, people from both groups ate and drank together. On July 2 white officers persuaded the Cherokees to perform a Green Corn dance—a Cherokee ritual—in exchange for which the whites held their own dance. The whites observed the Fourth of July with a parade, volleys, the firing of great guns, a speech to the Cherokees about its meaning, and whiskey. The young warriors closed the entertainment with a dance.[22]

Cherokee speakers reaffirmed the importance of a present connection at the treaty grounds through the use of repetitive acts. Like other eastern woodland peoples, the parties sat in a circle, lit the sacred council fire, smoked the pipe of peace, and shook the hand of friendship. The Cherokees added their own symbols to these observances. During the years when the parties treated at Long Island, the commissioners and headmen sat on the white benches of peace. The meetings took place outdoors so that the hundreds of attendees—both Cherokees and settlers—could participate in the experience. The Cherokee women sat in a women's circle. Wampum served in a variety of ways to advance the creation of a peaceful, present relationship. During talks, the Cherokees, like other American Indians, preserved a record of their important points by offering strings of wampum. Many speakers offered the beads as proof that what they said came from their heart. Cherokee headmen also used wampum belts to create a relationship. The Cherokees invited the commissioners to hold one end of the belt while they held the other. This allowed both parties to feel physically and present visually, to the assembled audience, the chain of friendship that stretched from the Cherokees to the settler community. These acts were more than the mnemonic devices and symbolic statements that historians describe. Because large portions of the Cherokee and white communities attended the talks, the chiefs and Beloved Men and Women intended the visual ceremonies and physical actions to draw the participants into a visceral commitment to each other.[23]

In addition to ceremonial practices, the Cherokees used the content of the discussions to facilitate the creation of a present relationship of friendship and peace. To accomplish this, the parties avoided past grievances and made speeches of good talks. Good talks were statements of peace and friendship. Another mechanism that aided in good talks was to assign blame for misdeeds to a third party. This was most commonly, though not always, an individual or group from outside the Cherokee nation. During the Revolutionary War, the British were often the cause of troubles. Later, it was the northern Indians,

Spanish, and Creeks. Upper Town chiefs frequently pointed to the Lower Towns as the source of murders and thefts.[24]

As scholars have noted, the present connection sought by the Cherokees was one of international kinship. Numerous Cherokee speakers designated the white commissioners as elder brothers and brothers and the governor of Virginia as their father.[25] Less explored has been the specific meanings of these diplomatic kinships for the Cherokees. As the Cherokee diplomats fashioned their new neighbors as fathers, elder brothers, or brothers, they did not imagine relationships that imputed as much power to their international kin as did the Euro-Americans or the northern Indians. In white patriarchal society, the father was the head of the household and, at the political level, the head of government. Algonquians in the North envisioned the fictive father as someone whose children obeyed his orders. The Cherokees did not assign this much authority to their diplomatic father. The matrilineal and matrilocal Cherokees placed the mother at the center of the household and gave women a voice in government. Further, the significant male figure for young Cherokees was from the mother's clan—usually her older brother. He taught and disciplined her sons and assumed the care of the children on the mother's death. The father was a more benevolent figure, who treated his children kindly and provided for them while nurturing their independence. The Cherokees transposed this relationship to the international sphere. In 1782 a messenger sent by the Cherokee chiefs to Indian agent Joseph Martin explained that the Cherokees were disposed to call the headmen of America their fathers so that the Cherokees could engage in trade that would feed and clothe them.[26]

Similarly, the elder brother in the English patriarchal arrangement stood to inherit entailed estates and exercise considerable power over the household on the death of the father. Although white Americans modified this hierarchy to some degree, oldest sons generally remained more powerfully positioned in relationship to the other children. Among northern Indians, the elder brother received deference from the younger brother. From the Cherokee perspective, embedded in the relationship of elder brother and younger brother was the doctrine of reciprocity and, on the part of the elder brother, protection and respect but not the expectation of deference. If one brother had what the other needed, the more fortunate brother gave to the other. Onitositah relied on this concept to reproach the North Carolina commissioners in 1777 when, out of greed, they threatened the livelihood of the already impoverished Cherokees by asking for Cherokee land: "I have been often told that my elder brothers were naked and had nothing. I said if so I will be naked also." Because the elder brother was stronger, he was more likely to be the one to supply the younger brother's needs. The Cherokee characterization of whites as elder brothers was in part a courtesy and in part a recognition that whites had greater access to goods and, as the more privileged party, should provide security to their younger brothers.[27]

After clearing the path of past misdeeds and establishing a present connection by establishing kinship and obligations between parties equally entitled to respect, the Cherokees stressed the importance of carrying that connection into the future. Traditionally, chiefs had no control over what young warriors might do, and so they rarely made future commitments. Nevertheless, they attempted to perpetuate a conciliatory state of mind by utilizing a concept of renewal. To do so, diplomats would invite the parties to continually reaffirm a harmonious relationship.[28] Their promise of peace was a wampum belt that stretched across time. In this metaphor, the belt was more than a symbol of present connection; it was a constant reminder of a commitment imposing obligations on unborn generations. Holding such a belt, Savanukeh in 1777 spoke to both sides of regeneration: "This is the bright chain of friendship which we have hold of, not only for us but the young ones on both sides, even the children yet unborn have hold of it through us, and shall be linked together by it. . . . It is a light for those yet unborn to walk by, that they may see the path of peace and know what is done at this place." In order to enhance the prospects for a stable future relationship, Cherokee spokesmen encouraged both sides to urge compliance on those not at the treaty. In pressing their listeners to continually refresh their friendship, Cherokee negotiators drew on a concept of renewal familiar to Cherokee people through the annual purification and thanksgiving festival. At the Green Corn ceremonies, which marked the start of the new year, the Cherokees gathered for several days of celebration and connection. Each person forgave past injuries, except murder, and began anew their relationships, in harmony with each other and the spiritual world.[29]

After the peace conferences and land losses of 1777, Cherokee negotiators continued to strive for a peaceful state of mind but modified their conception about how to achieve this. Traditionally peace treaties without land cessions, when broken and remade, left each party in roughly similar positions as they met to renew bonds.[30] Treaties that included land cessions transformed the dynamics of the process. As the Cherokees sacrificed land in an effort to create a harmonious balance between Real People and land hunters, they continued the practice of making the way clear but revised their ideas about how the parties took hold of each other by emphasizing mutual obligations of pity and justice and by altering their thinking about presenting grievances in conferences.

Cherokee spokespeople had made claims for pity for some years, but requests for pity increased with the invasions of the Cherokee towns. The use of the word "pity" is almost certainly a poor translation. In the American lexicon at that time, pity carried an edge of contempt and an assumption of inferiority. Nothing in the context in which the word was used by the Cherokees suggested a sense of shame or inferiority. In the 1770 Treaty of Lochaber, Oconostota indicated he was willing to give up lands that his white brothers needed because he pitied them, but whites did not pity him because they kept the price of trade goods high and encroached on Cherokee lands. Oconostota clearly saw pity as the fulfillment of a reciprocal duty—a kind of entitlement. In 1782 warfare between the settlers and Cherokees left many of the Cherokees starving and unable to hunt without fear of attacks from white hunters. The chiefs informed white officials that it was the responsibility of the white people to take pity on the Cherokees, who had become a weak people. Their reasoning for requiring assistance from their attackers was that they were once a strong people who took pity on the white colonists when they wanted help against the French and therefore the settlers should reciprocate. Because the kin relationship was a mutual relationship, it also imposed duties on the Cherokees. For example, when the Chickamaugans responded to overtures of peace in 1791, they showed pity by refraining from killing James Hubbard, a notorious Indian hater, and others who attempted an illegal settlement at Muscle Shoals.[31]

The sense of entitlement contained in the Cherokee appeals for pity was strengthened by its frequent linkage with demands for justice. A concept emphasized by diplomats as their lands became part of treaty bargains, justice required the restoration of lands unfairly ceded and the removal of intruders. In asserting that Americans had the obligation to protect Cherokee lands, the Ani-Yun Wiya did not speak in European terms of treaty rights but in a language of relationship. Numerous Cherokee negotiators over the years insisted that the diplomatic kinship imposed obligations onto the more powerful party that received land to do justice.[32]

As negotiators linked pity to justice, the Cherokees modified their traditional doctrine of putting bad thoughts behind and engaging in good talks. This concept met a serious challenge in the white belief that grievances should be stated and resolved. To the Cherokees, the discord inherent in such a procedure jeopardized the peaceable mind that the treaty talks should foster. Although the Cherokee headmen did articulate complaints, they preferred to do this largely in private conversations or talks outside the treaty process. For white diplomats, this was the heart of the peacemaking procedure. Over time, the white insistence that grievances not stated were waived worked a change in the Cherokee response, with the Cherokee spokespeople becoming more forthcoming about grievances. However, the Cherokees, while largely accommodating the white approach, did not permit it to supplant all their own goals. They continued to stress the importance of putting bad thoughts behind by incorporating their grievances into good talks. Onitositah in 1785 responded to the commissioners' remarks by noting he was pleased with their talk and gave beads as a symbol of friendship. After listing his grievances, he introduced Nan-ye-hi, who talked of peace and friendship.[33]

Although historians have focused almost exclusively on male voices in foreign affairs, the Women's Council and individual women made strong contributions to the new diplomacy. Following traditional practices, Nan-ye-hi and the Women's Council conducted international relations by incorporating useful white allies into Cherokee society through marriages and by using their important role as mothers to strengthen diplomatic kinships. Nan-ye-hi's most direct access to powerful whites came through the marriages of her daughters to important white traders and diplomats. Alliances with merchants were essential, because traders connected Cherokees and their skins, cattle, crops, and silverwork to businessmen with weapons and ammunition for hunting and protection, clothing, and other goods. Traders often spoke and wrote English, making them valuable as scribes and translators in communications and conferences. These roles heightened the importance of converting commercial men into trustworthy allies. Nan-ye-hi's older daughter Ka-ti married John Walker and later Ellis Harlan. Walker was a white trader who provided access to goods during the early years of white settlement. Harlan was particularly involved in Cherokee affairs as a trader, interpreter, and emissary for Nan-ye-hi. Nan-ye-hi's younger daughter Betsey made the most influential match, marrying Joseph Martin, North Carolina's and Virginia's agent to the Cherokees after 1777. Following a common practice, Martin had a Virginia family who was aware of the arrangement. The marriage probably took place in 1778 and the couple had dual residences —one home at Long Island near the white settlements and another with or near Nan-ye-hi, Ka-ti, and Harlan at Citico. Their son James was born in Citico in 1780, and after that they had a daughter, Nanny. The Wolf clan recognized Martin as a relation, giving him connections to the most influential clan of the nation.[34]

Relying on her clan connections, Nan-ye-hi become more actively involved in diplomatic negotiations after Attakullakulla's death and Betsey's marriage in 1778. Nan-ye-hi's growing influence built on the already active roles that women had taken in diplomacy after newcomers began claiming Cherokee lands.[35] Scholars have devoted considerable attention to the reluctance of young Cherokee men to part with their hunting grounds. Much of this work studies the importance of these lands to Cherokee livelihood and masculinity. But the loss of lands affected women as well as men, both because it threatened their own well-being and because land cessions impaired the livelihood of the children they reared.[36] Acting on the expectation that a marked line would prevent encroachment, two Cherokee women joined forty-five men to supervise the running of Donelson's line in the early 1770s. During pretreaty negotiations in 1774 between Richard Henderson and the Cherokees, the Cherokees sent an envoy of two men and one woman to North Carolina to view the goods Henderson offered for the treaty. At Henderson's treaty, Cherokee negotiators argued that their children would have reason to complain if they sold the lands. Many of the older Cherokee women at that treaty opposed a signature on any document that might transfer property. Women often served as messengers, carrying requests for peace conferences, sometimes at considerable personal risk.[37]

Like Nan-ye-hi who had alerted the settlers about Tsi-yugunsini's attack in 1776, some women brokered peace by intervening in order to lessen the chance of full-scale war. During peace talks in 1777, women hid the weapons when some drunk Cherokee men became unruly and threatened to disrupt the negotiations. A number of women among the eighty-five Cherokees attending peace talks in 1778 warned the trader, Thomas Price, that the talks of the chiefs were a delaying action while the warriors procured ammunition. Undercutting part of the war strategy, the women disclosed that the chiefs planned to blame Tsi-yugunsini's actions on the Creeks. When Savanukeh transferred his allegiance to the British in 1780 and planned to kill some American traders, several other women joined Nan-ye-hi in aiding the traders' escape. Cherokee women also attended peace conferences in large numbers, were consulted by the men at private caucuses during the conference, and sat together in a women's circle during the treaty talks.[38]

In order to protect their lands, Nan-ye-hi and the Women's Council undertook a more visible diplomatic presence during the 1780s. An increase in Chickamaugan attacks after settlement of the Cumberland region in 1780 led settler militias under Arthur Campbell to invade the Overhill country, destroying many towns and their provisions. Nan-ye-hi brokered peace by offering food and intelligence to Campbell and his troops.[39] The women then spoke publicly at several peace conferences. They brought a special voice to diplomacy—one that aimed to restore balance in two areas. They positioned Cherokee women as diplomatic mothers in order to urge peace in the face of warfare conducted by young men on both sides, and they sought to assert a common humanity between Cherokees and whites. Female diplomats believed that warfare would lead to forced land cessions and that agreement about the equality of the two peoples was critical to a recognition of Cherokee property rights.

The women spoke first at the talks convened in 1781 by General Nathanael Greene, commander of the Continental army in the South, to reestablish peace after the militia campaign of 1780. Described by Commissioner Joseph Martin's white son William as "one of the most superior women I ever saw," Nan-ye-hi addressed the white negotiators to plea for peace based on a kinship between the parties. Nan-ye-hi broke with traditional negotiation practice that avoided assigning blame in order to create an atmosphere conducive to peacemaking, prefacing her remarks with an explicit indictment of the land hunters' conduct that led to war. While male negotiators fashioned whites as fathers and elder brothers, Nan-ye-hi named them as her sons, placing them under her considerable matriarchal authority: "We are your mothers. You are our sons. Our cry is all for peace. Let it continue because we are your mothers. This peace must last forever. Let your women's sons be ours; our sons be yours." By extending her metaphor of motherhood to include all men, Nan-ye-hi's embrace suggested that native and white men should consider themselves to be the sons of both races, an image that dissolved racial constructions to imply parity.[40]

When Arthur Campbell, now one of the American commissioners, desired a land cession from the Cherokees as compensation for their aggressions, Nan-ye-hi responded that land cessions impaired Cherokee survival: "We know that the white people are more and stronger than us, but will you take everything from us and leave us to starve?" Nan-ye-hi followed her plea with the presentment of five strings, rather than the customary one string, emphasizing the strength of the constituency supporting her words. Nan-ye-hi's appeal, coming shortly after her gestures of support to Campbell during his military campaign, spared the Cherokees from pressures to make land cessions. Nan-ye-hi followed up by using her influence the next year to broker a prisoner exchange with Governor Harrison of Virginia.[41]

Nan-ye-hi's assertion of a universal humanity rooted in a diplomatic motherhood was affirmed by five older members of the Women's Council, who addressed Greene's conference on behalf of the women at the conclusion of the 1781 peace talks. They sought to bolster their authority by having a male chief, Scolacutta, accompany them. They whispered their speech to him, which he delivered to the assembled audience. Unfortunately, only part of their remarkable address was preserved:

> We the women of the Cherokee nation now speak to you. We are mothers, and have many sons, some of them warriors and beloved men. We call you also our sons. We have a right to call you so, because you are the sons of mothers, and all descended from the same woman at first. We say you are our sons, because by women, you were brought forth into this world, nursed, suckled, and raised up to be men before you reached your present greatness. You are our sons. Why should there be any difference amongst us? We live on the same land with you, and our people are mixed with white blood: one third of our [people are] mixed with white blood.[42]

Building on Nan-ye-hi's construction, these women imagined a diplomatic motherhood linked to Selu, the first woman and a powerful spiritual figure. They reminded Anglo men of the importance of women, a point that was critical because women's energy was needed to balance male forces. Responding to white notions of superiority, they stressed the similarities between Indians and settlers.

Speaking at the Treaty of Hopewell convened by the United States in 1785, Nan-ye-hi articulated an important implication of her 1781 assertion of a common humanity when she told the commissioners: "I look on you and the red people equally as my children." In verbalizing the equality of the two peoples, Nan-ye-hi added a new note to her speech: "The talk I have given, is from the young warriors I have raised in my town, as well as myself. They rejoice that we have peace, and we hope the chain of friendship will never more be broke." Nan-ye-hi's commission to speak for the warriors established that she had acquired and was exercising authority beyond that traditionally bestowed on Beloved Women, who spoke only for the women. At Hopewell, Nan-ye-hi and Onitositah dissuaded the federal government from extending American boundaries beyond those set in the 1777 treaty, except for some areas in Cumberland and in eastern Tennessee with numerous settlers, while convincing the government to void claims to Cherokee lands made by North Carolina in 1783 and by settlers in eastern Tennessee in 1785. Their success prompted William Blount, the North Carolina commissioner, to file a strong dissent.[43]

Following the lead of Nan-ye-hi and the Women's Council, other Beloved Women spoke publicly to fashion white men as their sons in order to forge peace. In a message to the Continental Congress addressed to President Benjamin Franklin in 1787, Katteuha, the Beloved Woman of Chota and probably the maternal niece of Oconostota and sister of Savanukeh, declared herself a mother to Congress:

> I am in hopes that if you rightly consider it that woman is the mother of all and that woman does not pull children out of trees or stumps nor out of old logs, but out of their bodies, so that they ought to mind what a woman says, and look upon her as a mother—and I have taken the privilege to speak to you as my own children and the same as if you had sucked my breast. . . . The great men have all promised to keep the path clear and straight, as my children shall keep the path clear and white. . . . The talk you sent to me was to talk to my children, which I have done this day, and they all liked my talk well.

Onitositah and Scolacutta endorsed Katteuha's speech.[44]

In a Grand Talk from the headmen and warriors of the nation addressed to the governor of North Carolina in 1789, the women stressed a new point—that peace was important for the children: "Now, this is our beloved women's talk; they say they have heard our great talks, and they hope to live at home in their houses in satisfaction, and they have told their warriors to be at peace from this time out, that they may raise their children in happiness." It was very likely the concerns of women for their children's heritage that long prompted Cherokee diplomats to complain that the goods whites gave for lands were fungible while the lands they received lasted forever. Implicit in this argument was a desire to preserve a heritage for future generations.[45]

Not limiting their entreaties to white men, Cherokee women believed that they could protect their land rights by appealing to white women to balance male energies for war, a practice that they had used in the past with other indigenous communities. Although aware that women in white society did not occupy the same positions of power as in the Cherokee world, Cherokee women did direct gestures of peace to white women. In 1776 Nan-ye-hi exercised her authority as the War Woman to save the life of a female captive, Mrs. Bean. In exchange, Mrs. Bean taught the women to make butter. When Nan-ye-hi spoke as a mother for peace to the commissioners at the 1781 treaty, she addressed the women specifically by proclaiming: "Let your women hear our words." Katteuha voiced a similar sentiment in 1787 when she told Franklin: "I am in hopes you have a beloved woman amongst you who will help to put her children right if they do wrong."[46]

While female negotiators positioned the settlers as their sons and sought to enlist women to control their children, congressional interest at Hopewell encouraged the male chiefs to revise their kinship to the representatives of the new state of Franklin. They reimagined the settlers as brothers, not elder brothers or fathers, giving the Cherokees an equivalent status to white settlers in relationship to the federal government. Many of these leaders also recast their kinship with the state governors, relegating them as well to the role of brother. Upper Town chief Oskuah established equality with a different strategy, characterizing the Beloved Men of Chota and the governor as his elder brothers, thus elevating the Cherokee chiefs to a status equivalent to that of the white leaders.[47]

In addition to reformulating their relationships with the frontier people, Cherokee negotiators expanded the diplomatic version of the concept of renewal beyond its original intention of perpetuating a peaceful state of mind. Persistent treaty breaches by the westering people resulted in new treaties, with whites claiming that the more recent treaties superseded the older ones. Cherokee headmen were unable to revive white promises made in earlier treaties, and they lost lands without any diplomatic or legal mechanism to regain them. Negotiators began to include the perpetuation of prior treaty covenants as one of the obligations of diplomatic kinship. Underlying the revised doctrine of regeneration was the idea that claims for justice with respect to older boundary lines did not expire. Drawing on the spiritual source of relationships, the Cherokee headmen made the treaty relationship —not unjust treaty terms—durable, holding out to the hundreds of young men present and to their white kin the belief that whites could and should, in the future, change their ways, take pity, and do justice. This was an important lesson, both for whites and for their own young warriors, advocating that human beings can reestablish peaceful and just relationships even in the face of broken promises.[48]

Cherokee success at General Greene's 1781 treaty in avoiding a land sale and at Hopewell in 1785 in regaining some of their territory encouraged them to believe that the confederated government might observe the responsibilities of a diplomatic father more reliably than state officials, but their reliance on the new federal government was misplaced. The weakness of the government under the Articles of Confederation and the failure of North Carolina to cede its western claims left Congress virtually powerless to control Indian affairs in the Southwest. Onitositah continued to broker a peace diplomacy but by 1787 became discouraged. That year, he condemned Virginia for sending him letters threatening "fire and sword" when the Virginians had taken almost all of the Cherokee lands without their consent and had failed to honor treaty boundaries.[49] Along with Onitositah, most Upper Town Cherokees wanted to preserve the remaining ancestral lands and to engage in trade with the settlers, but they struggled with the failure by many farmers, townspeople, and speculators in the state of Franklin to respond to Cherokee ideas about reciprocity and justice. Even with the conceptual modifications to traditional doctrines made by the peace chiefs and the Women's Council, ideas about fictive kinship and how to develop it were strained to the breaking point by tensions between peacemaking as a goal in itself to achieve a state of mind, the failure of international kinship to contain encroachment, and white demands for land cessions as part of the peace process. The vacuum created by the intellectual inadequacy of the Upper Town peace ideology made room for the more assertive conception of Cherokee diplomacy being developed by the Chickamaugans.

The frontier people brought a radically different cultural and ideological heritage. These land hunters represented a diverse group of backcountry farmers. Included in their number were people of English, Irish, Scottish, and German ancestry.[50] More than two and a half centuries of contact between Europeans and the first peoples of the Americas informed the thinking of the settlers about the original inhabitants. During this period, the colonizing Spanish, French, English and local officials struggled to develop positions about the native polities they encountered in the Americas, Africa, and India. At early contact in the Americas, Europeans ignored native governments and claimed both political jurisdiction and legal title to lands, which they viewed as vacant on grounds of *vacuum domicilium*.[51]

Following its European predecessors, England at first viewed the New World as *vacuum domicilium*, but Native American resistance forced them as well as other imperial powers to recognize the indigenous occupants. Joining other European theorists, English thinkers built on a medieval discourse from the Crusades that permitted the pope to override the natural-law rights of infidels in order to protect their spiritual well-being. Modifying and secularizing this doctrine, the English ground their empire building in theories that recognized the natural rights of aboriginal inhabitants but found exceptions in doctrines of conquest that justified their assertion of political control over the population and entitlement to the land. Unlike Spain, however, England had relatively little sustained interest in ruling the native peoples. Generally recognizing the sovereignty of independent Indian nations over their own peoples, Britain entered into treaties with them as they would European nations. Rights to land claimed more imperial attention. Initially,

England claimed the right to land by conquest but, by the eighteenth century, Britain recognized the natural right of occupancy of the native nations. In order to obtain land, England increasingly purchased it. Like other European nations, England restricted Native American sovereignty by asserting that indigenous peoples could sell only to Britain and not to other European powers in the sphere claimed by Great Britain. After the costly Indian allegiances with the French during 1756–63, the British attempted to lessen Indian tensions by restricting settlement west of the Appalachians in the Proclamation of 1763 and by prohibiting private purchases of Indian lands.[52]

While European conquerors imposed various forms of control over indigenous Americans, Africans, and East Indians, Enlightenment theorists in the sixteenth, seventeenth, and eighteenth centuries struggled to articulate a rational theory of international law. Writing during the emergence of the nation-state, they organized their constructs around a discourse of nationhood. These thinkers wanted to create a systematic framework that would embed international relations in principles of natural law. In the mid-eighteenth century, Emmerich de Vattel crafted a code that met with tremendous success. Published in 1758, *The Law of Nations* became the most widely read and accepted enunciation of principles for the conduct of international affairs in Europe. Vattel's work was extremely popular in the American colonies and early republic. It went through multiple printings, and colleges in the new United States commonly used his work as a text.[53] Many Tennesseans were familiar with it.[54]

Unlike the Cherokees who constructed their polity around clan ties, Vattel placed the nation at the heart of his system. To Vattel, a nation was a society of men who compacted to join together for mutual advantage. To be sovereign, a nation must govern itself by its own authority and laws. Vattel positioned the nation as similar to an individual in a state of nature, but contended that the laws of nature applied differently to nations than to individuals. Unlike individuals who consented to yield authority to the state, a state was potentially independent of other states. Each nation that governed itself without dependence on a foreign power was a sovereign state that had the right to make its own internal policies. In contrast to an older European view that states primarily exercised sovereignty over people—the king's subjects—Vattel described nations that controlled territory. He did not distinguish between civilized and uncivilized nations or between European and non-European states. However, he made one accommodation to the European realpolitik that was of great significance to Indian nationhood. According to Vattel, under natural law nations had a duty to cultivate the soil, because the earth furnished subsistence. Overpopulated nations had the right to occupy the territory of those who did not cultivate their lands.[55]

Vattel drew on diverse intellectual traditions to articulate his exception that permitted cultivators to appropriate lands in another nation not used for farming. The discourse that favored agrarianism originated in the idea that the earth belonged to all of humankind. John Locke and other liberal philosophers described a state of nature in which men owned property in common. The Scottish Enlightenment thinker Thomas Reid argued that the Creator gave the world to humankind with all property equally available for occupation by everyone to be used for the general good. Individuals had the right only to such material goods as they needed to provide for themselves and their dependents. Many Europeans understood that the best use of the earth was one that supported the greatest population growth, a goal realized through tillage. By the mid-eighteenth century, agrarian views about the common good were modified further and incorporated into a philosophy of civilization. Scottish philosophers articulated a progressive view of society that located civilization as the highest stage. Civilization was characterized by cultivation and commerce, advances that recognized private property rights in land. To Europeans, Native Americans were in an earlier phase of human development. As the European gaze turned to the Americas, these observers saw natives who lived by the hunt, wandering over large areas of land that they utilized for nonagricultural purposes.[56] Excluding indigenous peoples from European land rights, Vattel's theoretical compromise left unresolved the meaning of nationhood for such unproductive states.

The separate and autonomous political sovereignties that constituted nations made diplomatic connections with each other in significant part through the mechanism of treaties. In Vattel's analysis, this process was the best means for states to obtain benefits. Unlike the highly relational and holistic spiritual approach used by the Cherokees in making connections with foreigners, the European cognitive universe was ground in a more analytic epistemology. As participants in a movement toward secularization, Europeans tended to differentiate objects and to reason analytically about them, classifying them and using rules about categories to regulate and understand behavior. The object of peacemaking was to produce a treaty, a compact that contained agreements about specific issues. Treaty partners interpreted their agreement based on principles of Roman *jus gentium* or natural law and on analogies to private law, especially contract law.[57]

In fashioning their understanding of, distinctiveness from, and relationship to the peoples who preceded them, governmental officials and frontier people in North America drew on Vattel's principles of the law of nations, on the doctrines of agricultural use, on treaty protocols and land purchases, and on the European discourse of conquest. Like the Cherokees, the newcomers envisioned mental and physical boundaries between the two peoples, but of a different kind. In the political realm, they saw the Cherokees as a distinct sovereignty. With the exception of those whites who lived in Cherokee towns, the westering people did not consider themselves subject to Cherokee law, nor did they expect to intercede in Cherokee affairs or to contest the sovereignty of Native Americans over their own people. Although there were occasional references to Indian tribes, generally the pioneers considered that they were dealing with Indian nations who possessed a country. These borderland people expected to make a contractual connection through treaties and trade agreements, not to enter into a relational web of kinship obligations. Believing the early Tennessee settlements to be within its boundaries, Virginia signed a treaty with the Cherokees in 1770 that reflected its recognition of a separate Cherokee nation.[58]

Underlying this construction of separate societies lay tensions that threatened those boundaries. By 1774 the new farmers challenged the right of the Cherokee people to their country. In common with backcountry people elsewhere in British North America, most of the early land hunters in the Tennessee region believed in the right to appropriate lands used by the Indians primarily for hunting. Leaders like east Tennessean John Sevier, son of a wealthy Virginia planter, and James Robertson, a first man in the Cumberland settlements, contended that no nation could claim more lands than it could occupy or cultivate. Privileging cultivation, Sevier paraphrased Vattel when he proclaimed: "By the law of nations, it is agreed that no people shall be entitled to more land than they can cultivate. Of course no people will sit and starve for want of land to work, when a neighboring nation has much more than they can make use of."[59]

Sevier located the source of this doctrine in the law of nations. Robertson agreed, and buttressed his position with the laws of nature. Contrary to the assertions by historians that land hunters failed to recognize Indian farmers, the proponents of this doctrine in Tennessee did not ignore the fact that Native Americans also lived on and farmed their lands but objected to the reservation of large tracts of land for hunting. Robertson noted that Indian villages had title by nativity to lands, "but [there] ought to be some limitation to their bounds." As one German occupant explained, the Indians possessed "more land than they cultivated."[60]

Although many settlers in the Tennessee watershed held agrarian views, these early adventurers envisioned the Cherokees as a people in a variety of ways. While most fashioned a separate nationhood, some advocated for a transformation of Cherokee society, and many advanced a view of the natives as cruel savages who should be eliminated. Facing significant numbers of Native American residents, most early settlers opted to enter into treaties with the Cherokees as a distinct political entity and to respect the greater part of their territorial integrity. Many pioneers recognized Cherokee sovereignty and imagined an authority in chiefs that exceeded their actual powers in order to further their own interests. Seeking a peaceful accommodation, some of these settlers leased or purchased land directly from the Cherokee "nation." However, these designations reflected a compromised form of sovereignty. In contrast to prevailing notions of European nationhood, white purchasers and lessees did not suppose that their acquisitions of land in Cherokee country subjected them to Cherokee authority.[61]

Taking another stance, some settlers accepted the European Enlightenment doctrines of a common humanity and of progressive societies and believed that indigenous people could be civilized. Their belief was an early example of a doctrine prevalent during colonization in Neo-European settlements throughout the world from the late eighteenth to the twentieth century. Long before the federal civilization policy of 1789, these borderers contemplated arrangements that would transform Cherokee society by promoting civilization and Christianity. The persistence of these early settlers earned them a rebuke from Onitositah in 1777:

> Indeed, much has been advanced on the want of what you term civilization among the Indians; and many proposals have been made to us to adopt your laws, your religion, your manners, and your customs. But, we confess that we do not yet see the propriety, or practicality of such a reformation, and should be better pleased with beholding the good effect of these doctrines in your own practices than with hearing you talk about them, or reading your papers to us upon such subjects.

At boundary line discussions two years later, commissioner Daniel Smith recommended to the Cherokee diplomats that the Cherokee men farm to support their wives and children and hunt only for family needs. In the peace talks in 1781, the parties engaged in considerable discussion about the possibility of a school for the education of young Indians.[62]

Other westering people fashioned a different view of Native American peoples. The first backcountry settlers brought with them largely negative images of savages. To many frontier people, especially pioneers whose family members had been killed by Indians, indigenous peoples were bloodthirsty, cruel, and untrustworthy. Because many newcomers viewed Indians as more beast than human, these borderers refused to extend any political recognition or grant any rights to the Cherokees. Instead, they advocated extermination of the indigenous people.[63]

With American independence, the Continental Congress largely left the conduct of Indian affairs to the new states. That year North Carolina recognized the transmontane settlements as within its claim. When the Cherokee peace faction met the white negotiators at Long Island in 1777, the commissioners from North Carolina and Virginia treated with the Overhill Cherokees as though they were a separate European nation. Although the treaty protocol was Native American, the ensuing Treaty of Long Island at Holston continued to cast the Cherokees as a sovereign nation. It specifically referred to the Cherokee "Nation" and provided for the issuance of passports to whites who traveled in the nation. The treaty also contained mostly reciprocal provisions of criminal justice that supported views of separate polities, with whites executing whites who murdered Cherokees and Cherokees putting to death Cherokees who killed whites.[64]

The decision by the Chickamaugans to continue to associate with the British after 1777 led to a profound shift in the meaning many of the frontier patriots gave to Cherokee nationhood. These patriots reclassified the Cherokees as the enemy, acting as an agent of the British government. For these borderers "of all ranks," this classification of the Cherokees justified appropriation of their lands. The American victory over Great Britain encouraged the United States and the North Carolina government and most of its settlers to view the Cherokees as conquered. The United States abandoned this theory in the mid-1780s, when resistance from the northern Indians proved its inaccuracy, but North Carolina persisted in asserting it. North Carolina degraded native sovereignty over Indian territory by two unilateral legislative acts. In 1777 and again in 1783, the state, without negotiations, appropriated huge portions of native lands into its western district. A statute in 1783 issued warrants to claimants, many of them veterans, for land right up to the Indian villages. In 1784 the settlers of the eastern counties of North Carolina's western district organized themselves into the separate state of Franklin. According to one settler, their purpose was to appropriate the Indian lands. After military incursions, leaders of the "New State" purportedly negotiated with the Cherokees as a separate nation at Dumplin Creek in 1785 and at Coyatee in 1786. The language of both treaties that they crafted invoked a doctrine of conquest against the Indian nation based on victories in the Revolutionary War and on recent invasions of Indian country by militias.[65]

The borderers who propounded a doctrine of conquest were divided about how to apply it to the Cherokees. As in the earlier period, many whites assumed a license to murder Indian people, either out of hatred or a desire to seize native lands. A few leaders, driven less by hatred than the belief that white and Cherokee societies were incompatible neighbors, floated the idea of voluntary removal. Colonel Alexander Outlaw, in transmitting the Treaty of Coyatee to North Carolina's Governor Caswell in 1786, claimed that the Cherokees were willing to "leave the country entirely," if they were paid for their lands. In 1789 Brigadier General Daniel Smith, commander of the Mero District in the Cumberland region, corresponded with Governor Estevan Miro of New Orleans about Nashville's Indian problems. Governor Miro advised him that the Cherokees in May 1788 had asked permission of the Spanish to settle west of the Mississippi, which was given. Some Cherokees moved there at that time. Governor Miro believed that this would be the best result for the west Tennessee inhabitants. By 1793 the Cherokees complained to the English that American encroachment was forcing the nation to consider crossing the Mississippi.[66]

Some whites after the Revolution refused to recast the Cherokees as Britain's ally or as a conquered people without rights. Although the Tennessee lands were part of North Carolina's claim, Virginia continued to negotiate with the Cherokees, at times jointly with North Carolina, to protect its claims in Kentucky. At the Treaty of Long Island at Holston in 1777, Virginia negotiators tried unsuccessfully to alleviate North Carolina's harsh stance against the Cherokees for uncompensated land by right of conquest. During the 1780s, Indian agent Joseph Martin frequently provided supplies to the Indians at his own expense. Often reviled and occasionally threatened by the frontier people for his support of Indian rights, Martin pleaded their case to the North Carolina legislature and to various Virginia and North Carolina governors. In response to Martin's efforts, Virginia's Governor Benjamin Harrison recognized Indian claims and equated their entitlements to those of white people. Condemning encroachers and speculators who wanted more land than they could cultivate, Harrison wrote to Governor Martin of North Carolina: "Indians have their rights, and our justice is called on to support them. Whilst we are nobly contending for Liberty, will it not be an eternal blot on our national character if we deprive others of it who ought to be as free as ourselves?"[67]

Joseph Martin and Governor Harrison were not alone in fashioning the Cherokees as a nation entitled to rights and justice. Responding in part to friendships formed with Cherokee chiefs in peace councils and in other interactions, some leaders joined others who feared the effects of an Indian war or who believed peace would promote settler prosperity. Although many of these men agreed with the doctrine of conquest, they sought a negotiated arrangement that recognized native sovereignty and often worked against policies of extermination. In 1781 William Christian, one of Virginia's commissioners to the Cherokees, wrote the governor of Virginia to recommend that he do justice to the Cherokees with respect to their lands and support the Cherokee families if he wanted the Cherokees to treat with them. By 1787 the courts in Sullivan, Washington, and Hawkins counties in eastern Tennessee opposed the Franklin land grabs. In the fall of 1787, Arthur Campbell wrote Governor Randolph of Virginia, arguing that extirpation of the Indians "is a wrong policy at this day and in the present circumstances." At the same time, James Robertson dissuaded an army from invading the Cherokee country, creating considerable hostility against him by many of his white neighbors.[68]

By befriending the Cherokees, more ordinary pioneers also challenged the notion that indigenous peoples should be exterminated. Because of the kindness of Samuel Sherrill and his family, the Cherokees viewed them as friends and Beloved People and spared them in their attacks in the region. After Cherokee raids in early 1788, frontiersmen in Hawkins County restrained angry neighbors who wanted to plunder the Cherokee towns. Relying on goodwill built up between the Cherokees and settlers, Major Colby and another frontiersman in the French Broad area traveled to the Cherokee villages a year later and made peace after the unprovoked murder of a Cherokee man by one of the settlers in 1789. Pioneers like these managed to impose some limitations on violence against Native Americans.[69]

Westering people in the post-Revolutionary era who resisted the cries of their neighbors for extermination or removal of the Cherokees contemplated coexistence by imagining a variety of models for Cherokee-settler accommodation. Some, like North Carolina governor Alex Martin, proposed to segregate the Cherokees in small settlements in white country. Surrounded by whites, "their power [would be] reduced to the harmless and inoffensive situation of the Catawbas." In the summer of 1782, a group of North Carolinians attempted to raise a force of men to move the Cherokees near to the white settlements and to compel them to live by farming. Acting on a different vision, other citizens in the new state of Franklin in 1785 discussed incorporating the Cherokee people into Franklin's sovereignty. They negotiated with the Cherokees on three occasions to incorporate them into Franklin but the chiefs refused. Their motives are disputed. This movement may have had its origins in the religious zeal of a young minister. Joseph Martin reported that Franklin planned to get representatives from the Cherokee towns into its assembly to augment its numbers in order to get congressional representation, but the attempt was thwarted. However, one Franklin citizen wrote privately to a friend that the purpose was to make the Cherokees useful citizens. A third group of reformers favoring coexistence echoed earlier calls to civilize the Cherokees. Virginia governor Patrick Henry encouraged arts and manufacturing among the Cherokees. Joseph Martin, joined by other U.S. commissioners at the Treaty of Hopewell in 1785, recommended teaching the Cherokees useful branches of mechanics and how to raise, spin, and weave flax, cotton, and wool. By the mid-1780s, according to one resident of the French Broad area, many Cherokees who lived near the pioneer settlements were "undergoing a sensible reformation." A number engaged in commerce with the westering people. Cherokee women wanted to send their daughters to white women to learn to spin.[70]

With the adoption of the Articles of Confederation, a new government entered the picture, contesting with the states for authority to handle Native American affairs. Nathanael Greene's conference with the Cherokees in 1781 resulted in pledges of peace. The Congressional Proclamation of September 22, 1783, forbade settlement on or purchasing of Indian lands without federal consent. In the Treaty of Hopewell in 1785, treaty provisions placed the Cherokees under the protection of the United States. Angered by unfavorable boundary lines in the Treaty at Hopewell that located many settlers on Cherokee lands, most North Carolinians did not impute any authority to the treaty. Because North Carolina did not cede its western lands to the national government until 1789, the confederated government had no power to enforce its promises or to conduct Indian affairs in the state's western region. Consequently, the state of Franklin, operating under the doctrine of the sword, disputed Cherokee sovereignty and sold lands in the Indian territory.[71] Although the Franklin settlers who favored a discourse of conquest prevailed in the mid-1780s, the more extreme wing dedicated to extermination was not successful. Cherokee resistance and white moderates prevented the conquest and annihilation of the Indians. Though broached, the idea of removal remained a minor theme. As the decade moved to a close, the cession of its western lands by North Carolina to the newly formed United States rendered the predominant rhetoric of conquest problematic.

CHAPTER TWO

Ungrateful Brothers
and an Uncivilized Nation
The Cherokees and Settlers Reconceive
Their Relationship, 1776–1796

Onitositah and John Sevier met for the last time as spring waned in 1788. In May, when the men in the family were absent, several Cherokees killed the wife and ten family members of an encroacher named John Kirk, prompting an invasion of the Cherokee country by Sevier and his militia in early June, in part to avenge the massacre of Kirk's family. Sevier saw Onitositah at the Little River town where Onitositah lived. Accepting Onitositah's professions of peace, the war chief marched on to attack Hiwassee. Upon its destruction, Sevier dispatched Major James Hubbard, a notorious Indian hater whose entire family had been killed by Indians, and John Kirk Jr., along with other troops, to destroy Chilhowie, hometown of the Cherokee man who had murdered the Kirks. En route, Hubbard lured peace chiefs Onitositah, Oskuah, and several others into Oskuah's house under a flag of truce for talks. Once inside, Hubbard placed guards at the door and windows, gave a tomahawk to young Kirk, and authorized him to "take the vengeance to which you are entitled." Kirk did. Whether Sevier ordered or permitted this action has never been resolved.[1]

The massacre of Onitositah and the Upper Town peace chiefs galvanized many of the Cherokee people to reunite with the Chickamaugans in war. By 1788 most of the Upper Town inhabitants were disenchanted with their white brothers, who continued to violate the demands of the fictive kin relationship by expanding their land encroachments. Historians have uniformly portrayed the Lower Town residents as warriors, ignoring or belittling their peacemaking initiatives.[2] During the 1780s, however, the growing prosperity of the Chickamaugan Lower Towns encouraged some of their leaders to seek a negotiated solution to their differences with the settlers. The Treaty of Hopewell in 1785 introduced the Cherokees to a new potential ally—the confederated government. The massacre of the Kirk family and the Upper Town peace chiefs temporarily derailed these efforts to maintain peace and marked a critical turning point in the way that the Cherokee people constructed their relationship with the settlers. The murders of the peace chiefs brought the Upper Town leaders into the more aggressive Lower Town peace movement. Led by the Chickamaugans, this united Cherokee front reconceived its understanding of diplomatic kinship with the borderers and the United States. When white settlers persisted in ignoring what the Cherokees believed were prior commitments, the Cherokees recast them as misbehaving brothers.

In its first treaty with the reconstituted federal government in 1791, the Cherokees negotiated with Governor William Blount, the federal Indian superintendent who advanced local interests more strenuously than federal policy. Cherokee diplomats publicly countered white assertions of savage inferiority and insisted that peace be conditioned on their concepts of equality and justice, an assertive claim of Cherokee self-worth. Their statesmen received assurances of equality and of the perpetual existence of the Cherokee nation, but Blount pressured them to sign a treaty that contained land cessions. Unhappy warriors responded with violence. Although forced to make peace in late 1794, the Cherokees did secure the appointment of a more disinterested Indian agent in 1796.

Like other transmontane people, postcolonial citizens in other colonies, and inhabitants of regions claimed by more than one nation, Tennesseans negotiated the meaning of nationhood.[3] North Carolina ceded its western lands to the federal government in 1789. Flouting federal directives forbidding offensive war, territorial militias supported by Governor Blount responded to Cherokee attacks in 1793 and 1794 by waging a series of illegal assaults on the Cherokees. These violations of the federal mandates generated extensive debate about the nature of nationhood. Supporters of the militia actions argued that local citizens had the right to countermand federal authority and to determine their own Indian policy in cases of self-defense. Opponents stressed the importance of the rule of law to society. As citizens understood nationalism to require restraints on their actions, they revisited their understanding of Indian nationhood, rejecting the belief that native nations were entitled to the same prerogatives as civilized nations. This change was the outgrowth of a modified understanding of the doctrine of savagery. White farmers and townspeople translated their beliefs that the

Cherokees were a bloodthirsty, cruel, and untrustworthy people into a new view of the Cherokee polity—that of an uncivilized nation. As such, they concluded that the Cherokees should not enjoy parity with civilized nations, creating a distinction between uncivilized and civilized nations that Vattel's *Law of Nations* did not recognize.

The formulation of the newcomers as diplomatic kin, articulated by the Upper Town peace faction, was not universally accepted by the Cherokee people after 1775. Many Cherokees engaged in a different discourse about the new borderers. Rejecting them as fictive relations, these dissidents cast them as "rogues" or "Virginians"—encroachers who stole Cherokee lands. Those who resisted diplomatic kinship responded in a variety of ways. Many women and men withdrew into the Cherokee community, often in remote areas, and continued to live a traditional life with as little contact with the newcomers as possible. In the 1780s others initiated an exodus to the territory west of the Mississippi River, hoping to perpetuate Cherokee ways in a country uncluttered by white encroachers. Many, however, joined Cherokee warrior Tsi-yugunsini in resisting.[4]

Historians characterize the period from 1776 until 1794 as one in which the Lower Towns, joined by Creeks, some Upper Town Cherokees, and various northern Indians, engaged in more or less continuous warfare with the frontier people. These scholars portray Tsi-yugunsini and the Chickamaugans who followed him as defenders of the Cherokee nation, whose mission was to drive out the intruding settlers. Arguing eloquently that white usurpations of Cherokee land would continue until the Cherokees were extinct, Tsi-yugunsini had opposed Henderson's Treaty in 1775. By characterizing the white community as banditti and worse, the dissidents created a wide latitude for a variety of actions against it, justifying the killing of white women and children and slaves as well as white men. Tsi-yugunsini molded a war strategy designed to eliminate the weaker Cumberland settlements, established on land claimed by Richard Henderson, while harassing the eastern stations and farms. Meanwhile, the unhappy Upper Town Cherokees defended themselves against angry settlers by pointing to the Lower Towns as the perpetrators of mischief. The Chickamaugans, Shawnee, and Creeks made serious efforts to unify the southeastern tribes, especially in 1792, but the Chickasaws refused to join.[5]

This narrative overlooks several complicating features. Although many warriors fought to eliminate settler presence in the Tennessee Valley, from the beginning the motivation of the Chickamaugan warriors was more complex.

Physically withdrawing from the encroaching settlers enhanced the prosperity of the dissident Cherokees. During the American Revolution, they enjoyed trade opportunities with the British, and their incursions against the settlers yielded horses, slaves, and other goods. As they expanded their commerce to include more European and Native American partners, the Chickamaugans began to define their autonomy as a people in economic as well as military terms. Their pursuit of increasing wealth was at times at odds with their campaign against the "Virginians." On several occasions, Chickamaugan warriors sacrificed critical military goals in order to secure plunder.[6]

Growing prosperity encouraged the dissenters to envision their international economic connections as a counterbalance to American aggression and spurred a Chickamaugan peace movement that historians have ignored or belittled.[7] The dissident peace faction began tentatively, as Chickamaugans communicated with the Virginia commissioners and developed a relationship with Indian agent Joseph Martin, passing on intelligence, airing complaints, and attempting to maintain peace. At the same time, they strengthened their ties with the chiefs of the Upper Towns. Tsi-yugunsini wrote the Virginia peace commissioners in 1777 pledging peace. Onitositah delivered a peace message from the Chickamaugans in the conference with General Nathanael Greene of the Continental army in the summer of 1781, and the Chickamaugans had two representatives at the conference. Later that year, Chickamaugans warned Martin of impending problems from that region. Honoring a peace brokered by the Upper Town chiefs, the River People gave up prisoners to Martin in 1782. The next summer Martin and William Christian met with a Chickamaugan delegation of four chiefs, six women, and twelve young men. Martin and John Donelson concluded a peace treaty with the Lower Towns later that year. Exercising a peacekeeping role similar to that of many Upper Town women, a few women in 1783 warned travelers suspected of being speculators of plans by some of the men to kill them. Numerous Lower Town residents passed information on to Martin in 1784. John McDonald, a former British agent who lived with the Chickamaugans and was very influential in their affairs, established a correspondence with him in 1785.[8]

Although some Chickamaugans were taking tentative steps toward peace, their influence was still quite limited. White aggression and encroachment and the refusal by many young Chickamaugan men to accede to white treaty claims or to acknowledge white settlers as their kin rather than as rogues thwarted the peace movement. Asserting their right to Cherokee lands by conquest, the leaders of the new state of Franklin in eastern Tennessee destroyed the 1783 peace agreement when they unilaterally sold Cherokee lands in 1785. Some Cherokees turned to the United States for assistance. The Chickamauga peace faction sent representatives to the Treaty of Hopewell with the United States in 1785, though they did not participate in negotiations with the federal government in any significant leadership capacity. Wyuka of Lookout Mountain and Newota of Chickamauga signed the treaty. Newota spoke after the parties signed the treaty to report that he was happy to hear the talks and be under congressional protection. He intended to rely on the commissioners to do justice with respect to their lands. Two years later, Tsi-yugunsini's brother Ookoousdi and two other Cherokee negotiators from Nickajack held a peace conference with General Robertson in Nashville but with no result.[9]

The massacre of the Upper Town peace chiefs in 1788 marked a turning point and solidified a commitment between the chiefs of the Upper and Lower Towns. During the bitter war that followed the murders, most of the Upper Town residents united with those of the Lower Towns to still crying blood. In October, Lower Town warrior Kunoskeskie, Onitositah's maternal nephew, joined Nentooyah and Atawgwatihih in attacking Gillespie's Station, where they killed a number of men, women, and children. Shortly after this, the Cherokees became aware of the congressional proclamation of September 1, 1788, ordering intruders off Cherokee lands. The warriors saw this as a promise and disbanded.[10]

In subsequent peace talks, the Chickamaugans joined other Cherokee chiefs and warriors as active participants. Although historians emphasize the devastating effect on the Cherokees of Sevier's campaigns throughout the 1780s and particularly in 1788, the Chickamaugans in no sense considered themselves conquered. Sevier's campaigns destroyed the Upper Towns but left the Lower Towns untouched and in a position to assume the lead in diplomacy. The Cherokees interpreted the congressional proclamation as a marker of the confederated government's willingness to broker a just solution to their land losses. Cherokee statesmen now publicly positioned the settler polity as the unruly brothers who destroyed the peace, while some Cherokees continued to maintain more amiable private relationships with those who acted as allies.[11]

Emboldened by the support they anticipated from Congress, Lower Town statesmen brought with them forceful ideas about how to revise the fictive kin relationship, concepts rooted in a strong vision of Cherokee self-worth. At the heart of their message was the belief that kinship required justice—in particular, the restoration of their hunting grounds. A few weeks after Nentooyah's message, a number of chiefs and warriors from the Lower Towns, including Tsi-yugunsini's brother Ocunna, Nentooyah, and William Elders, joined Upper Town chief Scolacutta and others to negotiate peace with Martin. William Elders sent a string of white beads from Kunoskeskie. These talks signaled a new alliance between the Chickamaugans and chiefs and warriors of the other Cherokee towns. In a response that heralded a harder line of Cherokee peace diplomacy, the statesmen eschewed lengthy talks aimed at establishing connection and putting bad thoughts behind. Instead, they blamed the state of Franklin for starting the war and stated that, having heard from Congress that the encroachers would be removed, they were willing to broker a peace.[12]

In a rare diplomatic appearance, Tsi-yugunsini and other Chickamaugans, including Lower Town negotiators Kunoskeskie, Atawgwatihih, and Kenneteag, joined Upper Town chief Scolacutta and others three weeks after the meeting with Martin to respond to peace overtures by Richard Winn, the superintendent of the federal government's Southern Department. They thanked him for doing justice by protecting their hunting grounds and for brokering peace talks with Governor Samuel Johnston of North Carolina. In February 1789 the Cherokee nation held a Grand Talk at Coosowothee, a town associated with the Chickamaugans, to receive and answer peace talks from Governor Johnston. Setting aside prior Cherokee ideas that peace was a state of mind independent of other issues, the chiefs told their "friend and brother" that they wanted peace but that peace was conditioned on justice. They required that North Carolina stop its encroachments and murders. They also refused to meet at French Broad, as the governor requested, and demanded instead to hold the conference at Linekaa, a Cherokee site. In March, Tsi-yugunsini again spoke jointly with Kenneteag and Scolacutta to respond to Governor Johnston's peace talks. Acknowledging with approval the governor's recognition that the "unruly" overmountain people caused the late war, they offered peace but again refused to meet at French Broad, because it was "too near to those who have injured us." They proposed Seneca or Hopewell as sites. Kunoskeskie wrote the governor of North Carolina, offering peace only if white encroachers left Cherokee lands. He characterized "white warriors" as "rogues and liars." After various delays, the treaty was postponed when North Carolina ceded its lands to Congress.[13]

Upon North Carolina's cession of its western lands to the United States in 1789, the federal government assumed control of treaty negotiations. The Indian policy of the Federalists, continued later by the Republicans, recognized Indian jurisdiction over its people in many matters but aimed to "civilize" them by encouraging agriculture and useful arts. Disavowing a discourse of conquest, government officials believed that with civilization the Indians would have less need for land and would sell it to the United States. Under the plan envisioned by Secretary of War Henry Knox, eventually Indian nations would disappear as civilized Indians were absorbed into the superior and more advanced white society.[14]

In 1790 the United States organized the area that is now Tennessee into the Territory South of the River Ohio, known as the Southwest Territory. Washington appointed William Blount as both governor and Indian superintendent of the Southwest Territory. Blount was a North Carolinian with huge land speculations in Tennessee who, as commissioner for North Carolina at the Treaty of Hopewell in 1785, had formally protested against what he considered congressional generosity to the Cherokees. His efforts at treaty talks and elsewhere to advance his land interests earned him a Cherokee name—the Dirt Captain.[15] At the Treaty of Holston in 1791, the reconstituted national government met with the Cherokees for the first time. Although a federal representative, Blount advanced his own and local interests at least as strongly as those of the federal government. He ignored Knox's instructions to him by demanding far more land from the Cherokees than the federal government desired, and he insisted upon the North Carolinian theory of conquest, which the federal government had repudiated. Although the headmen professed to suspend their doubts about Blount at the beginning of negotiations and accepted him as an elder brother, his unacceptable demands for large land cessions angered them and almost terminated negotiations. The Cherokee statesmen quickly perceived Blount to be a spokesperson for the local frontier people. Several of the chiefs were so uncertain as to whether Blount acted as a national or local representative that they traveled to Philadelphia a few months after the treaty to speak to the president on the subject.[16]

The new coalition of Cherokee leaders unveiled a sophisticated reformulation of Cherokee diplomacy to counter Blount's promotion of frontier views as federal policy. The Native American diplomats assembled at Holston were part of a new generation of Cherokee headmen kindling the council fires. Savanukeh died in 1784 and Oconostota in 1785. Onitositah, Oskuah, and several other Upper Town peace chiefs had been murdered in 1788. After Onitositah's death, the peace faction split. Although the Upper Towns selected Scolacutta to replace Onitositah, the towns in closer proximity to the Lower Towns recognized Kenneteag as their peace chief. Kenneteag did not attend the conference but sent Chulcoah, one of the chiefs of Kenneteag's town. Nentooyah also represented the Chickamaugans, and Kunoskeskie, although not a chief, participated in the talks. The vigorous diplomacy conducted by this new coterie of leaders belies historical narratives that picture the Cherokees in 1791 as a weak and declining people.[17]

Virtually all historians of the Cherokees have failed to consult the minutes to the treaty proceedings taken by Daniel Smith, the secretary of the Southwest Territory. Consequently, their accounts overlook the remarkable shift in the Cherokee construction of their relationship with the settlers and the critical role played by Lower Town negotiators, particularly Chulcoah, at this conference.[18] The new headmen began by exercising precautionary measures. They selected interpreters in whom they had considerable confidence. They reduced their major speeches to writing. When they traveled to Philadelphia several months later for extended negotiations, they demanded that the government transcribe all speeches and give them a copy.[19]

Of greater importance, the coalition revived a sense of Cherokee power among the 1,200 Cherokee men, women, and children attending the treaty and countered white misconceptions about Cherokee diplomacy. In the face of persistent white encroachment and expansionism, the emerging leadership acted to reinstill a vision of Cherokee spiritual strength. The chiefs opened the treaty with the eagle tail dance. The Cherokees had frequently performed the dance for the British, and Governor Blount understood that they were bestowing an honor not previously accorded an American commissioner. While true, the Cherokees regarded the eagle as a great adawehi or spiritual leader. The eagle figured prominently in their rituals, especially those related to war and heroic exploits. A ritual that instilled a strong sense of pride, the eagle tail dance was held to inculcate a warlike spirit in the young and to symbolize victory. Drawing on this source of distinctly Cherokee spiritual power, the Chickamaugan-inspired leadership signaled its intention to challenge Eurocentric assumptions that denigrated the Real People. They confirmed their more aggressive stance when they had their interpreter introduce each of the forty-one chiefs to Blount by his Cherokee name. The chiefs appeared in Cherokee dress while the warriors wore eagle feathers on their heads.[20]

Central to the redefinition of their international kinship was a plan to correct settler misperceptions that denigrated Cherokee sovereignty over their lands by asserting white notions of superiority. At the outset of negotiations, the chiefs delayed good talks to address two areas of misunderstanding —the interpretation of fictive kinship and the white assumption of racial superiority. Cherokee leaders continued to cast the white polity as their kin, but in the face of white failure to reciprocate the relationship on Cherokee terms, these headmen clarified their meanings for the white negotiators at the same time that they rearranged their roles:

We are met all together here expecting to hear good talks as they come from our father and delivered by our elder brother as we have stiled him. But that is only a Title of Friendship, we being the oldest people on this ground, and it hurts our hearts very much to see the people who have grown up on our land now taking it away from us. It is just like an ungrateful child robbing his father.[21]

In this view, the diplomatic kinship continued, but with local whites in the role of children. Linking their position as fathers of the whites to their status as original possessors of the land, the Cherokee chiefs neatly asserted their claims both to respect and to justice, although the Cherokees continued to cast the president as their father. The headmen's position reflected a wider view in Cherokee society about the land hunters. Arcowee, a Beloved Man of Chota, observed to missionaries in 1797 that the whites had come to be called the older brother and the Native Americans the younger, but "the naming should have been reversed, for the red people dwelt here first."[22]

The new Cherokee diplomats also addressed white racial hostility. Large numbers of frontier people considered Native Americans to be cruel and bloodthirsty savages, more beast than human. Cherokee chiefs and women had handled this issue before in talks and peace conferences by contending that white and red men were brothers, although of different colors. White diplomats agreed but frequently tied their view to God's common creation of red and white peoples and his desire that they share American lands. This double-edged sword promoted peace by separating the commissioners from the racial prejudice of many of the settlers, but it also suggested that whites had entitlements to Cherokee lands. The commissioners at talks at Long Island in April 1777 delivered this explicit message: "We were all born in one land, the Supreme being hath placed us in the same neighbourhood and country, without mountains or great waters to divide us. We ought therefore to live like friends and brethren. . . . We should . . . become one people."[23]

The underlying dual assumptions made by white commissioners created an untenable position for the Cherokees. Most Cherokee speakers ground their claims to land in the notion that the Great Spirit, far from placing reds and whites in the same neighborhood, gave red people the lands on this side of the water and whites lands on the other side. To accept the premise of a single creator who desired the indigenous peoples to share their lands affirmed a common humanity but risked compromising claims to priority in land rights. To reject the doctrine might add fuel to white claims of racial superiority. In working out the implications of this doctrine over the years, the Cherokee chiefs had articulated different positions on the issue of a common creator. Most Cherokee diplomats, relying on traditional Cherokee beliefs, spoke frequently of the spiritual laws invoking brotherhood and peace without wedding these principles to a view of creation. Among those who did, the Cherokees were divided on the racial basis of creation. Most of those who utilized rhetoric about origins agreed that the Great Being above made all people. As Onitositah said, "The Great Man . . . made you and he made us; we are all his children." Travelers report that many Cherokees espoused this view.[24] Some Cherokees advocated polytheism. At the Treaty of Lochaber in 1770, Attakullakulla noted that there were three Great Beings above—one in charge of the white people; one, of the red people; and one, of the black people. Some views of creation were race-neutral. Oostope'teh of Great Hiwassee described a beloved man and a bad man sent by the Great Being. The bad man put bad thought into the heads of evil men, while the beloved man makes minds peaceable.[25]

In response to Governor Blount's statement that whites and Indians should become one people, the headmen countered with a direct question designed to establish common ground about the nature of the relationship between the Cherokees and the white peoples. Adhering to their view that the Great Spirit gave the red people the lands on this side of the great waters, the Cherokee headmen acknowledged the Great Spirit's common creation and relied on the doctrine of a single creator to advance principles of racial equality as part of their doctrine of international kinship. Addressing the commissioners verbally and taking the unprecedented step of concomitantly delivering a written copy of the speech, the chiefs inquired about the reason whites continued to encroach on Cherokee land:

> [I]s it because we are a poor broken nation not able to help ourselves? or is it because we are red people? Or do the white people look on us as the Buffaloe and other wild beasts in the woods, and that they have a right to take our property at their pleasure? Though we are red we think we were made by the same power, and certainly we think we have as much right to enjoy our property as any other human being that inhabit the earth. If not we hope our brother will not screen any thing from us, if we are to have our land taken away at the pleasure of any white man that chuses to go and settle on it.[26]

Their question forced Governor Blount to articulate white agreement that the peoples were equal: "Neither your great father nor myself do consider your people as buffaloes or wild beasts but as good as ourselves, not one better than the other."[27]

As in 1788 and 1789, the new statesmen no longer considered the achievement of a peaceful state of mind to be the primary goal of the conference. For these leaders, justice was a precondition of peace. The Chickamaugans and other Cherokees continued to maintain that the diplomatic kinship that Cherokees and whites had established obligated the parties to reciprocity, including an expectation that the more powerful whites had a duty to exercise their power responsibly: "We look on [Washington] as a father. . . . It is to him that we have looked up to for justice, and he has for a long time past, been promising us that we should have it."[28]

As part of their demand for justice, the outspoken negotiators in 1791 did more than respond to a request for grievances. They used the public forum to initiate demands for accountability from the white government. Although not attending as a chief, Kunoskeskie interjected questions to Governor Blount about the status of Long Island. The parties at the peace conference of 1777 agreed to preserve Long Island, the site of the conference, as a sacred meeting ground, but whites appropriated the land. Although Kunoskeskie's translated words read, "I love to explain such matters publicly," the context of his questions suggests a better interpretation would be, "It is important that you publicly account for your broken commitments."[29]

More significantly, the robust diplomacy reasserted the traditional belief that treaty covenants were part of a permanent bond that must be continuously renewed, points previously advanced by Upper Town negotiators. The Cherokees obtained an important concession at Holston that confirmed white agreement in the durability of the treaty kinship. When white settlers began to demand land in exchange for peace after 1768, women's concerns that land sales traded their survival and the inheritance of their children for fungible goods fueled protests at land cessions. Prodded by Cherokee negotiators, Governor Blount proposed a plan of payment that would satisfy these demands: "I will give goods to you, your young men, and children in every year. Children yet unborn will receive them." The United States sealed this commitment by agreeing to make annual payments in perpetuity for Cherokee lands rather than a single lump-sum payment as it had done in the past. In forging this compromise, Cherokee women and men gained more than financial recompense. They obtained a commitment from the federal government that the United States had a perpetual obligation to the Cherokees—a commitment that implied permanent recognition of the Cherokee nation.[30]

The survival of the Cherokee nation adjacent to a growing white community required that future generations remember their obligations. Cherokee spokespeople emphasized the duty of each party to renew vigilantly the ties between them. Addressing more than 1,500 Cherokees and whites, Scolacutta, now one of the oldest people on the treaty ground, closed the conference by drawing on a powerful Cherokee image. He positioned himself "as a mother more than anything else—my land raised and produced you." Scolacutta linked Chickamaugan demands for justice as a condition of peace with the older Upper Town notion of the spiritual durability of treaty agreements about land. Echoing the theme of renewal articulated by Onitositah and Savanukeh fourteen years earlier and restated on numerous occasions by other Upper Town diplomats, Scolacutta pleaded passionately with both sides to honor the agreement. He chided the settlers for imposing on the Cherokees by taking their lands. He represented that the Cherokees made peace based on "heart" and the promises of justice from George Washington. Holding a belt in his hand, he continued:

> This was formerly my land though you have now grown strong on it. Falter not from the agreement between us. Our children may be better raised. Use your utmost and let us see how many ages shall pass away while we have hold of this the token of friendship and trust. This belt is lasting; paper is not so. . . . The young seed as they come into the world will hold this. . . . Our successors must attend to what we do and always keep the friendship.[31]

Scolacutta's reiteration of the theme of regeneration to the younger men, to the Chickamaugans, and to the Cherokee's new treaty partner, the federal government, reflected his belief that a diplomatic kinship, symbolized by the belt, forged a stronger bond than contracts written on paper. Recognizing that many of the settlers would not honor these obligations and believing that the Cherokees could not perpetuate treaty agreements by force, Scolacutta sought to establish the kinship relationship, with its attendant obligations, with the representative of the United States. Scolacutta's efforts to perpetuate the treaty relationship throughout successive generations injected a part of the Upper Town tradition that retained vitality into the Lower Town diplomacy. Central to this concept of regeneration was the notion of justice, a theme that resonated with the new Chickamaugan diplomacy. Such justice must occur, even if one party was weaker than the other. The converse of this doctrine was a refusal to accept injustice. Many of the Cherokee headmen never conceded the land cessions made decades earlier. In 1785, 1791, and again in 1797, they asserted claims dating back to the 1770s. They saw justice as a spiritual principle that operated outside of white legal constructs. The failure by the settler governments to do justice did not end the relationship between the treaty partners but left it incomplete. Scolacutta's exhortation represented his belief that the parties could acknowledge past treaty violations and honor their commitments and that future generations could do the same.[32]

In spite of the accomplishments of their diplomats, the Treaty at Holston was in many ways a disaster for the Cherokees. While the treaty revoked two Franklin treaties signed under duress and omitted a clause in the Treaty of Hopewell granting the United States the right to regulate all Cherokee affairs, the Cherokees signed a document that conveyed considerable land to the United States. Daniel Smith's treaty notes indicate that the chiefs did not come to the treaty expecting a request for land cessions. To the contrary, the Chickamaugan-led delegation hoped to secure a return of lands previously taken from the Cherokees. The negotiations nearly collapsed when Blount pressed for major grants. Inexplicably, the Cherokee diplomats reversed their position and agreed to a cession. The treaty notes taken by Daniel Smith are silent on the reasons for the capitulation, which occurred abruptly and without explanation after the Cherokees threatened to leave. A Cherokee delegation to the president, led by Nentooyah, was sufficiently disturbed to undertake the long trip to Philadelphia a few months later to appeal the results. Nentooyah reported that they requested that a conference in Philadelphia be arranged during the treaty negotiations but that Blount asked them how they would pay for it. Because the government had always underwritten such trips, the Cherokee headmen interpreted this as a manipulation of their vulnerability and an abridgment of the government's obligations to the weaker Cherokees. Fearing that Blount's willingness to withdraw customary protection would extend to endangering those at the treaty grounds, the Cherokee diplomats may have placated him with a land cession. Their concern was reasonable, because the treaty took place only three years after the massacre of the Upper Town peace chiefs, and the murderers were present on the treaty grounds. In a private communication two years later, however, British agent George Welbank related that the chiefs claimed not to have fully understood the treaty articles they signed.[33]

The Cherokee delegation to Philadelphia was unable to reverse the land cession and succeeded only in securing a larger payment for the ceded lands. As a consequence, most of the Cherokee people united around war. Kunoskeskie, part of the peace delegation, assumed the mantle of war chief in the

Lower Towns upon Tsi-yugunsini's death in March 1792. Although some Upper Town chiefs counseled peace, Kenneteag and many other chiefs were deeply dissatisfied with the treaty line. Unhappy warriors throughout the nation joined the young Chickamaugan men in a renewed campaign to drive the whites out of the Southwest Territory and to plunder their settlements. Their insistent clamor for war, along with Spanish encouragement, prompted many of the chiefs, including Kunoskeskie, to join them. A scorched earth campaign by the territorial militia against many of the Upper Towns brought a Cherokee delegation led by Chuquilatague back to treat with the federal government in 1794. Before the results of the peace agreement between the parties reached Tennessee, militias destroyed the Lower Towns of Nickajack and The Running Water. Distraught that their captive children might be killed, Cherokee women dissuaded the warriors from pursuing the attackers and prolonging the war. Shortly after, the Chickamaugans joined Chuquila-tague in peace talks.[34]

Although the Cherokees were unable to prevail militarily, they did achieve one victory. At Holston, it became clear to the chiefs that Dirt Captain William Blount represented his own and other local interests rather than the federal position. Cherokee diplomats complained about Blount's conflict of interest to national officials. One of Blount's own agents, Leonard Shaw, confirmed Cherokee suspicions. After marrying a Cherokee woman, Shaw became attached to the Cherokees. He alerted them to Blount's land specula-tions and urged them to deal directly with the president. Although Blount dismissed Shaw, Cherokee criticism continued. As Blount's dual loyalties became more apparent, Washington's administration grew increasingly dis-pleased with him, particularly after Timothy Pickering replaced Henry Knox as secretary of war. Upon the expiration of Blount's commission in 1796, Congress selected disinterested outside agents.[35] With these appointments, the Cherokees finally gained a treaty partner to whom they could address their complaints about their misbehaving brothers, the settlers.

The overmountain people came under federal jurisdiction when North Carolina ceded its western lands to Congress in 1789. As territorial residents defined their understanding of their relationship with the federal govern-ment, they reconstructed their views about their Cherokee neighbors. In European terms, the arrangement between the Cherokees and the federal government created a unique problem. Americans were familiar with Euro-pean alliances in which a weaker state associated with a stronger one for protection against other powerful foreign nations.[36] However, the United

States protected the Cherokees from its own citizens, not from foreign nations. The stress that this tripartite relationship produced prompted the frontier people to craft notions of federalism and nationhood that permitted considerable local autonomy in Indian matters.

The federal commitment to the indigenous peoples ensured that Tennessee's adjustment to territorial status and to statehood was truly wrenching.[37] During the first two decades after permanent white settlement in 1768, the colonists had experienced a kaleidoscope of shifting governments by Britain, Virginia, North Carolina, and the confederated states and, in eastern Tennessee, Franklin. When North Carolina ceded its western territories to Congress in 1789, the weak national loyalties of the citizens in the new territory were immediately tested. Although Tennesseans challenged federal authority on other issues, the primary conflict between the United States and its local citizens in the 1790s and the early 1800s concerned policies relating to Native Americans. From the first white settlement, the overmountain men asserted the right to exercise considerable control over Indian relations. If frontier people believed diplomacy failed, the traditional redress was local—invasion and destruction of Cherokee towns by the militias. Frontier leaders in the 1780s commonly invoked this remedy without authorization from North Carolina and at times in defiance of orders forbidding offensive operations. When William Blount accepted the positions as governor and superintendent of Indian affairs for the new Southwest Territory in 1790, he assumed the unenviable task of reconciling the frontier people to a federal policy on southern Indian affairs that many abhorred. Earlier congressional proclamations forbade white settlement on lands that the federal government, but not local landowners, recognized as Indian country. The Cherokees and Creeks retaliated for encroachments and violence against Indians by stealing from and killing white farmers. Determined to avoid an Indian war in the Southeast, Secretary of War Knox issued strict orders against any offensive operations against the indigenous people. As the Indians declared war and stepped up their attacks in 1792 and early 1793 in response to the Treaty of Holston, many of the frontier people railed at the federal restraints. Despite Blount's strenuous efforts to convince federal authorities to authorize offensive operations, Knox notified him again in May 1793 that Congress refused to authorize war against the southeastern Indians.[38]

Like borderland peoples in locales as diverse as the Pyrenees, South Africa, Australia, and New Zealand, the frontier people rebelled against the assertion of what locals believed was too much authority by the metropole, although Tennesseans responded with greater violence than in most other regions. In the summer of 1793, the anger of the settlers exploded into a backcountry insurrection against the federal injunction against war.[39] On June 12, 1793, Captain John Beaird and his militia not only entered Cherokee territory but attacked Cherokees and federal agents assembling in a Cherokee town to travel to Philadelphia for treaty negotiations, killing several Cherokee men and women and one white man and wounding Nan-ye-hi's daughter, Betsey Martin, and Scolacutta's wife. Beaird's massacre prompted renewed hostilities during which General John Sevier mounted a major fall offensive campaign against the Cherokees, destroying a number of Cherokee towns. Daniel Smith, the secretary of the territory acting in Blount's convenient absence, flouted the federal prohibition on offensive war to authorize Sevier's campaign. Illegal forays into Cherokee country continued into the next year against the Upper Towns. Finally, on September 7, 1794, the militias struck the Chickamaugans. In the face of a specific federal directive prohibiting an assault on the Lower Towns, a combined force of 550 militiamen from Cumberland under General James Robertson, from eastern Tennessee under Major James Ore, and from Kentucky under Colonel William Whitley attacked two of the major Lower Towns. They destroyed Nickajack and The Running Water.[40]

Governor Blount dissociated himself from the illegal actions of the troops in his public letters to the secretary of war and to the local militia commanders but his private correspondence and the accounts of participants indicate active complicity on Blount's part, at least in the expedition against the Lower Towns. As early as 1792, Blount began to advocate for offensive war, both publicly and privately. In contrast to his restrained official facade, his personal correspondence shows that he chaffed at the federal government's injunction against war.[41] As the Cherokees escalated their attacks in response to the militia invasions of their towns, Blount in June 1794 again sought permission from Secretary of War Knox to launch offensive operations against them. On July 26, 1794, President Washington specifically denied Blount's request.[42]

Meanwhile, the Cumberland area in the west prepared its own campaign. According to Colonel Robert Weakly, the planning for the attack on the Lower Towns originated from Nashville in the spring or summer of 1794. Colonel Weakly and Captain Sampson Williams of the Cumberland settlement went to Kentucky to recruit. Colonel Whitley of Kentucky agreed to bring some men. Williams furnished rations for more than 100 men from Kentucky for thirty-four days before the Nickajack expedition. On August 9, Val Sevier, who lived in the Cumberland area, wrote his brother John Sevier in east Tennessee that Kentucky troops were in Cumberland, where the local militia would join them to attack the Lower Towns. Shortly thereafter, in Knoxville, Blount dispatched an expedition headed by Major James Ore, ostensibly to scout for Indian marauders on the Cumberland and Kentucky roads. Blount looked the other way while Ore and his men helped themselves to supplies and arms from the federal arsenal. Ore immediately proceeded to the Nashville rendezvous without engaging in any scouting. Colonel Weakley believed that Blount sent Ore to join the expedition against the Lower Towns. So did two of Ore's men, the Reverend John Kidwell and Philip Combs. According to these men, Ore's militia first marched to Knoxville where Ore held private talks with the governor. The governor's demeanor persuaded them that he was aware of the real intent of the expedition.[43]

On approximately September 1 near Nashville, Major Ore and his men rendezvoused with 200 men from Kentucky. Joined by 250 militiamen from the Cumberland settlements, the force made its way to Nickajack, which it attacked on September 7. The month after the attack, Abishai Thomas, a Philadelphia business associate of the Blounts who was visiting Knoxville at the time, wrote Blount's brother that Blount was "highly gratified" by Ore's actions under Robertson's orders. Because the action was offensive, he "*as Governor* is bound to disapprove it." Although Blount publicly disclaimed the expedition and asked for Robertson's resignation, he encouraged Robertson to provide an explanation for his actions. Robertson characterized his invasion as defensive in light of alleged intelligence that the Lower Towns were about to attack the settlements. This accounting partially placated Knox, who did not revoke Robertson's commission. Blount's complicity at the highest level of territorial government, known to the militiamen, reinforced a pattern of local willingness to belittle federal preemption—a pattern that continued long after permanent peace with the indigenous peoples was achieved.[44]

The open rebellion against the federal government triggered by Beaird's massacre and the subsequent invasions stimulated considerable public debate about the nature of federalism and exposed conflicting theoretical positions. Article I, Section 10 of the U.S. Constitution provides that "no state shall enter into any treaty, alliance, or confederation," a provision that most historians assume appropriated to the national government the sole authority to conduct Indian relations. Many Tennesseans thought otherwise. They disagreed with the federal government's policy of treaty making and proposed that the state disregard federal treaties. One issue of contention was whether the treaties with the Indians should be honored when, according to almost all whites, the Cherokees and Creeks did not honor them. Locals had expressed reservations about placing treaties outside popular control during the ratification debates in 1788. Arthur Campbell, the militia commander of the 1780 campaign who was very prominent in western affairs, argued that treaties should not be the supreme law of the land. Claiming that Indians will "make infractions at [their] pleasure," Campbell contended that treaties should be general laws, subject to modification by the legislature.[45]

Connected with the question of honoring treaties was the issue of whether the state had the right to declare war. Angry Tennesseans chaffed against the federal prohibition on offensive war and described several rationales that permitted war in the absence of a congressional declaration. Their theories supporting the rebellion constituted more than simple disobedience of a federal order—settlers challenged the federal government's authority to issue a binding order. The ideas of the frontier people were ground in notions of self-defense. William Cocke, who later represented Tennessee in Congress, argued an exception to congressional war-making power. If a state was actually invaded or in imminent danger, reason and the safety of the citizens required that it have the right to go to war. Some writers proposed not an exception to Congress's war-making power but the more radical theory of abandonment in which citizens became "absolutely" free to protect themselves if the state "abandoned" them.[46] Although relying on different justifications, all of these thinkers envisioned a limited form of federalism, one that allowed local citizens the authority to declare war to protect themselves. Countering these voices, judges, townspeople, and some frontier people issued pleas to abide by the rule of federal law. These appeals often connected themes of peace and the protection and security provided by the government with the advantages proffered by a law-abiding society.[47]

The response by the federal government to the frontier rebellion can best be described as tepid. Although not countenancing the disobedience of its orders, the national government was happy with the result. In sharp contrast to the Whiskey Rebellion, President Washington made no attempt to enforce the federal mandate against the fifteen-month offensive war and made little effort to punish the whites involved. The secretary of war did refuse to pay the militiamen for their services in Sevier's campaign and the Nickajack expedition. After Tennessee's admission to the union, Tennessee congressman Andrew Jackson succeeded in reversing even this rebuke.[48]

Intertwined with the struggle of Tennesseans to articulate their relationship with the national government around Indian policy was their effort to redefine their understanding of and connection with the Cherokee people. The views about native sovereignty held by those favoring extermination or

removal of the Indians under a theory of conquest and by accommodation-
ists who contended that the indigenous people had rights in the preterritorial
years underwent significant transformation after 1790. The theory of conquest was rejected by the federal government. After peace, the influx of
people and rising prosperity persuaded large numbers of citizens that violence would damage their economic prospects. Publicly abandoning the right
of the sword as a doctrine of land entitlement, land-grant settlers joined the
peace advocates of the earlier years, while some squatters continued to farm
Indian land based on agrarian doctrines.[49]

Desiring to create conditions that would accommodate population growth
and prosperity, the accommodationist group argued for the importance of
the rule of law and governmental security. Generally agreeing that Indian
claims had to be extinguished, they sought a more stable and controlled
method of doing so. Their discourse about native rights was not informed by
an agrarian rationale based on an individual right to soil but by the more
efficient use—efficient, that is, for the newcomers' society—that an agrarian
economy, working hand in hand with commerce, could make of the region.[50]

As Tennessee's population exploded in the 1790s, Tennesseans supporting
the rule of law began to wrestle seriously with whether and how its economy
could accommodate a separately organized indigenous population. Some
leaders and settlers saw native society as malleable. With the coming of peace
in the mid-1790s, these local whites expressed optimism about civilizing the
Indians. Writing in 1793, Daniel Smith, secretary of the territory, assumed
that a commercial mind-set would dominate the disposition of Indian lands.
He contended that the government would buy river lands from the Indians
because increased commercial activities and settlements would render the
land necessary to whites and useless to the natives. The Indians could then
live in a degree of affluence they would not otherwise experience. During
peace talks in 1795, many Indians applied to have their children educated at
federal expense. Blount recommended to Washington that they be schooled
on the frontier, where they could learn friendship with white youth and
could be Christianized. Supporting these benign views, a few frontier people
articulated a vision of the common humanity of whites and Indians. One
early pioneer advocated setting aside "all prejudice and distinction of colour"
and viewing Indians "as the creatures of the same creator."[51]

Even the writers who supported civilization for or the rights of the indigenous populations stopped short of recommending absorption into white
society, the goal of the federal civilization program. But most Tennesseans had
little enthusiasm for the civilization program. Forgotten were earlier pioneer

proposals that Native Americans adopt white ways. In its early stages, many Tennesseans interpreted Washington's civilization program as a program of gift giving designed to win the friendship of the native people, an effort they believed had backfired. In their view, Indians perceived it to be a sign of weakness on the part of the whites. Most Tennesseans probably agreed with the sentiments of one settler who characterized it as an "absurd chimera." With this dismissal went any possibility that local whites in the territorial period would agree to incorporate Native American society into their own.[52]

While almost all Tennesseans saw the native populations as separate, many of the proponents of a legal solution, whose ranks were now swelled with those who denigrated Indian rights to land, increasingly questioned the equivalence of their new nationhood with that of Indian nationhood. Embedded in the contested formulation of their own nationhood were ideas about the rule of law and the benefits, responsibilities, and costs of civilized government. Many Tennesseans contrasted this new understanding of nationhood with their images of the unreliable political organization of Cherokee society. As the citizens of the territory negotiated their beliefs about nationhood with the federal government, Tennesseans began to denationalize the Native American polities. The rejection of the civilization program and the denigration of Native American nationhood was an outgrowth of changing views on the indigenous people as savages.

White outrage after coexisting with Native Americans for twenty-five years, many of which were marked by warfare, had deepened and transformed the concept of the savage with its three tropes of bloodthirstiness, cruelty, and infidelity.[53] One of the dominant characteristics of the image of the savage in Tennessee by the 1790s was its bloodthirsty quality. The frontier people frequently lamented the tendency of Indians to kill, scalp, and torture innocent people. This fed into images of Indians as beasts. At the heart of much of the image of the Indian as bloodthirsty and bestial was white outrage at contrasting cultural practices around warfare and retaliation. Whites abhorred Cherokee attacks on women and children, although they engaged in similar practices themselves. Nonetheless, borderers early distinguished their style of violence from Indian wars, "intolerable among civilized nations."[54]

Many white farmers and townspeople reinforced the portrayal of Native Americans as bloodthirsty with a second potent image. Responding from European notions about gender differences, westering people decried the cruelty of the treatment of captives by Indians. The white media railed about the captivity of citizens and slaves by Indians and about the treatment of the white captives. Most of these captives were women and children. Writers singled out the treatment that women received for particular condemnation, at times based on sexually tinged accusations. For example, the Knoxville paper reported that one young woman had been repeatedly threatened with death for refusing to cohabit with her captor's son.[55]

In addition to deepening images of bloodthirsty and cruel savages, whites in the 1790s modified a third trope—that of infidelity—that devalued Indian nationhood. The long-held view of the Indian as perfidious intensified as many whites viewed the American Indian strategy of making alliances to balance one power against another through their own cultural lens. Untrustworthy Indians who easily changed alliances would not honor treaty agreements. Underlying this complaint after the American Revolution lay a more explosive assumption. Many frontier people perceived that the British during the war manipulated the Cherokees, a view that weakened their belief in the independence and sovereignty of the Cherokee nation. The Cherokee diplomatic practice of assigning blame to a third party for their actions in order to advance a peaceful state of mind inadvertently contributed to the white image of the Cherokees as dependent. When Bever of Chickamauga made peace overtures to Virginia in early 1784, he followed the traditional practice of locating the source of the problem outside of the negotiating parties: "It was never our desire to shed the blood of our brothers the Virginians, but our father over the great water told us to do it. Said he was our father . . ." After 1783, dissident Cherokees shifted their alliances to France and Spain. Americans characterized these relationships as dependent ones as well. After numerous communications from Governor Blount on the subject of Indian infidelity, Secretary Knox concluded that there could be "no permanent arrangement of peace . . . with the savage tribes, liable as they are to . . . other policy than that of the United States."[56]

Characterizing the Cherokee people as dependent had profound resonance in a new republican culture that regarded dependency with considerable suspicion. In their political, personal, and economic lives, men strove for independence, mastery, and competency. Dependency assumed submission to the will of another and consequent inability to make disinterested decisions. Subordinate people—women, children, and slaves—could not responsibly exercise political rights.[57] Casting the Cherokees as pawns seriously undermined the viability of independent nationhood. During the 1780s, the theoretical implications of this construction were overshadowed by the doctrine of conquest. As its proponents abandoned that argument, at least publicly, in the next decade, the perceived Cherokee dependency operated to erode the white understanding of Indian political sovereignty.

The imagining of American Indians as perfidious reworked white views about Native American nationhood in another way. In the white view, the unreliable behavior of the young men jeopardized the efforts of the chiefs to maintain peace and to honor their treaties. As the settler government strengthened, white officials became increasingly concerned that native governments could not control their young men. In the European understanding, a group of men who united together to promote mutual safety and advantage constituted a nation if the group governed itself by its own laws and authority. Contrasting the inability of the headmen to govern their societies with the growing control that government exercised over the westering peoples, white leaders concluded that native governments were fundamentally flawed. Governor Blount labeled them "Jacobin." In charging a Tennessee grand jury in 1794, Judge Anderson noted that under a republican government citizens forgo some natural rights. He cautioned the jurors that, although it was well known that some Indian nations were faithless, whites must nonetheless refuse to take revenge. In so attempting to restrain white men, Judge Anderson differentiated the republican society governed by laws from the inferior, ungovernable Indian nations.[58]

The white discourse with its stronger demarcation of the savage and uncivilized nature of indigenous government occurred in spite of significant countervailing forces and requires explanation. Although the paradigm of Native Americans as savages assumes a one-dimensional quality to the white perceptions of Indians, white interactions with indigenous peoples produced a far more complicated picture. For decades, the boundaries between Native Americans and westering peoples were quite porous. In addition to the treaty meetings, Cherokees and other native peoples commonly visited white farms, taverns, and towns, socialized with their neighbors, traded with them, warned them of impending attacks, helped them when they were lost in the woods, and lived with them. They stole horses and committed other crimes in interracial gangs. Former hostages and captors visited each other. Whites traded in Cherokee villages and attended Green Corn dances there. Individual Cherokees as well as the Cherokee nation occasionally used the white newspapers to assure the white community of their peaceful intentions, to return lost or strayed white property, to advertise for escaped slaves, to air their differences with whites, and even to engage in intratribal disagreements. In 1795 the General Assembly gave corn to the starving Cherokees of the Upper Towns. Hundreds of whites lived in the Cherokee towns, as government agents, traders, interpreters, or villagers. Many nonnative men and some women had Indian spouses.[59] Responding to the wide variety of contacts with Indians, many Tennesseans did not perceive all Native Americans through the simple lens of Indian. They commonly differentiated between the tribes and understood intratribal divisions as well.[60]

Why did so many of the settlers, who engaged in positive interactions with Native Americans and who discriminated between friendly and unfriendly Indian nations and towns, persist in maintaining a generally derogatory image of Indians as bloodthirsty, cruel, and perfidious savages? The answer lies in the gendered assumptions that Tennesseans imposed on their construction of the savage—one that militated against perceiving Native American society as compatible with white civilization. The settlers' own patriarchal gender arrangements encouraged them to universalize, as the Indian image, their picture of its young men. Faced with bloody deeds that they did not believe grew out of land intrusions and lacking modern theory about cultural differences, the settlers adopted a male-referent explanation for Indian actions. For example, whites reckoned Indian populations by the number of warriors. When Daniel Smith, the secretary of the Southwest Territory, wrote Secretary of War Knox that the Indians "were warlike because they could only distinguish themselves by feats of war," he spoke of the male warriors, not all Indians. By the same token, the settler belief in the bloodthirsty nature of Native Americans did not reside primarily in traits they saw in Indians but in those of their young men. Although at times suspecting duplicity, often frontiersmen accepted the statements of chiefs that they wanted peace but that their young men did not. Governor Blount reflected these male-referent assumptions in a letter to Secretary of War Knox in 1792. According to Blount's view, the Cherokees believed that all national honors were acquired by shedding blood, a view that was primarily that of the young warriors. This theory, of course, placed the actions of young Indian men at the center of this construction of the Cherokees' image. In his Message to the Territorial Assembly in 1795, he linked the incorrigibility of the bad young men with an ominous prediction: "I believe, that while there is a tribe of Indians remaining on this side of the Mississippi, uncircumscribed by the citizens of the United States, that a description of them by the chiefs, denominated bad young men, will continue, more or less, frequently to commit murders and thefts upon the frontier inhabitants."[61]

These same young men were also a large part of the reason the indigenous people were characterized as "perfidious." Whites saw their acts of warfare, retaliation, and horse theft as violations of the treaties, proof that savages could not keep civilized agreements. In spite of the fact that older chiefs frequently spoke against warfare in counsel and that women articulated concerns for peace, white writers tagged the entire nation with this label.[62]

In addition to portraying the bloodthirsty and perfidious action of the warriors as a Cherokee trait, the white community parlayed activities of young Indian men onto a universal picture of savagism in another critical way. The paradigm of the savage was bound up in the picture of Native Americans as hunters. This trope conjured up images of the beast, the wandering Indian, and the use of large sections of land for nonagricultural purposes. Although women increasingly accompanied men on hunting trips, hunting was primarily a male activity. In the Cherokee nation, women performed most of the work of farming and raising families. The myth of the savage as hunter occluded this more complicated social reality.[63]

These gendered constructions and vocabularies supported the downgrading of the nationhood of a society that was bloodthirsty, cruel, and unreliable. In dealing with nations composed of savages, many Tennesseans began to contemplate that they were dealing with not "nations" but "uncivilized nations." They increasingly concluded that such bodies did not have the character necessary for treatment as nations. In 1793 one gentleman from Cumberland captured several gendered expressions that informed his view of Cherokee and Creek nationhood in a private letter:

> You will no doubt, have acquired information of the many recent injuries we have sustained here, in the loss of our citizens and property, from the unrelenting cruelty and perfidy of the merciless savages. The Creeks, and some Cherokees . . . are the nations who entered into treaties of peace with the United States, at New York, and Holston! treaties attended with great expense, ratified with all that pomp and solemnity which civilized nations have adopted, but violated with as little ceremony as the untutored son of nature would observe upon parting with his *squaw*, in order to engage in his ordinary pursuits of hunting. . . . Rapacity, infidelity, and love of war, are prominent features in the character of uncivilized nations.[64]

The deepening images of Indians as immutably bloodthirsty, cruel, and faithless savages who could not be civilized contrasted with the optimistic view of white society that many Tennesseans took during the rapid growth following peace in 1795. Post-Revolutionary white westering people turned their attention to ideas that would enhance prosperity, a touchstone of civilization. As the white population increased and thrived, its members came to perceive native nations as fundamentally different from civilized nations.

Characterizing indigenous communities as uncivilized persuaded these settlers to begin to denationalize Indian polities at the same time that they were defining their own national loyalties in terms that permitted local autonomy.[65] For the borderers, as for the Cherokees, the process of reimagining their own society and the society of the other during the territorial period was stimulated, in significant part, by the presence of a third sovereignty—the United States. As Tennesseans entered statehood in 1796, these three political entities established a largely unexplored triangular relationship.

CHAPTER THREE

Fictive Father and Federalism

Cherokees, Tennesseans, and
the United States, 1796–1810

Bloodless bullets punctured the bitter last years of the two-decade intermittent conflict between the Cherokees and the pioneers in the region soon to achieve statehood as Tennessee. Chronicled by the *Knoxville Gazette*, numerous frontiersmen recounted attacks against them by Indians in which bullets passed through their clothes without touching their flesh. The first published report in 1792 originated near Clinch Mountain when a man hunting horses related that a party of Indians fired on him. Four balls passed through his clothes and shattered his powder horn without injuring him. Settlers subsequently described similar incidents throughout eastern Tennessee. By late 1793 these mysterious happenings had spread to Nashville. During the next year, the episodes became commonplace, and reports continued for two more years. The record for the greatest number of close encounters survived unscathed seems to have been held by a man named, ironically enough, Ball. Between September and December 1793, Nicolas Ball's apparel absorbed a total of seven bullets on at least three different occasions, the last on December 2, 1793. His luck ran out three weeks later when Indians killed him.[1]

This bizarre chain of events terminated in 1796 when Oconostotee, a Cherokee chief, responded to the *Gazette* that the settlers attacked the Cherokees. The white men removed and fired into their own clothing to establish self-defense in order to escape prosecution by the national government, which was pressuring the frontier people to keep the peace under the federal treaties.[2] Oconostotee's story persuaded at least one white reader. George Roulstone, the *Gazette*'s publisher, printed no further accounts of bullets that pierced clothing but not flesh.

The ploy, Oconostotee's response, and the *Gazette*'s publication of his letter revealed significant tensions in the tripartite relationship between the Cherokees, Tennesseans, and the federal government as Tennesseans entered statehood—a triangular linkage largely overlooked by historians.[3] This chapter explores the ideas and assumptions underlying the construction by the Cherokees and the settlers of their relationship with the United States and with each other from the recognition of statehood in 1796 until 1810. My focus is on local perceptions and the dynamic ways in which these ideas informed and were transformed by events. I study federal thought only inasmuch as it impacted Cherokee or settler formulations.

During this period, the Cherokees and frontier people each supported their claims for autonomy within a federal relationship. Oconostotee's letter to the *Gazette* reflected his confidence that the Cherokee's new treaty partner offered protection from unruly settlers. In this developing relationship with the United States, many Cherokee leaders cast the president as their diplomatic father. They built on Upper and Lower Town concepts to redefine the meaning of this term by importing five obligations onto the protective relationship—their father agreed to regenerate the bonds between the parties, to act justly, to provide for Cherokee needs, to recognize Cherokee equality, and to support Cherokee sovereignty. Because aspects of the Cherokee doctrine resonated with Federalist Enlightenment principles, the general government responded with its own views of just treatment of the indigenous peoples. In 1783 Great Britain formalized a policy that it was the sole sovereign power in East India, governing under a trust in which Britain protected the non-Christians in its care until they could achieve the full rights of British citizens. The United States rejected the idea of absolute sovereignty and recognized the Cherokees' right to govern themselves. The federal government offered some protection and aid but, in response to pressures for land cessions from Tennesseans, eroded promises of equality and autonomy by recasting the Cherokees as wards who required a guardian. In the ensuing negotiation about the meaning of the Cherokee relationship to the United States, Cherokee ideas contributed to the formulation of a unique doctrine of separation and connection, one that has informed the characterization of the legal connection between indigenous peoples and colonizers throughout the world.[4] As the Cherokee leaders strengthened their relationship with the federal government, they reassessed their links to their Tennessee neighbors, reclassifying them as "friends" rather than "brothers."

Frontier people and townspeople also struggled with how to construct a relationship with the national government. After statehood in 1796, most

Tennesseans supported American nationalism in significant part because local whites needed federal support for their efforts to obtain Indian lands and for prosperity but contested the meaning of nationhood. Tennesseans imagined an expansionistic but limited nationalism in which the state had a strong voice. The success of the illegal frontier rebellion encouraged the state government to maintain a local three-pronged Indian policy under which the state conducted direct diplomatic relations with the Cherokees, urged the federal government to purchase land and road rights, and occasionally restrained its own citizens from illegal acts. In justifying their right to deal with their native neighbors, Tennesseans constructed a doctrine of constrained nationalism with long-range implications. As their own conception of a limited federalism solidified, the settlers reclassified the Cherokee people, downgrading them from an uncivilized nation with a country to a tribe with a territory or, worse, to tenants at will with extinguishable or no claims to land. Tennesseans now viewed Native Americans as obstacles to progress, a belief similar to that of many settlers in Neo-European colonies.[5] Because the Cherokee presence interfered with the economic expansion of westering people, many Tennesseans promoted the idea of removal of the Cherokees to the west of the Mississippi.

With the advent of statehood in 1796, Cherokee diplomats constructed a relationship with a new group of federal officials. Responding to Cherokee concerns that Indian agents be disinterested in land acquisition, the United States selected Benjamin Hawkins, a North Carolinian with no significant landholdings in Tennessee, to act as agent to the Cherokees and Creeks. Hawkins appointed Silas Dinsmoor as his assistant to live with the Cherokees, and Hawkins resided among the Creeks. Major Thomas Lewis replaced Dinsmoor in 1798 for three years. Jefferson appointed Return Meigs, a staunch Republican, for the job in 1801 and Meigs served until 1823.[6] These men, Federalist and Republican, continued to pursue the Federalist civilization policy that was initiated in the Territorial period.

Prior to the reunification of the Cherokee nation in 1810, the federal agents met with numerous Cherokee leaders. The variety of men and women sitting at peace talks with the federal officials reflected the localism and disorientation of the Cherokee people after their agreement to end warfare in 1795. In the earlier period, statespeople like Onitositah and Nan-ye-hi constituted a visible leadership. From 1795 until 1809, a cacophony of voices spoke for the Cherokees on international affairs. Indian agents endorsed and promoted men amenable to land and road concessions as leaders, but their strategy was only partly successful. In addition to the chiefs cultivated by American officials, numerous delegates from the Upper and Lower Towns and from various factions within those regions represented less visible constituencies.[7]

Among the many diplomats were several women.[8] Although Joseph Martin returned to Virginia when his appointment expired in 1789, Nan-ye-hi retained considerable influence. As late as 1819, Indian agent Reuben Lewis related that Nan-ye-hi's "advice and council borders on supreme." Other women remained active in diplomacy. In 1796 a delegation of ten Cherokees, including one woman, went to Philadelphia to consult with the president. A number of women accompanied their husbands in attending the marking of the boundary line in 1797. Early the next year, several women, including Kunoskeskie's sister, Sally Vann, and Betsey Shepard, joined Cherokee men in attending preparatory meetings for the upcoming treaty negotiations. The federal government paid the expenses of the women as well as the men. Two women and three men constituted the advance party that met the boundary line surveyors in 1802. Six years later, two women joined thirty men in a visit to Washington. In early 1809 two women and six men consulted with Jefferson. Although white norms meant that federal officials often ignored the presence and voice of the women, local leaders took notice. When Governor Sevier discussed the goods he needed for the upcoming treaty in 1808, he penned a rare acknowledgment of the women's presence and authority: "The goods would have a pleasing and alluring effect on the Indians, particularly the females and young men, who have their weight and influence."[9]

Not all Cherokees desired to maintain an alliance with the United States. Some of the Real People opted to move across the Mississippi. Others withdrew into isolated locations in Cherokee country or turned to alcohol.[10] Those Cherokees who chose to stay and pursue peace with the federal government could have revived earlier efforts to ally with the Spanish further south, with the French, or with the northern Indians. They selected the United States for several reasons. The defeat of the northern tribes and a change in policy toward conciliation with the United States by the Spanish government weakened the attractiveness of alliances with those peoples. Leaders and warriors also anticipated that the new government would respond more reliably than did the local whites to the Cherokee formulation of diplomatic kinship.

The men and women who conducted diplomacy with the new federal agents built on their traditional relational style of diplomacy by seeking new ways to remedy the imbalance in their foreign relations created by unreliable local treaty partners.[11] Although some of the chiefs adopted European notions of self-interest, most negotiators labored to realize Cherokee goals from a traditional cosmology that emphasized a relational kinship, rather than an arm's-length contractual arrangement. They could have followed the European practice of fashioning the United States as a contractual treaty partner, but instead they positioned the president as their father. The parties were linked by mutual obligations. For their part of the reciprocal connection, the Cherokees agreed to keep the peace, to refrain from alliances with other foreign powers, and to punish treaty transgressors.[12]

In forging a relational kinship, diplomats reached out to a partner that responded in part to their efforts to create mutuality and reciprocity in a treaty relationship. The Cherokee mental world and the Federalist vision had a significant feature in common that made some of the positions taken by federal policymakers of the 1790s attractive to the Cherokees. Both systems rested on suppositions of harmony. In contrast to the contentious interests and aggressive individualism of many of the settlers, Cherokee notions of balance required reciprocity, with each party fulfilling prescribed functions. Federalists imagined a society with mutually compatible interests in which all men had certain rights, an outlook that permitted the Federalists to envision a country that included both Cherokees and white settlers and to incorporate notions of justice into its view of how such different peoples should interact. In allying themselves to the new republic, the Cherokees reaped an unexpected advantage. American political leaders of the 1790s were concerned with the reputation of the United States in the European community. In their view, Europeans looked to the new country's Indian policy as one indicator of its republican values. Eager to be respected, each of the first four administrations—both Federalist and Republican—struggled to fashion a relationship with the indigenous inhabitants that conformed to its ideals while realizing its other policy objectives.[13]

Operating from frameworks containing some common impulses, both Cherokee spokesmen and agents for the United States understood that their connection involved a reciprocal, protective relationship. Neither party entered the relationship with fully realized ideas about how to conceptualize their new trust arrangement. Although the federal government agreed that it assumed a protective relationship, it often defined the relationship by reference to contractual principles, relying on the interpretation of written treaty provisions.[14] In response to federal efforts to define the relationship by contractual rules, Cherokee spokespeople insisted that the connection was governed by kinship standards of reciprocity as well as by treaty commitments. Drawing on some familiar concepts and articulating new ones, Cherokee men and women molded five roles for their new father. In their view, he agreed to honor and renew the fictive kinship, to do justice to the Cherokees, to assist them in times of difficulty, to treat them as equals with his white children, and to recognize their autonomy.

A concept developed by the Upper Towns and articulated by Scolacutta at Holston, the doctrine of regeneration was critical to all of the other obligations imputed to the United States.[15] Included in the idea of revival were two tenets—the Cherokees understood that the covenant between the parties was permanent, and they believed that the bonds had to be vigorously renewed. The most significant challenges to the Cherokee claim that the fictive kinship was perpetual were the efforts by the United States to acquire Cherokee lands and federal assumptions about the civilization program. Without land, the Cherokee nation would not exist. After Jefferson assumed office, the federal government reopened the Treaty of Holston to pressure the Cherokees to sell their lands and to grant road concessions. Under American contractual doctrine, parties operated at arm's length and proposals to renegotiate an agreement were perfectly acceptable. In the Cherokee mental world, attempts at excessive persuasion constituted coercion. Such actions were a violation of the independent spirit highly prized by the Cherokees. As Chuquilatague explained in refusing to grant road concessions: "I expect you will think we have a right to say yes or no as answers, and we hope that you will say no more on this subject; if you do, it would seem as if we had no right to refuse."[16]

In addition, the United States had assured Cherokee delegates that the boundaries set at Holston were firm and that the national government would not request additional land. The unwelcome efforts of the Indian agents after 1797 to obtain more land abridged the spirit of previous covenants. In 1807 negotiator Selukuki Wohellengh rejected Governor John Sevier's proposal to purchase additional lands by arguing that the loss of additional lands would interfere with the Cherokees' ability to pursue the civilization program established by Washington. He invoked the durability of early promises to admonish Sevier for attempting to breach the agreement reached by the deceased Washington: "[By asking us for more land] you render inconsistent, the advise of your late Beloved Man [Washington], which ought not to be; for though he is no more, yet his word should remain."[17]

The loss of their land was not the only threat to Cherokee existence. Federal Indian policy presupposed that, once Indians were civilized, they would be absorbed into white society. Although some of the Cherokees accepted the tools and looms offered by the government, few contemplated that they would utilize these gifts to assimilate into American life. They frustrated federal officials by adapting aspects of the civilization program to accommodate Cherokee ideals and goals while refusing to accept fundamental American tenets that offended indigenous values.[18]

Regeneration required that the perpetual bonds be frequently renewed. Succeeding generations must actively nurture a diplomatic relationship in order for it to survive. Cherokee diplomats fostered the kinship by frequent reminders to the United States about its obligations and by numerous visits to the president. Speakers persistently urged a relational view of the treaty connection and referred to American responsibilities when they addressed governmental officials. In addition to talks aimed at maintaining their connection with their father, Cherokee statesmen and stateswomen observed the traditional practice of diplomatic visiting. On numerous occasions, men and women traveled to see the president—a journey that took months—to make a personal connection as well as to air their grievances.[19]

As Cherokee statesmen and stateswomen renewed their permanent ties, they reminded their father and his agents of their obligations to act in accordance with his promises—the older idea that they captured under the duty to "do justice." This responsibility was relational, not contractual. A commitment survived subsequent treaties that modified it, if the later treaty wrongfully obtained the concession. Soon after the first land transfers, Cherokee peace chiefs began to fashion the doctrine of justice and had restated it throughout the years to North Carolina and Virginia agents. With their new treaty partner, the chiefs again sought to recover their lost lands. In 1797 the chiefs attending the boundary line survey made a last attempt to recover the territory they contended had been wrongfully taken from them in the Treaty of Holston. They were no more successful than in prior attempts. A few years later, some of the Cherokees revived old claims, dating back twenty-five years, to Long Island on the Holston River. After the execution of the 1777 Treaty at Long Island, Onitositah articulated his understanding that Long Island was not part of the cession. Most local whites ignored this contention. When the Cherokee revived the claim in the early 1800s, the federal government purchased the land to silence the Cherokees. After the purchase of Long Island, the headmen abandoned claims to lands ceded by treaty and concentrated on retaining their remaining lands.[20]

Negotiators responded to pressures for land sales by linking treaty commitments by the United States to notions of justice. Such justice must occur, even if one party was weaker than the other. Making frequent visits to the president, the chiefs had some success in their appeals to protect their territorial integrity. When federal agents proposed that the Cherokees grant road rights through their nation in 1801, Chuquilatague reminded the commissioners of former talks in which the national government promised to preserve Cherokee lands. Responding to Chuquilatague's "pathetic appeal to the justice and magnanimity of the government respecting the roads, and the pressing demands . . . for the fulfillment of existing treaties," the commissioners decided not to press further at that time. Later in the decade, Governor John Sevier, acting as commissioner from Tennessee, broached the possibility of further transfers, but Selukuki Wohellengh refused to consider land cessions.[21]

Responding to bribery, pressure, and internal divisions, some of the chiefs, acting without authority, sold considerable lands, but the Cherokees reunited in 1809 and 1810 and refused to part with additional property. Meanwhile, diplomats had more success in protecting their treaty boundaries from encroachers. They persistently framed the federal government's obligation to protect their lands in terms of justice. Their complaints about intruders not infrequently produced results. In 1797 they successfully relied on the "justice" of the government to prevent a group of speculators from settling on Cherokee land near Muscle Shoals. That same year Benjamin Hawkins oversaw surveyors who marked the line established by the Treaty of Holston in 1791. Despite an enormous outcry from the state government and its citizens, President Adams sent the U.S. Army to remove Tennesseans located on the Cherokee side of the line. Throughout the first decade of the 1800s, the Cherokees turned to the United States to remove intruders as part of its obligation to "do justice." Meigs on numerous occasions responded to these kinds of demands. In 1803, 1804, 1805, 1808, 1809, and 1810, Meigs ordered federal troops to remove encroachers, and the army did so. Although the Cherokees were well aware that the government's responsiveness was usually linked to its hope for concessions at upcoming treaties, these actions nonetheless bespoke an agreement that some mutuality in honoring the treaty relationship existed, a protection that many Cherokees appreciated. In 1809, John McDonald, the former British agent who resided with and maintained considerable authority among the Lower Towns, praised the efforts of the federal government to a visiting Mohawk man: "The Government of the United States pledged themselves to guard [the Cherokee territory] inviolate, and they have sacredly observed and guaranteed the Treaty ever since."[22]

In addition to ensuring justice, a diplomatic father provided goods to his needy children. As they had with Virginia and North Carolina, the headmen expected assistance from their fictive father in times of need. When drought ruined the crops in 1804, some of the headmen appealed to Return Meigs for assistance. They informed him that "if our father grants us this relief then we shall know he is a father in reality." Meigs obliged, but the United States operated with a different cultural logic. The president expressed his "fatherly concern" while using the potential indebtedness created by the distribution as a bargaining chip in future negotiations. Undoubtedly aware of these differences in perception, the chiefs rarely asked for this kind of aid after 1796. Their new father responded more approvingly to requests for supplies that furthered his civilization program. Consequently, the headmen generally solicited these items.[23]

The lead taken by some women who used the civilization program to learn white ways of making clothing strengthened the Cherokee view of the president as a father who provided for his children. Benjamin Hawkins buttressed these leanings when he impressed the women by being the first governmental official to speak with them and inquire about their needs. When contacted by Hawkins in 1796, the women at Etowwah expressed a strong desire for peace and voiced satisfaction that the government planned to furnish them with supplies. Accepting aspects of the federal civilization program that met their needs, many women embraced the federal father who taught them to spin and weave and who gave them cards and wheels.[24]

Hand in hand with renewal, justice, and assistance was an expectation of equality as part of the federal father's obligation, a concept that had been strongly promoted by Upper Town women and Chickamaugans. Reflecting Governor Blount's commitment at Holston in 1791 that the government considered red and white people to be equal, spokesmen frequently reminded Indian agents of their father's promise to treat his red children as fairly as his white children. These leaders received confirmation from the national administration that the federal government intended to treat both Cherokees and whites equally. As Cherokee negotiators firmly embedded their connection to the United States in principles of equality, their chiefs reconceived the nature of their entitlements. In their earlier dealings with Virginia and North Carolina, the chiefs and warriors framed their claims for parity in the logic of mutuality and the rhetoric of pity. For their contribution to this balanced relationship, the Cherokees had fought the French on behalf of the English, provided food for the hungry pioneers, and struggled to minimize violence against the settlers. In exchange, they requested white governors to "pity" them and do justice.[25]

By the 1790s, it was clear to the leaders that this rendition of mutuality was not persuasive to the Americans. Their federal treaty partner felt no allegiance to Great Britain and no longer depended on the Cherokee crops, and the growing white population lessened the need for the assistance of the chiefs in restraining their warriors. At the Treaty of Holston in 1791, the Chickamaugan-led negotiators adopted a language more familiar to the settlers. Appropriating a republican discourse of rights, statesmen transformed the entitlement aspects of pity into the more autonomous concept of rights. Successfully pressing Governor Blount to concede the humanity and equality of the Indian people, they claimed "as much right to enjoy our property as any other human being." At the same time, their requests for "pity" became more infrequent. The delegates who attended the running of the boundary line in 1797 wrote the president that, with the establishment of the line, they hoped no one would disturb them "by intrusion on our rights." Some years later, the chiefs wrote the president that their nation claimed the "right" common to all nations to ratify or reject treaties.[26]

Unlike many American theorists, the Cherokees did not speak of natural or contractual rights. Invoking a specifically Cherokee kind of mutuality, they located the source of their rights in their relationship. They positioned themselves as equals to the American people and contended that rights enjoyed by Americans belonged to them. Realizing that the federal government believed that their rights originated in treaty commitments, they understood their fragility and worked assiduously to protect them. After correspondence from Governor Sevier threatened to take land and ferry entitlements from the Cherokees in 1801, Jobber's Son, speaking to the other chiefs, urged them to visit Jefferson to prevent Tennesseans from "intrud[ing] upon our rights still more."[27] By reformulating their entitlements in the rhetoric of rights, negotiators asserted their equal status while appealing to the federal government for protection.

Cherokee demands for rights resonated with the self-conscious republican ideology of post-Revolutionary white society. Grounded in Enlightenment notions about humanity, most national leaders posited that all human beings had certain rights. Secretary of War Knox believed these natural rights extended to Native Americans and could not be divested, except by a just war or through the legal process. In response to Cherokee appeals for protection of their rights, Indian agent Return Meigs worked diligently to ensure a fair claims process. In explaining why he accepted Indian testimony—inadmissible in the courts—in his claims hearings, Meigs noted that the government could hardly assert that it had the Indians under its protection if it deprived them of their rights by considering them incapable of giving evidence.[28]

The Cherokee insistence on equality, the foundation of their claim for rights, exposed most sharply the divergence between the indigenous and federal doctrines of protection. Although both Cherokees and Federalists spoke of social harmony and rights, their ideas of harmony contained crucial differences. The Cherokee understanding of balance—whether between humans and nature, women and men, or Cherokees and strangers—presupposed an arrangement of equals, with participants having autonomy within their spheres. For the Federalists, interests were hierarchically arranged, with the more powerful having a duty of protection that precluded substantial independence of the lower orders. The Federalists may have publicly positioned their "red children" as equal to their "white children," but many early leaders believed that all these children needed a disinterested gentleman to lead them. Their position was underscored by a view of savagery as the childhood of the human race, thus importing another inequality into the relationship. Although the Republicans brought a different paradigm to the national government, their more democratic ideology did not embrace Native Americans, and early Republican administrations fashioned Indian relations based on their own similar assumptions about Indian inequality.[29]

The federal protective doctrine contained another set of incorrect assumptions and tensions. The government balanced a promise to protect Indian rights against its desire to acquire Indian lands. Federal policymakers assumed that, upon civilization, Native Americans would no longer need hunting grounds and would consent to sell their lands. When the Cherokees, along with other Native Americans, failed to follow this trajectory, the conflict between Indian rights and white desires grew. In addition, the federal government mediated between the Cherokees and the settlers, a position that produced its own strains. During the territorial period, both settlers and Cherokees breached the peace treaties. This placed the national government in the uneasy position of attempting to placate the Cherokees without alienating its own citizens. After Tennessee was granted statehood in 1796, many local farmers lacked the patience of the federal government to await the results of a long-term civilization program and used their new congressional clout to force treaties.[30]

Consistent with its promise of equality to the Cherokees, the federal government initially stressed to the Ani-Yun Wiya that they were free to accept or reject offers for the sale of their lands. After Jefferson's election, the tensions within the federal position became more apparent, and the government began putting increasing pressure on the chiefs to sell. When they refused, Meigs advanced a new view of indigenous rights that denied equality. In 1805 Meigs reasoned that Indian nations east of the Mississippi relied on the

United States for care and protection. If the United States did not assist them, they would become extinct. Although the United States should recognize their just rights, it incurred an expense in protecting and civilizing them. Accepting the frontier argument that the Indians did not have tenure in the land "that they pretend to hold," Meigs contended that they could not refuse cessions, especially when the purchase money would fund improvements. Their intransigence about selling their hunting grounds demonstrated their inability to make responsible decisions. From this perspective, the United States had the "just right to determine and are the best judges of what lands they can spare." Meigs revised the government's initial opinion about the nature of Cherokee rights and equality to reach an ominous conclusion: "From the above observations I would not infer that [the Cherokees] have no rights, they have rights by compact, but it is such a compact as a minor makes with his guardian; their rights are limited."[31] Alluding to the image of savages as children, Meigs thus transformed Cherokee rights from those grounded in natural rights between equal parties to contractual rights. He further diminished those contractual entitlements by imputing a hierarchical power relationship between the contracting parties.

These very different understandings of the Cherokee spokespeople and federal officials about Indian equality created critical tensions around the related but distinct issue of Cherokee autonomy. In Cherokee society, each person was connected to others through the mother's clan, and the father did not have rights to the custody or raising of his children. The primary male connection for a woman's children was her brother. The Cherokee concept of fatherhood continued to be a man entitled to respect who provided for his children while encouraging their independence. Cherokee leaders fashioned their diplomatic kinship from this perspective. In the early stages of the new relationship, some Cherokee diplomats agreed to permit their federal father to give them advice or to make a few decisions for them. Chiefs saw these actions as part of a web of connection in which a father best offered guidance or made some decisions. They did not intend to surrender their sovereignty to their federal father.[32]

The Cherokees learned that their new kin imagined the role of father to be a more intrusive one than the Cherokees supposed. In the years prior to the articulation of his theory of federal guardianship, Return Meigs exhibited considerable ambivalence about his assumption of authority to make decisions about the regulation of internal life in the Cherokee community. Meigs assumed office in 1801 believing that the Cherokees had complete authority to manage their domestic affairs: "The internal regulation of the Cherokees lies solely within their own jurisdiction and we have no right to interpose, except from principles of benevolence to advise them to live in peace and do justice to one another." He deferred frequently to the Cherokees, stating that he could only advise on internal matters. At the same time, Meigs assumed considerable control over council politics when the Cherokees made decisions involving the United States and its citizens. In 1802 Jefferson's administration initiated efforts to restrict visitations by the chiefs to Washington to those favoring land cessions for roads. Soon the government began to bribe some of the chiefs in order to obtain favorable treaty terms. This meddling in domestic decision making to control international relations spilled over into other internal matters.[33]

Numerous Cherokees responded to the federal assertions of paternalism by contending that they had not endowed their diplomatic father with this kind of authority. The question of Cherokee independence to exercise political sovereignty played out primarily in the arena of immigration and border control. As the Cherokees grappled with the demands of white traders, sharecroppers, visitors, and residents in the early 1800s, they increasingly asserted their right to define their physical borders and the flow of goods and human traffic into their lands. Upon the unification of the nation in 1809, the new National Council lost little time in asserting its right to govern Cherokee affairs.[34]

As statesmen and stateswomen negotiated their kinship with the United States, their relationship with Tennesseans weakened. Although they occasionally referred to the white borderers as "brothers," Cherokee chiefs cast them as brothers who failed to obey the United States. With growing frequency Cherokee speakers weakened the kin relationship by calling them "white people" or "friends and brothers." The Cherokee leaders increasingly maintained diplomatic distance from the settlers, urging the government to issue passes to control the entrance of white visitors onto Cherokee lands, handling most of their grievances through the federal agents, and resisting local efforts to obtain more lands and roads.[35]

Although leaders found a more viable treaty partner in the federal government, the Real People did not completely abandon their efforts to make present connections with the westering people. Chiefs corresponded with their white brothers and friends through talks and letters in the white newspapers. The communities met on other occasions. For example, numerous whites attended the Green Corn festivals held in locations near white settlements. The Cherokees continued to recognize the possibility of connection with individual whites, encouraging those with skills to come into the nation, permitting some white tenants to farm, and placing their children in schools run by white missionaries.[36]

Some local whites responded favorably. Traders and Cherokee neighbors often opposed Tennessee's efforts to remove the Cherokees. White judges sometimes found in favor of Cherokees over their white countrymen. On occasion, white citizens on their own initiative contacted the Cherokee agent to alert the Cherokees to white wrongdoers. Thus, as the century changed, the Cherokee people fashioned a protective relationship with the United States as they reconceived their relationship with the settler community, weakening their kinship while they informally pursued selected connections.[37]

While Cherokee negotiators labored to fashion a kinship with the United States that granted them sovereignty as a nation, Tennessee leaders formulated a doctrine of limited federalism that permitted vigorous state involvement in Indian affairs.[38] After Tennessee achieved statehood in 1796, local leaders and ordinary people supported nationhood as critical to expansionism. As with many postcolonial nations, local citizens negotiated ideas about national identity. The Tennessee vision was one of a nation with strong state authority, especially in Native American affairs. The failure of the federal government to rebuke Tennesseans seriously for their illegal war against the Cherokees encouraged the new state government to construct an expanded doctrine of constrained nationalism and to fashion and implement its own Indian policies. During the 1770s and 1780s, overmountain men frequently conducted direct diplomacy with the indigenous peoples of the region, sending community leaders to make peace when violence threatened to erupt. Drawing on this tradition, the legislature and John Sevier, serving as the state's first governor, adopted an official position on the general government's authority to engage in treaty making. Shortly after taking office in 1796, Sevier wrote the secretary of war that he and the legislature were "disposed" to honor the treaties ratified by the federal government "so far as they are not pernicious, odious nor inequitous." The state's condition represented an expansion of earlier thinking that locals could ignore treaties when necessary for self-defense. Tennesseans now reserved the power to protect their property as well as their lives. Governor Sevier informed the secretary of war that he spent a good deal of time on "Indian business."[39]

The courts and ordinary settlers agreed with state leaders, extending their notion of state involvement in Indian matters to a myriad of situations. Articulating a constitutional rationale for limiting federal authority, Judge John Overton held that the United States obtained only the authority expressly delegated by the states. Under the Constitution, the federal government regulated trade and made treaties with the Indians. The states retained all other rights, including the right to issue judgments against lands within the Cherokee boundaries. Judge Campbell argued that the federal government was required to honor the North Carolina grants on Cherokee land. One hundred five male and two female heads of household living on land near Muscle Shoals articulated the views of numerous white borderers about the limits of federal authority when they petitioned Congress to countermand the federal orders to remove them from Indian land. The petitioners held themselves "willing to obey the command of our country if the public good require it"—a conditional obedience to the federal government.[40]

The evolving connection between the United States and Tennessee faced its first major challenge early in 1797. The Treaty of Holston in 1791 called for a boundary line between the Cherokees and settlers to be run with Cherokee representatives present. After various delays, the United States sent federal commissioners to mark the correct treaty line in April 1797. Unhappy Tennesseans witnessed the placement of a boundary that situated hundreds of farmers in Cherokee country. As usual, the settlers on Cherokee property did not budge. For the first time, the federal government sent the army to Powell Valley and to the Clinch River areas in eastern Tennessee to enforce the treaty lines. Twelve hundred troops under Colonel Thomas Butler removed hundreds of settlers living on the Cherokee side of the line, at times burning their cabins and destroying their fences. The removals continued in 1798, with the government prosecuting some recalcitrant settlers. When the state failed to protect them, a number of settlers again resorted to force.[41]

Although violent, the level of illegal protest was muted compared with that of the earlier years. George Roulstone's publication of Oconostotee's letter exposing the bullet hole ploy illustrates a rift in settler attitudes about the acceptability of violence against the Native Americans. Local political leaders were no longer interested in joining unhappy farmers in a war that might discourage immigration. To protect the property rights of its citizens without resorting to rebellion, the political leadership of Tennessee developed a three-pronged Indian policy—one of direct diplomacy with the Cherokees, pressure on the federal government, and sporadic efforts to control its own constituents. Although the United States claimed the sole authority to conduct Indian relations, local lawmakers dealt with the Cherokees without federal authorization. The assembly authorized Sevier to appoint an agent to approach the Cherokees about a land sale. At Sevier's urging, the citizens on Indian land south of the French Broad River elected Samuel Handly as their representative to deal with the Cherokees. Sevier also sent James Ore on a secret mission to ascertain the intentions of the Cherokees and to attempt covertly to persuade them to sell. Tennessee pursued a second avenue by pressing the general government to purchase the disputed territory. Finally, to placate the state's own citizens, Governor Sevier assumed a direct diplomatic role by issuing passes in hardship cases that allowed dispossessed citizens to return to their farms to harvest crops. When challenged by Colonel Thomas Butler, the U.S. Army officer in charge of settler removal, about his power to intervene in federal operations, the governor obtained the opinions of two attorneys general who confirmed his authority. Meanwhile, the leading men urged restraint on the homeless. The federal government, on its part, acted with considerable tact in accomplishing the removals. Observers credited the diplomacy of Colonel Butler as the salve that averted more serious violence. A treaty in 1798 did not accomplish all of Tennessee's grandiose objectives, but the Cherokees did sell almost all of the disputed territory from which settlers had been removed.[42]

Tennessee's success encouraged its political leaders to continue its three-pronged Indian policy into the next century. Acting on their doctrine of limited federalism, local government leaders stepped up their diplomacy with their native neighbors on the theory that Indian affairs required their expertise to obtain justice for their citizens. Sevier, who served six terms as governor, maintained a direct correspondence with many of the Cherokee chiefs. He assumed overt diplomatic powers by threatening war if the Cherokees retaliated for unpunished white murders, by ordering them to cooperate in various prisoner exchanges, by sending for slaves held in the Cherokee nation, and by authorizing white citizens to travel to Cherokee land to recover stolen property. In 1801 the General Assembly passed a resolution granting the state jurisdiction over debtors or criminals that fled to the Cherokee nation. Tennessee officials assiduously attended treaties, conferences, and Cherokee council meetings.[43]

In conjunction with direct diplomacy with the Cherokees, Tennessee politicians pressured the federal government to obtain land and road concessions. In 1799 the assembly passed a law ordering the governor to communicate with the president to open a road contemplated by the Treaty of Holston in 1791. By 1806 Tennessee congressmen had persuaded the United States to purchase all of the Cherokee hunting grounds. Reflecting a growing confidence in its doctrine of limited federalism, the General Assembly in 1807 initiated a more remarkable action, authorizing $20,000 to purchase lands directly from the Cherokees before the state had obtained federal approval for the purchase. The 1802 Trade and Intercourse Act permitted the states to negotiate with the Indians with the approval of the federal agent. After the appropriation, Governor Sevier notified the federal government of the state's plans in language that presupposed federal approval. In his view, "there cannot be any reasonable objections in the legislature of the United States" to Tennessee's assumption of treaty-making powers. With the federal government's consent, the governor and his agents arranged the treaty. The state agreed to pay all expenses, except those incurred by the federal agent, Return Meigs. Because of various delays, the treaty was not held until 1809, by which time the legislature had reconsidered a purchase from state funds.[44]

As the state and federal governments moved toward greater agreement, state leaders as their part of the accommodation bargain exercised occasional control over unruly farmers. Many Tennesseans characterized the federal government as favoring the Indians over its own citizens. While sympathizing with these complaints, state officials responded at times by ordering local leading men to control outbreaks by whites. The intruders on Cherokee lands mounted the most significant challenge to the restraint exercised by the state. Although the state typically left this sticky problem to the Indian agent, local leaders occasionally intervened. In 1802 Meigs attempted unsuccessfully to placate residents of Sevier County, when Cherokees retaliated for a Cherokee death by killing a man there. Meigs's letter to Colonel Samuel Wear, one of the county's leading citizens, was unsuccessful. Governor Archibald Roan spoke to the people and reassured them.[45]

The illegal frontier rebellion, supported at the highest level of territorial government, paved the way for state officials to conceive a local role in Indian affairs. As these leaders advocated a form of federalism that recognized their right to involvement in Indian policy, many Tennesseans modified their concept of Native American sovereignty to provide the intellectual content for the expansionistic course that state leaders pursued.

In the postwar period, many newcomers arrived without a history of bloodshed with the Indians, and attitudes toward the indigenous peoples softened. The vast bulk of the population no longer sought to eliminate Native Americans by violence or to take their land by force. Tennessee's population increased from 77,262 in 1795 to 105,602 in 1800. Many Tennesseans by 1800 had little personal history with the aboriginal peoples. Their diaries, correspondence, and legislative petitions indicate that they gave Indians very little thought. Newspapers after 1795, unlike the earlier period, provided minimal coverage of Native American affairs. Most immigrants preferred to maintain peace. Some citizens traded with the Indians or, living nearby, otherwise benefited from the Cherokee presence. Many of these frontier people maintained a good rapport with their neighbors and some of the state's leaders became more optimistic about the possibility of civilizing the Cherokees. Blount in 1799 thought the Cherokees had improved remarkably, although they still were not civilized enough to embrace Christianity. At Aaron Burr's dinner in Nashville in 1805, General Daniel Smith, the territorial secretary who authorized Sevier's illegal expedition of 1793, offered a toast to the Cherokee nation: "May they speedily come into the measures of the United States." Sevier approved of civilization plans by 1807. Indifference or even optimism about Cherokee progress did not mean that Tennesseans supported Cherokee sovereignty. At the same time that Cherokee diplomats initiated a discourse about Native American rights, many settlers argued that Indians did not have rights. Most considered the concept of Indian rights to be "visionary"—a theoretical notion nullified when their rights conflicted with white entitlements.[46]

Bringing with them a strong desire for material improvement, new arrivals joined old-timers in a drive toward prosperity. Moving away from hatred of Native Americans as bloodthirsty, cruel, and untrustworthy, white thinkers in this period identified Indians as obstacles to progress. Building on the concept that Indian political communities were not equivalent to civilized nations, the published responses to the settler removal crisis in 1797 further whittled away at the construct of Indian nationhood. Situated in the early stages of an economic boom, John Sevier juxtaposed the "rights" of Tennessee citizens against the "indian claims" that interfered with the enjoyment of these rights. In this neat reversal of logic, white encroachments became Cherokee encroachments. At the heart of this argument was the belief that white enterprise promised the greatest economic development of natural resources. As John Sevier articulated it to Congressman Joseph Anderson:

> I am happy to learn, that the Secretary of War gives assurances that he will expedite and forward on the [proposed] treaty [of 1798], as it is a thing much to be wished; the people being very uneasy and greatly distressed occasioned by their removal. I earnestly hope that Tennessee River will be made the line, nothing short of which can possibly place the State on a footing adequate to the welfare and cultivation of its local and natural advantages.[47]

In determining that Native Americans were obstacles to rather than potential beneficiaries of civilization, Tennesseans were early proponents of an influential argument with international reach. Australians in the 1830s frequently noted the parallels between the United States and Australia with both continents chosen by God to be civilized by the British. By the next decade, aboriginal failure to embrace civilization persuaded Australian settlers, like Tennesseans, to reimagine indigenous people as barriers to progress. Colonialists elsewhere who needed natives' labor rather than their land were more likely to persist with civilization programs.[48]

Tennessean rhetoric promoted the shift from Cherokee to white land rights in a movement that reconstituted the Indian sovereign unit as a "tribe" with territory or, worse, as "tenants" with mere claims. Although Congress referred to Native American corporate bodies as "tribes" in the 1780s, Tennesseans rarely spoke of "tribes" during that decade to refer to the Indian nations. By the mid-1790s, the term moved vigorously into the official vocabulary. Governor Blount used the term "Indian tribes or nations" in his 1795 Message to the Territorial Assembly. In an address from a Joint Committee of the Tennessee legislature to William Blount in 1796, the chairman of the committee adverted to "the adjoining Indian tribes." Blount's response framed the Indian bodies as "tribes." Judge Campbell referred to the Indian "tribes" in condemning settler removal.[49] Governor Sevier further weakened the authority of native sovereignty by reducing their land rights to "claims." In a Remonstrance to Congress in 1796, the Tennessee legislature argued that the Indians had no fee simple title to land; if the Indians had "any kind of claim" to Tennessee lands, it was, at best, "the lowest kind of tenancy, namely that of tenant at will." The legislature pressed the federal government to secure the "owners and grantees" of the disputed lands their constitutional rights by extinguishing the Indian "claims."[50]

The Tennessee legislature took the next step in November 1803. After the Louisiana Purchase, Jefferson flirted with the idea of moving the cis-Mississippi Indians west of the Mississippi. Thus encouraged, the Tennessee Senate and House of Representatives, in a rare show of agreement, unanimously passed a Memorial to Congress urging the extinction of all Indian "claims" to lands in Tennessee and advocating their removal west of the Mississippi. The idea of removal had a long history in Tennessee. The concept had taken hold with the frontier people, some of whom actively tried to drive the southeastern tribes west. By the 1780s numbers of Cherokees were beginning to migrate. In 1795 Governor Blount revived the removal discourse of the previous decade when he contended that Indian depredations would continue as long as there were Indians east of the Mississippi not constrained by whites. Although the 1803 memorial stopped short of advocating forcible removal and reassured the national government that the state planned to respect Indian "rights," it clearly repositioned the relationship between the native and settler polities. Unlike the United States, the Indian political body was not a "nation" but a "tribe," whose land base was not a "country" but a "territory." The memorial did acknowledge "rights," but it spoke primarily in terms of Indian "claims" and "privileges."[51]

Several years later, new governor Willie Blount, half brother and former secretary of William Blount, renewed proposals for removal. Blount reasoned that the state of Tennessee had an undivided interest in the vacant lands west of the Mississippi held in common with the other states. Consequently, it had the right to exchange its interest in territory there for Cherokee and Chickasaw claims to Tennessee lands. Blount revived the argument of the occupant-claimants on Cherokee property that Tennessee owned the Indian lands by conquest and under the terms of the North Carolina cession act. Blount's original contribution was to propose that, because the state did not have the money to purchase the Cherokee claims, the Cherokees should exchange their lands and move.[52] Blount's demands for removal were predicated on the erosion of the concept of Indian sovereignty. By denationalizing native communities without incorporating them into the white polity, the settlers created pressures to develop an alternative classification for indigenous peoples to Vattel's category of nationhood.

Ideas generated by the Cherokees, settlers, and federal government about their connections to each other during the period before 1812 found their way into the intellectual vacuum created by the denationalization of the Cherokees, as these ideas joined larger national discourses a generation later. Of course, later theorists modified some of the earlier concepts. The thinking of Native Americans and the federal government contributed to the solution articulated by Chief Justice John Marshall in the Cherokee cases decided in the 1830s. In those cases, the Cherokees contended that they were a foreign nation and not subject to Georgia law. The state of Georgia argued that the Cherokees had no sovereignty but were entirely subject to the laws of Georgia. By the time of the Marshall cases, Great Britain had extended its assertion of absolute sovereignty in East India to its colonies in Australia, New Zealand, and Canada. British policymakers imagined that England had a trust relationship with indigenous wards who were its subjects with limited rights until they became sufficiently civilized to exercise the full rights of British subjects. Marshall articulated a fourth position, one that relied strongly on the premise of a relational mutuality between the United States and the indigenous peoples. In *The Cherokee Nation v. Georgia* in 1831, Marshall characterized the Indian nations as domestic dependent nations, a classification that acknowledged a potentially enduring relationship between separate nations and granted the first peoples a limited recognition of sovereignty. Echoing the language used by Return Meigs twenty-six years earlier, Marshall formulated a doctrine that created a trust relationship of guardian and ward between the United States and the Cherokees. The next year in *Worcester v. Georgia*, he cited Vattel as authority for his holding that weaker states did not surrender their sovereignty when they came under the protection of stronger ones. Tracing the relationship of protection between the Cherokees and the United States to the Treaty of Hopewell in 1785 and to the Treaty of Holston in 1791, he confirmed that the Cherokee nation was not subject to Georgia's laws.[53]

Marshall found that the relationship between the United States and the Indians was one of guardian and ward because the Indians looked to the United States for protection, relied on its kindness and power, turned to it for aid, and addressed the president as their great father.[54] However, in contrast to Vattel's stronger state that protected its dependent states from other nations, the United States promised the Cherokees protection from its own citizens.[55] The concepts of fatherhood, guardianship, kind treatment, aid, and protection from a nation's citizens suggest domestic and familial ties rather than contractual bargaining between autonomous nation-states. They are not constructs described by Vattel, nor is this the British wardship that granted no sovereignty to native peoples but incorporated them as English subjects. The Cherokees and the federal government negotiated their connection at the treaties of Hopewell and Holston and in later meetings using the framework of a diplomatic family rooted in Cherokee values. Indigenous concepts invoking claims of kinship and mutuality, a duty to the weaker party, and the autonomy and permanence of the Cherokee nation and Federalist notions of harmony, humanity, and paternalism forged the meaning of the protective relationship. In this familial connection, the United States as the stronger party offered more than the protection that Vattel's European nations supplied to weaker ones—the national government made annual payments to the Cherokees rather than the Cherokees paying tribute to the United States, and the federal father provided aid as part of his civilization program.

Lost in Marshall's pronouncement of the trust doctrine was the express recognition of Cherokee equality promised at the Treaty of Holston in 1791. Subverting the commitment to consider the Cherokees "as good as ourselves, not one better than the other," Marshall created a pupilage relationship. Yet in the face of the widespread white belief that Native Americans were disappearing, Marshall placed constitutional obstacles in the way of those states seeking to deny Native American sovereignty and to take Indian lands. Marshall's ruling reflected in important though limited ways the fictive kinship that had been negotiated between the Cherokees and the United States. The concept of domestic dependent nations continues to inform and complicate much of American Indian law.[56]

By imagining limited sovereignty in Native Americans, Marshall presented an alternative to the British policy, a construction that interested rulers in the British colonies, though for reasons different from the impulses that motivated Marshall. Government leaders in England argued that its policy ensured better treatment to natives than Marshall's formulation, because Britain gave native people some rights as British subjects. In spite of the metropole's policy, local officials in the mid-nineteenth century in Australia, Canada, South Africa, and New Zealand were not interested in risking native resistance to the destruction of their sovereignty in order to confer British rights on them, nor were they eager to incorporate indigenous people into their society. Often referring to the widely publicized Cherokee cases, they adopted variations of Marshall's approach by recognizing that tribes controlled their own affairs, unless they consented to British authority.[57]

The Cherokees, the national government, and Great Britain were not the only parties seeking to fill Vattel's void. Tennesseans created a broad-based state role in Indian policy while they evolved a philosophy of limited federalism in response to the Native American crisis. Ominously, as they forged their concept of a civilized nation, they linked it to the denigration of Cherokee sovereignty. Along with other western Americans, they initiated a discourse of incompatibility between the civilized American nation and the savage Indians that generated another alternative to Vattel's theory, different from that of Chief Justice Marshall's. Their early expansionist proposals of removal became national policy with the Trail of Tears, when this solution was imposed over Marshall's ruling under a doctrine of constrained national authority by Tennessean, then president, Andrew Jackson.

PART TWO Intracommunal Relations

CHAPTER FOUR

"The Name of My
Nation Is Cherokee"

*The Reformulation of
Cherokee Identity*

As the troubles between the Cherokees and the settlers intensified in mid-1793, the *Knoxville Gazette* filed a remarkable story. In its routine feature on the latest Indian attacks on frontier farms, the *Gazette* reported in amazement that Indians had scalped some hogs. Nonplussed about the motive, the publisher could only speculate that "superior dexterity in scalping gives preeminence to Indian warriors." But this explanation is implausible—warriors' pausing in the midst of the white settlements to practice or demonstrate their scalping technique would be needlessly risky. More likely, the gesture reflected the disdain with which Cherokee men viewed the "Virginian" agricultural norm of men raising domesticated animals. The Cherokee warriors celebrated the superiority of their cultural ways of hunting wild animals by scalping the pigs. As part of the traditional role that women played in agriculture, Cherokee women had for decades adapted the European practice of raising hogs along with other stock.[1]

Postcolonialists are interested in the moments and processes that occur when people from different cultures become intertwined.[2] The scalping episode captured Cherokee men and women in a hybrid space at a crucial time in the refashioning of their identity and exposed tensions underlying the transformation of Cherokee society. Scalping and raising hogs serve as a microcosm of the cultural disarray that prompted the Cherokees to reinvent clan rules, government, and economic relations. At times, they used elements of both cultures as described by theorists of transculturation and in some cases embedded customary arrangements into new structures in ways that signal retraditionalization.

Scholars describe the Cherokees as a factionalized people as a result of the division between the Upper Towns and the Chickamaugans in 1776.[3] The overemphasis on Chickamaugan military goals by historians contributes to an inaccurate portrayal of the relationship between the Upper and Lower Town residents.[4] Although divided, the two sections of the nation retained much in common. People in both areas denied the validity of the sale of land to Richard Henderson and supported hunting as part of their way of life. The men and women in both Upper and Lower Towns also retained a traditional government of numerous local chiefs and decision making by all people that reflected indigenous values.

The division among the Cherokees occurred because of ideological differences about how best to constitute a Cherokee identity in the face of rapid change. What was a borderland struggle for Euro-Americans was a transformation in the heartlands for Cherokees. The Upper Towns ground their self-concept in their belief in the importance of retaining ancestral lands. In an effort to create a harmonious balance, they established economic and social alliances with the settlers. The Chickamaugans separated because they believed that they could best preserve Cherokee autonomy by maintaining distance from settlers and by balancing American pressures with international trade to protect their autonomy and to avoid the dependency created by trade relations with only one partner.

With the advent of peace after 1795, the Cherokees confronted similar pressures from the postcolonial expansionist United States that the northern Indians faced—to surrender land, to civilize, or to relocate to the west. In response, the Cherokee people continued to understand the universe as a balance of opposing forces and used this principle as they imagined a stronger national identity to offset American aggression. They retained their clan system but modified their understanding of their social structure to include individuals without clan ties who could assist the Cherokees. Extending the law about captives, Cherokees gave employers and masters, like captors, complete authority to control and discipline their employees and slaves. This reliance on a traditional doctrine avoided European Enlightenment and Christian concepts about a universal humanity with natural rights and a social contract theory that imputed civil rights to non-Cherokee residents.

Although they were not colonized, pressures from the United States and Tennesseans prompted the Cherokees to move away from the localism of the past and to create a unified government with genuine power over all Cherokees. They nationalized not to become civilized, as some historians have suggested, or to support expansionism, as did Tennesseans, but to protect

Cherokee sovereignty.[5] The Cherokee concept of nationhood did not copy American national models but tapped into important components of Cherokee identity in a movement similar to one that postcolonial historians have observed in colonized countries.[6] Utilizing the processes of transculturation and retraditionalization, the Cherokees constructed a National Council that required unanimity rather than a majority to act and that included older chiefs and the Women's Council in its decision making. While Tennesseans crafted localism into their views of nationhood by urging a strong role for the states in a federal system, the Real People incorporated localism by deferring to traditional practices when they adopted and enforced their new laws. Cognizant of the experience of the Chickamaugans, the Cherokees embraced a strong economy as an important component of autonomy. By 1810 many of the Cherokee people formulated the outlines of a new concept of themselves as a nation rooted in a modified version of the clan system, in a stronger Cherokee-controlled national government, and in expansive economic relations that countered American pressures.

After Henderson's Treaty, the dissidents led by Tsi-yugunsini removed themselves from the Upper Towns and ended Chota's authority as the town that conducted diplomacy and regulated trade for the Real People. In constructing the picture of a sharply divided people after 1776, however, scholars have been overly influenced by the efforts of the Upper Town chiefs to maintain peace with white negotiators and on later white memories. Relying on a traditional tactic to promote a peaceful frame of mind by assigning responsibility for misdeeds to third parties, Upper Town diplomats frequently blamed violence and theft on the young men of Chickamauga. As part of the white reimagining of Indians as proud defenders of a doomed culture, mythmakers in later periods envisioned Tsi-yugunsini in the heroic but futile role of savior of his people.[7] While the accepted rendition casts the Upper Town peace chiefs as acceding to white pressures and the Lower Town residents as traditionalists fighting to preserve Cherokee ways, paradoxically historians describe the Lower Towns as the region that most quickly embraced the federal civilization program after 1795.[8]

The Chickamaugan narrative is misleading because it overlooks considerable agreement among both factions, the presence and role of women and older chiefs in the Chickamaugan towns, and the economic and diplomatic goals of the Chickamaugan women and men. After the Henderson sale, the Cherokee people agreed on significant points. Frequently avowing that "we love our land," all Cherokees saw the possession of their land as part of a spiritual attachment to the earth. The land was the source of their livelihood through farming and hunting. Their forebears were buried there. Most considered that the sales of land diminished the "country life of [our] ancestors." The land was also their heritage to the future generations. Both Upper and Lower Town residents believed that the Cherokees had superior rights to the land. When whites claimed title to lands the Cherokees saw as theirs, thinkers from both regions located their entitlement in the Great Spirit's bestowal of the lands on the Cherokees and in the right of first possession. They also claimed lands by treaty rights. In the view of many Cherokees, white people lived on their land as their "friends"—that is, as guests without ownership claims.[9]

Almost all Cherokees agreed that many of the alleged land sales were fraudulent. Onitositah, the peace chief of the Upper Towns, told the federal commissioners in 1785 that Richard Henderson forged names on the deeds ten years earlier. According to Onitositah's account, the Cherokees believed that they were giving Henderson a little land on the Kentucky River for his cattle and horses. Under pressure from white negotiators at Hopewell, Onitositah agreed "to say nothing more about Kentucky, although it is justly ours." The Chickamaugans, of course, agreed.[10]

In contrast to the Euro-American view that the Cherokees could not claim lands that they did not cultivate, all Cherokees believed that the Great Spirit gave them a property interest in the wild animals in their forests. Responding to the white vision of land as the source from which farming and domestic husbandry produced increased population and civilization, Onitositah bespoke a common belief when he argued that the Creator intended varying uses for diverse peoples:

> The great God of Nature has placed us in different situations. . . . *We are a separate people!* He has given each their lands under distinct considerations and circumstances; he has stocked yours with cows, ours with buffalo; yours with hog, ours with bear; yours with sheep, ours with deer. He has, indeed, given you an advantage in this, that your cattle are tame and domestic while ours are wild and demand not only a larger space for range, but art to hunt and kill them; they are, nevertheless, as much our property as other animals are yours; and ought not to be taken away without our consent, or for something equivalent.[11]

In addition to agreement about land and hunting, Upper and Lower Town Cherokees continued the traditional governmental system of village chiefs who relied on influence, not compulsion. The Upper Town government was primarily local government. Numerous small villages each had their own headmen. Women retained their traditional sphere of influence under the formal government, with the Women's Council and Nan-ye-hi actively participating in affairs.[12]

Contrary to scholarly accounts that Tsi-yugunsini headed the unified Lower Towns, the Lower Towns did not embrace a different form of government but, like the Upper Towns, listened to numerous local chiefs. Contemporaries saw Tsi-yugunsini as one of a number of war chiefs. Indian agent Joseph Martin in 1786 described Tsi-yugunsini as "one of the chiefs" and British agent George Welbank in 1791 as "one of the head warriors of this nation." Although an important war chief, Tsi-yugunsini was not the only one. During the war in the summer of 1788, Lower Town warriors Tsi-yugunsini, Nentooyah, Catigiskey, Kunoskeskie, Atawgwatihih, Uwenahi, and the Tsi-yugunsini's brother Ookoousdi were among the Cherokees who defeated troops led by Joseph Martin against the Chickamaugans. In October 1788 it was Nentooyah, Catigiskey, and Atawgwatihih with about 200 men, led by Kunoskeskie, who launched a major assault on Gillespie Station. Tsi-yugunsini's views did not dictate Cherokee policy. For example, the council split over Tsi-yugunsini's refusal to kill women at Eaton's fort. As in the Upper Towns, the Lower Towns also had peace chiefs. During the extensive peace negotiations carried on by the Chickamaugans prior to 1795, numerous diplomats from the Lower Towns spoke. Wyuka and Newota represented the Chickamaugans at the 1785 Treaty of Hopewell. Ookoousdi went with two other Cherokees in 1787 to Nashville for peace talks. Chulcoah was the principal Cherokee diplomat at the Treaty of Holston in 1791. Governor William Blount understood that Tsi-yugunsini was second to Kenneteag as head of the nation and second to Kunoskeskie as a warrior. By 1790 Tsi-yugunsini's mind and probably his influence were slipping.[13]

Because Upper and Lower Towns maintained customary governments, the traditional practices of embracing individual independence continued. Cherokees in both parts of the nation did not expect or want the chiefs to govern them, and many chiefs observed traditional practices of consulting all their people before making decisions. Many Cherokees in both parts of the nation rejected white efforts to assign authority to their chiefs. White diplomats pressed peace chiefs to enforce treaties by controlling the warriors. In spite of the entreaties of their chiefs, numerous young men from the Upper Towns traveled to the Lower Towns to join the Chickamaugans in assaults on white farmers and travelers. Although Governor Blount characterized Kenneteag as the head of the nation in the 1790s, Kunoskeskie, the maternal nephew of Onitositah, working behind the scenes, was the most powerful man in the nation. Women also operated independently. When captive Samuel Handly humiliated a Cherokee woman who tortured him, she traveled a hundred miles to the white settlements many years later to attempt to kill him. Some women warned traders of plans to kill them.[14]

By the late 1780s, the Upper Towns, pressed by their proximity to white neighbors, began to restrict the Cherokee tradition of independence. To keep the peace, the Upper Town residents enacted formal laws around 1789 that made murder, horse theft, and any other violation of treaty provisions punishable by death and that prohibited the use of alcohol. They appointed Toowayelloh to ride the circuit to enforce the regulations and exiled several men who disobeyed the ordinances. Faced with individuals who disclosed secret governmental operations, sometime before 1792 the Cherokees passed a law "that any Indian, a native of the Cherokees, who should give intelligence to the whites of any orders which the nation took in council, or otherwise, he should forfeit his property, and be banished from the country." Even these efforts to restrain the Cherokees had limited success, because enforcement was spotty.[15]

Despite their many areas of agreement, the Real People did divide after the loss of lands to Richard Henderson. Some historians suggest that the division reflected differences between old chiefs and young men.[16] While age and gender may have played a role in the separation, such accounts exaggerate the importance of young men in the Chickamaugan community by overlooking the presence and contributions of older chiefs and women. Kitegiska, the brother of Oconostota who was the principal chief of the Cherokees in 1775, associated with the Chickamaugans. Oconostota remained friendly with them. Peace chief Onitositah remained with the Upper Towns, but his brothers Chuquilatague, Iyahuwagiatsutsa, and Talotiskee fought with the Chickamaugans. Nan-ye-hi's brother Tuskegateehee lived in Chickamaugan towns until 1783. Ostenaco and Scolacutta, both older chiefs, allied with the secessionists, although Scolacutta later returned.[17]

Women also joined the Chickamaugan cause and pursued roles in their military efforts. During the Chickamaugan attack on John Donelson's party on the Tennessee River in 1780, women and children colluded with the men in attempting to lure the party ashore. When Nentooyah, one of the principal chiefs of the Lower Towns, traveled to Florida in 1792 to obtain arms from the Spanish in order to wage war on the settlers, his wife accompanied him. After the attack on the Lower Towns in 1794, women, fearing that their captive children would be killed, dissuaded the warriors from pursuing the militiamen. Women also exercised their customary authority to incorporate out-siders into Chickamaugan community by marriage and adoption. Almost all traders married Cherokee women. A Lower Town Irish trader took in Joseph Brown, a young boy saved when his family was killed. The trader was married to a French woman adopted by the Cherokees after she was taken prisoner as a child. River women used their power over their homes and children to influence Chickamaugan decisions. When Cutleotoy, an important man in the town, decided to kill Brown, the trader's wife refused to allow the killing in her home. Bowing to her authority, Cutleotoy removed Brown from her house. Women and children tortured Samuel Handly during his captivity.[18]

A result of neither age nor gender divisions, the separation had ideological roots. The split reflected divergent views about what values were central to the identity of the Cherokees as a people. The Upper Towns pursued an accommodation with the newcomers in order to retain their ancestral lands, whereas the Chickamaugans sought to establish independence by physical separation through which they initially pursued military success but came to believe in the importance of economic autonomy. Attached to their country, the Upper Town men and women refused to relocate in the face of white encroachment. Their cognitive world was rooted in a spiritual attachment to the land as their gift from the Great Spirit, as the burial grounds of their ancestors, and as the heritage for their children. They sought to create a balance between Cherokees and settlers by establishing relationships with the newcomers that would permit the separate peoples to exist in harmony.[19] To do so, they forged ties through economic and communal connections with the frontier people, but these relationships operated as more than mecha-nisms for material advancement or social intercourse. As was the case with diplomatic ties, these bonds in the Cherokee mind existed in a web of mutu-ality that bound the parties together in a common universe in which each party assumed obligations.

Women in the Upper Towns fashioned many of the connections with the settlers by converting their traditional role as farmers for their community into trade relationships with whites. Incoming settlers and travelers needed food. As the producers of crops, women sold food to the village traders and to the white community. Nan-ye-hi prospered by raising crops and cattle, some of which she marketed to settlers. By 1785 the Upper Town settlements lived primarily on the strength of the sale of their crops to the new settle-ments, an activity largely carried on by women. After the Cherokee war of 1788, women continued to deal in the buying and selling of corn. The wom-en's efforts were not without risk. The Hubbards shot at four women and a man in a white settlement, Cherokees who were probably there to trade.[20] In addition to marketing produce and cattle to exchange for goods, women were eager to acquire skills to permit them to manufacture clothing, a task that required white assistance. Years before the federal civilization program, some women had learned to spin, and many wanted to raise flax, cotton, and wool and to master weaving. The Cherokees in the French Broad area in eastern Tennessee, particularly the women, had established considerable trading connections with the settlers. The relationship was strong enough that the women planned to send their daughters to the white women to learn to spin. Sevier's attack on the peace chiefs and Upper Towns in 1788 derailed these plans.[21]

Men also formed a variety of connections with settlers. Some Cherokees and white diplomats maintained close personal ties. Cherokee men as well as women traded with the immigrants. Cherokee and white men drank together, and the Cherokees engaged in competitive sports with the newcomers, including racing and shooting. Hunters occasionally socialized at each others' camps. Former hostages and captors at times visited each other. White men often attended Green Corn dances and occasionally scalp dances.[22]

Both the Cherokees and some whites believed that these economic and social exchanges integrated the separate peoples in larger networks of connection. Peace chiefs described the provision of corn to be one of the Cherokee contributions to the reciprocal kinship between the parties. One ordinary white man in eastern Tennessee recognized the mutuality created by the interactions between the parties: "A sensible reformation has taken place with the Cherokee since the white people have lived so nigh them. . . . The manner of the Indians is also become more natural to the white people by frequent intercourse."[23]

While the Upper Towns envisioned the preservation of their ancestral lands through the creation of reciprocal bonds, the Chickamaugans imagined a Cherokee identity of autonomy and independence. Tsi-yugunsini and many of his followers believed that it was the intention of Virginia and the Carolinas to destroy them as a people. The invasion of Virginia, North and South Carolina, and Georgia militias into Cherokee country during the war of 1776 pointed to the difficulty of a military victory against white encroachers and their eastern allies.[24] Whereas many Chickamaugans believed that the rogue land hunters should be dispelled by force, others envisioned a counterweight to the pressures from white settlers in distance and an autonomous Cherokee economy that did not depend on the largesse of the encroachers.

Like Native Americans who played off European powers against each other for diplomatic balance, the River People used trade with a variety of nations to maintain symmetry and to avoid dependency on one nation. They sought to enhance Cherokee independence by preserving their hunting grounds, claiming animals and property on land that they contended whites unlawfully seized, diversifying the products that they brought to market, and developing multinational trade connections.

Because hunting remained the principal economic activity of the Lower Towns, the major concern of the Cherokees was to protect their hunting grounds so that hunters could supply skins for trade. Their greater distance from the encroaching Americans gave them access to more territory. The Chickamaugans agreed to peace in 1783, but they attacked land hunters when North Carolina opened its land offices and entered lands north of the Tennessee that included "the greater part of all the corn plantations belonging to the Chickamaugo . . . together with the principal part of their hunting grounds." Their second move downriver further expanded their opportunities for game. In addition to pelts, the Chickamaugans began producing silver products. Their silverwork drew Creek and French traders to their towns. The Lower Town women sold crops and cattle.[25]

Unsuccessful in securing the return of the land sold to Henderson, the River People contended that the property of illegal settlers on their land and waters belonged to them. Cherokee law and often British and American policies allowed the Cherokees to seize the property of traders who behaved dishonestly and of intruders who poached on Cherokee lands. The dissidents extended the law of forfeiture to those that they considered encroachers. As Chulcoah, one of the principal diplomats at the Treaty of Holston in 1791 with Chickamaugan connections, explained: "Those people who came over the line we took their horses. If they had not come over the line it would not have been done." Based on this doctrine, the Chickamaugans freely robbed white farms, confiscating horses and slaves, and seized boats on Cherokee waters. As part of the appropriation of property on their lands, the secessionists developed extensive horse theft rings that took the horses of settlers in the Cumberland settlements and elsewhere on lands that they claimed. They sold the horses to traders in their nation who needed pack animals, to other Native Americans, to the Spanish and French, and to settlers in the Carolinas and Georgia. Slaves were a special target and a source of wealth. Chickamaugan marauders often killed whites and took blacks as prisoners. Numerous settlers attempted to reach the Cumberland settlements by traveling down the Tennessee River through Cherokee country. The residents of the Lower Towns seized boats traversing Cherokee waters without authorization, especially at Muscle Shoals.[26]

Laden with furs, merchandise, and plunder, the residents of the lower part of the nation sought to maximize their economic opportunities by establishing wide-ranging trade relationships. Americans in 1776 wanted to restrict Cherokee commercial relations by forbidding intercourse with Great Britain. The Chickamaugans believed that the Real People should seek more extensive trading contacts. As they distanced themselves from the American settlers by relocating, they controlled access to the Tennessee River. Initially, they turned to British allies for goods. After peace with the Chickasaws in the early 1780s, the River People sought better commerce with them. The Chickamaugans traded with the Spanish in Pensacola and with the French and Spanish in New Orleans.[27] The Lower Towns welcomed merchants into their towns. The French established posts in Cold Water in 1786, and the Creeks traveled there to trade. Spanish, French, and Canadian traders built stores at Muscle Shoals. The Lower Towns warmly received a trader from Baltimore.[28]

The economic goals of the Lower Towns came to eclipse their military mission, as many residents began to enjoy their prosperity and to see it as a balance to the influence exerted by the overmountain people. In the 1780s the dissidents increasingly viewed the "rogues" as sources of wealth as well as enemies to be driven out or killed. Motivated by the prospect of material gain, Chickamaugan warriors sacrificed critical military goals in order to secure plunder. During a major attack by Tsi-yugunsini and his men on the Bluffs near Nashville in 1781, the frontier people routed them because the Cherokees were more concerned with stealing horses than with fighting. After 1785, as civil war broke out in eastern Tennessee over the state of Franklin, the Chickamaugans forsook the military opportunity the turmoil created in order to seize property. During the Cherokee war of 1788, the Cherokees raised an army of 2,000 Cherokees and 1,000 Creeks to drive off all of the white settlers south of the French Broad River. Upon arriving at Gillespie's Station, the Chickamaugan warriors seized so much plunder from the fort and surrounding farms that they abandoned their military mission and returned home. In 1792, after the successful attack on Ziegler's Fort in the Cumberland settlements, the victors awaited a party that had gone to Nashville to steal horses. When the Nashville contingent appeared without booty, the Cherokees drew knives and quarreled violently among themselves.[29]

Chickamaugan entrepreneurship made the river towns the wealthiest part of the nation. Believing that commerce offered independence from the encroaching Americans, many women and men left the Upper Towns. Governor Randolph of Virginia complained that the young men of the Upper Towns, seeing the benefits that the inhabitants of the Lower Towns received from their war on the settlers, frequently joined the Chickamaugans. In 1792 Governor Blount reported that many Cherokees from other parts of the nation had settled in the Lower Towns. Here they had access to a variety of merchandise, including luxury items like wine and striped silk shirts. The enterprise of the Chickamaugans and their distance from white intruders during their first two decades meant that they were more prosperous at the time of peace in 1795. As The Nephew explained in 1795, "the river people who are near the hunting grounds are well clothed; the upper towns are naked."[30]

As the Chickamaugans sought autonomy in international trade, the Lower Towns attracted numerous foreign residents. Whites and blacks joined Creeks and other indigenous peoples in participating in the economic life of the nation. A number of Spanish people, mostly deserters, lived in the area. The multiethnic population gathered in a cosmopolitan effort to participate in commerce and to share in the higher standard of living in an environment freer from compulsion. The creation of a cosmopolitan trading center resulted in more residents who were unrelated to the Cherokees by clan connections and not governed by clan law. Joseph Brown's captivity narrative indicates that the Creeks residing in the Nickajack area in 1788 were not connected to the Cherokees by clan ties. In spite of Brown's adoption by the influential Wolf clan, the Creeks pursued him and forced him to exercise precautions to avoid being killed.[31]

Although the residents of the Upper and Lower Towns fashioned different concepts about how to maintain their Cherokee identity, there was much movement between the two regions that kept the Real People connected. Young men from the Upper Towns moved downriver for more than improved economic opportunities. Their mixed diplomacy of peace and war allowed Chickamaugans to retain the ancient custom of blood revenge, while the Upper Town chiefs urged restraint. Not only clan revenge but also clan connections bridged the factionalism of the Real People. Tuskegateehee, the brother of Nan-ye-hi and the maternal uncle of Joseph Martin's wife, left the Chickamaugans in 1783 because "Colonel [Joseph] Martin sent for me to come away; being his relation I came." A member of the Wolf Clan, Tuskegateehee became chief of seven Upper Towns, and thirteen others listened to him. Kunoskeskie, the most influential man in Chickamauga in the early 1790s, was the maternal nephew of the Upper Town peace chief, Onitositah, called Old Tassel by Euro-Americans. Onitositah was one of the diplomats killed under a flag of truce in 1788. Also known as Young Tassel, Kunoskeskie was extremely close to his uncle who, in the Cherokee kin system, served as his male parent. Kunoskeskie frequently traveled back and forth between Chickamauga and the Upper Towns. Kunoskeskie was so overcome at seeing his uncle's murderers at the Treaty of Holston three years later that he withdrew from negotiations. Numerous such close relationships suggest that clan connections bound the Lower and Upper Towns in spite of political differences.[32] Such connections allowed the philosophical orientations of both the Upper and Lower Towns to contribute to the identity that the Cherokees created when hostilities ceased.

After peace in 1795, the Cherokees responded to the rapid changes in their world from their traditional spiritual orientation toward balance. They also continued to turn to rituals, shamans, and conjurers for spiritual help. Although a few Christian missionaries entered the nation to preach salvation, the vast majority of Cherokees rejected this approach, including Nan-ye-hi and her family.[33] Rather than salvation, the Cherokees sought to reestablish balance. They did so by reimagining what it meant to be Cherokee. They fashioned ideas about Cherokee identity that emphasized expanded interaction with the non-Cherokee world, nationhood along with local connection, and autonomy.

The infusion of unrelated outsiders transformed Cherokee society. Although clan connections retained much of their importance, challenges to the clan system arose from two sources—from white men who married Cherokee women and from slaves, servants, laborers, mechanics, and tenants in the country who did not have clan connections. During the period after permanent white settlement, white traders and diplomats with Cherokee families became more insistent on observing European patriarchal customs. On death, the property of Cherokee men traditionally passed to their brothers, as their closest relatives, but many white traders trained their sons in their business and devised property to them. Some wealthy Cherokee men accepted these practices. The National Council of 1808 passed new inheritance laws authorizing regulators to protect the wife and children on the death of the husband, but these leading Cherokees were unwilling to accept white patriarchal notions that favored the eldest son. The council rewrote the will of a wealthy *métis* decedent who left most of his property to his oldest son to provide greater protection for his wife and other children. However, most Cherokees paid little attention to recorded laws. The regulators, the body of men charged with enforcing the laws, had great discretion in adjusting conflicts and probably relied on traditional values in settling inheritance issues and other problems created by white intermarriage. As late as 1817, inheritance law remained unsettled.[34]

While whites with Cherokee spouses had a link to the clan system through marriage, the multicultural environment of the Chickamaugan towns brought numbers of people into the nation who had no clan connections. A few were adopted into a clan, but most were not. After 1794 the Upper Towns also accepted mechanics, laborers, tenants, and slaves with no clan ties. The 1809 census located 341 whites in the nation, whose Cherokee population was 12,395. Two-thirds of the whites were not married to Cherokee women. Several wealthy individuals in both regions owned most of the 583 slaves.[35] The influx of significant numbers of people into the nation who had no clan identification prodded the Cherokees to formulate ideas about how to classify and govern these strangers.

Scholars have argued that the Cherokees and other southern Indians adopted European ideas about race to restructure their thinking about people without clan connections.[36] Although this was increasingly true after the unification of the nation in 1810, in the earlier period the Cherokees initially relied more strongly on a different scheme to cope with the intellectual challenge of incorporating non-Cherokee residents into their social structure —they categorized them based on status, conduct, and cultural practices. Considering themselves superior to servants and slaves, the Ani-Yun Wiya constructed a special classification for bonded people—one based primarily on status rather than race. A fiercely independent people that valued personal autonomy highly, the Cherokees disdained bonded men and women because they hated servile subordination. The earliest slaves in Cherokee country were Native Americans taken captive during war. Prisoners who were not adopted remained outside the clan system and were called *atsi nah sa'i*, a word that applied to all living beings, including animals, owned by a person. Because they did not belong to a clan, the owner had complete authority over the Indian slaves, who had no rights. Traders introduced black slavery into the nation in the early part of the eighteenth century. By the time of the Revolution, the Cherokees viewed slaves as a degraded species. During the 1776 expedition, a Cherokee man attacked the slave of a British colonel, "thinking to have a Negro to wait on him." The Cherokees owned and sold black slaves in significant numbers after 1776, when the Chickamaugans began to seize slaves. The Cherokees sold or transferred slaves with such frequency that travelers reported that the Cherokees marketed slaves as whites did in Carolina and Virginia. Not surprisingly, slaves often ran away from their Cherokee owners.[37]

Although there may have been a racial element underlying the disdain that the Cherokees expressed toward slaves, the primary impetus behind the Cherokee scorn of slaves was not racial animus. African Americans who were adopted became members of a Cherokee clan and were treated like other Cherokees. The Cherokees also did not denigrate blacks who maintained a status as free. One of the best-known of the free black people living in the nation was Jack Civils. According to some accounts, he was a free man who came to the Tennessee region with Richard Henderson and was taken prisoner by the Cherokees. Others claim that he was a slave of John Donelson captured by the Cherokees. Another account claims that Civils married a Cherokee woman and distinguished himself in battle. Nickajack, the most prominent of the Lower Towns, may have been named for him, as a variation of "nigger Jack." Civils ran a tavern and store and acted as a messenger for the Cherokees to the federal government. A proud man, he resisted white efforts to denigrate him because of his race. Indian agent William Lovely derided Civils for failing to defer to whites. To Lovely's disgust, the Cherokees treated Civils as an equal. His Cherokee identity encouraged his self-assertiveness in dealing white officials. At his death in 1805, Civils left a white wife and a sizable estate.[38]

While they molded their characterization of slaves around their status as beings without freedom of will, most Cherokees constructed different categories for the various peoples of European ancestry outside of the clan system. Although they often referred to Euro-Americans as white, the Cherokees did not use the word "white" as a racial marker in the same way that whites used the word "red."[39] The Cherokees made ethnic distinctions among European groups based on their conduct and cultural practices, rather than on racial identity. Most Cherokees readily distinguished Europeans and Tories from the settlers. They denigrated speculators and farmers as Virginians, while they welcomed Scotch, French, Spanish, and English traders. The important distinction to them became which European group cheated them in trade, took their land, or attacked their villages. Some Cherokees did come to hate or fear "whites," by which they usually meant Americans. At other times, when Cherokee speakers used the word "white," they used it as a diplomatic or a cultural marker—to distinguish the original inhabitants with spiritual or possessory land rights from the newcomers and to classify communities based on whether men relied on hunting or farming. Because the definition of white did not harden as a racial category for most Cherokees, Cherokee men and women could marry and bring white spouses into the nation, apparently without significant discrimination. Sick-quo-in-ne-Youchee married Ann Jane Durant on February 5, 1797, in Philadelphia. A *métis* trader married a white woman and lived in the Cherokee nation in 1799. Some Cherokees adopted aspects of white culture. By 1809 English dancing and music were quite popular in the nation. Although most men retained traditional dress, almost all women wore European-style clothing.[40] More importantly, Cherokee leaders were able to incorporate white traders, mechanics, laborers, and tenants into the nation.

Although Indian agent Return Meigs exercised considerable control over who entered Cherokee society, Cherokee law governed the non-Cherokees while they resided in the nation. As more unrelated people located in Cherokee country, Cherokee men and women transformed their law concerning residents who were not part of the clan system. Their law was not based on racial theory, European ideas about a common humanity, or settler theories about a social contract but was an outgrowth of the Cherokee law of captives. Traditionally, prisoners were the property of the captor, although warriors often turned prisoners over to the Women's Council for disposition. If a captor kept a prisoner, he determined the fate of the prisoner, including whether the captive lived or died.[41]

As the Cherokees began to utilize the services of other strangers outside the clan structure, they extended the law concerning captives to the relationship of master or employer. In contrast to white slave codes, the slave owner or employer governed their bondspeople and workers, who had no recourse to legal protection by local or national councils. Given the authority to discipline slaves, servants, and employees, many masters reserved the harshest discipline for those of the most servile status. When James Vann, a wealthy and unusually harsh Cherokee farmer and trader, suspected his Irish servant of involvement in a theft, he tortured her severely with impunity. Her ultimate fate is unknown. His slaves who stole from him faced "death at least." When White Man Killer died in 1800, his sons were free to abuse or kill his female slave and her children.[42]

Employers had similar power over employees but exercised it more sparingly. Undoubtedly, they realized that mistreatment of white employees would dampen their prospects to entice future workers. Even so, the power to discipline resided in the employer. Jonathan Lowry whipped a white carpenter who worked for him when the man tried to persuade one of his female slaves to escape. Lowry justified his discipline of his employee as authorized by the nation's laws, which allowed the master to determine punishment: "Our law is that when a man lives in the nation for him to abide by the laws of the nation. And we only give him the law of the nation and I think that all villains ought to be punished let them be in what country they may."[43]

While employers and slave owners governed useful outsiders, the United States put pressure on Cherokee leaders to control the conduct of Cherokee men that jeopardized the peace. The most serious problems were horse theft and international killings to still crying blood. With no political mechanism to resolve problems created by Cherokees who violated treaties, the National Council began to exert control. At the turn of the century, the council adopted a law punishing thieves with whippings and began to pardon unintentional killings, obviating the need for blood revenge. Shortly after assuming office in 1802, Meigs suggested to the National Council that it appoint a representative in each town to monitor the conduct of the townspeople but initially nothing was done. In 1808 the National Council authorized the establishment of regulating parties to suppress horse theft and robbery. Two years later, the council unanimously passed an act forgiving all lives for which anyone was indebted and nullifying permanently the law of blood revenge. In practice, the regulators decided virtually all controversies among people in the nation. Because of the lack of compulsion other than their own physical prowess and influence, they likely functioned primarily to enforce the traditional values acceptable to those whom they governed. As one contemporary observer noted: "In the unsettled state of the community, the want of forms, and the absence of precedent, much was left to their discretion; and after all, these decisions were enforced rather by the number, energy, and physical power of the judges, than through any respect paid to the law itself."[44] Consequently, it is likely that they deferred to a large degree to customary practices and to ancient clan law.

The expansion of governmental authority to handle matters that the clans were no longer able to regulate corresponded with a wider recognition that the Cherokees as a people needed to embrace a more unified national government to respond to external pressures from the United States. The federal government's Indian policy aimed to assimilate Native Americans into white society by civilizing them—a process that would persuade them to sell their lands no longer needed for hunting and to reject their cultural ways and accept civilized values and practices or to move west of the Mississippi. With assimilation, separate Native American nations would no longer exist. After years of division and weak regional coalitions, the Cherokees responded by quickly asserting their distinctiveness and cohesiveness as a nation during the peace talks of

1794. The Chickamaugan chief Nentooyah distinguished the Cherokees from other indigenous peoples when he informed peace commissioners that "the name of my nation is Cherokee." Insisting on Cherokee unity five years later, Dick Field, a *métis* man, stated that all the people were Cherokees and did not make distinctions between Cherokees and Chickamaugans.[45]

While they identified as one nation, most Cherokees continued to imagine government as local or clan authority. A coterie of chiefs in the Lower Towns exercised the strongest influence in dealing with the United States. Kunoskeskie led the Lower Towns until his death in 1802, but numerous men participated in governance, including Chuquilatague, Nentooyah, Chulcoah, Atawgwatihih, Uwenah, and Tolonteskee, the nephew of Kunoskeskie who married Chuquilatague's sister. Enola and Selukuki Wohellengh later gained prominence. The Upper Towns splintered. One group of people lived in considerable isolation in the Appalachian Mountains. The most politically active part of the Upper Towns lived in eastern Tennessee. Among the important chiefs representing these people were The Nephew, Jobber's Son, and Kanetetoka. Some of these men alternated between supporting the federal position and articulating the concerns of more ordinary Cherokee people as part of the popular government.[46] Pushed from South Carolina and parts of Georgia overrun by whites, another segment of people living in northwest Georgia exercised little influence in national affairs. Although the historical record masks their presence, women retained their political sphere of influence. The fact that so many women attended diplomatic conferences attests to the continued importance of the Women's Council. James Vann's mother spoke to the chiefs at a ball play in an effort to persuade them to permit Moravian missionaries to remain in Cherokee country. The annuity list submitted by the Cherokees in 1803 consisted largely of items for women. As John Sevier noted, women had their influence.[47]

As they did successfully with the northern Indians, the United States assiduously cultivated men, especially the Lower Town chiefs, who could be swayed or bought as the leaders of the Cherokee people. The secretary of state and his agents utilized their designated chiefs to obtain land grants and road privileges. They manipulated arrangements so that those supporting federal programs held positions of power and received favors. The United States refused to recognize Cherokee claims that the chiefs did not have the power to convey lands without the consent of the nation.[48]

Cognizant of the role of women, the United States courted prominent women as well as men. During the period before the critical treaty negotiations of 1798, the federal government paid for the boarding and surgical expenses of Nancy Martin, probably the daughter of Betsey Ward and Joseph Martin and the granddaughter of Nan-ye-hi. The government also paid boarding expenses for Lower Town chief Kunoskeskie's sister and purchased cotton goods for her and provided housing and meals for Betsey McKee and Sally Vann for thirteen weeks and Betsey Shepard for three weeks. Kunoskeskie's sister most likely accompanied her brother, who visited Governor John Sevier to hold preliminary talks. Sally Vann was related to James Vann, a wealthy and influential Lower Town chief. Betsey McKee was probably the Cherokee wife of John McKee, the Indian agent. Because diplomats and traders tended to marry into prominent clans, Betsey McKee was likely a woman of considerable influence. These women almost certainly were important members of the Women's Council, visiting in preparation for the peace conference in 1798.[49]

Faced with federal attempts to consolidate power in selected headmen and to influence important women, the Cherokees were more successful than the northern Indians in countering the federal strategy. They did so by relocating power formerly exercised by the clans and local chiefs to the National Council. In addition to controlling behavior that jeopardized the treaties, the 1808 council authorized regulators to try misdemeanors, to collect debts, and to protect children and widows on the father's death.[50]

More significantly, the Cherokees established a unified nation that eventually undermined corruption by the United States by relying on and ultimately by transforming their democratic ideology. Cherokee councils traditionally consulted all the people before making decisions. Confronted with federal efforts to bribe their leaders, Cherokee opponents used public festivals, including annuity distributions, treaties, Green Corn ceremonies, and ball plays as occasions to conduct business with popular participation. Out of a nation of about 12,000 people, 3,000 to 5,000 attended the annuity gatherings until the United States managed to reduce the numbers to about 1,000 in 1808. Several thousand people also attended the treaty talks, and similar numbers attended ball plays and the Green Corn dances. By 1805 younger Lower Town and many Upper Town women and men constituted much of the emerging leadership. The young warriors and chiefs began to agitate to replace the Lower Town chiefs seen as especially susceptible to American pressure, particularly Atawgwatihih, Uwenahi, Selukuki Wohellengh, and Enola. James Vann and Atawgwatihih tried to accommodate the differences but were only partially successful. In the 1806 treaty, several Lower Town chiefs accepted bribes to sell the last of the hunting grounds. Chuquilatague and Tolonteskee accepted private tracts of land. Enola received a lifetime annuity of $100 per year "for his merit and amiable character." Atawgwatihih also participated in the covert deal. With this treasonous behavior, the dissidents gained adherents, including Nan-ye-hi's brother, Tuskegateehee.[51]

The democratic coterie of leaders staged a coup in August 1807. In May of that year, the Willstown Council, now controlled by Meigs's chiefs, requested that Meigs remove James Chisholm, a white man popular with the opponents of the annuity chiefs. Chisholm had implicated Atawgwatihih in the sale of the hunting grounds. When the army attempted to carry out the removal several months later, a party opposed it with armed force. Meanwhile, at a ball play at Hiwassee, assassins killed Chuquilatague.[52] Further armed resistance occurred throughout the next year. When Enola, designated by the United States as the primary chief of the nation, and some of the other Lower Town chiefs pressed for relocation west of the Mississippi, large parts of the nation again rebelled. At the September council meeting in Broomstown, some of the Lower Town chiefs met secretly and voted to move. Discovering the plot at the council meeting held at the annuity distribution in October, the warriors and chiefs at the October council convicted Enola, Atawgwatihih, and Tolonteskee of treachery, removed them, and declared them unfit to hold any future office. As he stepped down, Enola alluded to the difficulty of establishing national rule in one man: "I have led you to battle and to victory. I have grown old in your service and have now learned that ingratitude is not peculiar to the whites; and that the man is yet unborn, perhaps will never come into existence, who can give general satisfaction to the Cherokee nation."[53]

Enola's chastisement illustrates the intellectual confusion among the Cherokees about political authority. In the years after 1795, men and women reconceived their understanding of the characteristics of leadership. The advent of peace disrupted the process for selecting headmen, who customarily achieved status by their success at war. The possession of wealth did not translate into influence in Cherokee society as readily as it did in other countries.[54] New chiefs acquired authority not from their military exploits or their assets but from their ability to advance Cherokee interests in the face of federal pressures.

The dissidents agreed with Enola's assessment that one man should not head the nation, although their reasons differed from his. The nation unified at the National Council at Willstown in September 1809, at which leaders rejected white models of governance that conferred authority on one king or president to serve as head of the nation. Aiming to establish a more representative leadership and to avoid the corruption of a small coterie of chiefs, the successful insurgents appointed thirteen men to manage the affairs of the nation. Unlike the Americans, the National Council invoked traditional values of decisions by consensus and the acquiescence of the old chiefs and the Women's Council, headed by Nan-ye-hi. This concept that authority should be dispersed among a wide range of leaders imported traditional Cherokee notions that all people possessed power in varying degrees. The activists in the reconstituted government compromised on one significant item. Remolding their democratic style of governance to a representative one, the council constituted itself with the authority to take action without obtaining the widespread agreement of the nation. By embarking on this defensive nationalization program, the Cherokees established a National Council that they and not the Indian agent controlled and answered the American objection to consulting all the people on decisions and treaty ratifications.[55]

Although the Cherokee leaders and many dissidents embraced a national political structure with considerable authority at the top, most Cherokees, including the chiefs, preserved their belief in the value of individual will. Some continued to dissent from council actions. Many withdrew from whites and lived in remote areas—a decision consistent with traditional Cherokee practices that more cosmopolitan Cherokees did not oppose. A substantial number of Cherokees concluded that they were so incompatible with the land hunters that their best option was to move west of the Mississippi River—an action that each member of the nation was free to undertake. Encouraged by the federal government, about 1,000 Cherokees made this choice during the fifteen years after peace. Although the National Council refused to subdivide Cherokee lands to create land rights in the emigrants, there was no significant stigma attached to relocation. As one old chief explained, people had the "liberty they received from nature" to choose where they lived.[56]

The unified national government immediately advanced a stronger version of Cherokee sovereignty. A few months after their assumption of power, the headmen of the National Council previewed their agenda to Meigs. The council advocated two related concepts—the right of the Cherokee people to their communal lands and the autonomy of the Cherokee people in political matters. The new leadership reinstated traditional spiritual beliefs that the land belonged to the Real People in common and could not be individually parceled and sold. They stated that they would not cede more lands. The chiefs stressed the importance of the separation of the Cherokee nation from that of the whites. They asserted their right to determine who resided in the nation by demanding that all whites be removed except those that the council permitted to remain.[57]

Mirroring the efforts of the Cherokees to balance American threats to their sovereignty and identity by transforming clan and political structures, many Cherokees conceived of an economic system that relied on international trade to protect Cherokee independence from American control. Women and men in both sections of the nation engaged in commerce. Skins remained an important product in trade, for cultural as well as economic reasons. As Chuquilatague explained to the federal diplomats in 1794, "we are a people that do not make our own clothes as our brothers do. We are a people that depend on our gun to support us and our families." As their hunting grounds shrank, the Cherokees extended the hunting season by adding a spring hunt to the traditional winter hunt. Following the lead of the Lower Towns, they sought to improve on the efficiency of the hunt by including more women who cooked for the party and skinned the animals.[58]

The declining animal population and the collapse of the European market for furs in the late 1790s led women and men to tap other markets. The hundreds of thousands of new settlers streaming into the southeastern region after 1795 created significant new markets for food. Lower Town women joined Upper Town women in selling cattle and produce to settlers and travelers and in providing goods for wider export markets and for army posts. Some of the women raised cotton, learned to spin, and took an active role in business. In addition to exporting cloth, by 1809 women manufactured most of the clothing for the nation. Women also received money and goods for sexual services at the army post. Some women, particularly in the Upper Towns, accumulated significant estates. With her considerable property, Nancy Maw, the wife of Scolacutta, supported her daughter and her daughter's husband, John Watts, the son of the chief Kunoskeskie. She purchased slaves, including one from John Sevier, and rented to sharecroppers. Nan-ye-hi maintained extensive holdings, including a plantation, cattle, and slaves. Her daughter, Betsey Ward, lived in the Upper Town area on a fine plantation with furniture, numerous dwellings, cotton cards, and a number of slaves. She grew corn, wheat, and other crops and raised livestock. Nancy Falling, James Vann's sister, managed a farm.[59]

The federal agents pressed Cherokee men to farm, but most men persisted in observing the balance of moieties and hunted, herded wild cattle, or stole horses for their livelihood. The influx of immigrants created new sources of revenue for men. Men joined women in taking advantage of the demand for food by the newcomers by selling meat as well as skins from their hunts to white settlers and travelers and to the federal trading post. Men marketed horses, saddles, and silverware and rented horses to the traders. Along with women, men raised cattle. By 1809 the sale of cattle brought in considerable cash each year. They extracted and sold saltpeter and erected sawmills and gristmills. With the support of the federal agents, the Cherokees also leased the rights to operate ferries and roadhouses. The Cherokees rented land to American tenants, often under a sharecropping arrangement.[60]

Some Cherokee-born traders envisioned greater autonomy by acting as merchants. In earlier periods, virtually all store owners were Europeans or Americans, married to Cherokee women. After 1795 some Cherokees, both full bloods and sons of white traders, established stores. Chuquilatague, a full-blooded Cherokee, and his kinsman, Tolonteskee, sold excellent goods at lower prices than Tennessee traders. Their success stemmed partly from the fact that the American trading posts stocked inferior goods and did not pay good prices for skins. Chuquilatague acquired considerable wealth trading produce, cotton, and cattle to New Orleans for manufactured goods that he sold at home or to other Native American nations. James Vann, the son of white trader John Vann, inherited his father's business and improved his fortune through his mercantile businesses and farms. More experienced at international trade and strategically located to interact with numerous Native American nations and to access Pensacola, Mobile, and New Orleans, the Lower Towns continued to maintain extensive commercial relations. Their long history of foreign enterprise explains why the Lower Towns, pictured by historians as traditionalists, were the part of the nation that most enthusiastically embraced the aid proffered by the civilization program.[61]

The Cherokees persisted in converting white property into Cherokee ownership. Supported by federal law, the Cherokees appropriated the property of unlicensed traders and divided it. The chiefs assumed authority to remove encroachers and to burn their improvements. Some of the young men still engaged in horse stealing. Refusing to concede that whites owned the Cherokee lands on which they lived, these young men insisted that the animals on the lands belonged to the Cherokees. As Indian agent Meigs understood it, "the Indians steal horses from the white people and the white people steal their lands; this is their way of expressing it." Considering horse appropriation a substitute for wild game, Indians from areas in which game for hunting declined were particularly likely to take horses. The young men sold the horses in western Tennessee or Alabama.[62]

In addition to trade, the annual annuity represented an important economic resource to the Cherokees. The annuity increased over the years from $1,000 in 1791 to $7,500 in 1810. After instituting the annuity in 1791, the Cherokees struggled with how to characterize and divide the payments. The tensions implicit in their confusion were a microcosm of stresses in the larger society about how to balance communal sharing, the individual pursuit of wealth, and other traditional values associated with property. These philosophical issues underlay the debate about whether the annuity should be divided pro rata by population or whether the poor, future generations, or the hunters should be favored. In one view, the annuities represented reimbursement for lands that were communally held. Cherokee leaders and the Indian agent established a pro rata distribution process, which presupposed that all shared in the annuity. Some viewed the annuity as a distribution of wealth to the poor. Kunoskeskie refused a share in 1799, saying that he did not need it. Because the annuity was to relieve hardship, the Cherokees instructed the government not to supply luxuries but practical goods. Chuquilatague opposed the use of annuity funds to pay the debts owed to private traders, because the annuity was "intended for our old helpless people and children." Established because of concerns that the sale of lands eviscerated their children's heritage, the annuity for some represented a source of funds from which to support future generations. In order to provide for the "young seed," they envisioned that the annuity should support economic improvement. The greater part of the 1803 list contained articles for women, many of which were items that women needed to enhance economic development by producing cotton or clothing. The payments also constituted consideration for the animals that Cherokee men could no longer kill—an individual property loss to hunters. Three years after Chuquilatague cast the annuity as relief for the poor, he joined three other men to propose that part of the annuity be reserved to pay off traders. Although Chuquilatague's change of heart may have been based on self-interest, the implicit logic of reimbursing hunters for the declining game is plausible. Even so, some young chiefs resisted handing their annuity over to traders, claiming that they had a year to pay their debts. By 1809, as leaders united the nation and reaffirmed a commitment to Cherokee lands as communally owned and not transferable by individuals, most Cherokees came to see the annuity as communal money.[63]

The Cherokees were not the only people who were pressed to respond to white hegemonic ideas about civilization. A substantial number of the newcomers were black, mostly slaves. Emerging white ideas about civilization also shaped, in different ways, their African American worldview.

CHAPTER FIVE

"The Nigger-Trader Bought Me"
African American Community

Like many slaves transported to Tennessee, Mary lived with a family group. Abraham and Patsy Tipton, Samuel and Joanna Tipton, and James, Polley, and Isaac Tipton and their slaves clustered in a neighborhood near each other. Mary was originally Abraham and Patsy Tipton's slave. In 1805 Patsy Tipton told Mary, now on loan to Samuel and Joanna Tipton as a house slave, that Patsy's husband Abraham planned to sell the Tipton slaves along with the slaves' share of the cotton crop. After complaining that James Tipton would never give his slaves up to Abraham, Patsy instructed Mary to come to her house so that she could deliver her to her husband. Mary spread the alarm, warning both the slaves and James Tipton of the plan. No doubt angered, one of the slaves stole cotton from Joanna Tipton. The sale never occurred. Mary reimbursed Joanna for her loss with a like amount of Mary's cotton, probably seeking to allay anger on Joanna's part about the theft. Two years later, Joanna reciprocated by sending a letter of explanation to Mary's church, exonerating Mary from charges of theft of the cotton and certifying to her honest character.[1]

This incident points to social relations between black and white women and men embedded in notions of patronage and reciprocity. Patsy Tipton trusted Mary when she relayed sensitive information to her. Switching patrons, Mary felt confident enough in her connection with Joanna that she spread the news. Mary strengthened her relationship with Joanna when she replaced Joanna's cotton, allowing Mary to draw on the mutuality implicit in her link to Joanna to clear herself with her church.

Although historians have examined the charter generations of Africans and creoles in early British, Spanish, and French settlements in North America, few scholars have explored the ideas and assumptions of African Americans in later American frontier regions, where most slaves were transported from mature plantation societies rather than from Africa.[2] Writers who study the charter generations of black inhabitants in the early European settlements of Virginia, Maryland, Florida, Louisiana, and South Carolina contend that slaves and free blacks had fewer restrictions in these environments but have little to say about how this informed their ideologies. One exception is Ira Berlin, who describes the logic of such freer relationships in early Virginia, Maryland, and South Carolina as that of patronage. African historians have noted the importance of social ties and patronage in African life, and Berlin draws on this work to illuminate the role of patronage in the cognitive worlds of charter generation Africans and creoles.[3] With the development of a plantation society, historians note that masters rejected sponsorship and formed patriarchal, then paternalistic, and later liberal capitalist connections with their slaves.[4] Scholars of American slavery find that blacks of various African ancestries crafted distinctively African American values about family, community, and religion in these plantation societies in the eighteenth century and later.[5] Recently, writers have chronicled the mobility of the beliefs of African, Caribbean, and American slaves and free blacks in the Atlantic world, showing that peoples of African ancestry had access to a larger palate of ideas than those negotiated with their masters.[6]

Most African Americans in frontier Tennessee came from Virginia and North Carolina, where generations of patriarchal and paternalist relationships between master and slave had long replaced an earlier system of patronage. Faced with disrupted family and communal ties and the dispersal of some power downward on the frontier, black residents in pioneer Tennessee relied on African American values about black society and, in a process similar to retraditionalization, recalled and modified older ideas about patronage to weaken the paternalist structure. They placed affective bonds with the black community and clientage connections with white sponsors and allies at the heart of their views about sociability, governance, and economic relations. While the Cherokees reluctantly opened their society to some individuals outside the clan structure, slaves and free blacks revised the African understanding of patronage as a relationship between patron and slave to seek sponsors and sympathizers among a wider range of nonfamilial white contacts.

Like some communities in postcolonial nations, enslaved African Americans in Tennessee formulated their values in black and white societies without relying on the nationalizing ideologies that informed the ideas of the Cherokees and free Tennesseans.[7] Slaves negotiated social relationships based on a cultural logic of black communal connections, white sponsorships, and, in the case of Christian slaves, spiritual equality. Bondspeople viewed the government as a second master entitled to no loyalty—one to be strategically managed where possible, often with the help of white supporters. With no voice in government, slaves were a community with no allegiance to laws.[8] In their economic relations, slaves relied on patronage with important white contacts and on market networks to exercise their own will in decision making and to experience some degree of freedom and an improved standard of living.[9] Tennesseans ultimately responded from a cognitive worldview that envisioned slavery as essential to prosperity and civilization—an outlook that represented a liberal capitalist depiction of slaves as a commodity. The difference between these constructions limited the success of African American slaves.

A tiny fraction of the population, free blacks chose regions in which they could establish connections with other free blacks and with white allies. They combined their African understanding of clientage with Christian teachings of a common humanity and an American belief in political and economic rights similar to that of white Tennesseans. From this perspective of entitlements from multiple sources, they created an African American concept of freedom rooted in their individual efforts that remained, at the same time, intimately linked to their connections.

Although Africans displaced to the Americas came from numerous and diverse African states, many shippers transported slaves from a limited number of countries to British North America. The slaves exported to Virginia came from different locations than did those of North Carolina, but most slaves in both states came from approximately half a dozen countries in West Africa. Although their cultures were different, slaves shared an African ideological orientation that allowed the transmission of significant parts of the African worldview through the Middle Passage. At the heart of African social life was a particular notion of personal bonds, connections made through kin and through the larger social world. Many African societies emphasized relationships as the source of identity and freedom. Liberty, in those cultures, meant connection to a kinship group, to a patron, or to power, rather than individual freedom, which could result in less connectedness and influence. For most Africans, the basic unit of attachment was kin. The family included the unborn and the dead, as long as they were remembered. Extended horizontally, kinship related people to each other and to the nonhuman world. Vertically, kinship connected the present to the past and future. Africans lived their lives for their kin, living and dead. At death, the spirit survived, either on earth or nearby, but slaves could not join this spirit world. Most West Africans believed that ancestors and divinities were attached to particular places and that the land held power. Nights were times of celebration in Africa but also dangerous times when spirits were more likely to be present.[10]

The African cognitive world of connection also included important attachments and organizations that were not based on kinship, although kin linkages often played an important role in these structures. Many African cultures were organized around a variety of dependencies, including junior age-sets and pawnships—connections often created by ties other than blood. Africans also structured larger social institutions on ties other than kinship. Precolonial Africans belonged to an extensive religious network of localized cults, distant shrines, and hunter societies. Virtually all Africans had some experience of slavery. Individuals in subordinate positions relied on fictive kin relationships with patrons to move into African life. Responding to these expectations, owners generally incorporated slaves into their kinship structure. These linkages—hierarchical rather than affective—created a relationship of mutuality in which masters often trusted their slaves. In return, reliable slaves attained positions of responsibility and status and frequently acquired greater freedom. As with religion and slavery, Africans organized governments of elected officials, armies, and secret societies around principles other than kin. Slaves brought ideas about flexible social networks with kin and with unrelated individuals and about the meanings and obligations of dependencies to the Americas.[11]

Like their white counterparts, the early slave and free black transplants in Tennessee came largely from Virginia and North Carolina. In the seventeenth-century Chesapeake region, masters and slaves established patronage ties, rooted in the creole culture of the transatlantic world. The plantation culture in the early eighteenth century replaced patronage with patriarchy, and patriarchy with paternalism. The distinctions between patronage, patriarchy, and paternalism were meaningful for the cognitive worlds of both African Americans and influential whites. A patronage relationship supposes an arrangement in which a powerful person offers advantages to a less powerful person in exchange for services or loyalty by the sponsored person. Clientage relies on trust by the sponsor and creates a sense of entitlement in the slave. A patriarchal relationship is one in which both parties imagine a patriarch whose slaves are familial dependents in an organic society. As the century advanced, masters recrafted patriarchy into paternalism, replacing an early attitude of severity by masters with one of sentimentality. In both regimes, slaves labored for and subsumed their wills to the master in exchange for protection and care.[12]

By the mid-eighteenth century, the growing population of native blacks in the Chesapeake colonies had created an identity as African American, syncretizing elements of African culture with their American experience and identifying as a black community, thus weakening the ties of patriarchy. As a result of the Great Awakening in the mid-eighteenth century, some African Americans and Euro-Americans shared religious experiences and church life. For several decades, African Americans voted and preached in Baptist churches. These slaves modified their African view of the afterlife that excluded slaves to imagine a heaven that included all Christians. The American Revolution created a larger class of freed blacks in the upper South, and some of these freedmen and women moved west to Tennessee. With the growth of the internal slave trade in the 1790s, traders imported larger numbers of Chesapeake slaves to the Southeast through slave markets. Viewing slaves primarily as property, Virginia masters began to imagine themselves as liberal capitalists rather than affectionate paternalists, while bondspeople resisted their hardening classification as property.[13]

Black slaves lived and traveled in the Tennessee region prior to first white settlement.[14] In the first half of the eighteenth century, the Cherokees captured some black slaves, and a number of the traders living in the Indian villages kept African slaves. Slaves occasionally accompanied explorers and long hunters. Some of the earliest white settlers brought bondspeople. In the spring of 1769, several wealthy Virginians from Culpepper settled in Powell Valley with their slaves. By 1778, whites complained about the shortage of slaves for purchase.[15]

The convergence of Cherokees, African Americans, and Euro-Americans on the frontier prompted the Cherokees and free Tennesseans to imagine their communities as nations, but they excluded slaves from their deliberations. Bondspeople focused on constructing their own communities based on the African belief in the importance of ties to kin and African American values of attachment to the black community and also formed clientage relationships with whites. Tennessee frontier conditions created severe challenges for enslaved people seeking to imagine and construct a system of connection with each other. During the period before 1790, most slaves in the Tennessee region dwelt in isolation from other blacks. In Virginia and North Carolina, slaves lived in small houses with their families. In contrast, the transmontane slaves generally resided with whites on farms where they were the only slave. Data from eastern Tennessee in 1779 and 1780 suggest that about 11 percent of the taxpayers owned slaves, with the largest holding being ten or eleven slaves and the vast majority owning one or two.[16] The first census in 1790 showed 3,417 slaves in the territory, 9.6 percent of the total immigrant population. During that decade, prominent Tennesseans, including Governor William Blount and Indian agent and trader John Chisholm, acted as slave traders, importing slaves from the East Coast, particularly the Chesapeake region. The growing immigration of whites, the internal slave trade, and the growth of cotton production swelled the number of slaves. By 1800 slaves numbered 13,584, 12.9 percent of the population, and by 1810, 44,535, 17.0 percent of the population. The highest concentration of slaves was in the Cumberland area. By 1810 slaves constituted 21.9 percent of the inhabitants in Cumberland and 9 percent in eastern Tennessee. While middle Tennessee had larger numbers of slaves and a greater proportion of the households included slaves, the majority of bondspeople there lived on farms where there was only one or two black adults plus children.[17]

While most of the enslaved men, women, and children in Tennessee were African Americans from Virginia and North Carolina, a few slaves were African-born people, most of whom apparently arrived in Tennessee after 1795. Although they were foreign to each other, African Americans as well as Africans held some African ideas. Many slaves viewed night as a time to socialize and believed in the presence of spirits attached to the land. On their death, they believed that they would return to Africa.[18]

In addition to their isolation and ethnic mix, bondspeople dealt with other disruptions as they crafted their ideas and cultural logic about sociability. All newcomers to Tennessee faced transitions as pioneers and immigrants, but slaves suffered from far more instability in their family relationships than did their white owners. They had no input in the decision to migrate to Tennessee and had little voice in whether family members accompanied them. Some became homesick and returned to the country familiar to them. White families often migrated in waves, with some family members moving a year or two before others as men traveled to find land and to put in a crop before returning for their families. Slave families were parted as some were sent ahead and others remained behind. These transitions multiplied because slaves lived with white immigrants, a very mobile set of people. In creating communities, enslaved people were forced to construct new social arrangements in Tennessee among other blacks from varying backgrounds with whom they often had little history.[19]

Slaves also confronted significant challenges after their settlement. During the Revolutionary War, slaves of suspected Tories were confiscated and often sold. Throughout the pioneer period, bondspeople were captured or killed by Indians. As the economy expanded, slaves often moved around when their owners hired them out. John Sevier's journal describes multiple instances in which one man left his slaves for weeks or months at a time with another. In many cases, slaves were loaned as gifts, as was Mary, the Tipton's slave described at the beginning of this chapter. In other cases, masters moved slaves so that they could be trained. Of course, the most traumatic injury arose from slave sales. Anita S. Goodwin's study of slave sales in Nashville from 1784 to 1803 showed that the overwhelming number were sales of one slave, suggesting that most owners did not attempt to transfer families intact. More than one-half of the sales that included age data involved children under sixteen. This movement of people made the continuity necessary for community extremely difficult.[20]

In the face of the frontier obstacles, enslaved people in the Tennessee region like slaves elsewhere labored to make and to maintain family connections. A number of runaways sought to return to family and kin. In addition to forming families, some African Americans forged communal connections with each other through informal social networks, at work, and in taverns and churches. In towns, many slaves often lived in kitchens or in lean-tos near white cabins. Their quarters became a gathering spot for other slaves in the area. Knoxville slaves visited in their owners' kitchens or in uninhabited houses on Sundays and in the evenings. Similarly, in Nashville, slaves congregated in their masters' houses or kitchens in the evenings to dance and play music. Slaves seeking to socialize in venues off the plantation ignored, where possible, white laws aimed at restricting their movement.[21]

Although the small size of slaveholdings in Tennessee meant that enslaved blacks were more likely to work with whites than with other blacks, the growth of the commercial economy stimulated the formation of businesses in which some slaves labored in largely black workplaces. One of Virginia's largest slave owners, David Ross, utilized slave labor almost exclusively in his Virginia ironworks. In order to encourage good work, he developed a system of incentives and used whole families, including women, children, and older people. Ross established one of the first furnaces in the Tennessee region in 1789. Other ironwork owners followed his practice by frequently employing slaves and free blacks. It is likely that the large number of blacks, the family connections, and the incentive system facilitated a sense of community among the workers. In 1799 Cherokee hunters murdered a slave who worked at James Robertson's ironworks. The Cherokees recognized the bond between black workers. When they returned to hunt near the ironworks the next spring, they felt impelled to speak to the other black laborers to ensure that they would not retaliate against the Cherokees if they hunted there. Other businesses also hired slaves in significant numbers. A baling factory in Cairo hired ten African American boys from ten to fifteen years old for a term of five years. Owners of a hemp factory at Mitchellsville advertised to hire ten boys, ten to twelve years old, and ten men from sixteen to twenty-five years old, for terms from three to five years. These long-term hires of boys and young men may have created a site for community with their co-workers even as they disrupted the family relationships of these young men. Acting on this, hired slaves occasionally chose to escape in pairs or groups.[22]

Enslaved Tennesseans crafted other venues in which to meet outside of informal gatherings and commercial workplaces. Some slaves ran taverns, which became one of the social centers for the slave community. In 1800 Nashville had 345 people, of whom 136 were slaves and 14 were free blacks. Robert Renfroe and Caesar Prince both ran taverns in Nashville as slaves in the 1790s. After hiring their time from their owners, other slaves relocated to Nashville, where they also operated houses of entertainment. Slaves gathered, intermingled, and traded at these sites.[23]

While slaves socialized in their homes, work, and houses of entertainment, they formed in churches a more institutionalized location for community. As elsewhere, many slaves in Tennessee joined Christian churches. Enslaved congregants occasionally constituted the majority or a substantial plurality of the membership. In the Bethel Communities Zion Church, 103 of the 160 members in 1809 were black; 46 of 108 worshipers at the Mill Creek Baptist Church in 1800 were African American, as were 26 of 95 members of the Zion Presbyterian Church during the first decade of the nineteenth century. In common with the national trend, most slaves probably favored Baptist and, by 1805, Methodist over Presbyterian churches.[24] Church practices encouraged a sense of black community within the congregations. White members often segregated slaves in church seating, creating the occasion for closer connection and identification among blacks. Occasionally, black members met separately in disciplinary committees. With almost half of its membership black, the Mill Creek Baptist Church spent considerable time dealing with its African American members. White church members made special efforts "to accommodate the servants." They often appointed slaves to cite other slaves to disciplinary proceedings and at times deferred their decisions about fellowship matters until they heard from the black members who met separately.[25]

As slaves struggled to create black families and communities under the constraints imposed by a transient white slaveholding society, some initially turned to Native Americans as potential allies. Throughout the southeastern borderlands, the relationships between indigenous peoples and African Americans were ambivalent. In the period of early settlement, runaways occasionally headed for Indian territory. During the Revolutionary War, two slaves escaped from the Holston settlement and settled deep in Cherokee country, improving land and planting. Others followed their example. White leaders designed policies to create animosity between the two races, and the southeastern native peoples began to adopt white practices of black slavery. The first peoples frequently obtained slaves by kidnapping blacks from the settlers. The Cherokees and Creeks also killed slaves in their attacks on frontier farms and stations. Many pioneer slaves developed considerable antipathy for Native Americans after facing the dangers of Indian attacks. After peace in 1795, Indian country became less appealing to escaping slaves. Native Americans in the Tennessee region were likely to retain slaves as their own, to sell them to other tribes, or to return them to their white owners as part of the peace settlement. Not surprisingly, these actions reinforced the mistrust and hostility between slaves and Indians.[26]

In addition to social connections with each other and, in limited ways, with potential Native American allies, the enslaved community forged a modified patronage system of sponsors, sympathizers, and allies from a wide segment of white society. The borderlands in pioneer Tennessee offered a setting that permitted the reappearance of patronage rather than the perpetuation of paternalistic relationships. The dangers and hardships of frontier life forced free people and slaves to protect and care for each other, reversing the patriarchal tenet that the master provided for his dependents. Bondspeople defended themselves and whites against wilderness dangers and Indian attacks. Enslaved men fought with their masters when attacked by other white men. They often shared the work of raising houses and cultivating land.[27]

Unlike the more structured patronage systems of West Africa, power on the frontier was more dispersed, creating more possibilities for sponsors. A part of the fabric of frontier social life, slaves interacted with whites more powerful than themselves in many settings. They migrated with whites through the wilderness. Black and white children socialized together on farms and in towns. Black boys ran races, wrestled, and played ball and marbles on Sundays with white boys. Huddled in close quarters, many bondspeople lived in kitchens or slept in the room with their masters. They participated with white neighbors in barn raisings and cleared newcomers' fields. At corn huskings, it was slaves who "raised the corn-song," signaling the commencement of work. When hired out, slaves worked with white laborers. Slaves also struck up acquaintances with transient whites, such as passing boatmen. Christian slaves worshiped with white Christians. As elsewhere, some slave women had sexual relationships with white owners.[28]

The immigrants and slaves crafted their dependency into a frontier patronage system—with an inequity in power between the parties, trust bestowed by the slaveholder, a belief in entitlements for loyal service by the slave, and the unimportance of the affective relationship imagined by paternalism. The bonds forged between slaves and powerful whites constituted the more obvious adaptation of the patronage relationship. Unlike sponsorships in Africa, wealthier whites did not recognize their slaves as fictive kin, but the personal ties between slaves and whites, although not sentimental, often generated confidence on the part of slaveholders. Fighting together created strong bonds. Some bondspeople handled the master's business. Occasionally a slave owner assigned a slave sufficient responsibility in running the farm that the slave became "his own master." In the absence of reliable mail service, masters used their slaves to carry important messages. Many masters entrusted their slaves with money to buy supplies for them. In addition to relying on slaves to carry out business, masters discussed personal and business affairs in the presence of and at times with slaves.[29]

While some whites envisioned a relationship of trust with dependable servants, many slaves believed that the reliance that masters and other influential whites placed in them created a connection in which slaves had the right to expect reciprocity. Slaves solicited assistance from more powerful whites as part of the mutuality inherent in their relationship. For example, when Molley, like Mary at the beginning of this chapter, faced an accusation in her church, her master defended her, contending she was falsely accused.[30] Some bondspeople utilized their connections to create a variant on the custom in the middle Atlantic region and parts of the upper South of choosing another master if they did not get along with their owner. In that tradition, slaves acted at times with the written acquiescence of their owners and at times on their own, to seek an acceptable owner who would purchase them from their masters.[31] In the Tennessee practice, slaves rarely if ever received written permission from their masters to seek a new owner. Instead, they drew on personal connections to arrange a transfer. In his position as messenger, Bob met John Overton, Andrew Jackson's partner and one of Tennessee's most prominent lawyers, who liked him. When Bob did not want to return to an old mistress, Overton offered to take him. One eighteen-year-old slave and his sixteen-year-old sister impressed Colonel King sufficiently that he interceded on their behalf when he used them to discharge a bond to the secretary of the Southwest Territory, Daniel Smith. When the girl wanted to go with her brother, he instructed his agent, Governor William Blount, to attempt to persuade Smith to take both.[32]

Occasionally, the owner's trust in a slave impelled the master to locate a more acceptable situation for his bondsperson. When John Irwin's slave Aaron escaped, Irwin considered Aaron honest enough that he would acknowledge Irwin as his master if captured. Irwin believed that Aaron sought to join his wife who had been removed to Natchez by her owner. Irwin authorized his business agent in Natchez to sell him there if caught. Although Irwin's decision may have been entirely practical, his confidence in Aaron's honesty suggests that the relationship between the men contributed to Irwin's willingness to permit Aaron to live in the vicinity of his wife.[33]

In the most radical cases, enslaved people made connections that brought them freedom. Slaves turned to white allies to aid their escapes. In other cases, the personal bond that developed between masters and their bondspeople persuaded white owners to liberate their slaves. Recognizing the humanity of his slaves, William Nodding sought to emancipate them because he came to believe that "the door [of opportunity] ought not to be kept shut against them more than any other of the human race." Sam's master freed him when he risked his life to save the family that owned him by warning them of a flooding river.[34]

Although masters often trusted their slaves and bondspeople anticipated reciprocity, frontier conditions discouraged masters from embracing the sentimental familial attachments of paternalism. Masters assigned slaves the most dangerous jobs in times of Indian attacks. They also used slaves, not just for labor and capital, as historians have recognized, but as specie and collateral in the frontier's cash-poor and undercapitalized economy, where slaves were taken in lieu of cash and pledged to secure loans and bonds.[35]

Like their masters, slaves in Tennessee generally did not see their ties with whites as familial. The Tipton's slave Mary, whose involvement in talebearing was described at the beginning of this chapter, engaged in a series of actions as she made decisions about spreading gossip that suggested she saw the black community, not the Tiptons, as her family, and Joanna as her patron. Mary made the decision to relay the knowledge of the sale of the slaves to protect herself and the slave community and their property. Access to private intelligence created and destroyed bonds of trust, and Patsy Tipton left herself vulnerable by imparting sensitive information about the slave sale to Mary, disclosures that Mary parlayed into a stronger bond with her new mistress and sponsor, Joanna. Mary cemented this tie by replacing Joanna's cotton. This connection surely contributed to Joanna's willingness to support Mary in her church disciplinary hearing.[36]

Although bondspeople did not seek sentimental familial attachments to their masters, they did convey implicit messages to their owners and sympathetic whites to treat them not as property but as human beings. Slaves at cornhuskings sang songs like "The Nigger-Trader Bought Me" and "I'm Gwine 'way Down the River," melancholy tunes that implicitly argued against the slave trade. "Fare You Well, Miss Sarah" may have reminded white owners of the ties that they sundered when they sold slaves. Blacks raised their voices in order to be heard at a distance by whites, and white listeners perceived "a tone of sadness" in the corn songs. One Baptist woman was expelled from her church in part for permitting slaves to dance at her house "if they behaved themselves like white people." In her willingness to tolerate dancing, which her religion condemned, she tacitly acknowledged her slaves as human beings with human desires. Her condition about behavior, while laden with racial judgment, revealed an assumption that slaves could act like whites, a logic that reflects an awareness of the common humanity of the races.[37]

In addition to ties forged with their owners or other individual white men and women, some slaves created strong attachments to whites in churches, where, at times, they crafted a different kind of relationship with their Christian brothers and sisters—one that presupposed spiritual equality, not patronage. Religious slaves were very concerned with promoting their thinking about how Christian teaching applied to the institution of slavery. Tennessee slaves challenged white doctrine and argued for greater freedom and better treatment for African Americans in three areas—marriage, fellowship, and preaching. Underlying these contests was an assumption by slaves that God's authority represented a higher power than that of white church people or of their masters, a doctrine held by many northern and southern slaves in the late eighteenth century.[38]

Slaves forced Baptist congregations to consider the tension within Christian theology between doctrines supporting marriage and tenets that upheld the slaveholder's right to require obedience from his or her slaves. The conflict arose frequently around the master's practice of separating married couples. The Tennessee Holston Association referred the "pernicious" practice of separating married Negroes to the local churches for input in 1791. A year later, the association advised churches to avoid parting black couples, where possible. The Red River Baptist congregation answered a query about whether it could admit an enslaved man who had been sold away from his wife in the East and who married another woman. Baptist churches excluded white women from fellowship for taking another spouse if their husband abandoned them. Even so, the members of Red River Baptist Church accepted the man. Bondspeople also challenged the slaveholder's authority over the Christian slave's choice of spouse. When her church suspended Bess for marrying a man against her master's orders and living with him before marriage, Bess refused to leave her husband. She forced the congregation to decide whether to enforce the Christian doctrine of the slave's obedience to the master or to uphold the Christian doctrine of marriage. After numerous debates over the course of a year, the majority of the church members concluded that she was justified. The minority agreed to accept this decision. Slaves also forced churches to deal with situations in which slaves were compelled by their masters to live in relationships not sanctioned by the gospel. Apparently recognizing that Becky might not be able to make the decision, a disciplinary hearing acquitted Becky of living in an "improper way" with an unnamed man but "advised" her to move.[39]

Christian slaves sought to apply gospel teachings to more than the doctrine of marriage. Protestant denominations relied strongly on ideas about fellowship—a precept that existed in an uneasy relationship with the institution of slavery. Issues about fellowship arose in two contexts. The first concerned the inclusion of slaves in the church community. Operating under the constraints of slavery, some slaves promoted more liberal policies for the admission of black members to fellowship and urged tolerance for lapses in behavior deemed disorderly or immoral. A large number ultimately found Christian rules about membership as interpreted by whites to be too confining. Because of their reluctance to follow white interpretations of the gospel, slaves were much more likely than white members to be the subject of discipline. They were also much more likely to refuse or fail to make satisfaction, excluding them from fellowship.[40]

In addition to questions of inclusion, the fellowship doctrine was concerned with how Christian congregants treated each other. Tennessee Methodist and Presbyterian conferences mandated more humane treatment of slaves, and some churches required gradual emancipation. Although Baptist churches sanctioned slavery, some religious slaves successfully interpreted spiritual fellowship to place restrictions on the discipline that their masters could impose on them. When Baptist minister Isaac Todevine preached near Clarksville in 1807, he told the slaves that they should be thankful to have someone to whip them when they needed it and that this was worth more than a new set of clothes. The slaves were very offended and called him ugly names. Responding to these types of disputes, the Tennessee Association in 1808 decided that it was wrong for owners to whip Baptist slaves. The convention referred masters to the procedure in Matthew 18 that called for private verbal confrontations with a wrongdoer and, if unsuccessful, criticism by the church.[41]

As slave members argued for their understanding of the gospel of Christian marriage and fellowship, some pursued their own spiritual path of public preaching. In many African spiritual traditions, Africans received revelations continuously. Some Christian slaves had the same experience and believed that they should respond by proclaiming the messages imparted to them. On occasion, these slaves convinced their white brethren and sisters to accept their gifts. At Mount Olivet Baptist Church, 9 percent of whose founders were black, George persuaded the congregation to place him "at liberty to exhort among his black brethren." In the same meeting, church members revoked the credentials of a white preacher. When faced with white opposition, some slaves nevertheless obeyed their calling to spread God's word. One such slave, Sam, waged a five-year struggle to persuade his church to sanction his preaching. Sam was a member of Mill Creek Baptist Church, in which 43 percent of the members in late 1800 were black. After numerous disciplinary actions against Sam, the white members capitulated in November 1806 and passed a resolution granting black members the same liberty to preach and lead public worship as white members. Sam's victory was a limited one, as the church excommunicated Sam on February 15, 1807, with no explanation given in the record.[42]

As inhabitants without political rights, bondspeople were not positioned to shape a concept of nationalism as did the Cherokees and Tennesseans. Enslaved men and women experienced most of their governance in the household. To the bondspeople, the government constructed by white men represented a second master, one that controlled their conduct outside the plantation. The early pioneer period may have been somewhat more lenient. Prior to 1790, North Carolina laws about the conduct of slaves were seldom enforced. By 1795, peace with Native Americans, the population explosion in the region, and the assertion of the rule of law by leading men persuaded political authorities to enact more intrusive restrictions on slaves. State and local regulations forbade travel without papers, trade without a pass, travel at night, congregating in the kitchens, and insults to whites. The government organized patrols and prescribed punishment for escaping. Patrollers had the power to search houses and other places where they suspected slaves might be concealed. The town regulations were particularly invasive. In Knoxville slaves could be whipped for being drunk on Sunday, quarrelsome, fighting, disturbing the citizens, or assembling at night outside of the kitchen. The Nashville commissioners forbade slaves from hiring themselves, settling in town, or keeping a tippling house. Slaves had to have a permit to be in town after dark and on Sunday. Slave patrols in the town of Franklin could also whip slaves found without a pass.[43]

Situated without direct power in political affairs, many slaves learned to view government as a force to manipulate in order to advance their interests where possible. Echoing African notions of the connection between patronage and freedom, African Americans relied on personal bonds with black and white sponsors and allies to develop several options that offered limited freedom. Blacks exploited political boundaries to create free status, capitalized on their role in Indian defense and as part of militia training to arm themselves and escape, and used the law and their patronage connections to expand their choices about where to live.

Governments marked landscapes for bound men and women in critical ways. The woods on one side of the Tennessee, Mississippi, and Ohio Rivers meant freedom. On the other side, they represented servitude. Frequently assisted by white sympathizers with whom they traded or socialized, many slaves took advantage of governmental lines to liberate themselves. Numerous advertisers for escaped slaves in the Tennessee papers noted the likelihood that the slaves were headed for a jurisdiction where they would be free, including Natchez, the Louisiana territory, Pennsylvania, and Ohio. Slaves occasionally exploited jurisdictional limits between Indian nations and the United States. This practice was more common in the earlier period but tapered off after 1790 as native attitudes about slaves hardened. Even so, some slaves did flee to Native American country.[44]

Bondsmen acted more autonomously in their self-liberation when, similar to Euro-Americans and to Caribbean slaves, their militia service transformed their sense of self-worth. During the years of Indian attacks, slaves commonly carried guns as they worked in the fields or traveled. Although laws in North Carolina prohibited slave service in the militias, Native American attacks forced white Tennesseans to include enslaved men in their companies. Slaves claimed authority through their militia experience, promoting their identity as militiamen over their status as slave. During the civil war in the state of Franklin in 1788, the antistate forces captured Tobe, the slave of Franklin

Stop the Runaway.

FIFTY DOLLARS REWARD.

ELOPED from the fubfcriber, living near Nafhville, on the 25th of June laft, a Mulatto Man Slave, about thirty years old, fix feet and an inch high, ftout made and active, talks fenfible, ftoops in his walk, and has a remarkable large foot, broad acrofs the root of the toes--will pafs for a free man, as I am informed he has obtained by fome means, certificates as fuch— took with him a drab great-coat, dark mixed body coat, a ruffled fhirt, cotton home-fpun fhirts and overalls. He will make for Detroit, through the ftates of Kentucky and Ohio, or the upper part of Louifiana. The above reward will be given any perfon that will take him, and deliver him to me, or fecure him in jail, fo that I can get him. If taken out of the ftate, the above reward, and all reafonable expences paid—and ten dollars extra, for every hundred lafhes any perfon will give him, to the amount of three nundred.

ANDREW JACKSON,
Near Nafhville, State
of Tenneffee.

Escaped slave notice placed by Andrew Jackson, 1804. Jackson's offer to pay an additional reward for a severe whipping of the escapee, who would undoubtedly be whipped again on his return, was very unusual. No other ad in this period offered this type of reward. The brutality of Jackson's offer suggests his rage that the unnamed slave would thwart his master's will and represents a public assertion by Jackson of his will and authority. (*Tennessee Gazette*, October 3, 1804, 2; photograph courtesy TSL.)

governor John Sevier. When asked to whom he belonged, Tobe responded "to the Sullivan County troops, sir." Empowered by their identity as fighting men, many slaves used their military expertise to advance their own radical ideas of freedom. Two-thirds of runaway slaves in Tennessee through 1810 were young men between the ages of eighteen and thirty. During the period prior to mid-1797 when militiamen trained for potential Indian attacks, 33 percent of the male escapees were armed. With one exception, none of the men who escaped after 1797 carried weapons. Thomas Wynne alerted white Tennesseans to the subversive possibilities of military training. In describing a North Carolina slave uprising, he warned the white community in Tennessee that blacks seemed to be organizing militia-style.[45]

A few slaves negotiated with white sponsors to use laws in equally radical but more peaceful ways—they paid for their freedom and obtained legislative or judicial recognition of emancipation. Robert Renfroe purchased himself from Nashville commissioner Robert Searcy in 1801. Philip Thomas of Nashville, a free man of color, bought his wife Nancy from Joseph Greer of Knoxville. Recognizing that freedom after slavery remained precarious, some free blacks used the legal system to protect themselves. When Nelly in Nashville purchased herself from William Taitt, the parties signed an agreement that Nelly could never become a slave again but would be forever free.[46]

Most slaves were not able to free themselves by escape or purchase. In less dramatic ways, a number of slaves took advantage of the law on adverse possession in combination with their personal connections with white patrons in order to expand their options about where and with whom they lived. The law recognized a claim for the adverse possession of a slave in a master who retained the slave for three years in defiance of the legal owner. Some bondspeople used this law to choose their residence on the theory that they could create adverse possession of themselves in the owner of their choice. Gambling that the interest and attachment of a former master would support their decision, slaves not uncommonly escaped to return to an old owner, probably because they had family or connections there. The runaways undoubtedly realized that the original owners had little incentive to return them. In other cases, slaves sought to create possession in a new owner, perhaps because of better treatment. In many cases, slaves whose masters reported them as stolen may in fact have gone willingly with their "captor," preferring him or her to their owner. Many owners were unable to ascertain whether slaves left voluntarily, suggesting that some "stolen" slaves chose to go to create possession in their new masters.[47]

Occasionally, bondspeople stretched the logic of the law beyond the theory of adverse possession in another owner by breaking their master's chain of possession without acquiring a new owner and without escaping from the jurisdiction. These slaves envisioned a form of quasi emancipation. Samuel Smith's slaves refused to return to him after his wife hired them out to Elijah Witt. The slaves hid in the woods in an unsuccessful effort to avoid being transferred back to their owners. Abraham Martin's slave refused to move with him to the Mississippi Territory. Ignoring his legal status as slave, he freed himself from Martin's possession by laying out until Martin left and then returned to his job at the ironworks where he had been employed.[48] This man's example was extreme in its result but typical of the slaves' conception of government and the legal system as a second master with no claim to slave loyalty.

Like slaves elsewhere, enslaved men and women in Tennessee translated their connections with other blacks and white allies into some degree of freedom in the fluid frontier marketplace.[49] They did so by relying on patronage ties and on business relationships. Bondspeople traded their goods, hired their time, ran their businesses, developed economic networks, and occasionally used market connections to assist their escapes. In doing so, they developed a view of the economy as a site in which blacks could, in limited ways, make their own decisions and create economic opportunity and freedom. In acting as both producers and consumers, albeit in limited ways, they engaged white men and women in a wide range of relationships that persuaded them to see African Americans as human, not property, and to give them greater latitude in their economic lives. Asserting their own will in economic matters gave slaves an experience of freedom that their masters sought to deny them.

Early slaves in the Tennessee region migrated primarily with Virginia and North Carolina backcountry settlers. Bondspeople in both states had considerable freedom to engage in marketplace activity. Many Virginia slaves were accustomed to earning cash from self-hire and overwork payments. Although plantation slaves worked in gangs for their masters during the week, many had Saturdays off and were given a garden plot to raise grain, poultry, and occasionally pigs for themselves. They traded among themselves and with their owners and other whites. Backcountry North Carolina slaves worked under a task system. Each day, the owner or overseer allotted the tasks, which the slaves generally completed by early afternoon. During the balance of the day, they worked in their own private fields, consisting of five or six acres. On some plantations, they raised hogs and poultry. Because the slave owner fed and clothed them, their production was for their own profit, which they realized largely by selling any excess to their owners.[50]

Because the majority of Tennessee slaves lived on farms with at most only one or two other enslaved adults, most owners utilized the task system. Although a master could make the task system onerous, generally tasking created a reciprocal relationship between owner and enslaved workers that offered industrious slaves the possibility of more free time. Some Tennessee masters used a "task week" rather than a daily task assignment, to stimulate production. One lenient owner, Sampson Williams assigned jobs and let the slave community decide how to perform them. On his farm, the older slaves organized the tasks and persuaded the younger ones to work. In addition to time after completing work, plantation slaves had free time during inclement weather. In 1803 the legislature enacted a statute prohibiting slaveholders from working their slaves on Sunday. Tennessee manufactory owners, like those in Kentucky, also used the task system. A few years prior to his arrival in Tennessee, William Blount investigated the feasibility of using slave labor in a nail factory. He found it desirable, because black workers could be kept at the same spot and at the same work and could be tasked. Ironworks owners in Tennessee relied heavily on slave labor, probably tasking them as Blount described. Virginian David Ross established the first foundry in Tennessee. Ross's laborers were primarily slaves. He operated his businesses under a modified task system long used in the Chesapeake region in which slaves got cash or credit for overtime work. Ross granted his slaves considerable latitude: "'Tis well known that I demand moderate labor from the servants. . . . I have in great measure left them free only under such control as was most congenial to their happiness." Ross utilized men, women, and children in his furnaces. He kept families together and stationed them near each other. Artisans often taught their skills to their sons. Other foundry owners adopted Ross's reliance on black labor and may have utilized his management style.[51]

As did slaves in Virginia, North Carolina, and elsewhere, many in Tennessee used the free time made possible by the tasking system to tend their own gardens and cotton, corn, and other crops, to raise stock and poultry, to hunt, and to make alcohol. The Tiptons' slaves owned a share of the Tipton cotton crop. Slaves traded the produce and goods that they failed to consume. Many relied on their masters for assistance and on a network of local connections for customers. In many cases, of course, the trading partner was a master or mistress. In other cases, the owners cooperated with and controlled slave trading through an arrangement with the mills. When slaves brought their cotton to the gin, millowners credited the amount delivered to a special account with their masters. Off the plantation, slaves found trading partners in local merchants, boatsmen, tavern proprietors, participants at revival meetings, and the general public. Some slaves made businesses of selling cakes, butter, and other products to the public.[52]

Subject to North Carolina jurisdiction before 1789, slaves faced a variety of laws that attempted with little success to regulate their economic activities. North Carolina statutes regulating slaves contained restrictions on raising livestock, hunting, and trading. After North Carolina's cession of its western lands to Congress in 1789, Tennessee utilized North Carolina law, except as its legislature adopted new laws. The Tennessee legislature in 1799 passed a bill that prohibited trading with slaves who did not have a pass. Although Knoxville made no effort to limit slave enterprise, the Nashville commissioners were more restrictive. They imposed a fifty-cent fine on anyone who dealt with a slave without the written permission of his or her owner. They also established market rules that required vendors to purchase stalls on market days and forbade selling elsewhere during market hours, an action aimed at undercutting black merchants who operated off market grounds. However, the efforts of the government to control the slave economy were ineffectual. Believing that they had a customary right to engage in economic relations and feeling no loyalty to white laws, slaves ignored the legal constraints on their market participation. White producers and consumers in the nascent economy supported slave involvement. Notices in 1801, 1803, 1805, and 1807, forewarning the public against trading with slaves, testify that slave businesses persisted throughout the state, and particularly in the Nashville area, largely unabated.[53]

In the labor-hungry economy of Tennessee, many masters hired slaves out on a temporary basis. As elsewhere in the South, some slaves viewed the lease relationship as one in which they had the right to expect reasonable treatment and acquired some power to enforce their expectations. If the hired owner mistreated them, they often ran away, either back to their masters or elsewhere. Their actions created a dilemma for the owners—although the slaveholder had a contract to honor, they had an interest in avoiding injuries to their slaves and in discouraging escapes. Equally important, they did not want slaves to acquire a reputation for being runaways, thus making it more difficult to hire them out in the future. Using this leverage, some slaves placed masters under constraints to arrange satisfactory employment situations. When William Faith hired Nelly out in 1793, the contract with John Gordon specified that Nelly washed and cooked for Gordon and that he had "no further authority over her."[54]

In addition to the leasing of slaves by masters, bondspeople in Tennessee hired themselves out in spite of a law forbidding the practice. Historians use the term "self-hire" to cover a number of arrangements. In some cases, the slave obtained a job in his or her free time, often with his or her owner or, at times, with an outside party. In others, the master sent the slave out with a pass to obtain employment, with the bondsperson to pay a specified amount of the earnings to the owner.[55] As when they traded, slaves generally relied on the relationships that they formed with whites and other blacks to find employers. Local merchants often hired black workers on a temporary basis. Travelers, a constant feature in Tennessee life, paid slaves to perform personal services for them and to care for their animals.[56]

Enterprising slaves in Tennessee converted trusting relationships with masters to fashion creative uses of the self-hire custom in order to enhance their earning potential and increase their personal freedom. In this form of sponsorship, a slave acquired enough assets to hire a significant block of time from his or her master. With the owner's pass, the slave then owned all of his or her time and retained all earnings during the period of hire. The master trusted that the slave would return at the end of the lease period.[57] One Virginia slave, Sam, a good fiddler, managed to lease four years of his time from his owner. Using his master's pass, he traveled throughout the South, playing for compensation at school dances. Sam's example was known in Tennessee. In spite of a North Carolina law prohibiting self-hire, slaves in Tennessee hired themselves from their owners and lived independently. York, a slave in Sumner County, worked under this arrangement. York's situation comes to us through a court case. Although the case does not discuss York's labor arrangement, York sued his owner, Isaac Pearce, for false imprisonment. The suit suggests that York owned his own time and had sufficient resources to hire an attorney and to bring a court proceeding. Other entrepreneurial slaves ran their own businesses by buying their time from their masters and moving into Nashville, often operating taverns with the consent of their masters rather than hiring their time. Both Robert Renfroe and Caesar Prince hosted such tippling houses in Nashville. Renfroe maintained a running account at Andrew Jackson's Nashville store at least as early as 1795, from which he purchased items, including tea and chocolates, probably for his tavern business. Renfroe also hired black help and had an arrangement with Jackson's store to pay his workers and to charge the advance to his account.[58]

As elsewhere, many slave owners disapproved of the practice of slaves hiring their time and conducting their own businesses, because it created an aura of freedom for the slaves. The leading figures of Nashville, including its founder, James Robertson, petitioned the state assembly in 1799 to enact legislation prohibiting slaves from keeping houses of entertainment and masters from allowing it. The assembly rejected the bill but two years later empowered Nashville to pass a local ordinance against slaves hiring their own time or keeping tippling houses. The ordinance enacted by the town of Nashville in 1802 indicates the extent of freedom some slaves enjoyed when they hired themselves out. The regulation forbade the slaves to hire their time to any citizen of Nashville, with or without the consent of their owner. The bylaws authorized the town sergeant to seize any slave violating the ban and to hire him or her out to the highest bidder for one month, subject to redemption by the master for the amount of the bid. The ordinance imposed the same penalty on any slave who hired himself or herself from his or her own owner twice and attempted to settle in town or to keep a tippling house.[59]

As in Africa, where freedom meant connections to people with power, slaves formed bonds with influential people, relationships that they tapped in order to increase their prerogatives. Unlike Africa, participation in a frontier market economy meant a wider circle of sponsors and contacts—gentlemen, suppliers, customers, co-workers, and criminals. Slaves drew on their business connections with leading men to sponsor petitions for emancipation. Forty-six men from Davidson County requested the legislature to free Robert Renfroe, whom they had known for a number of years. Originally purchased at an execution sale, Renfroe impressed his sponsors by his enterprise in industriously raising the money to reimburse his owner through the tavern he owned. As did other bondspeople in the South, slaves developed social connections with poorer whites and boatmen with whom they traded. Runaways occasionally turned to the white men and free blacks with whom they had formed economic relationships for aid in escaping. The problem was severe enough that North Carolina and later Tennessee regulated it by a law prohibiting the harboring of slaves.[60]

Some slaves formed partnerships with white criminals. Arthur Howe, a white man with Nashville connections, persuaded Mustapha, a North Carolina slave, to join him on his journey north. The parties agreed that Howe would sell Mustapha several times en route to Virginia, after which Mustapha would make his way further north as a free man. In a variation on this scheme, a Tennessee black man, James, worked with a white man, William Simpson. Simpson sold James as a slave, then paid him $150 to return to him to repeat the scheme. Daniel, a Jonesborough slave who escaped with his former "owner," may have been a party to a similar scheme.[61]

Nashville's town fathers who sought to regulate slave economic activities correctly diagnosed the threat posed by slave enterprises. Enslaved people obtained more than material rewards and greater freedom when they made alliances with whites, operated businesses, and received compensation for their work. Unlike the African system of slavery, American slave owners sought to subsume the will of the slave to that of the owner. In their forays into the marketplace, African American slaves forged self-esteem and power as they functioned as producers and consumers rather than as property subject to the will of their master. As wage-earning laborers and business people, they made more of their own decisions and reaped the rewards for their efforts. In extreme cases, their connections, confidence, and improved financial position led to their decision to free themselves. Robert Renfroe and Caesar Prince acquired the fortitude, financial base, and white connections through the taverns they owned as slaves to purchase themselves legally. Others emancipated themselves through escape. As elsewhere, considerable numbers of runaways had special skills or conducted their own businesses. These slaves likely developed a sense of self-worth through their active participation as producers in the marketplace that played a role in their decision to leave.[62]

Entrepreneurship also allowed slaves to exercise their own will as purchasers. Slaves with money or goods to trade could choose which items they bought and thus could improve their lives with products like blankets, salt, blades, and sugar. Slaves occasionally obtained luxury items, acquisitions that signaled their belief in their own self-worth. Robert Renfroe, while enslaved, purchased silk, handkerchiefs, linen, and tobacco from Andrew Jackson's store. When house slave Isaac ran from his owner, he risked carrying with him his identifiable silk hat, perhaps a symbol to him of his entitlement to respect and a better life.[63]

Although enslaved Tennesseans believed in modified African concepts that linked freedom to kinship and sponsorship connections, they had less success in creating an expanded realm of opportunity than did slaves in Africa. Peace with Native Americans and the explosive growth of slavery after 1795 greatly weakened the possibilities for patronage connections. Tennessee masters came to understand their role as slaveholders to be one in which they asserted their will over their slaves, not one in which they rewarded talented and dedicated slaves. Frontier slaves expanded their notions about patronage by reaching out to middling whites with some success, but most white Tennesseans, wealthy and ordinary, embraced ideas about a civilized society that relegated the role of slave to be one that produced prosperity.[64]

Free black Tennesseans responded to frontier conditions by drawing on and reframing both African and American premises in molding their cognitive landscape about social relations, government, and the economy. They did so in a region in which they composed a very small minority of the population.[65] At the time of the first census in 1790, there were approximately 361 free blacks in the Southwest Territory, about 1 percent of the settler population but almost 10 percent of the black inhabitants. By 1810 the free black figure had grown to 1,317 people, with free blacks about one-half of 1 percent of the larger population and 3 percent of the black inhabitants.[66] As black frontier people constructed a life for themselves in Tennessee, most fashioned a cognitive world centered on the importance of community with other free blacks. They demonstrated this by taking advantage of the freedom offered by the frontier environment to cluster in areas with other free people and to avoid regions that had few free blacks. They were willing to be quite mobile to achieve these goals.

In 1790 30 percent of free blacks collected in Sullivan County, one of eight counties in the Southwest Territory. In 1795 the majority of free blacks lived in two of the territory's eleven counties. By 1810 the majority clustered in three of the thirty-eight counties. Each of the other thirty-five counties had fewer than 100 free blacks. As free people gathered in some regions, they avoided others. The 1790 census records a total population of 35,691 and at least a few free blacks in each county. In 1795 Blount County listed no free blacks and Sumner had only one. In 1810, with a population of 261,727, seventeen counties reported less than 10 free blacks. A number of free blacks migrated to Indian lands. They probably sought the prospect of free land, a community of other free blacks, and a region in which racial restrictions may have been relaxed out of a need to present a common defense against the Chickamaugans. Of all free blacks in the Tennessee region in 1790, 18 percent lived in Cherokee territory south of the French Broad, joining 11 percent of the white population. In 1795 Sevier County, located in Indian country, had almost no slaves but contained the largest aggregation (28 percent) of free blacks in the territory.

Like free blacks in the Chesapeake region, black Tennesseans generally sought to distance themselves from slaves, avoiding settlements that would permit them to establish communities with slaves.[67] Tennesseans had greater success than their Chesapeake counterparts. In 1790 the largest aggregation of free blacks lived in Sullivan County, which ranked sixth of the eight counties in slave population. Hawkins County, with the largest number of slaves, had the second largest free black population, but the region south of the French Broad, with almost as many free blacks as Hawkins County, ranked seventh in slave count. More than one-half of the free blacks in the 1795 census lived in Sevier and Washington counties in eastern Tennessee. Neither area was a large slaveholding county. By 1810 most free blacks lived in the Cumberland region, where, except for Davidson County, home of Nashville, free blacks continued to circumvent the counties with the largest slave populations. Their resistance is probably the result of several factors—they identified strongly as free and they sought to avoid racial prejudice and the possibility of mistaken enslavement. Regardless of the reasons, this choice meant that free blacks negotiated their relationships and shaped their ideas and values primarily among free people.

As they settled in areas near each other, free African Americans created families in which a significant number of households contained more than two adults. Occasionally they lived in white homes that also included slaves. On very rare occasions, free blacks owned slaves. Large numbers of single men lived in towns. The diversity of their living arrangements did not preclude a sense of community. Many free blacks came together in their homes, taverns, and churches.[68]

Although black Tennesseans created most of their intimate kinship connections in the free black community, free blacks also fashioned ties to white men and women. They mingled with white neighbors at farm work parties, erecting buildings and harvesting crops. African Americans and white men socialized extensively at militia musters, where the men drank, played cards, and engaged in fist cuffs. Christians of both races sought fellowship in churches. Black businessmen and businesswomen sold goods and provided services to blacks and whites and were customers of white enterprises. In making these attachments, African Americans engaged in a precarious social world defined in significant part by racial classifications and met with a variety of responses from acceptance as an equal to denigration.[69]

As did free blacks in South Carolina and Georgia, a number of free people envisioned their connections as part of a patronage system from which they could expect assistance and protection. From this perspective, African Americans turned to their white connections for support in order to undercut racial restrictions. When Gaspar Lott requested the right to sue on his accounts—a procedure denied to blacks because they could not take oaths—148 men signed the petition, including such influential men as slave owners John Sevier, David Campbell, and Charles Robertson. Samuel Hamilton of Washington County submitted the signatures of fifty-seven men on a similar petition several years later. Robert Renfroe, who ran a tavern in Nashville for many years, first as a slave and later as a free man, developed a bond with his owner, Nashville commissioner Robert Searcy, who considered him industrious and allowed him to work his way out of slavery. Renfroe was popular with both races. In 1802 citizens put out a fire in his new building. Four years later, Dr. Watkins advertised that he had moved his shop next door to "Black Bob's."[70]

Gaspar Lott and Robert Renfroe envisioned a world of connection that included white people and one in which individuals responded to barriers by calling on their attachments. Their success was unusual, but their perspective was not. The story of Betty Lucust and her family suggests some of the more typical constraints operating on free blacks and the ways in which these Tennesseans conceived of alliances with influential white connections as their foundation for a response. Betty was the daughter of Mary Lucust, a free black woman. Mary had at least four children—Betty, Val, Austin, and Poll. Betty, Val, and Austin were free. In 1802 Betty's seventeen-year-old daughter was seized and probably transported to New Orleans for sale. Betty turned to more powerful friends for help. Nenian Edwards published a notice in the Nashville paper about the kidnapping of Betty's daughter in an effort to secure her return and to safeguard the other children. Although it is unlikely that Betty recovered her daughter, Edwards's action may have protected some of her other children. Two year later, Betty had two free children and three children who were held by William M'Ado as slaves in Logan County, Kentucky. M'Ado twice appeared in court in connection with the children, where he acknowledged their freedom but persuaded the judge to bind the children to him as orphans. Governor John Sevier held Poll, Betty's sister and Mary's fourth child, as a slave. In 1804 John Powers, in whose household Betty lived, appealed publicly to Sevier to release Poll. Because her siblings were free without manumission, he argued that she also was free. Pointing out that Poll did not have the resources to secure a court judgment decreeing her freedom, he urged Sevier on Poll's behalf to recognize her status. The records do not indicate whether Sevier freed Poll, but the connections Betty made with Edwards and Powers gave her a limited social voice, one that reached to the governor.[71]

Although patronage arrangements offered mutual entitlements, some free black men and women, like slaves, joined churches where they pressed for equal treatment under Gospel doctrines that preached the universality of humanity and the importance of Christian fellowship.[72] One such congregant was John (Jack) Gloucester. Reverend Gideon Blackburn, a prominent Presbyterian minister, freed Jack because Blackburn believed that Jack had special preaching talent and a charitable disposition. With the assistance of his local congregation, he overcame church barriers to become an ordained minister. Other free blacks used their mobility to seek out churches in which they could engage in a spiritual union with accepting whites and blacks.[73]

While free African Americans revived elements of African-based principles of relationality in their social world, they combined their notions of sponsorship with American ideas about entitlement in their views about governance and economic relations. Revolutionary theories informed the thinking of black frontier people, as well as whites, persuading them to assertively claim their political space. A literate George Gabriel signed his name to a petition to the North Carolina Assembly in 1787 for recognition of the state of Franklin. He joined hundreds of white men to claim that "it is our undeniable right to obtain for ourselves and posterity a proportional and adequate share of the blessings, rights, privileges and immunities allotted with the rest of mankind."[74]

Like poorer and middling white men, the participation of free black men and women in sacrificing for and fashioning a political community in a frontier environment created an expectation of earned rights. Black men and women faced the dangers of settlement in the pioneer period. Free black men voted, served in the militia, and performed roadwork. Translating their contributions into rights, free people disputed the assertion of white men that their authority to create rights permitted the inclusion of racially based categories. Instead, they believed that black people, like white people, created entitlements by their efforts. Moses Brown of Davidson County believed that he earned the right to citizenship by his actions as an honest and useful citizen, who "supports the character of an honest man, and useful member of society." Brown's bill to obtain the privileges of a citizen was rejected in the state senate in 1804, but Brown persisted and the assembly passed a law the next year recognizing that he was "entitled" to the privileges of the other citizens of the state. Other free people envisioned that their efforts earned them the right to expect judicial protection and pursued court cases against whites who abused them, often assisted by white witnesses or lawyers.[75]

Black Tennesseans brought their African notions of connection and American ideas about rights to their understanding of market relations. While many white Tennesseans pictured commerce as an impersonal mechanism working in tandem with agriculture to advance civilization, black Tennesseans imagined economic life from a more relational perspective.[76] During the frontier years, free blacks moved as a group to take advantage of connections with white patrons, cheaper land, and commercial opportunities. In 1790 81 percent of the free people lived in eastern Tennessee, with a large plurality in Sullivan County. By 1795 the percentage in the east had increased to 97 percent, although most were choosing residences in Washington County and the remote Sevier County and had deserted Sullivan County. The Cumberland counties in middle Tennessee, with 15 percent of the total population, recorded only twenty-six free blacks, less than 3 percent of the free black population. By 1800 the free black percentages in the Cumberland settlements began to increase, but 89 percent of free blacks continued to live in eastern Tennessee. During the next ten years, free people in much larger numbers chose middle Tennessee with its growing commercial center in Davidson County, where white employers were willing to hire black labor. In that decade, free blacks had almost abandoned Washington County. The largest plurality, 36 percent of those in eastern Tennessee's seventeen counties, lived in Grainger County. The major demographic change was in the Cumberland area. The 34 free blacks in 1800 increased to 807 ten years later, placing 61 percent of the state's free blacks in clusters in middle Tennessee.

Faced with legal restraints that inhibited their ability to participate fully in economic life, black communities responded by constructing a marketplace using implicit sponsorships by more powerful whites and by networking with black connections. By necessity, the minute free black population dealt with white people, who were their employers, creditors, customers, and associates. In a labor-hungry economy, many business people were eager to hire black workers and apprentices, often on terms that created greater dependencies than those crafted with white workers. Many black workers bound themselves for a period of years, as did Mary Lucust to Thomas Barker for seven years. In other cases, employers engaged entire families, increasing the reliance by both parties on each other. Turning to white connections as creditors, some used loans from supporters to secure their emancipation. A few free blacks managed their own businesses. Whites as well as blacks patronized these enterprises.[77]

Relying on the personal and business connections that they made, African Americans refashioned the economy into a sphere in which they promoted a vision of greater racial equality among free men based on merit. Rallying against the application of the law against oath taking to honest black merchants, the 148 men that successfully petitioned the assembly to grant Gaspar Lott the right to prove his accounts in 1803 argued that the law deprived an industrious man of the common benefits of a citizen. A number of other black men submitted similar petitions.[78] When free blacks formulated a cognitive world around intimate links and sponsorships by powerful white men, they shared the worldview of slaves. When free blacks crafted notions of entitlement based on their own efforts and merit to participate in white institutions as equals, their intellectual perspective converged with that of westering whites.

By the eve of the War of 1812, the organizing principle of the mental worlds of most black Tennesseans was a modified African-influenced web of personal and patronage relationships. Slaves created an expectation of reciprocity in their relationships with whites, connections that slaves associated with the possibility of greater freedom. Free blacks utilized these ties to realize their American vision of entitlements and equality in political and economic spheres in which racial restrictions were increasing. Meanwhile, in contrast to the Cherokee project of imagining a defensive national identity or the black vision of familial connections and clientage, white men and women positioned a cluster of ideas about civilization at the heart of their cognitive universe.

CHAPTER SIX

"A Never-Failing Resource in the Benevolence of Society"

Sociability and Family in the Euro-American Community

When Judith Phillips of Knox County, Tennessee, contracted gonorrhea during her husband's absence in 1797, she turned to her neighbors, Polly and John Boley, for assistance. She described her sexual contact with laborer William Small to Polly Boley to determine if Small could have passed the disease. After Polly assured her that it was possible, she persuaded John Boley to find out if Small had gonorrhea. On learning that he did not, she asked John to dress as a woman and to get her husband drunk. Her plan was to persuade her husband that he was the source of her infection. In making this request, Phillips crossed a moral boundary. The Boleys not only drew the line at neighborly assistance, but they filed depositions for Small when Phillips lodged a rape complaint against him.[1]

This episode exposes some of the human complexities that made up the deep webs of connection woven by white women and men in Tennessee. Historians have largely neglected the exploration of the ideas and assumptions of backcountry people about family and sociability. Social historians have emphasized the isolation of pioneers, with some crediting religion and Native American wars as forces creating community.[2] This work neglects the European ideology about social life that informed settler thinking and practices. In contrast to the Cherokee cognitive universe of community centered on clan and balance and the African view of social relations as spiritual connections to ancestors and as familial, associational, and patronage attachments, the frontier people of European ancestry in Tennessee brought assumptions from the Atlantic world about sociability linked to civilization. Americans articulated the purpose of the civilized life to be to produce happiness. Using the native peoples they encountered as a counterpoint, most pioneers pictured their society as a more advanced stage of civilization, in part because of their belief that they enjoyed a richer social life. Modifying European notions of social connections arising from an organic hierarchy, transmontane women and men sought happiness through voluntary familial and social relationships in which merit created entitlements.

Because women situated domestic and communal relations at the center of their cognitive world, they were central to the development of ideas and logic about sociability. Although intellectual historians of gender and women in the early republic generally focus on how gender intersects with other relations of power or on the impact of women on politics or business, pioneer white women in Tennessee were much more concerned about maintaining thick social relations, an issue that has drawn less attention.[3] This chapter follows their concerns by examining their cultural premises on this topic. Pioneers framed marriages as contractual affairs embedded in a dense communal web, a view that allowed intellectual space for several types of familial arrangements. As women defended themselves and their children from Native American attacks and engaged in the hard work of settlement, they saw themselves as partners in the wilderness enterprise. Acting on this new authority, women crafted networks of community to maintain standards of nonviolence and, for some women, morality.[4]

Men contributed more substantially to the logic of wider social relations. Although many ordinary men migrated because they envisioned freedom from oppressive political authority and patriarchal control by big men, they advanced a vision of egalitarian social relationships that relied on connections with and the opinions of others. In addition, small farmers pushed prominent men toward norms of achievement over hereditary status by insisting that leading men be able militia commanders.

The decade of the 1790s brought significant challenges to the social world of the pioneers. With the promise of permanent peace, an influx of immigrants came with a new set of gentry values that drew on discourses about refinement and republicanism to advocate for legalized marriage and to imagine the wife as the emotional helpmate of her husband. In the newspapers that proliferated in Tennessee beginning in late 1791, columnists made character an individual achievement of self-control, producing a model for the self-made genteel man. Women and men accepted some of the propositions of polite literature and rejected or remolded others. Asserting themselves as part of a marital partnership, most women accepted the morality of marriage but persisted in viewing their domestic role as more akin to that of a vocal participant than a submissive helpmate, promoting their values about harmony and wider communal ties and creating expectations about their entitlements to property and custody that conflicted with legal norms.

As women sought virtue, harmony, and social networks, many leading and middling men became concerned about discord between men. Polite values of self-mastery aimed to contain passions, but some gentlemen disagreed with the refined vision of self-control that restricted traditional forms of social demonstrations, such as dueling, gambling, and drinking. Increasingly visible assertions of social hierarchy spurred ordinary men to redouble their efforts to assert their vision of social leveling. As tensions between leading and middling men increased, both gentlemen and middling men sought harmony in voluntary associations by crafting a larger meaning of brotherhood that embraced unrelated strangers with whom they imagined a connection and from whom they sought approval. As they extended their circle of connections, some men began to expand their vision about ideological and philosophical differences, evincing a growing belief that a community could contain members with diverse ideas.

The white people who crossed the Appalachian Mountains into the Tennessee Valley from 1768 through 1810 were of various ancestries, with substantial numbers of Ulster Irish, Scotch, Germans, and English. The newcomers arrived with a variety of ideas about communal life and about household autonomy. Scottish Enlightenment theorists formulated a concept of civilization as a system that organized the natural sociability of human beings in order to create happiness. They embedded these ideas in a progressive view of human history that considered that humanity had moved through stages of development—from hunters to pastoralists to cultivators to commercial society. Scotch-Irish Presbyterian educators spread the Scottish Enlightenment philosophy in the Tennessee region through their schools. Of the four classical schools in the area before 1796, Presbyterian ministers trained at Princeton—a stronghold of Scottish Enlightenment theory—founded and ran three of them. A Princeton graduate taught the founder of the fourth school.[5] Other European Enlightenment philosophers described a similar progression of human development to be savagery, barbarism, and civilization, with the societies associated with this schema moving from a state of nature to the thick sociability of the city. The Revolution spread the ideas of civic humanists—an ideology that located a rich human life in the *civitas*—and Lockean assumptions about consensual social relations and individual autonomy.[6]

Relying on these transatlantic ideological traditions, many pioneers viewed their community as a civilized one, rooted in a progressive human history, with their agricultural and commercial society as the more advanced form of societal organization. In formulating a concept of civilization in the cis-Mississippi woods, borderers turned their gaze to Native Americans, whom they viewed primarily as hunters. For most Tennesseans, as for many whites elsewhere in the country, the trope of the isolated savage was a counterpoint to the rich communal life offered by civilization. The *Knoxville Gazette* in 1792 contrasted the savage and civilized ways of life, depicting the savage life as carefree, abundant, and natural and civilized society as full of toil, anxiety, chains, and scarcity. A reply the next month contended that the savage life was full of want, was precarious, and had few pleasures and little chance for improvement, whereas the civilized man enjoyed security, arts, expansive ideas, and society. Another columnist commented that "the civilized man has a never-failing resource in the benevolence of society," whereas the woodland inhabitants survived precariously by isolated hunts. With the possible exception of a few hundred white people who chose to live in the Cherokee towns, virtually all white settlers perceived their way of life to be a more advanced and superior stage in a progression of human society that located Indians in the savage stage.[7]

The use of Native Americans as a foil against which to define the superior sociability of civilized life is particularly telling since this was not the only possible contrast. The numerous ethnic groups that populated the Tennessee region were quite foreign to each other. Immigrants with ancestors from the British Isles were especially likely to target the Germans for scorn or dislike. Newspapers parodied German language speakers, suggesting that they were stupid. Contrasting the disposition of those from Holland and Hamburgh to the liberality and good fellowship of the French and English, John Sevier believed that "narrowness, meanness, and a selfish disposition" characterized the Germans. Tennesseans traveling around the state often commented on German households, some finding Germans greedy or inhospitable. A popular song cast them as "dirty." Yet writers did not describe the Germans as barbarians or uncivilized. Instead, setting aside their distinctions, the different ethnic groups found common ground against the indigenous peoples.[8]

Westering people believed that civilized people organized more advanced societies with a purpose in mind. Unlike Africans, who envisioned connections stretching backward and forward in time and horizontally bonding humans with each other and the rest of the earth as part of their metaphysical worldview, Europeans related attachments to a specific human goal—happiness realized in a civilized life. In the *Law of Nature*, sold in Tennessee, C. F.

Volney characterized the improvement of social systems and human faculties as the source of happiness. Like Volney, white men and women of almost all ranks placed happiness at the center of their personal, social, political, and economic universes, and frequently related happiness to their social connections with others. As John Donelson, one of the founders of the Cumberland settlements, wrote his son Johnny in 1785, "Your mama's ease and happiness . . . your and your brothers' and sisters' well-being and happiness . . . is the most ardent desire of your most affectionate father."[9]

The experience of the pioneers reinforced views about the importance of sociability. Like settlers up and down the Appalachian spine, most of the newcomers who crossed the Appalachians into the Tennessee Valley from 1768 through 1810 maintained their social vision by moving in clusters of families, neighbors, friends, or religious communities. Numbers of single men often attached themselves to these convoys. Although some of the early settlers attempted to settle separately from others, many of these loners did not survive. Consequently, most people settled in neighborhoods, where one family constructed a station. During periods of Indian threats, families crowded into the stations, where they shared farming and household jobs.[10] In times of peace, a variety of social events reflected the interdependence of the settlements. Neighbors worked, socialized, and assisted each other at parties, quiltings, barn raisings, logrollings, stores, taverns, childbirth, school exhibitions, sugar camps, cotton picking, and corn shuckings. John Sevier's journal shows that, even as governor, he attended house raisings, corn shuckings, logrollings, quiltings, and apple-butter boilings. One study of the material culture that examined probate records found that individual farmers owned few tools, apparently borrowing from each other. Even the more transient workers considered a social life important. Boatmen drank, played cards, ran races, swam, gambled, and engaged in shooting matches with whites, Indians, and blacks.[11]

At the center of communal relations was the family. Most pioneers saw the family as an autonomous patriarchal social unit deeply embedded in a communal network. Early settlers imported the philosophy of the North Carolina and Chesapeake marriage laws, which contemplated a contractual relationship between the parties. Parental approval was important but not essential.[12] Casting intimate relationships as a compact between the parties, many pioneers tolerated several kinds of familial arrangements. Both leading and ordinary men and women envisioned that parties could establish their own relationships outside of traditional marriage. Men and women had sexual relations or lived together without holding themselves out as married. Judicial efforts to enforce marital rules met with limited success when the case required a jury verdict. Big men also fathered illegitimate children. General James Winchester, the leading man of Sumner County and one of five members of the Territorial Legislative Council, sired at least seven children with Susan Black before he married her. He legitimized his children by special legislative acts. Other men, both leading men and ordinary farmers, recognized the children of similar relationships. A form of serial bigamy was not uncommon, as men and women left spouses and entered into new marriages without a divorce. Ministers as well as laypeople engaged in these forms of relationship. Secular and religious challenges to the construction of marriage as a private matter of agreement between the parties during the pioneer period were infrequent. Courts were most likely to intervene only to provide for support of illegitimate children.[13]

When whites crossed racial lines to marry Native Americans, they triggered broader communal concerns about civilization that potentially imposed restrictions on their autonomy to contract intimate relationships. White men with business in the Cherokee nation developed a custom of taking Indian wives. Some of these men engaged in bigamy, taking a Cherokee wife with whom they had a family in addition to their white wife and family. Arguing that they engaged in this practice to secure personal protection, trade relationships, and diplomatic ties and to advance their white families economically, white men largely avoided criticism about uncivilized behavior by articulating rationales that advanced the security and prosperity of civilized society. Such men included Joseph Martin, the Indian agent for Virginia and North Carolina during the 1780s; Bryan Ward, a trader; Joseph Sevier, John Sevier's oldest son and a trader; John Chisholm, a trader and important Indian agent for Governor William Blount; and John Benge, a longtime trader.[14] Lacking a community-based rationale for rejecting civilized society to marry a "savage," white women did not experience the same permission to cross racial lines to marry. Nonetheless, some white women did wed Cherokee men. As white womanhood came to symbolize virtue and refinement, such unions increasingly threatened the Euro-American vision of civilization. In addition to lacking justification for these marriages, whites had a second concern about white women choosing native husbands. As the masterful head of household, white men could potentially bring civilization to the union with an indigenous woman. As a dependent without her own will, a white woman became native.[15]

Differences in the ways whites viewed cross-cultural marriages with Indians reflected larger understandings about gender arrangements in civilized society—a set of social relations that women were transforming in other ways. In a region in which more than 90 percent of all settlers lived on small farms, the home was the center of domestic and work life. By law and custom, free men governed the household.[16] Over time, the social reality became more complicated. In the frontier period, women faced considerable danger from raids when their husbands were away. When settlers were forted, women's care of cattle often took them out of the encampment early in the morning, making them prime targets. Along with children and slaves, women faced the rigors of being taken prisoner. Such women often relied on their own efforts to protect themselves and their children. Women also assisted in common defense efforts.[17] More significantly, on numerous occasions men fled or hid in the face of attack, leaving women and children to protect themselves. In some cases, women succeeded in defending themselves and their children, but usually they were killed or captured. Hoping to protect their families by alleviating racial tensions, some women made efforts to decrease the violence between Native American and settler men by maintaining cordial personal relations with Indian visitors. During the late 1780s, a Mrs. Kirk, squatting on Cherokee land in the French Broad area with her family, offered food and hospitality to friendly Indians. At the request of the Cherokees, other white women in that area agreed to teach Cherokee women how to make clothing.[18]

While defending their households, women worked as hard as men to build a life for their families. Women and men saw women as yokefellows, working in tandem with their husbands in a team driven by the husband or, in his death or absence, by the wife. In offering advice on marriage, Andrew Jackson acknowledged the importance of the wife's efforts: "Seek a wife, one who will aid you in your exertions in making a competency and will take care of it when made." In the pioneer period, the efforts expended by women to handle the heavy work of the farm caused many to value women for "masculine" traits. Women frequently ran households on their own. In the Cumberland settlements, two-thirds of the wives of the original settlers were widows by 1795. Most remained but did not remarry. Even when the husband was alive, he was often gone, leaving his wife to manage the farm and her husband's affairs. During the Revolutionary War, militiamen in the Holston area captured a Tory and took him to the home of Colonel Benjamin Cleveland for disposition. The men turned to Mrs. Cleveland in her husband's absence, and she ordered the man hanged.[19]

Expected to provide protection and support for their families, many women assumed informal but real authority in the home. Some women decided whether the family would remain at home or move to the station during periods of Indian threats. Religious women convened services in their houses over their husband's objections and made decisions to baptize their children. The power that women exercised in homes legally governed by men became the subject of popular lore and humor.[20]

Many women used the power that they claimed in the family to embed their households in a larger social world. In the view of these women, their role was to spin webs of connection. Households frequently included members outside the nuclear family. Single, separated, divorced, and widowed women and men often lived with family members or neighbors. Related families clustered together in the same neighborhoods. To nurture community and family, women were deeply involved in births, illnesses, problems, injuries, and deaths of relatives and connections. Living together, visiting, and corresponding, women defined communication and shared communal knowledge as central to social relationships.[21]

Within their networks of family and sociability, women promoted ideas about nonviolence and morality. Wives and mothers sought to moderate fighting and drinking. When several men began to brawl in the house of farmer George Martin and threw him out of the house, his wife intervened by scorning one of the combatants, stopping the fight. In 1782 Captain Samuel Handly got into an altercation with a German man at the man's farm. When Handly began to beat the man, his opponent's two brothers stepped in against him. Believing the fight to be unfair, the brother's wives attacked their husbands with shovels. Dr. Morgan Brown's wife and his son watered down his alcohol in order to diminish the effects of his drinking.[22]

In addition to alleviating violence, women played a prominent role in obtaining and using information about community members to maintain standards of morality and respectability through gossip. Historians have given much attention to the gentlemen's code of honor but less attention to the cultural assumptions underlying gossip. Gossip is the outcome of an implicit belief that a person's conduct has communal implications and may be a matter for public censure, disapproval, or praise. In the small interdependent frontier communities of Tennessee, women and men crafted a world in which reputation was vitally important. Small farmers relied on their neighbors to make social connections and to obtain assistance and credit. For big men, reputation was critically linked to honor.[23] Relying on the importance of reputation, women and men used gossip and scandal to enforce norms about sexuality and honesty. Their generation of gossip was so widespread that slander cases became one of the staples on the legal calendar in the pioneer era. Many of the slander cases brought by women and some men implicated sexual morality, such as fornication, bestiality, rape, and murder of a bastard child. Men were more likely to prosecute for accusations of charges involving property, like forgery and theft, or violence. Other women and men enforced standards of morality and conduct through their church disciplinary procedures.[24]

Most men agreed that family and communal life were important and considered themselves to be the heads of the household, a role that included the protection of and provision for their family. Their activities took them away from their families, and men often tried to minimize their absences. Many farmers refused militia service because they had to protect their families. Their resistance persuaded leading men to avoid drafting married men or to release them early, where possible. Along with small farmers, first men expected to provide for and protect their families. James Robertson, who saw his son killed, cried that it "unmanned" him. Thomas Hutchings declined to attend a council of officers during a time of Indian troubles, because he had to take care of his family. Hunting songs portrayed one way in which men transformed an activity that isolated them from their families into a tender familial link. In one song, the father reminded himself of the infant he protected: "Bye you baby bunting / your daddy has gone hunting / To catch a rabbit skin / to wrap the baby in." Another hunter's song recalled the father's domestic life: "O you little deer who made you breeches / mammy cut them out and daddy sewed the stitches, sewed the stitches."[25]

When they moved in the social world outside of their families, the heads of households brought a different set of cultural assumptions to their relationships. Rejecting deference as they had in the North Carolina and Virginia backcountry, frontiersmen formulated a version of connection that emphasized the leveling of social ranks. William Tatham, an Englishman who moved to eastern Tennessee in 1776, described the backwoodsmen as quick "to treat the appearance of arrogance with contemptuous roughness." Ordinary farmers also elevated values of accomplishment and skill—such as bravery, strength, and fighting and hunting acumen—rather than status based on birth or wealth. When men met for house raisings, they linked the values of social leveling and recognition of skill by voting on the first four corner men.[26]

Gentry men advanced their vision of community by creating and maintaining a social order that emphasized harmony supported by ranks of people. This notion of harmony altered over time. In the pioneer period, first men supposed that their wealth and control of resources—particularly land and stores—entitled them to head a harmonious social order. Militia farmers, however, expected their gentry leaders to display leadership and bravery and refused to serve under men who did not measure up to their standards.[27] These changes in the political sphere had social consequences, as men of good birth had to earn the right to exert authority.

The influx of population into Tennessee in the 1790s brought challenges to the understandings of sociability developed by frontier women and men. In 1790 there were 31,913 white people in the Southwest Territory. Ten years later the figure had almost tripled to 91,709. By 1810 whites numbered 215,875. When William Blount arrived in eastern Tennessee as governor of the Southwest Territory in 1790, he brought with him the life-style of the North Carolina gentleman. During the next two decades, increasing numbers of wealthier people began to move into the state, particularly into the Cumberland area. With the advent of the publication of local newspapers, the voices of some of the leading men reached ordinary farm women and men and people of substantial means in a new way. Solicited by Governor Blount to move from North Carolina to the Southwest Territory, George Roulstone established the *Knoxville Gazette* in 1791. Roulstone was the spokesperson for Blount during Blount's tenure, and the *Gazette* continued publication for several decades as one of Tennessee's most influential papers. During the period before war in 1812, numerous other papers came and went. The most prominent was the *Tennessee Gazette*, renamed the *Clarion* after 1808, which was printed in Nashville and appealed to the Cumberland region. The publishers of most of these papers represented a newer order of gentry—one that associated civilization with a particular set of refined and republican values.[28] In common with writers throughout the United States, they made significant efforts to further their discourse of civilization by redefining the roles of women and men of both small and substantial property in the family and community.

Promoters of gentility sought to elevate the legal family as the guardian of civilized happiness and to detach it from the thick communal networks created primarily by women. During and after the 1790s, advice writers argued more insistently for legalized marriage as "necessary to the existence of civilized society." The Tennessee legislature underscored the growing view that state-sanctioned marriage was critical to a virtuous civilized state. Disturbed by "frequent" applications to the legislature to legitimize children that "expose the morals of society," the legislature in 1805 sought to remove this blight from public view by creating a procedure for the courts to legitimize children. Similar motives prompted the legislature to curtail legislative divorce and to refer divorce to the courts for decision.[29] Like polite literature throughout the United States, gentry papers in Tennessee ignored extended familial relationships and imagined the home as the scene of domestic quiet where the best improvements of social life enriched people. Returning from a trip to find a ten-day old son, Judge Joseph Anderson proclaimed: "I . . . felt about a thousand guineas richer. . . . Thus my friend do the springs of industry increase our wealth, some in one way, some in another."[30]

Historians have recognized that the newly imagined family structure was that of a republican family. As the *Knoxville Gazette* explained, "every family is a little republic." According to the *Gazette*, the prosperity and happiness of the larger republic depended on good family management. Columnists in Tennessee as elsewhere in the United States formulated a role for mothers that emphasized their duty to instruct their children about republican principles.[31]

Advice writers encountered some difficulty in carrying the political analogy into the domestic sphere. In their view, the heads of the family should govern their children carefully. As one of the heads, women were located in a decision-making position, yet these men did not intend to delegate such political authority to women. The frontier setting exacerbated this quandary, because women and men saw women as helpmates. Writers in the refined mode along with many gentry men sought to contain these tensions by assigning the wife a new function—to bolster the governing capabilities of her husband by catering to his emotional needs. Theorists wanted wives to accomplish this by subsuming their will in order to achieve a pleasing amiability. Gentlemen sought a woman who had a sweet temper and good understanding that would yield to her husband's persuasions. Will, a matter of central importance to men, became unseemly in women—its sacrifice a trivial consideration for the sake of family harmony. Editors in obituaries and marriage notices portrayed the ideal wife as dutiful, amiable, and endearing, affectionate to her relatives and charitable to her neighbors. An important requirement for amiability was that women accede to men without complaint. Columnists and others mounted a determined campaign to restrain women's power by discouraging their voices. By the mid-1790s writers frequently warned women against arguing with men, practices that undercut the vision of a peaceful home in which the woman sought to soothe the cares of her husband and model the virtues of amiability to her family.[32]

In tandem with the wife's role as emotional helpmate, the best marriages, according to some writers, were those based on esteem and love. Alluding to the distaste for monarchical rule by republicans, many urged men not to see themselves as "over" their wife but as partners in a relationship in which they appealed to their wife's reason and amiability to persuade her to their views.

One obituary praised a woman for her masculine understanding. Many gentlemen anticipated that they would continue to rule the home by appealing to the reason and sweet temper of their wives.[33]

At stake in this redefinition of the female role was a reimagining of the meaning of civilization—one that conflated it with republicanism and placed women at its center as the socializing force that created civilized men. According to polite authorities, women were the mainstay of civilization. Although not born to conquer or rule the senate, one author explained, women promoted the rule of law and the advancement of civilization, because their virtue inspired men to obey the law and to mind their manners. By teaching the young, women moved the secret springs of government and fixed the manners, customs, and character of nations. Although refined gentlemen promoted women's education, most believed that women taught primarily through their character. By 1801 gentlemen in Tennessee toasted the "American Fair" and honored women as the source of virtue, which they dispensed to "all sons of liberty."[34]

Advice writers sought to remold men as well as women. Prominent among the traits of the genteel man was self-government. At the same time that writers dampened will in women, they urged it on men. In promoting self-mastery, they reshaped the concept of character. Loosening character from its moorings in breeding and wealth, thinkers relocated it in the realm of achievement. In conjunction with self-mastery, the new man displayed other genteel qualities that could be attained by any industrious man. He was caring of his family and exhibited an amiable nature. Obituaries praised gentry men for their minds and accomplishments. By making character dependent on self-mastery and achievement, republican writers diagrammed a program for self-made gentlemen.[35]

Both ordinary and elite Tennessee women and men adopted very selectively the ideas of the new theorists. Rather than picturing the home as a hearth of domestic comfort, most women and men continued to view it as a productive space. In the face of the outpouring of articles defining women as deferring wives, kind neighbors, and pious Christians, numerous women conceived of a more active role for themselves. Some declined to marry. Many married women refused to function primarily as their husband's emotional support or to accede amiably to their husband's reason. Reflecting on her long marriage, Rachel Henderson, the wife of a postmaster in Sumner County, wrote that one of the advantages of marriage was that she began "to think and act for myself." Married to a prominent Nashville merchant, Mary Deaderick angered her husband because she invited people to the house and attended dances and entertainment without his consent. The reasons listed by men for their wives' elopement in separation notices and divorce petitions indicate that many women did not accept the roles advanced by refined men. Ordinary men lost wives for reasons such as "refuses to return to her duty," "imprudent behavior," or "can't agree as man and woman ought to." A male relative of the husband in one divorce case characterized the wife as "insolent."[36]

As in the pioneer period, many women believed that sources of conflict should be addressed by personal communication with their husbands that did not include deference. These wives promoted their own vision of the civilized republican family by voicing opinions and venting their feelings to their husbands. The numerous articles inveigling against scolding and nagging by women testify to the prevalence of these practices. Married to a man who believed that a woman should be humble and accommodate slight differences by yielding to her husband's reason, Polly Waterhouse lost Richard's esteem when she got angry.[37]

Not satisfied with scolding, women in this period exercised a greater role in decision making than advice columnists recommended and historians allow. Women often had a voice, frequently a deciding one, about where the family lived.[38] Once settled, some women refused to remain homebound. They often traveled considerable distances to visit friends.[39] Both gentry and ordinary women continued to act as yokefellows, managing households in their husband's absence. Wives commonly accepted payments on their husband's accounts. Recognizing their wife's role, most men selected their wife, often along with a male relative or friend, to act as administrator of their estate upon their death. In Wilson County from 1802 to 1810, two-thirds of the married male decedents named their wife to serve as an administrator of their estate. In 50 percent of the cases, married men named their wife along with a male executor as coadministrators while 17 percent chose their wives as sole administrator.[40]

Contradicting the model of the amiable wife, some unhappy women went beyond scolding and claimed authority within the marriage by leaving their husbands. The decision to leave a marriage produced tension between the understanding of marriage as consensual and the tenet that marriage served the public interest in civilization and morality. Women were particularly likely to assert that they had a right to solve marital problems without resort to the legal system by simply separating—a position consistent with the contractual view of marriage. From the time of the first local newspaper in late 1791 through 1810, fifty-five men advertised their separation from their wives in the extant copies of the papers. In 69 percent of the cases, the wife left her husband.[41] Many wives who decided to terminate their marital relationship considered themselves free to proceed with their lives. Without legal process, some women left with another man. Women had later relationships that produced children. Some refused to return, although asked.[42]

Women also asserted their right to leave unhappy marriages by assuming the lead in petitioning for divorce. From 1796 through 1810, at least eighty-eight individuals petitioned the legislature for divorce, 50 percent of whom were women, 41 percent were men, and 9 percent were joint petitioners.[43] Legislative divorces were only part of the story. In 1799 Tennessee enacted one of the most liberal divorce statutes in the country, granting the courts the power to decree divorce when certain statutory criteria were met.[44] Eight years later, religious voices persuaded the assembly to repeal it. Popular outcry, in the form of a flood of seventy-nine divorce petitions to the legislature in 1809, forced the assembly to revive the original statute. Female spouses led this revolt, filing 56 percent of the petitions. The sheer volume of petitions tied up the legislature and prevented a fair investigation of the allegations. Representative R. C. Foster wrote that the legislature was concerned about granting divorce by the petition method, because the opposing party had no opportunity to respond. Tacitly acknowledging both the compactual nature of nuptials and the public interest in marriage, the assembly directed the matter to the courts "to proceed as in civil contracts" and to impanel a jury to determine the merits of the divorce.[45]

The contractual understanding of marriage, their contributions to the family, and the emphasis on republican motherhood and civilization encouraged women to consider themselves part of a partnership in which they were more active in familial and interpersonal communal relations, while their husbands carried on legal and political business. Agreeing with men that entitlements were earned, republican women appropriated rights to property and children as they assumed the duties and burdens of the household. With the increase of prosperity, due in no small part to women's efforts and sacrifices, some women asserted a voice in determining how their gains would be spent. Elizabeth Snoddy sought to make purchases in excess of what her husband felt that they could afford, compelling him to notify the public to refuse credit to her. Polly Waterhouse's spending elicited a complaint from her husband about her infrugal habits. Appropriating a more proprietary interest in children, republican mothers often made decisions about naming and baptizing children, even in the face of differences with their husbands.[46]

In the process of separations and divorces, as during the marriage, some women asserted ideas about their inchoate rights to marital property and the children. By law, the husband controlled the property of the marriage and had the right to custody of the children. Relying on the sense of entitlement to joint property that women were developing, numerous women took property on separation that belonged legally to their husbands but to which they asserted moral claims.[47] Although men were legally entitled to custody of their children, republican mothers sometimes found a way to obtain de facto custody. In some cases, men left the children behind when they deserted. Cognizant of the deterrent of expensive and uncertain divorce procedures, some wives took the children and disappeared, obtained family assistance, or forced the husband to take action if he opposed her. Other women sought remedies through their churches.[48]

Women's efforts to obtain custody in divorce reflected a wider movement among affectionate mothers and mother surrogates to assert custodial rights. Upon the death of the father, children became orphans. If the mother could support them, she was often named guardian. If the mother appeared unable to support her children on the father's death, the court bound them out to someone who could. Occasionally, such mothers resisted by failing to appear in court. Others proved to the court that they could provide for their children "so much as is common for a person in her situation." Some women on death left the care of their children to a female relative or friend. These guardians often asserted their entitlement to custody in the face of legal obstacles. One such woman was Granny White. While she was in her late sixties living in North Carolina, a female friend died and left two small children to White's care. When the county orphan court threatened to take the children because she could not post security, White absconded, moving with the children to Davidson County, Tennessee, about 1799, where she raised them.[49]

Besides declining the role of amiable helpmate and converting their active involvement in consensual marriage to inchoate rights, many women refused to isolate their households from the larger community. Despite the efforts of advice columnists to locate women and men in autonomous homes, women imagined and fashioned bonds of sociability, forged in communal networks, gossip, and churches. Informal but powerful social networks provided assistance to women at the same time that they enforced multiple and often contradictory communal norms. Unhappy couples usually attempted to resolve their disputes outside the legal arena by calling on family members, neighbors, churches, and the extended community to mediate marital disagreements before they permanently separated. As described at the beginning of this chapter, Judith Phillips drew on neighborly ties but was thwarted when she tried to involve her friends in concealing her immoral conduct.

Mrs. Parker heard her neighbor, William Shaeffer, threaten to kill a Cherokee man who was visiting the Kingston area in 1809. When she witnessed Shaeffer beating an Indian later that day, Parker averted a potentially serious incident by rousting her family to rescue the man.[50]

One of the most controversial components of the network of sociability after 1790 was the persistence of gossip. Advocates of refinement complained about gossip, especially talebearing by women. The spread of rumors became a particularly serious matter for theorists promoting a polite civilization, because the dissemination of private information threatened to undermine reputations. As white society expanded and prospered, both women and men refashioned respectability—important for survival in pioneer years—as integrally linked to a civilized society, a connection noted by Judge John Overton: "The enjoyment of a fair and unsullied reputation is certainly the greatest blessing a rational being can enjoy in this sublunary state of existence; an attempt to deprive a person of it ought, and must, in all civilized states and nations, be considered as a serious injury."[51]

The concerns of polite writers and gentlemen about preserving reputation in an advanced society competed with other views about civilized social life. As they had in the earlier period, white women and men spread information about personal conduct to enforce cultural mores and to gain social power. Restrictions on talebearing struck women particularly forcibly, because women had less formal power than men to effectuate social norms. In spite of the invectives against the practice, women and men continued to talk. Among women, improper sexual behavior was often the subject of scandal as many women followed polite writers in promoting virtuous conduct. As the example of Judith Phillips and Polly Boley at the beginning of this chapter illustrated, beliefs about immoral conduct could strain female bonds. Men also participated in the world of gossip. Elizabeth Jackson claimed to have seen Rachel Hays nursing a child before her marriage to Robert Butler, a friend of Andrew Jackson—an intimation of premarital sexual conduct that caused Jackson to track the rumor to its source and secure a retraction.[52]

In addition to maintaining communal values, women and men who conversed about the personal and public behavior of others appropriated power by converting private information into social knowledge. While slaves used the leverage offered by gossip to strengthen their patronage bonds, white women and men found in gossip a social leveling opportunity. Rumors were empowering, since they could be spread by anyone and could be damaging to the most prominent individuals. James Mitchell, William Purnell's carpenter, gained the ear of Colonel William Donelson, for whom he also worked.

Mitchell told Donelson that, according to Purnell, Andrew Jackson's man Dinwiddie poisoned Purnell's stud horse. When the carpenter's rumor reached Jackson, it created a breach between Jackson and Purnell. Similarly, when someone told Jackson that Isabella Vinson, the mother of Robert Butler's wife Rachel, had insulted his wife, Vinson felt compelled to write Jackson with her account of the events, disclaiming any intent to injure Rachel Jackson's reputation.[53]

Although the greater part of the female universe of sociability operated through informal avenues of assistance and gossip, churches offered one institution in which some women could, in limited but important ways, vocalize and enforce their vision of communal norms.[54] Church membership was small in 1796. Most of the church people in Tennessee were Baptists, Methodists, or Presbyterians. With the population climbing above 75,000, the Baptists had the largest membership with approximately 2,500 adherents; the Presbyterians had 1,500; and the Methodists numbered fewer than 600. During the revivals of 1800, participation began to soar. Many women turned to the churches as a place to vocalize their values and find a community that supported their spiritual principles. Although men assumed much of the formal governance of churches, the large numbers of female members ensured them a voice. As elsewhere, women composed the bulk of the congregation in most churches. Of greater importance, in many churches the majority of founding members were women. Women did a considerable amount of the work of bringing in new converts. Women often traveled great distances to attend church, returning with renewed determination to encourage their families to follow "the narrow way." Women also contributed significantly to the financial life of the churches.[55]

As a result of their labors in establishing and supporting churches, women exercised considerable power in them. Baptists offered the most public institutional recognition of women. Unlike Methodists and Presbyterians, Baptists were congregational churches in which the members made many decisions about procedural and theological questions at the local level. This expanded the terrain for women to press local churches about the proper Gospel role for women. The Red River Baptist Church, a church founded primarily by women that maintained a predominantly female membership, agreed in 1794 that women could vote on all matters pertaining to fellowship and discipline, although they could not make motions or debate on the floor. The male members carried out the other church business. When a member submitted a query to the Wilson Creek Primitive Baptist Church—the bulk of whose charter members were female—about whether women could speak at conferences, the members voted in the affirmative by a large majority. Women had some public voice in other churches, making motions, calling witnesses, and carrying on church business. Women attended Baptist association meetings and passed on the preaching to women at home. Good ministers realized who constituted the majority of their audience. During the course of their sermons, revivalist preachers commonly engaged members of their audience—women as well as men—in dialogue to confirm their views. When the famous Methodist minister Lorenzo Dow discussed unhappy marriages, he addressed the problem from the woman's perspective first.[56]

Like slaves, white religious women did not always acquiesce in the theology and practices promulgated by men. They often refused to be passive at church, at times believing that they had the authority to question religious doctrines and to disobey church rules. Eliza Humphreys and her daughter resigned from the Sinking Creek Baptist Church when they concluded that the church was on "sandy foundation." Christian theology offered women an intellectual space that surpassed the authority of their husbands. Surrendering to the higher will of God, these women persisted in pursuing their spiritual views even though the influence that they wielded in churches sometimes split families and congregations. The Big Spring Primitive Baptist Church was rent by a controversy that began when William Stroud charged the Harpers and Lanes with following "fashion" by cutting their hair. The Harper and Lane women responded by arguing that the haircuts were a necessity. They spawned a debate that lasted almost two years and resulted in the expulsion and readmission of the contrite Stroud party.[57]

The strong position that white women held in churches gave them an important role in interpreting Christian theology—a task to which women brought their own values and ideas. As in the larger culture, church women were particularly concerned about issues of morality and destructive male behavior. Churches played a significant role in handling marital discord. Religious people cast marriage as a joining of souls by God in everlasting love. Ministers taught that the family was an interconnected unit in which the members had mutual duties to each other and to God. Following these precepts, religious members made strong efforts to support marriages. Responding largely to women's concerns, churches also tackled larger communal issues that touched primarily on male culture. In disciplinary proceedings, members commonly sanctioned men for actions that interfered with harmonious communities, such as excessive drinking, fighting, anger, and gambling. The most common disciplinary actions involving white members were taken against men for drunkenness and were particularly likely to occur in churches in which women composed most of the membership.[58] By taking an active role in enforcing their ideas about morality—concepts advanced in part through genteel literature—women accepted some and rejected others of the polite precepts.

While family, community, and spirituality were the central components of the mental universe of women and important to men as well, many men after 1790 evinced increasing concern about discord between men. In their view, disagreements arose from several causes—passions, tensions over social hierarchy, the contentiousness of politics, and the competitiveness of the marketplace. Advice writers equated disharmony with passions, including anger, envy, pride, vanity, intemperance, and avarice. They targeted dueling, gambling, and drinking as particularly undesirable expressions of passion. According to one writer, passions caused duels, which were a feudal practice, one founded on superstition. They urged men to form themselves into virtuous men and good citizens, emancipating themselves from the "slavery of pride." Gambling, they asserted, wasted time and ruined men. Intemperance was the worst of vices, because it was particularly likely to make men a dupe of their passions. Numerous writers cautioned against it.[59]

Gentlemen wavered between two competing visions of civilized life. Some men of property supported the movement against expressions of passion. Invoking images of Native Americans, one opponent of dueling condemned it as a "savage passion," one that destroyed families and took talents from the country. Similarly labeling dueling a "barbarous practice," another pointed to its origins in medieval life and contrasted it to the rational life of the free man in America. These gentlemen attempted to detach dueling from honor. Imploring Andrew Jackson to forgo a duel, James Robertson admonished him that "no honor can be attached to the conquered or conqueror." The solution of many writers advancing refinement and of some big men to the excesses of emotion was self-mastery. Gentlemen should manage themselves as they managed others. Their model reified passion, placing men's desires outside of themselves. Like the control men exercised over the natural world, slaves, women, and dependents, men were to control their own natures through their will.[60]

Not all big men accepted the new moral code of self-mastery advanced by authors promoting refinement. Many men continued to adhere to an older code of honor that had its roots in a different philosophy of what made a gentleman. In contrast to notions of self-mastery rooted in the doctrine that men mold their character, the older perspective considered character as the essence of a gentleman, revealed in a set of behaviors that displayed status. Important qualities were the public exercise of will, bravery, indifference to money, and hospitality. Will—the assertion of mastery over dependents—was at the heart of what separated gentlemen from the rest of humanity. Gentlemen asserted and displayed will against dependents; they did not use it to control themselves. In the mental universe of traditional gentlemen, dueling, gambling, and drinking were occasions for demonstrations of courage, wealth, and hospitality. Dueling, for instance, was not a test of skill, but one of bravery between social equals, in which men sought to maintain self-esteem.[61] Dueling followed a set of agreed-upon rules that forced each party to face death. One of the rules required the challenger to select a mode of fighting that allowed the parties to duel on relatively equal terms, rather than to arrange a contest in which the challenger excelled. High-stakes gambling allowed gentlemen to exhibit their wealth publicly. Intemperance in the wealthy suggested indifference to values of industry and was an integral part of hospitality.[62]

The disagreement among the gentry about self-mastery reflected larger regional trends in the South and the North. As a slave-owning class, many wealthy men in Tennessee brought with them values of the older South that were inextricably intertwined in the set of social relations that perpetuated slavery. This ethos emphasized the importance of character and denigrated labor. Other gentlemen embraced more modern values of liberal capitalism that promoted self-discipline and industriousness. Like other western slave states, Tennesseans adopted a quixotic mix of these values. The newer breed of gentry that advocated industriousness and weighed the personal and social cost of activities like dueling, gambling, and drinking undermined an old order still adhered to by many gentlemen. The contest created a public tension that was not resolved in this period.[63]

Although gentlemen disagreed about the role of passion in establishing character, many leading men in both camps advanced the importance of other displays of wealth as a promotion of their own status and as a symbol of civilization. Big men, particularly in the Cumberland area, took on more visible manorial styles while assuming public and private leadership. Many built larger homes, purchased carriages, and dressed in the latest European fashions. General James Winchester of Sumner County and General James Robertson of Davidson County considered themselves to be such community figures. General Winchester erected Cragmont, the largest and most ornate home in the state. By reproducing his wealthy Maryland environment, Winchester saw himself importing civilization to the frontier. Both men held public offices and appointments and both assumed quasi-diplomatic positions, working as private citizens to preserve peace with the Indians.[64]

Corresponding with the new emphasis on refinement, imported luxury items appeared in greater quantities in the 1790s. John Somerville's store in Knoxville in 1798 sold imperial teas, chocolate, Italian sweetmeat, French brandy, Old Jamaica spirits, Holland gin, and Lisbon malags. Ten years later, Thomas Kirkman sold London fashions in Nashville. Some of the towns attracted forms of polite culture at the turn of the century. By the early 1800s, residents of Davidson County enjoyed plays, dances, and shows. A number of schools emphasizing refined culture opened in the Nashville area. These institutes taught French, dancing, Danasög, music, and fencing. Promoting the view that the expansive civilized life allowed for arts and culture, gentlemen patronized libraries, law societies, literary fairs, theaters, and jockey clubs.[65]

Like women who assumed authority and inchoate rights based on their contributions to family life, many ordinary men constructed social life around achievement-oriented values and believed that their accomplishments leveled the social hierarchy. Farmers continued to recognize strength and good fighting skills as the most honorable male accomplishments, with contests frequently occurring on court days and at elections and horse races. Mechanics sought the status of gentlemen based on their contributions rather than on self-mastery. While many middling and poor men did embrace religion, religious doctrines frequently grated against elements of the male culture that supported violence and drinking. The aggressive pride that poorer men took in their skills encouraged them to counter elite displays with a continued insistence on a climate of social egalitarianism. Many ordinary men, along with women, assailed the material displays of the wealthy by reinventing refinement as a commodity available to those who earned the money to purchase it. They countered efforts to distinguish between people by buying refined goods as a material form of social leveling. Middling people also asserted equality in day-to-day encounters. When his hunting companion assumed a superior air and refused to do camp chores, Joseph Bishop, an ordinary young man trying to advance himself, prepared such poor food that the hunter got sick. After that, the pair shared the duties of "waitman."[66]

During the 1790s, passions and class differences, along with conflicts engendered by democratic politics and market competitiveness, created a growing perception of disharmony.[67] A desire for a sense of communal accord amid the increasing diversity of ideas in white society encouraged gentry and ordinary men to widen their understanding of social relations in two important ways—by creating new categories of communal relationships and by expanding their acceptance of diverse ideas. Many men sought to contain social tensions within their class by enlarging their concept of brotherhood to include men with whom they shared common values and might otherwise be in conflict. Institutionalizing this concept through voluntary associations, gentlemen established lodges, middling men organized mechanical societies and farmer societies, and religious men joined churches. These organizations were sites where men established and reinforced moral codes and made deep connections to manage the contentiousness of social, political, and business activities. The most significant of these groups among men of substantial property was the Masons. Prior to 1796, Masons in the Tennessee region belonged to the North Carolina lodges. The first lodge founded in Tennessee was the St. Tamany Lodge in Nashville in 1796. Between that date and 1812, gentlemen established twelve lodges in Tennessee. Nashville had a Masonic Hall by 1809. Valorizing honor, justice, virtue, and true friendship, they proposed a brotherhood that would teach men the moral sensibilities of civilized men. In the Masonic address in 1801, William C. C. Claiborne, then a congressman from Tennessee and later governor of the Mississippi Territory, eulogized the Masons for guaranteeing happiness and harmony by supporting each other in all honorable pursuits. Brothers, he said, sought to live in accord with all and to avoid passions. To this end, the Masons promoted congenial conflict resolution. When General James Robertson's men shot a French trader at Cold Water in 1787, he tried to save himself by calling out, "Liberty man. Free mason." Masons encouraged each other to settle disputes by private arbitration with other Masons, rather than through the legal process. According to Mason Andrew Jackson, courts "create passions that never ought to exist between brothers."[68]

The mechanics in Nashville organized into the Nashville Mechanical Society sometime before February 1801. Like the Masons, their society formed around bonds of brotherly love and mutual benefit. Lauding the free representative government that granted them "the right to command our property and our time agreeable to the dictates of our own reason," they presented themselves as "gentlemen mechanics." Unlike the Masons' claim that their gentility arose from polite behavior, mechanics rooted their social equality in republican principles that made them masters of their property and labor. In a similar vein, the orator for the Farmer's Society on Drake's Creek on the Fourth of July applauded the decency, goodwill, and harmony of tillers. Recognizing that their "plain and homely cheer" invited the contempt of the "dissipated," the speaker rebuked the Masons by noting that farmers did not "ape the gaudy pageantry of a corrupted court" but celebrated liberty.[69]

Men, of course, also joined churches. As did the Masons and mechanics, religious men called each other "brother." They promoted churches as one means of encouraging conciliation among men and of attaching men to civil government. Many men resolved personal and business disputes in church disciplinary proceedings.[70]

At the same time that men advanced voluntary associations with their cohorts as a solution to disharmony, their wider connections persuaded some men to consider that ideological differences might not create social chaos. In the earlier period, citizens viewed divergent political ideas as threats to social harmony. The absence of deference created a culture of contentiousness, both between ordinary and big men and within each of those groups, leading many to suspect plots and schemes among those who did not agree with them. As family, ethnic, and religious groupings and communities developed ties with each other through the need for common defense, communal activities, and political and economic interactions, this overlay of mutual interests encouraged people to consider that differences in ideas might indicate something other than party design or factionalism. When Adam Pick requested additional time to perform his contract with the legislature to cut a road, he acknowledged that he and the commissioner appointed to oversee his work might differ on what was best. Unperturbed, he observed that "the idea of mankind is so various." Noting that human beings had different tastes and dispositions, Richard Green Waterhouse found in this a source of wisdom and industry, as "variety in Mankind is, of all things, the most essential." One religious backcountry resident accepted without rancor the assortment of preachers as a reflection of the diverse desires of humanity:

> I believe it is the nature of man never to be satisfied for we have a great variety of all sects of ministers here, such as old Mr. Clark, called Hell Redemptioners, Anabaptists, Antipedo baptists, Ranting baptists and a great many more that I cannot name at this time; so that they are all good people so that we have no need of no more sorts of ministers here.[71]

After four decades of frontier life, white women and men had distinguished their civilized society from their perceptions of indigenous communities by envisioning and fashioning dense and diverse social and family networks aimed at creating happiness. These connections relied on an emerging cultural logic embracing consent in contractual marriages, informal networks, and voluntary associations and on assumptions privileging merit, the basis for women's claims of authority and inchoate entitlements and ordinary men's assertions of social equality. The transformation of the assumptions and ideas of the inhabitants of the settler society was not restricted to the social sphere. White men and, to a lesser degree, white women molded ideas about consent and merit into compactual government and earned participatory rights as they conflated the discourses of republicanism and civilization.

CHAPTER SEVEN

"The Protection of
Civil Government"

*Governance in the
Euro-American Community*

During the economic crisis precipitated by President Jefferson's embargo, the Davidson County militia companies in February 1809 each sent two deputies to a citizens' meeting at the Davidson County Courthouse in Nashville to advocate for the suspension of state laws on debt collection. Nashville lawyers, merchants, clerks, and students packed the meeting and outvoted the deputies. Outraged at the subversion of the democratic process that allowed each town gentleman as much weight as one-half of a militia company, one irate citizen complained that "the people of the country should never be baffled out of their rights by the rabble of the town."[1]

The town meeting, the militia's actions in sending deputies, and their complaints about the manipulation of the process reveal a much more robust, participatory democracy than historians have suspected in the South in this period. In the North, particularly in the cities, a vibrant civic sphere featured voting, public festivities, and political and labor organizations.[2] Historians of the South portray the southern farmer as considerably less politicized than northern urban dwellers and farmers during the later colonial and antebellum years. Recognizing the critical role that slavery played in the South, most accounts of the southern white farmer contend that the man of small property acceded much of the political realm to slave owners. His reward was mastery of his own domestic sphere, universal white male suffrage, and the potential to hire or obtain his own slaves.[3]

Contrary to accounts of weak political life in the South, ordinary white rural and urban Tennesseans created a more democratic society than the ones they left in the East. Although frontiers do not necessarily nurture a more populist worldview, Tennessee's democratic ideology had many of its roots in the borderland experience.[4] During the first two decades of settlement after 1768, local men dealt with weak, distant governments. Trans-Appalachian white men drew on European and American discourses and on their own experience to formulate their ideas about governance. As was true elsewhere in the colonies, large landowners and ordinary farmers clashed over political arrangements, but poorer men wielded significantly more power on the frontier.

Historians have largely overlooked the importance of militias in borderland areas, but attacks by Native Americans made militia service by Tennesseans critical.[5] Farmers translated the leveling effects and sacrifices involved in militia service, along with governmental requirements that they build roads and pay taxes, into an earned right to participate as equals in political life. Rather than accept that natural law dictated their duties in an organic social order, small landowners and tenants translated transatlantic ideas about a fictive Lockean social compact into a doctrine of popular sovereignty based on an explicit social contract. Gentlemen ultimately acceded but maintained most positions of authority.

After the federal government organized the Tennessee region into the Southwest Territory in 1790 and created a stronger governmental presence in the region, men of consequence sought a rule of law and a republic led by property owners—a class potentially open to all ambitious westering men— that would protect speculators' rights to property and encourage population growth. Operating from a belief in an explicit social contract, men of small property contended that their role in political decision making should not be limited to the election of big men, or any men, to represent them. Articulating a claim for direct majoritarian input on matters of importance to them, they expanded the public sphere by engaging in a remarkable array of activities—public meetings, petitioning, fetes, militia organizing, and electioneering—to advance their views on local, state, national, and international issues directly to government.

White men conflated their new ideas about majoritarian democracy with a second discourse, that of civilization. The European theory of civilization envisioned societal development as progressive—an interpretation founded on inequality, because cultivators and merchants were more advanced than savages. Agreeing with this hierarchy, Tennesseans sought to distinguish their earned entitlements to political participation from potential natural-law claims of Native Americans and slaves. Troubled about the tenets of natural-law doctrine that extended rights to all human beings, they drafted a state constitution in which the social contract was the source of rights, rather than one in which natural rights were reserved to the individual.

The reliance on a theory of compactual government founded on majoritarian democracy had two important ramifications. Because the right to participate in the polis was earned, virtue lacked the importance it held in those states where ideologies were informed by civic humanism with its commitment to the public good. At the same time, the reliance by ordinary men on the social compact theory gave the majority of white men the intellectual space to import gendered and racially based views about a civilized society into their treatment of other constituents. Ironically, the theory that invested ordinary white men with political authority disempowered white women and black Tennesseans.

The great land rush that flooded the eastern and middle Tennessee region during the first two decades after white settlement in 1768 brought Euro-Americans with diverse understandings of government. Throughout much of western Europe, theorists conceived of government as founded on natural law and created by a social compact. Many of these thinkers saw individuals bound together in community by a set of duties, or "offices." In order to perform these obligations and thereby realize the common good, people had rights. Although European philosophers and lawyers differed on the meaning of the social contract, they generally interpreted it as an arrangement that permitted the realization of familial and communal duties imposed by natural law. In England, John Locke theorized that men formed the compact to protect life, liberty, and property.[6]

Natural-law discourse contained numerous tensions and ambiguities. Those who migrated carried with them unresolved questions about the nature of the social contract, the location of sovereignty, the constituency of the polis, the origins of rights, and the meaning of virtue. Most theorists treated the social contract as a legal fiction, but some contended that human will created it and could revoke it. Some thinkers described a deep-seated deference that made it natural to submit to rulers, whereas others posited an ultimate sovereignty in the people, who could rebel against unjust rulers. Natural-law theory left unanswered many questions about the relationship of diverse populations to government—an issue of considerable importance to colonies with male and female wealthy landholders, farmers, indentured servants, Indians, and slaves, representing numerous nationalities. Another ambiguity was the role that human moral authority played in the creation of rights. Although rights were linked to the common good and a moral order of offices, ideas about the possibility of improvement injected the potential for human agency and change into this cognitive world. Finally, trans-Appalachian men contended with ambivalent ideas about virtue—whether God was the only source of virtue or whether human institutions could, or should, reinforce virtue.[7]

European emigrants were often dissenters or people who were dissatisfied with their offices in society. Immigrants to the British North American back-country brought a concern about overreaching authority, a tradition of pro-test, a desire for liberty coupled with strong communal bonds, and a goal of material improvement through industriousness. The Ulster Irish imported a distrust of British monarchical government and an affinity for the radical Whig teachings of Francis Hutcheson of County Down. In Hutcheson's view, "the end of all civil power is the public happiness." A government that did not support this was unjust, and the people who constituted it could abolish it.[8] As one of the largest European immigrant groups in the United States in the eighteenth century, Germans comprised a considerable number of trans-Appalachian residents. German peasants brought a tradition of petitioning and direct action against local nobles who aspired to expand their power, associating liberty with freedom from governmental obligation, rather than a more positive liberty that promoted support for public virtue.[9] The back-country Scotch, mostly Highlanders, came to America for freedom from clan structures and the tyranny of landlords that stifled initiative. The Lowlanders diffused the doctrines of the early and midcentury Scottish Enlightenment, particularly the commonsense school, in the colonies and early republic. Most Scottish philosophers described human beings as sociable. Their moral and political philosophy focused on the common good, the realization of which provided the foundation for natural rights. The commonsense phi-losophers advanced an epistemology ground in the belief that the ordinary man had perceptions that were as valid as those of a philosopher. By applying inductive reasoning to those perceptions, any thinking person thus exercised common sense. Relying on a rich social life for authority, the commonsense outlook empowered the judgments of the community of citizens over estab-lished authorities.[10]

Theorists in the predominantly English culture into which the immigrants arrived were in the process of developing their own ideologies about govern-ment. In the pre-Revolutionary and Revolutionary era, these thinkers drew from multiple traditions. From Lockean and civic humanist theorists, they developed a belief in the social compact as the ideological basis for govern-ment, a penchant for written constitutions, an emphasis on virtue, a critique of arbitrary authority, and a belief in natural rights as a restraint on government. English constitutional and common-law traditions encouraged men to imagine rights arising from long-standing customs and from inherent principles of fairness. During the Revolutionary era, leaders molded these principles into a republicanism that located sovereignty in the people but placed authority in disinterested gentlemen responding to an ethic of civic virtue to represent them, with rights reserved to individuals to restrain governmental abuse.[11] Although most new arrivals spent relatively little time in the coastal areas where agitators promoted the English civic humanist and liberal traditions, they imbibed Revolutionary ideas and rhetoric. In addition, substantial numbers of the backcountry residents were of English ancestry. Many of the Ulster Irish, German, Scotch, and English immigrants who migrated to Tennessee spent a generation or two in the backcountry—primarily in the states of North Carolina and Virginia. In both places, local and distant leading men maintained some control over political affairs. However, backcountry settlers challenged the culture of deference that prevailed in the seaboard regions and insisted on independence. Ordinary backcountry men crossed the Appalachians to the Tennessee frontier to free themselves "from the shackles of the wealthy."[12]

Frontier settings do not necessarily nurture democracy. In Australia, for example, the democratic movement developed slowly over decades. A strong British metropolitan government and soil conditions that favored wealthy sheep herders on large estates rather than small farmers resulted in cautious democratic reforms.[13] Settlement patterns in the Tennessee region initially continued the Carolina and Virginia tradition of a two-tier white society in which gentlemen exercised contested power over men of small property. As elsewhere, many of the big men believed that "the multitude adopt no established principles of conduct" and needed restraint provided by their order.[14] But the leading men and small farmers who migrated west brought with them the unsettled tensions about the location of authority to rule and the relationship between governor and governed. Book inventories show that Tennesseans read from the multiple European traditions from which they originated, including works by David Hume, John Locke, Lord Chesterfield, Thomas Paine, and Voltaire.[15] Because of weak links to distant governments, an environment that supported small family farms, and the danger from Native Americans, the borderland setting created a situation in which, at least for a period of time, ordinary men forced the devolution of power downward. From the earliest white settlement, the most remarkable feature of political culture among white men in the Tennessee region was its robust participatory dynamic. Gentlemen, middling white farmers, mechanics, laborers, and merchants formed local governments, contested control of the militias, and voted. In these meetings and institutions, white men used their beliefs and experiences to rework their notions about governance. In doing so, most common men emphasized an explicit social compact and expanded its theoretical underpinnings, located sovereignty in all free men, and rejected the necessity for virtue enforced by the government.

Central to the transformed idea of political authority was the reinterpretation of the social contract, a process begun by the earliest pioneers. Throughout the period from 1768 through 1790, settlers tended to arrive in family or communal groups. These groups often coalesced around a local prominent man who decided to move, but each free man expected to have a voice in decision making. As travelers, they held "councils of war" to decide whether to proceed and how to deal with Indian threats. Before permanent peace with the Native Americans in 1795, these groups formed stations, in which the core of white men who initiated the migration assumed power. However, this authority relied on agreement by the other men in the station.[16]

Early frontier theories about the formation of government built on the notion that each free man had the authority to participate in the creation of government. During the years before the region became a federal territory in 1790, the transmontane people had weak ties to distant government. Before 1776 most thought they were part of Virginia's western region. When Virginia made no serious effort to provide them with government, local men took matters into their own hands. In 1772 the settlers along the Watagua River in eastern Tennessee met and unanimously agreed to establish a court system using Virginia law. In 1775 the inhabitants instituted a more comprehensive government. Responding to communications from the Continental Congress, the freemen from Watauga formed a committee that established rules for a militia and appointed officers. When a survey showed them to be in North Carolina's boundaries, the inhabitants petitioned North Carolina for protection. North Carolina responded by organizing its western lands into the Washington district, establishing a court there, and granting the district representation in the distant Carolina Assembly.[17]

The Watauga association became a model for other areas of the state. Led by Wataugans, the Cumberland settlers 150 miles to the west drew on the Wataugan agreement and on the revolutionary discourse of the era. Drafted in 1780 and agreed to unanimously, their compact established a court and made provisions for land distribution. Free men older than twenty-one at each of twelve stations elected a judge from their station to form a twelve-man court. The court made all legal decisions. Men older than sixteen were required to perform militia duty and were also entitled to receive land. Land was only available to those who signed the compact. Reviving the compact in 1783, settlers provided that any person who did not subscribe to the compact could not benefit from the courts. When North Carolina attempted to cede its western lands to Congress in 1784, the settlers in the eastern part of the state, fearing interference with land sales, quickly organized their region into the state of Franklin. The inhabitants held conventions in 1784 and 1785, at which they adopted a constitution. The state officials established courts and functioned as a government. When Congress and North Carolina were unable to agree on the terms of the cession, the North Carolina legislature repealed its grant, but many of the citizens of Franklin refused to submit to the North Carolina government until 1788.[18]

The Treaty of Hopewell in 1785 left the farmers south of the French Broad and Holston Rivers and west of the Big Pidgeon River in the eastern part of the region on what the United States, although not local whites, considered Indian land. Falling under no governmental jurisdiction, the inhabitants south of the French Broad followed established local precedent in 1788 by holding a convention and creating their own governing compact. Although stopping short of organizing an independent state, they adopted the constitution and laws of North Carolina, organized districts based on militia companies, provided for an elected legislative body called a general committee, established a legal system, and made plans to apply to North Carolina for protection. Early the next year, some of the leading men from Greene County, much of whose land was within Indian boundaries, met and adopted a voluntary plan for defense and engaged in numerous governmental actions, including the appointment of a council of safety to regulate their affairs. In addition to the larger quasi-governmental efforts to create compacts, communities organized to hire sentinels, and prosperous farmers formed contracts for defense with their tenants. Smaller bands of citizens, calling themselves Regulators, united to apprehend Tories and criminals.[19]

While the unorganized nature of the western region stimulated the formation of local government by consent of householders, poorer men developed their strongest experience of political involvement and sense of public self-worth through their militia experience. The militia was the central political institution in the lives of common men in these early years. Composed of white freeholders, servants, free blacks, and slaves, the militia companies, when mustered above the company level, also brought together Ulster Irish, English, Scotch, Germans, and others. With compulsory service, the militia embodied both elitist and popular elements. In North Carolina before the Revolution, as elsewhere in the colonies, the governor appointed the militia officers. Following the Revolution, however, concessions were made to the soldiers. After 1778 the North Carolina legislature appointed the general and field officers and the men elected the company officers, usually gentlemen, subject to the approval of the Provincial Council. The advent of the American Revolution and attacks by the Cherokees on the white settlements in 1776 increased the importance of the militia for the overmountain people and encouraged the westering people to adopt more democratic militia policies. When John Donelson's party established settlements in the Cumberland area in early 1780, the Cumberland compact allowed men to elect their own officers. An accomplished soldier could rise through the ranks. For example, John Buchannon, one of the early settlers, was known as a good soldier and hunter. He rose to the rank of colonel/major. Henry Bradford came to Tennessee in 1784 to claim his land bounty for his services as a soldier in the Revolutionary War. He became a major in the militia during the Indian wars and later served as revenue collector under presidents Adams and Jefferson.[20]

From the beginning, the ordinary men who composed the militia exerted considerable power in determining strategies and policies. When they disagreed with a decision by an officer, the men simply refused to follow. Poorer men also exercised considerable authority by refusing to serve or by deserting. With every man needed in times of trouble with Indians and Tories, their power flowed from the lack of any practical means on the part of local gentlemen to enforce militia directives. Consequently, gentleman listened and responded to the concerns of the farmers and junior officers. Officers frequently consulted with the enlisted men to determine military policy. When officers disagreed about policy, the views of the men often decided the issue. When men wanted a military response that militia commanders did not order, they composed themselves into voluntary militias and pursued their goals. In these volunteer companies, the men elected their own officers. This propensity toward their own action forced gentlemen to accommodate their desires.[21]

The militia battle philosophy and customary rules about captives and booty reinforced the authority of each soldier on the battlefield. Militia officers understood that the object of the militia was to get men in the field, but they did not expect to control how the men waged war. When the fighting occurred, it was every man for himself, including the officers. The best officers were the best fighters, "leaders rather than commanders." Men also made individual decisions about the disposition of captives. Under the militia norm, any men could claim captives. If other men refused to recognize the claim and killed the prisoner, this breach of the unwritten code generated conflict among the men. After making allowances for men who may have lost property in the campaign, the men divided plunder equally, regardless of rank. Officers or men who took more than their share were court-martialed or sued.[22]

Both leaders and poorer men incorporated the militia into political life, blurring the boundaries between militia service and county court government. During the pre-Territorial period, the courts used the militias for governmental duties. Militias guarded prisoners, and local men held trials at their officer's house. Gentlemen used the militia to mark county lines. The county courts divided the county into districts based on militia companies and called on militia companies to collect taxes. The judges assigned roadwork by militia company. In 1790 the court extended militia duties to require militiamen to serve as slave patrollers. Agreeing with the county judges that militias served governmental functions, farmers used their militia companies to organize politically. Militia units generated petitions on local issues and appointed committees of correspondence to respond to concerns of wider relevance. Powerful local men understood the political importance of the militia. Leading men often based proposals for governmental reform around the militia. William Christian, a prominent man, suggested that political conventions be organized not by voting at the courthouse but by balloting by militia company. This method would reach more people "from whom power flows."[23]

While local men exercised considerable control over their militias, the assumption of oversight by North Carolina in 1776 transformed direct political participation into representative government in areas under North Carolina's control. The long arm of government touched the lives of westering people through the courthouses and the North Carolina legislature. County courthouses functioned as the center of political life in the South, particularly in the tidewater areas of Virginia and the Carolinas. Their importance was diminished in the backcountry regions, but nonetheless they represented the government there. The location of power in judges appointed by a distant government reinforced the ideas of wealthier landowners that the frontier people needed government provided by men of substantial property. At the same time, this control by gentlemen relied on ordinary men to perform roadwork, jury service, and militia duties and to pay taxes. The election of legislative representatives offered middling landowners an opportunity to participate in the control of government and to shape the premises of the political culture. As elsewhere, gentlemen candidates solicited support from other gentlemen based on character and connection, but borderers began to undermine some of the assumptions of the older order. Unlike the practice in the cis-Appalachian region, candidates in North Carolina's western provinces offered themselves for office. Furthermore, the backcountry people, while selecting leading men for office, rejected the culture of deference in political life as they did in the social sphere.[24]

The robust political culture of quasi-governmental associations, militia companies, courthouse authorities, and electioneering, created by leading and ordinary men, built on and reshaped important assumptions about the origins of governmental power and the relationship between the government and its constituents. Many settlers in this period envisioned and lived an explicit—not a tacit—compact theory of government. The articles of association drafted by the inhabitants south of the French Broad in 1788 specifically acknowledged that they entered into a "social compact." Arguing that the United States could not force North Carolina to join the union, one citizen explained that the first principle of government was that all were free by nature and had an equal and unalienable right to enter a compact and erect government for their own happiness. They also had the right to alter or abolish the compact according to its rules. As the transmontane people set up these social compacts, they ground them in the idea that sovereignty resided in the people who created them. The Watauga compact, the Cumberland agreement, and the Greene County association offered benefits to, and made demands on, only those who signed them. The Watauga settlers formed their court in 1772 "by consent of the people." In Cumberland, "the people in general" could call new elections if they disapproved of the actions of their judges.[25]

By limiting its privileges to those who agreed explicitly to accept its responsibilities, the framers advanced a nascent notion of citizenship with two important implications. A man attained rights—land and access to the courts —based not on natural entitlements but on his own conduct in executing the contract and assuming its obligations. Furthermore, the signers of the compact retained the power to define who was included and excluded from their community. Participation in formulating these political agreements shaped the way in which men viewed the philosophical foundations of popular sovereignty. In Europe, natural law—either promulgated by God or perhaps coauthored by humans—embedded the duties and rights of political subjects in morally based relations of authority and deference. John Locke's social compact gave civil rights to constituents for their entry into the political community in exchange for their ceding some natural rights. In the colonies, some theorists relied on the evolving doctrine of popular sovereignty in English Opposition ideology—itself linked to natural law—as they disengaged sovereignty from the English Parliament and relocated it in the people. The trans-Appalachian frontiersmen constructed a different foundation for popular participation—a political quid pro quo reminiscent of the economic exchanges of the marketplace in which a member earned entitlements not merely by joining the compact but by contributing. The freemen in all the compacts committed to militia service. The Cumberland Compact explicitly linked political entitlement to a marketplace exchange. Under the terms of that agreement, the proprietors gave settlers who signed the agreement both land and a political voice in exchange for making homes, serving in the militias, and accepting other duties of the society. Farmers and others who served in the Continental army and in Indian campaigns perceived that their sacrifice and risks created similar entitlements.[26]

The domination by leading men of county courts dependent on middling men to carry out most of their functions had the unintended consequence of strengthening the poorer man's concept of popular sovereignty as a right that he deserved by virtue of his efforts. Gentlemen supposed that poorer men assumed the duties mandated by the courts as part of their station in life, but small farmers did not interpret these duties as part of a natural order. The onerous and unpaid roadwork was unpopular. Similarly, not all inhabitants were eager participants in jury service. Fines for nonattendance at jury duty were common. The most telling dissonance between the big man's premise of inherent duties and the small farmer's reinterpretation of his contribution was in the area of taxation. The county courts changed the tax structure during the 1780s, adding poll taxes to land taxes. In the state of Franklin, only those who paid taxes could vote. Although this change in tax assessment benefited the wealthy financially, it fed the political self-importance of all taxpayers. With every participant shouldering some of the taxation burden and with voting conditioned on the payment of taxes, each freeman saw taxation not as a natural duty but as a payment for which he expected some return from government. Echoing assumptions from the world of trade, ordinary men believed that their militia service, roadwork, jury duty, and payment of taxes created an entitlement to participate in civic life.[27]

In formulating their ideas about an explicit social compact founded on active participation, the inhabitants of the Tennessee region grappled with the question of whether government should demand virtue from those who earned their right to participation. Two factions in the state of Franklin revealed an early split in thinking about the relationship of government to virtue—a division in which neither side advocated the position of many eastern gentlemen that civic virtue was essential to republican government. Shortly after the dissidents established the state in 1784, they called a constitutional convention. A religious contingent, headed by Reverend Samuel Houston, proposed a constitution that imposed religious qualifications to hold office, limited officeholding to the virtuous, and imposed Christian principles on the populace. Associating virtue not with civic humanism but with religion, Houston believed this would "free [the citizens] from prevailing wickedness" and make them moral. Other state constitutions of the era offered an alternative by incorporating more political notions of virtue. Delegates rejected both philosophies and copied almost entirely the constitution of North Carolina that placed little emphasis on virtue but more on property holding as an assurance that elected officials would govern for the common good.[28] By detaching themselves from moral-based and civic humanist traditions that linked the performance of public duties with virtue, the leading men advanced the privatization of virtue.

The advent of the territorial period in 1790 brought tremendous changes to the organization of government. Within a year after North Carolina ceded its western lands to the United States in 1789, Congress organized the region into the Territory South of the River Ohio. George Washington appointed William Blount, the North Carolina speculator with extensive lands in the territory, as governor, and Daniel Smith, a surveyor in the Cumberland region who had also acquired considerable holdings in the area, as secretary of the territory. By 1794 the United States gave voters input into the appointment of a territorial council. With statehood in 1796, Tennessee voters elected their own state and local governmental officials and no longer looked to the state house in New Bern or to Philadelphia for provincial government.[29]

Speculators used the territorial period to attempt to solidify their control of the power structure. Many of the large landowners—including John Sevier, Stockley Donelson, James Winchester, James Robertson, and William Cocke —gained political posts in the new government. Station leaders now became officials in the county or state government. At the constitutional convention of 1796, speculators led by Blount clashed with proponents of popular sovereignty. Delegates responsive to the concerns of middling men tried unsuccessfully to limit the legislature to one house and, when that failed, to restrict the powers of the senate. Representatives favoring popular participation in government did succeed in expanding the franchise to all free men older than twenty-one.[30]

Most free men defined the role of government to be the promotion of happiness and prosperity. Men of consequence believed that order provided the foundation necessary to realize these goals. By the mid-1790s large speculators in the territorial government and later the state looked to population growth to spur prosperity. Believing that compliance with the treaties and laws would bring settlers and would protect their landholdings, they worked to persuade farmers and townspeople of the importance of the rule of law. Like poorer men, men of influence located the authority of government in a social compact of all men. Because they considered that people were more prone to vice than virtue, leading men theorized that the originators of the social compact assigned the powers of government to the better classes of the community. Jeffersonians all, most leading men nonetheless defined a republicanism that saw democracy, or mobocracy, as the binary opposite of monarchy. Andrew Jackson presided over a celebration among the gentlemen of Nashville on the Fourth of July in 1805 at which the fifteenth toast was to "the federal republic of America, destruction to aristocratic oppression and democratic misrule."[31]

Men of small property responded with considerable heat to the efforts of leading men to impose the rule of law from positions of authority. Their solution was not less government, as some historians have contended, but a greater share of participation in government.[32] Their belief in an explicit social contract in which all contributors had a voice persuaded them to act in spite of the antipathy to government in their European intellectual traditions. They challenged the onus that big men cast on democracy by insisting on the equality and dignity of the ordinary white farmer or worker. In December 1791 Judge David Campbell charged a grand jury that public preservation relied on the different "ranks of men." Citizens issued a correction a few months later, pointing out that "classes of citizens" would be more congenial language to "the American creed, THE RIGHTS OF MAN." As this modification articulated, Tennesseans made distinctions, but at least in the political arena, most did not intend that such distinctions were hierarchical. On the same Fourth of July in which Nashville gentlemen condemned democratic misrule, militiamen at the Robertson County fete identified anarchy, not democracy, as the dialectical opposite of monarchy.[33]

As big men filled most elective seats and assumed the reigns of state government, farmers and town residents contested the theory of representative government that limited citizen participation to casting a vote. Middling white men envisioned and fashioned a system of public meetings, petitioning, fetes, and militia activities in which the ordinary citizen not only elected candidates but also formulated and voiced opinions about local, state, national, and international affairs. After the United States organized the region under its dominion, citizens gathered regularly to discuss issues of government, to initiate legislation, to address their government directly, and to instruct their representatives in the state and federal governments. The *Carthage Gazette* in 1809 reported that these meetings were "very common." In the typical citizens' meeting, local inhabitants met at the courthouse, a tavern, or a militia officer's farm, elected a chair and secretary, and debated and passed resolutions on matters of public interest. The group often appointed a delegate to present the resolutions directly to the appropriate government body, rather than to their elected representatives. Participants at these community meetings covered a wide range of concerns, not limited to state legislative actions. Knoxville citizens met at Mrs. Chisholm's tavern to consider the constitutionality of the Alien and Sedition Acts. In a meeting in Carthage, the assembled men nominated presidential electors and offered a premium for a mechanic who made knives and forks. Nashville citizens in 1809 convened to condemn Europe's conduct.[34]

In addition to community meetings, ordinary inhabitants engaged in widespread petitioning to assert their opinions and grievances and to spur change. The tradition extended back to the earliest settlements, when pioneers solicited additional militia forces, new counties, land preemptions, and land offices from local leading men, North Carolina, the state of Franklin, and the territorial government.[35] The later years are the more extensively documented period. During the twelve-year period from 1799 through 1810, more than 18,000 signatures appeared on more than 300 petitions to the legislature.[36] Approximately one-half of the men over the age of sixteen who remained in the state through three legislative cycles—about five years—signed a petition.[37] The numbers are particularly impressive, because many of the petitioners stated that they were inhabitants living far from the courthouse. These documents represent a rare glimpse into the thoughts of the rural residents. The breadth of issues is remarkable. Citizens requested county divisions, more lenient debtor laws, changes in the militia law, public warehouses, and roads. They filed grievances on land laws, jury duty, obstructions to river navigation, and election procedures. Citizens also petitioned their county courts for relief in more local matters, such as road construction and milldams. Addressing themselves directly to the legislature or the court, these petitioners were not instructing their representatives. They reflected the ordinary man's belief that he had the right to speak directly to his government.[38]

Public meetings and petitioning represented only part of the expansive civic sphere. Like the North and larger cities in the coastal South, rural and town citizens created a popular political culture centered on festive celebrations.[39] The most prominent was Independence Day, but Tennesseans celebrated Jefferson's election, Aaron Burr's visits, St. Patrick's Day, and other occasions. The absence of a local newspaper until late in 1791 obscures the occurrence of earlier festivities. Although the first locally published report of an Independence Day fete appeared in the *Knoxville Gazette* of 1793, the account noted that residents honored the day "with the usual demonstrations of joy," suggesting that the celebration of the Fourth of July was a long-standing custom. In many respects, the observances paralleled those in the East. Hundreds of people commonly turned out to enjoy an array of festivities. As in other areas of the country, the newspapers published accounts of the celebrations and often reprinted the toasts, expanding the public sphere reached by these events.[40]

There were some significant differences between the fetes in Tennessee and those recorded elsewhere—variations that reflected the ideological differences between leading and ordinary men and the value placed on popular participation. Throughout the country, the ceremonies created a space in which participants constructed versions of national unity while advancing partisan and local input on national issues. Scholars have focused most of their attention on the contests between Federalists and Democratic-Republicans. In Tennessee, where the constituency was overwhelmingly Jeffersonian, the first men, farmers, and mechanics used the occasion to contest publicly their ideological and cultural differences with each other. For the festivities of the 1790s and early 1800s, different groups of local citizens planned the celebrations. Governmental officials organized some of the festivities, particularly in Knoxville, the capital. In the larger towns, local leading men coordinated events. In Nashville during the early 1800s, the mechanics society also sponsored its own ceremonies. In more rural areas, militia officers, the Farmer's Society, and ordinary citizens organized the fetes.[41]

Throughout the United States, committees scripted the toasts in advance in response to the custom that anyone who disagreed with a toast should not join. Because organizers prepared the toasts, their offerings reveal much about the political thinking of these hosts. An examination of the toasts given at Tennessee events highlights the differences in their orientations. Toasts organized by political leaders celebrated particular governmental officials by name, presented international concerns, urged obedience to the government, and pressed the federal government on local issues. Using the occasion to display and reinforce their status and power, leading men in the festivities that they orchestrated opposed both aristocracy and democracy. Mechanics were the most festive group, coupling their toasts with liberty poles and parades. They were more likely to celebrate ordinary soldiers, mechanics, and farmers. Although big men headed the militias, militia toasts tended to be different from other affairs run by the leading men, probably because ordinary soldiers elected many of their officers and constituted much of the audience. Militia toasts celebrated republicanism and opposed aristocracy. While they abhorred anarchy, they did not denigrate democracy.[42]

Celebrations also reveal the value Tennesseans placed on political expression by ordinary men. While the organizers of Tennessee festivities wrote most of the toasts, after 1795 guests—often leading men but occasionally ordinary citizens—offered volunteer toasts following the prepared toasts, a deviation from the national custom. At the Aaron Burr dinners, volunteers made all the toasts. In contrast to the practice elsewhere, they began with local issues. In another concession to popular participation, newspaper accounts sometimes recorded the number of cheers following each toast. Although hosts ordered the toasts to reflect their sense of priorities, the offerings engendering the most cheers rarely followed the sequence of the toasts and represented public sentiment on matters of concern to the celebrants.[43]

Though meetings, petitions, and fetes involved citizens in the public sphere, the militia remained an important institution in expressing a popular voice, even after peace in 1795. The state legislature made all free men, regardless of race, and all indentured male servants between the ages of eighteen and forty-five subject to military duty, with a few exceptions. In a number of locations, citizens, often the leading men, formed volunteer units. The Tennessee Constitution of 1796 continued the practice of permitting the men to elect their captain, subalterns, noncommissioned officers, and field officers. Disputed militia elections were common, especially from 1796 to 1802, suggesting that the outcome was important to the men. Because almost every free man between the ages of eighteen and forty-five met on the militia grounds, the militia became one of the major organizing forces behind a great number of the petitions that were filed during the early years of statehood. The link between militias and the political sphere remained so strong that one citizen in 1809 proposed that militia delegates nominate candidates for public office.[44]

Activists who sought to expand political participation to give ordinary men a more direct voice on the issues did not overlook the electoral system. Cultivators, mechanics, and laborers brought the popular emphasis on majoritarian democracy into electioneering to challenge the efforts of first men to maintain a representative republic managed by large property owners. At times, some leading men joined them. Although only partially successful, they worked to expand the number of offices and issues subject to popular vote, to liberalize the franchise, and to improve the responsiveness of candidates to their concerns. The passion for majoritarian rule led to efforts to increase the range of positions filled and issues decided by voters. In 1790 the freemen of Washington County elected wardens for the poor. In 1797 the people south of the French Broad chose a delegate to represent their interests to the Cherokee nation. Citizens on numerous occasions petitioned the legislature to permit them to decide the location of contested county seats by suffrage. In 1810 the public selected the board of a manufacturing company. Many ineligible voters insisted on casting ballots, creating disputed elections. Although some ballots were simply efforts at fraud, many of the contests concerned restrictions on voting that Tennesseans disliked, such as the exclusion of young men required to do militia duty and residency requirements. Exhibiting considerable leniency in the matter of voting, local and state officials nearly always resolved these challenges in favor of accepting the ballots.[45]

Political officeholders were caught in the sea changes as ordinary men worked to ensure that their representatives advanced more than the interests of the leading men. Historians have identified a wider change in northern political culture from older notions of deference to emerging values of open campaigning for voters, but the shift in Tennessee's political environment was more complex. As the region became a territory in 1790, voters altered the culture of selecting political candidates from among the big men based on family or character. While some candidates ran on these grounds, a newer group of politicians began to advocate for their election based on merit. Merit, for these men, did not have the modern definition of appropriate job skills. Rather, a man advanced a claim of merit by establishing his prior service and proper political orientation, traits based on his contributions and loyalty. Many big men were uneasy about these changes, fearing that they promoted dissension or "party spirit." Others viewed the necessity of parading their qualifications to the public as degrading to their status as civilized gentlemen. For these men, accustomed to holding office as a birthright, this kind of self-promotion smacked of savagery. Samuel Spencer, soliciting John Sevier's support for his candidacy in 1790, illustrates the trend and also some of the anxiety associated with it. After elaborating on his merits as a judge and his support for the American Revolution, Spencer closed by stating he did not want to resemble the Indian warrior, publicly recounting his exploits.[46]

Other gentlemen disagreed. A newer breed of leading men saw in the rivalry of electioneering a promotion of republicanism. William Claiborne, a young man on the rise in 1797, heralded election contests for their advancement of virtue and patriotism. By offering honors to candidates possessing these traits, "a spirit of emulation seems to pervade all ranks of people." By the mid-1790s most men recognized merit as the basis for officeholding. At the Independence Day toasts in Knoxville in 1796 organized by the big men in government, the men assembled offered a toast to "the citizens of Tennessee —may they reward every man agreeably to his merit."[47]

Although the ordinary voter preferred achievements and public service to birth in a candidate, these traits did not ensure that the representative understood or would carry out the wishes of the farmer or town dweller. By the turn of the century, insistence by rural and urban residents to be heard on the topics of the day persuaded candidates touting merit to add a new item to their repertoire—they campaigned on the issues. When Sampson Williams offered himself publicly for the state senate, he disdained to make promises and instead proffered his character. Nonetheless, he did state he favored reform of the judiciary. A more aggressive opponent defeated him. Responding to pressure from citizens dissatisfied with the court system, Thomas Harris successfully campaigned against Williams by taking a strong position on court reform, outlining the changes he embraced to improve the system. Writing in the same vein, one voter in another state election applauded Thomas Hart Benton and several other candidates who stated their views on matters of public interest, while disparaging a candidate who disclosed no plans to remedy problems.[48]

Ordinary men linked their ideas about majoritarian democracy to social compact theory, encouraging them to reconstitute their understanding of rights by moving away from doctrines about universal and individual natural rights toward constitutional public rights that supported a responsive government. Heirs to several European intellectual traditions as well as American Revolutionary thought, Tennesseans had available many sources for notions about rights. The strongest tradition was a natural-law philosophy that informed a good deal of Scottish Enlightenment and Lockean theory, although in different ways. Whereas the Scottish imagined rights as a vehicle for realizing one's traditional duties in order to enhance the public good,

Locke formulated entitlements available to all people that acted as a restraint on government.[49] The legacy of the explicit social contract from the pioneer period left many Tennesseans ambivalent about a natural-law philosophy rooted in traditional social arrangements that derived rights from duties, that imputed rights extended to all people, or that framed rights in terms of individuals. Their performance of duties was not an effort to fulfill a divine or human mandate embedded in natural law but was a quid pro quo action that created an entitlement to participatory, not universal, rights.

As Tennesseans embraced the idea of constituent-earned rights in a political compact, their ideas about Native Americans, slaves, and civilization further challenged a natural-rights philosophy that extended rights to all human beings. With the growing pressure to accept the rule of federal law, most citizens increasingly began to distinguish their civilized nation from that of the indigenous peoples. This discrimination informed their crafting of political theory as well as of diplomatic constructions. Part of their discomfort originated in the rejection of the "natural" way of life ascribed to "savages" in favor of that of "civilized" people who enjoy rights as part of familial and public life. One writer who made the comparison linked rights to civil government, not nature:

> The savage, disengaged from the chase, or war, leads a life of stupid insensibility. There can scarcely be said to be any progress, or succession of events, in his existence. 'Tis one perpetual *now*. The civilized man lives in himself, in his children, in the public, and as he participates in the labors, he enjoys the happiness of his country and of mankind. The savage feels no anxiety for the future welfare of his family. . . . [The civilized man] feels the protection of civil government, and he cheerfully contributes to its support, protected in his acquisitions by law, he contemplates the transmission of his name, his inheritance, his rights and privileges, to his posterity, with unspeakable pleasure.[50]

In this view, civilized government, not natural law, was the source of rights and those rights, rather than being universal, extended only to the constituents of the polis. Such government allowed a happier future in contrast to the savage life oriented entirely in the present.

For different reasons, Tennesseans also linked slavery and civilization to conclude that slaves did not have natural rights. By the late 1790s Tennesseans faced pressure from abolitionists, who linked emancipation to natural-rights theory, but many Tennesseans accepted slavery because they viewed it as integral to prosperity, one of the goals of civilization. In 1797 John Steele of

North Carolina, a former commissioner for the southern Indians and a friend of William Blount, supported a petition to Congress concerning the upcoming treaty with the Cherokees. A memorandum outlining his private thoughts expressed the feelings of many westering people on the extension of rights to Indians and slaves and on the source of rights:

> [Treaty commissioners] should not entertain sublimated notions of Indian Rights, and virtues, nor unreasonable prepossessions [against] the claims of the white people. Indian and negro rights are fine things to talk about in a quaker meeting, or in the house of Reprs. but when accurately analyzed they will be found to be theoretic and visionary. Their rights have no other foundation than the humanity and kindness of government and these are sufficient to protect them [against] fraud and violence.[51]

In Steele's analysis, Indians and black Americans have no natural rights, only those that the government may chose to extend to them.

The belief that rights originated in the social compact rather than that all human beings had natural rights informed the framing of the state declaration of rights by the constitutional convention delegates in 1796. Judge Joseph Anderson, a former Pennsylvanian, led the committee that drafted the declaration. The committee copied many of the provisions for rights from the Pennsylvania Constitution. In spite of this borrowing, the Tennessee committee members rejected the first section of the Pennsylvania declaration of rights that recognized that "all men are born equally free and independent, and have certain inherent and indefeasible rights." Relying instead on the authority that "all free governments are founded on [the people's] authority," the Tennessee declaration in Article XI followed with a list of rights, implying that these rights sprang from the popular contract. The framers articulated only one exception. They recognized "the natural and indefeasible right to worship Almighty God" according to conscience—the only instance in which they referred to natural rights.[52]

Because the convention delegates conceived of the social contract as the source of rights, they fashioned these rights primarily as public in nature, designed to ensure good government, rather than as natural rights reserved to individuals.[53] Like republicans elsewhere, Tennesseans were ambivalent about governmental authority. Tennessee's delegates were anxious about overreaching by government, but most believed that government served a positive role in promoting happiness, advancing prosperity, and protecting property. The framers intended that the political principles outlined in Article XI of the constitution improve the operation of government and discourage corruption. Eight of the thirty-two sections in Article XI's Declaration of Rights contained at least some clauses that enumerated public rights designed to strengthen government, many borrowed from Pennsylvania's constitution. For example, they copied Pennsylvania's provision protecting the right of the public to open courts—a right that subjected the judiciary to widespread scrutiny in order to ensure its honest and effective operation. Parts of twenty-four sections enumerated governmental limitations adopted to define good government, not to enshrine natural rights. For instance, again borrowing from Pennsylvania's constitution, the framers prohibited the governmental abuse of double jeopardy—a provision that avoided the misuse of prosecutorial powers by vengeful citizens. This section, like many, also protected the accused but was framed as a restraint on a contractual government, not the retention of a natural right of the accused.[54] In addition to the rights supporting good government, Tennessee's delegates added another category—communal rights to property. They crafted unique clauses preserving the common right to navigation of the Mississippi River and claiming the right of soil for the state. To protect the inhabitants south of the French Broad River on Cherokee land, they added a clause granting them preemption rights to their lands.[55]

While the logic of the social contract theory led to a written state constitution, both gentlemen and ordinary men were uneasy about completely committing their notion of rights to a written document subject to governmental control. Heirs to a revolutionary tradition that feared arbitrary government, most men were uneasy about political overreaching. Large-scale speculators and creditors feared majoritarian tampering with what they saw as their property rights. This was an old concern, articulated by William Blount in 1787 when he equated republican government with tyranny. He contended that property was not safe under that form of government. Anxious about the control that big men maintained over much of the government, ordinary men worried that courts or legislators would not respect their inchoate sense of customary rights, equity, and expectations attached to malleable concepts like "justice" and "republicanism."[56]

Caution about relying on the government to safeguard rights produced a unique provision—an unenumerated rights clause—that recognized a separate sphere outside the government as the repository for unwritten rights. Amendment IX to the federal constitution proclaimed that the enumeration of specific rights in the Constitution should not be construed to deny others retained by the people. No state constitution before Tennessee's contained such a reservation. Tennessee's provision declared:

And to guard against transgressions of the high powers which we have delegated, we declare that everything in the bill of rights contained, *and every other right not hereby delegated*, is excepted out of the general powers of government, and shall forever remain inviolate.[57]

Although legal commentators view these kinds of clauses as protection for individual rights, the reference to undelegated rights preserved both public and individual rights.[58] The thrust of the clause is to place unnamed rights that would ensure a free government in a private protected sphere outside of government. The ambiguity of the clause made it appealing to first men and poorer farmers. While future petitioners did not refer to this clause by number, they argued, as constitutional or inchoate rights, entitlements not listed in the constitution in their legislative memorials. For example, although he could rely on no specific constitutional protection, John Wallace, a debtor in prison who had a duty to support his family, requested the assembly to provide relief "consistent with the Constitution of this state, and consistent with the principles of a republican government." The heart of his appeal was not a plea to recognize his individual right to freedom but was a request to permit him to support his family, a public responsibility whose observance was necessary for republican government to function. Article X preserved these broader principles.[59]

The reliance on a constitutional theory of government based on covenantal rights and majoritarian rule carried two important implications—the doctrine undercut the necessity for civic virtue, and it empowered the majority of voters to limit the participation of other constituents. As white men reformulated their principles of government, most believed that consenting free men who formed the social compact earned its benefits by assuming its obligations. As in the frontier period, they found independent assurances of virtue to be unnecessary. Many white women and some men responded to these beliefs by proffering the need for governmental regulation of conduct. Women had long been concerned with male behavior that disrupted family and communal life and sought to regulate gambling, violence, and drinking through social sanctions. Some extended their efforts to the political sphere by casting this male behavior as a public problem. Religious women and men accomplished this by raising questions about virtue. Successors to those advocates of a theocratic constitution for the state of Franklin, these thinkers believed that the public sphere should be used to enforce standards of moral conduct. They linked peace, good order, and happiness with the suppression of vice and immorality. Their legislative targets were gambling, dueling, Sabbath breaking, and drinking. According to its opponents, gambling undermined industriousness and promoted idleness. Dueling cost families their provider and the country loyal citizens. Drinking encouraged crime and created an expense for taxpayers. These activists proposed legislation to restrict these vices and passed laws regulating gambling, dueling, and the observance of the Sabbath. Their attempts to regulate drinking were not successful.[60]

Although almost all the public figures associated with the morality movement were men, women likely worked off the public stage to promote these efforts.[61] Katherine Sevier may have been one of these women. Her husband, John Sevier, opposed Reverend Houston's efforts at the Franklin convention to enact a theological constitution. Sevier questioned importing religious sentiments into law. Although his journal entries are incomplete, none of his Sunday entries from the beginning of his journal in May 1790 until February 9, 1794, reflect that he attended church. His wife did attend. He began going with her on February 9, 1794, and went occasionally after that. The next year, Sevier, then a member of the Legislative Council that governed the Southwest Territory, introduced the first antigambling bill at the council to bar recovery for money won at horse racing. In one notable instance, women more openly entered the public domain. In 1809 152 citizens of Maury County, home to several vibrant church communities, submitted the first printed petition to the state legislature—a request that the assembly regulate drinking. The fact that the document was printed suggests that it was part of an organized movement to gather signatures. The most striking thing about the petition is that a large number of signers used their initials rather than their first names. In none of the other 296 extant petitions to the legislature from 1799 through 1810 was this practice followed. Virtually all of the 16,000 subscribers to those petitions were men. Quite likely, the signers of the 1809 petition using their initials were women, probably churchwomen.[62]

In addition to concerns about virtue, leading and ordinary men relying on a theory of compactual government faced the question of whom they should include as participants in the political covenant. White men saw America's civil and religious liberties benefiting all people "even from the bright european to the tawny Americans and from the swarthy Asiasic to the black African." This sanguine view did not address the questions about the relationship between the beneficiaries and their government. With the demise of monarchical rule and the adoption of state and federal republican constitutions, white men in the post-Revolutionary period grappled with a new concept—citizenship. On the national level, as monarchy yielded to republicanism, theorists transformed the station described by Scottish natural-law thinkers as "subject" into that of consent-based citizen. The term "citizen" came into growing use in Tennessee in the 1790s but was not defined. The state constitution used the term sporadically and apparently gave it no more meaning than "freeman." The constitution did not use it at all in setting out civil voting rights. Men signing petitions to the legislature commonly referred to themselves as "inhabitants." Claiming a stronger identity with their government, denizens of towns were more likely than rural inhabitants to refer to themselves as citizens in the earlier period. After 1800, country subscribers increasingly identified as citizens.[63] Whether they called themselves citizens or inhabitants, white men in Tennessee perceived their connection with government to be an interconnected package of rights and duties with voting being only one, and not the most critical, facet. The most important of the privileges and obligations for the ordinary man were militia service, jury duty and right to a jury trial, the right to take an oath and use the courts, petitioning and instructing representatives, the payment of taxes, roadwork, and voting and officeholding in civil elections.

Not all people in Tennessee had the full bundle of rights and duties extended to most free white inhabitants older than twenty-one. The early shift in cultural logic from natural law with rights in all people to earned rights under a social compact created intellectual space to import communal views about civilization, with its doctrines about gender and race, directly into political theory. The men who envisioned themselves as the makers of the compact believed that they had the right to determine how it functioned. These men viewed citizenship as a very malleable concept, assigning varying rights and obligations to different sectors of the population, although men at times differed on how to handle conflicting premises implicit in notions of rights, merit, and civilization. Because militia service was central to their reformulation of the source of authority, men viewed those who served as the core of the constituency of government. For many men, this group was free men of militia age or older. They assigned the benefits and burdens of citizenship largely from this prospective. Consequently, propertied adult white men enjoyed all the privileges and assumed the duties of citizenship. They served in the militia and on juries, accessed the courts freely, petitioned, voted, and held office, although some men of smaller property were ineligible to hold office. Younger white men could not vote for governmental offices, although this was a subject of controversy. In a close vote of 28 to 25, the constitutional convention delegates denied the right to vote in political elections to free men between the ages of sixteen and twenty-one who were required to serve in the militia. These young men were eligible to vote for militia officers.[64]

In accordance with the view that women were born not to preside over the senate but to use their virtue to advance civilization, Tennessee men barred white women from significant privileges of citizenship. Women's participation in building communities offered a challenge to the logic of their exclusion from political life. At the constitutional convention in 1796, two delegates from frontier Hawkins County, Thomas Henderson and James Berry, moved to reword the enfranchisement provisions to include women, but their motion was defeated. Women did participate in other ways in political life. Women paid taxes and could and did sue. Women did not serve as jurors but could take oaths. In 1806 the state appointed its first woman officer. Upon the death of her husband, the state printer George Roulstone, Elizabeth Roulstone defeated George Wilson by a vote of 28–7 in the state senate to win an appointment as state printer.[65]

The ways in which white men ascribed and refused to assign the entitlements and obligations of citizens to free blacks illustrate an ambivalence that suggests that whites were still in the process of reconciling views about rights accruing from the social compact with inherent natural rights. Advocates for black rights relied on natural law, human law, and merit-based conduct in assigning rights. When Nenian Edwards inserted an advertisement in the *Tennessee Gazette* in an effort to capture the slave traders who kidnapped Betty Lucusts's free black daughter, he deplored the abduction as "contrary to natural right, and in violation of every principle of law." Free blacks could not take oaths against white men, but they could use the courts—an entitlement that accrued by virtue of their free status rather than their participation in the polity. When James Gowan sued Isaac Baker for assault, battery, and false imprisonment for beating and detaining him for fifteen days, Baker countered by arguing that Gowan, a black man, could not maintain a suit. The Superior Court allowed the suit. After a mistrial, a second jury found for Gowan, "saying that the plaintiff is a free man." Interestingly, it awarded him six and a quarter cents plus his costs. The verdict, the amount of a "free" poll tax in contrast to a "black" poll tax, was undoubtedly symbolic.[66]

Other whites accorded free blacks political rights not because they considered the rights inherent, but because free blacks earned them. Probably because free black men served in the militias, the Tennessee Constitution granted them the right to vote.[67] The occasions at which the legislature granted free men of color the right to prove accounts are also instructive. Tennessee followed North Carolina law in refusing to allow any black person to take an oath against a white person. Responding to a petition signed by 148 men, many of them prominent citizens, the legislature in 1803 granted Gaspar Lott the right to prove his accounts by oath. The assembly agreed that a restriction on oath taking would discourage black business people from conducting their affairs honestly and would place Lott in a position to be cheated. The legislature's efforts to promote ethical business practices may have reflected a regard for the public good. However, its concern that Lott not be cheated suggests that it intended to reward merit. After rejection in 1804, the legislature the next year granted Moses Brown all the privileges of other citizens. Although there was some doubt about the degree of his blood, the legislature found him to be an honest and respectable citizen. As with Lott, Brown's efforts and character earned him his rights.[68]

During the period in which white men began to identify as citizens rather than as inhabitants, they increasingly used their rights as a majority to denigrate the position of free blacks in the social compact. The Tennessee Assembly in 1796 authorized a higher county tax for a few counties at twelve and a half cents on "free male citizens" and at twenty-five cents on "black polls," leaving ambiguous the taxation of free black men and women. By 1802 Nashville, Knoxville, and several counties clarified that "black" polls paid twice the tax of "white" polls, thus assigning free blacks the same classification as slaves. At the same time, state law restricted free black movement and trading. The General Assembly in 1804 exempted from roadwork "any free white person sending three slaves, or three other persons," again making racial distinctions that favored white men. In 1806 state law required free blacks to register. Between 1805 and 1810, the legislature denied all petitions by free blacks seeking the right to sue on their accounts. Slaves, of course, were outside the body politic.[69] Pursuing the logic of their social compact theory, a belief in their advanced civilized society, and their ideas about gender and race, white men were on the road to a *Herrenvolk* democracy.

In forming social and political relations, white Tennesseans recast European ideas about civilization to emphasize themes of happiness, human agency, consent, and merit-based rewards, while they distinguished their society from that of their savage neighbors and of their black members. In doing so, leading and middling men and women at times advanced conflicting ideas and cultural logic about how to constitute sociability and government. These intellectual stresses intensified as white men and women linked their views about civilization to their understanding of economic advancement, prosperity, and property.

CHAPTER EIGHT

"The Best Security
of Rising Greatness"
Economic Relations in the
Euro-American Community

When John Sevier delivered the inaugural address as the first governor of the new state of Tennessee in 1796, he lauded the government in Tennessee "so wisely calculated to secure the liberty and advance the happiness and prosperity of our fellow citizens." During that year, Sevier participated in Tennessee's prosperity by selling land and a lead mine, harvesting and marketing crops, and purchasing a man, Will. Sevier's wealth was tied intimately to his ability to assert property rights to the land, its products, and other human beings. Shortly after offering the sermon at George Washington's funeral memorial in Nashville, the Reverend A. Boyd traveled through eastern Tennessee. Lauding the natural beauty of a valley near Roaring River, Boyd immediately imagined an even more desirable scene as the wilderness gave way to private ownership and improvement. "The soil is rich, and the water good," he wrote, "so that very soon plantations will there abound. Already the wilderness begins, in that way, to blossom, and to assume the appearance of industry and wealth."[1]

Historians have produced few studies on how westering slaveholders and ordinary farmers conceived of the economy, prosperity, or property rights. Studying primarily northern farmers, historians of the early republic disagree about whether farmers pursued economic goals in order to advance family values or to realize financial reward. In contrast to their northern rural counterparts, scholars of the South largely concur that farmers participated eagerly in market production for profit—a goal made more attainable by slavery. These studies fail to explore the constellation of beliefs that persuaded white southerners to pursue happiness and prosperity, rather than other values, in their economic activities.[2]

Like John Sevier and Reverend Boyd, most white men and women conjoined republicanism and civilization with happiness and prosperity. Rejecting what they saw as the insecure life of their hunting Indian neighbors, Tennesseans envisioned a civilized economy but differed from European commercial models because they paired agriculture with commerce rather than exalting commerce as the most advanced stage of development. Although most white men and women linked prosperity to the free-market economy, some producers held religious views about a moral economy, conducting business based on ethical, not market, standards. In order to achieve prosperity, many citizens as well as leading men like John Sevier favored considerable governmental involvement in matters that spurred economic development.

One of government's most significant tasks was to structure a doctrine of property rights. Like most white Americans and western Europeans, Tennesseans believed that the right to private property encouraged individual enterprise and was key to the creation of wealth in a civilized society. In order to realize Reverend Boyd's vision, wealthy, middling, and poorer whites struggled with conflicting ideas about how to compose and distribute property interests in the environment and in and to human beings. Men and women disputed how to assign ownership of lands, which natural resources were communal, whether human beings were property, and whether individuals should control substantial wealth.

Detaching landownership from Native Americans raised the question of whether the authority to assign the right to land resided in individuals or the government. Like landless settlers in other parts of the world, occupant farmers in Tennessee and other American states forced the government to establish a more coherent system for land distribution that recognized occupant rights.[3] In contrast to European theorists, the westering people considered all navigable waters to be public highways to which farmers, fishers, and millowners could obtain limited usage privileges if they could establish a significant public benefit to their appropriation of the rivers.

The frontier people struggled with the most difficult renditions of the definition of property when some, like John Sevier, characterized human beings as enslaved property. During the frontier period, white families and slaves created sponsorship ties, but slaves became vital to the cash-poor economy, not only for their labor but also for the flexibility they offered as cash substitutes, collateral on loans and bonds, and temporary hires. Most opponents of slavery relied on religious, not political objections—arguments that failed to persuade men and women pursuing material gain. Growing prosperity also forced citizens to contend with the inequalities inherent in the aggregation of property by some speculators and merchants. Operating from a labor theory of value, middling men objected to "drones" who did not work and also feared the uneven impact that wealth had on the common person's access to the market and to the political system. The chaotic state of land titles created alliances across class lines, preventing men of small property from coalescing permanently against large speculators.

Enlightenment philosophers, Scottish thinkers, court proponents of civic humanism in England, and Lockean theorists created European ideologies that promoted commercialism and property rights. By the mid-eighteenth century, Adam Smith was lecturing in Scotland on the four progressive stages of society—hunting, pasturage, farming, and commerce. Philosophers in this tradition believed in the importance of populating the earth as part of economic advancement. Thinkers in England also promoted the liberating features of a commercial society and the significance of private property.[4]

The early Appalachian land hunters subscribed in large part to the European discourse that promoted a civil society bound by economic connections that laid the material foundation for a rich civilization. John Sevier's library included Adam Smith's *Wealth of Nations* and he was not the only Tennessean to read Smith. Hume and Locke were also popular. Tennesseans modified the Scottish understanding of civilization by combining Smith's third and fourth stages to envision a commercial society reliant primarily on agriculture. Most Tennesseans extolled the virtues of agriculture, commerce, and manufacturing in creating prosperity and happiness. The publisher of the *Tennessee Gazette* aptly captured the interrelationship between commerce and agriculture and political values: "Of all the objects worthy of our attention, none more forcibly present themselves, than the present state of our commerce and agriculture. Those ought to be considered as primary objects of civil polity, as combining the attainment of ease, happiness and independence."[5] Most white men gave priority to cultivation of the land. Leading men in 1797 touted population increase and agricultural improvement as "the best security of rising greatness, and respectability." However, agriculture went hand-in-hand with commerce. Tennesseans eagerly sought markets for their products. By the 1780s, stores in the Tennessee region were carrying goods from Baltimore,

Philadelphia, and Europe. In 1809 the *Carthage Gazette* summed up the views of many farmers when it praised commerce for exciting industry, stimulating agriculture, and creating revenues for the government.[6]

Tennesseans distinguished their advanced community from the uncertain survival inherent in the hunting society of their native neighbors. Assuming Native American land to be an undeveloped natural landscape, one Tennessean asserted the desirability of the commercial system:

> This is not a country matured and grown opulent by the advantages of commerce. It is an infant district which never knew the plastic hand of refinement, nor the inestimable attainments of social perfection; and since it is our peculiar destiny to inhabit it, it is our own industry and perseverance that must produce an order of things that will rescue us from contempt, raise us to the dignity and importance of any of the sister states, and to an equality with the other civilized sons of Adam.[7]

White women joined men in pursuing material betterment. These women saw themselves as actively involved in economic life. The expectation of both women and men was that women contributed to the maintenance of the family. When William Doherty filed for divorce from his wife, Lydia, one of his grounds for the suit was that she was "totally unwilling to be of any assistance to your petitioner in making a support for their family." Not uncommonly, husbands discussed business with their wives and both parties expected the wife to act in her husband's absence. Single, divorced, and widowed women owned property in their names, paid taxes, and in all other economic ways acted as head of the household. Gentry women often involved themselves actively in the management of their large plantations. In 1801 widow Nancy Benton moved her nineteen-year-old son, Thomas Hart Benton, his younger sisters, and six slaves from North Carolina to the Cumberland region. Settling in a sparsely populated area, Benton established a small settlement known as Benton Town by granting rent-free leases of seven years to tenants. The town included a mill, school, and meetinghouse.[8]

More than 90 percent of the white population were small farmers. In common with rural women throughout the United States, Tennessee women ran households, raised children, made clothes, cooked for all hands, tended gardens and the domestic animals, and at times worked in the fields. Seeking financial rewards for their efforts, women became entrepreneurs, turning farm products into cash in a series of cottage industries. Harvesting maple sugar on "good sugar days," women made maple sugar production into a significant business. By 1810 maple sugar was one of eastern Tennessee's most productive industries, generating more revenue than its fulling mill or furnace, and more than the manufacture of guns, shoes, flaxseed oil, paper, or cordage. Producing enough surplus that one legislator in 1801 introduced a bill to establish its inspection, women made another home industry out of butter.[9] The most economically productive enterprise was the production of cloth and clothing. A study of estate inventories concluded that spinning was the most extensive of the home industries. Many women ginned and sold cotton and made and sold cloth. Valued at $1,675,309, domestically produced cloth was the largest industry in both eastern Tennessee and the Cumberland region at the eve of the War of 1812, almost all of it prepared at home by white or enslaved women.[10]

The farm economy benefited from women's contributions in other ways. During the first four decades after white settlement, and particularly after 1790, the region experienced rapid growth. Tens of thousands of families immigrated to the state or to points beyond, numerous men traveled out of state and around the state on business, and thousands of soldiers and militiamen moved around the state. In a cash-poor economy, these travelers were responsible for much of the specie that flowed into the area. Most farm homes offered lodging and meals to travelers and fodder and shelter for their animals, and women were frequently the ones providing these services. They also washed, mended, and made clothes for those on the road. Women boarded public charges, receiving a government allowance for their services. Transferring their skills into the business world, a number of women carried on their own enterprises. Women extended the lodgings they offered at home by operating boarding homes and taverns. They ran these at times with their husbands and frequently on their own.[11] Women translated other skills they learned at home into paid labor, operating clothing stores, working with doctors or as midwives, and teaching. Married women frequently partnered with their husbands in commercial enterprises. William and Martha Atkinson of Jonesborough, a husband-and-wife team, were engravers who made the first state seal. Elizabeth Roulstone took over the printing business after the death of her husband, George Roulstone. The legislature appointed her state printer, and she married William Moore soon after that. He found the *Carthage Gazette* largely on her credentials. Several women ran schools with their husbands.[12]

As they worked with men to improve their material well-being, many ordinary women sought happiness by embracing the ethos favoring productivity. Along with men, women envisioned prosperity as one of their central values and imagined their wealth to be linked to the work ethic and the commercial society that they associated with civilization. Like so many white men, Eliza Campbell contrasted settler ideas with those of Native Americans to express the superiority of civilized pursuits of wealth: "The Indians will find it to be their interest in having a civilized people as their neighbors. They will teach them the arts and industry, which are more certain sources of wealth and happiness than hunting or military achievements."[13]

While most men and women believed in the pursuit of happiness and prosperity though tilling and trade, not all Tennesseans accepted market-driven ideas about how to conduct economic relations. Numerous individuals held notions about a Gospel order or other moral system that promoted a different set of values about business. The Mill Creek Baptist Church congregation voted that the Gospel did not allow its members to follow "all the wild extravagances of the world" in their business dealings. In order to maintain religious fellowship, growers in many churches lowered prices that they or buyers thought too high. The Red River Baptist Church agreed that Baptists could not take interest in excess of that allowed by law and sent a committee to the White Creek Church to discuss the matter with them. Church discipline also enforced honesty in business dealings.[14]

To encourage economic growth, most leading and republican men believed in a prominent role for government.[15] In Governor John Sevier's message to the legislature in 1798, he described the duty of the government "to advance the growth, better the police, and increase the happiness of our common country." From the earliest settlements, the local and state governments controlled ferries, set tavern rates, restrained loose animals, and inspected flour, tobacco, cotton, and other goods.[16] Ordinary men joined leading men in routinely requesting regulation of dams; government warehouses for tobacco, wheat, and other crops; bridges; and other assistance. The state purchased rights to the use of the cotton gin to assist growers in improving their cotton production. White Tennesseans understood that governmental and individual interests sometimes conflicted. In such cases, the common view was that the public good should prevail.[17]

One of the most critical economic functions of government was to define and protect property rights—a doctrine indelibly intertwined with the more advanced stages of civilization. According to Scottish theorists, hunters and gatherers, in the first stage of human development, had no property; herders had property rights in tamed animals; cultivators, in land; and commercial people, in mobile property. Tennesseans linked the movement from communal to private property on the ladder of social progress to their belief that private ownership was necessary in order to stimulate individual industry and population growth. But agreement on the significance of private property to civilized people raised more questions than it answered. While many Tennesseans shared the view that the earth was for the common use of humankind and that settlers could claim the untilled lands of savages, they disagreed about who had the authority to inscribe ownership of the land—commonly called the right of soil—in unfarmed territory. European theorists located the right to claim and assign the unproductive territory of a nation in other nations. As American thinkers relocated sovereignty from Parliament to the people, some Tennessee residents relied on this more democratic conceptualization to boldly articulate their theory about the entitlement to uncultivated lands. Conflating Vattel's theory of unproductive nations with more general ideas about the earth given to humankind, one resident on Clinch River recognized a common right of the soil in individuals, rather than nations:

> The right of this soil is in us all; that each man has an inheritance to a part, & that government, which for our general convenience, and to promote our general welfare we have consented to live under, has only a right to direct the mode of securing and quieting each citizen in the particular property he may entitle himself to, under such regulations, and to say what each individual of us must pay to the community as a compensation for their aggregate property."

Thousands of frontiersmen who occupied Native American lands in defiance of government proclamations against encroachment as well as squatters on other lands agreed. Opposing this view, leading men located the right of soil in the state, inserting the right into the 1796 declaration of rights of the state constitution. Federal authorities claimed the land for the national government. In the Land Compact of 1806, the state and federal government finally compromised their claims by awarding the state most of the land settled by American citizens in the eastern and central part of the state and reserving for the federal government the territory in the west.[18]

Underlying the disagreement about the location of the right to soil were different theories about how whites established individual ownership of lands. Those who espoused the doctrine that individuals could create the right of soil drew on a long tradition of backcountry squatting.[19] Possessors developed several theories premised on the idea that individuals can assert a right to soil. The Ulster Irish, immigrating in the earlier part of the century, were strong proponents of the rights of the landless. Irish squatters in backcountry Pennsylvania refused to pay quitrents, basing their resistance on two claims. One was reliance on an implied commitment by the government to free land. Because "the Proprietary and his agents had solicited for colonists and . . . they came accordingly," they took possession of the land. They also articulated a labor theory of value based on their work on vacant lands: "It was against the laws of God and nature, that so much land should be idle while so many Christians wanted it to labor on and raise their bread."[20]

In the early eighteenth century, large landowners in Virginia and later North Carolina encouraged landless settlers to migrate to the backcountry in order to form a defense against the native peoples to the west. The early farmers developed their own customary law about land claims. Marking trees created "tomahawk rights." The erection of a log cabin on the tract a farmer claimed gave him "cabin rights." Under "corn rights," a farmer received 100 acres of land for each acre he planted. If he erected a lodge and planted grain, he "took up land." In the backcountry of North Carolina, Irish Regulators fought for their "right" to occupy vacant land, regardless of the title of absentee owners. By custom, these inchoate rights came to be more than usufructuary. If another farmer wanted to settle on the tract claimed, he had to buy the rights from the possessor. The Irish and other settlers carried these ideas to the domain west of the Appalachian Mountains. The Virginia settlers who populated Kentucky in the 1770s and Ohio in the 1780s invoked the "ancient cultivation law" to assert rights based on their occupancy and improvement of land. In Kentucky, settlers also relied on Virginian and later Kentucky preemption laws to validate their claims.[21]

Large numbers of landless settlers also pushed into Tennessee. Although some of the earliest settlers in the Long Island area on the Holston River had legal title, all newcomers staking claims elsewhere prior to the Revolution were squatters on native lands. Some of the proprietors wanted to prevent squatting, because the intruders on Indian lands endangered the peace, but they were unsuccessful. In spite of efforts by the North Carolina legislature to prevent encroachment, as early as 1777 settlers flooded lands rumored to be subject to treaty negotiations. The state of Franklin opened land offices in 1785 to sell land claimed by the Cherokees. Their actions in encouraging settlement south of the French Broad River on Cherokee land opened the area to large numbers of occupant claims. The doctrine of occupancy rights was well established when the area came under federal control in 1790. In 1791 the *Knoxville Gazette* boasted that the region was an asylum for the oppressed. Claiming that the multitudes would find freedom and support, the paper advertised the land as divided on "agrarian principles." At that time, Governor Blount estimated that there were 300 families settled south of the

French Broad without title and that the first settlers in Davidson County had preemption rights on 309,760 acres.[22]

Occupancy of Native American lands continued well after statehood in 1796. Return Meigs, the Indian agent for the Cherokees, frequently complained about the encroachments of the squatters. Although the army removed them on a number of occasions, the farmers returned. In 1796, and again in 1806, the Tennessee House of Representatives almost passed laws prohibiting preemption rights for those on Indian lands. However, the legislature did grant preemption, and occupant claimants continued to farm native lands. The Surveyors Book for the Fifth District in eastern Tennessee from 1807 through 1810 contains considerable information about preemption claims. Of the surveys in the Fifth District Survey Book, 210 tracts (46 percent) were on lands claimed by occupancy. Preemption claimants even managed to establish rights to land set aside by the government for military reservations. In 1807 the report of the land commissioners for western Tennessee showed fifty-five preemption and guard right claims filed on such land. The commissioners found forty-three claims, or 78 percent of those asserted, to be valid. Although most of the claimants were men, women took up land as well. One list of intruders at Sims Settlement on Cherokee lands, compiled by Indian agent Return Meigs, listed six women as heads of household among the ninety-three homesteads.[23]

Landless men and women developed customary practices that created occupancy titles for claims on Indian, government, and private lands. In order to establish a claim, the claimant or his agent was required to take actual and peaceable possession. The farmer had to begin the first improvement without resort to force—usually cutting logs, raising a house, and clearing some land—before the legal owner came to take possession. By custom, the community expected the cabin size to be about fifteen feet square and at least two acres to be cleared. The improvements might be less if the legal owner used force to prevent the occupant from completing his improvements. Some early preemption claims were for 400 acres, following Virginia custom, but most were for 640 acres, the North Carolina tradition. After the turn of the century, the size of the claims decreased in response to legislation that restricted preemption to 300 acres. In the Fifth District in eastern Tennessee from 1807 through 1810, the acreage claimed varied widely from 12½ to 300 acres, with the average claim size 129 acres.[24]

Tennessee claimants relied on three concepts to create occupancy rights—custom, statute, and contract. Backcountry custom that justified "taking up" land was actually a cluster of doctrines. At the heart of the squatters' ideology was a belief that the landless could earn title to the land. The same men who structured the social compact around rights created by participation crafted a theory rewarding involvement that made the land productive. The most basic claim arose from the natural-law doctrine that people in crowded countries could occupy lands barely used. Those acquiring land under this theory established rights by marking boundaries or otherwise asserting possession. A connected and more commonly asserted doctrine was a labor theory of value, based on improvements and cultivation. Settlers claiming under this tenet contended that their labor created a title where none previously existed. One Tennessean located the source of this authority in God: "We claim it as a power inherent in us, and derived from the author of our existence, to cultivate and convert to our use, any unappropriated part of the habitable globe; and to make it bring forth the fruits of the earth." A third source for customary rights was a philosophy of entitlement based on the claimants' contributions to settlement. Unlike Pennsylvania settlers, colonial agents did not lure pioneers to Tennessee. However, as in the Virginia and Carolina backcountry, the early frontier people acted as an advance guard to assert claims over native lands. They considered that their hardships and sacrifices created special entitlements.[25]

Regardless of the theoretical basis for claims, the reliance on custom in asserting occupancy claims was so strong that the courts eventually accepted traditional practices as part of the legal rules governing land claims. The appellate court for the state, cognizant of "all classes being in the habit of taking up land," acknowledged that these communally created land rights could not be ignored: "When the rights of individuals and the rules of property become ingrafted on any general practice, long acquiesced in, it cannot be lightly set aside. In cases which would be doubtful on the law, such practice makes the law. And then the maxim implies, *communis error facit jus* [the common error makes the law]."[26]

In addition to entitlements based on custom, many settlers made occupancy claims under North Carolina and Tennessee laws or under a contract that recognized preemptive claims.[27] Unlike Kentucky and Ohio, occupants in the Tennessee region, North Carolina's western district, relied on stronger statutory law to support their rights against legal claimants. A 1779 North Carolina statute established preemption rights for claimants in possession of vacant lands for seven years on which no person had obtained a grant. The 1783 act setting aside lands for military warrants exempted those settled on the Cumberland River with a right of preemption. Another statute in 1784 extended the time for Davidson County residents to secure certificates to pay for their preemption claims. The Tennessee Constitution granted the inhabitants of the area south of the French Broad the right of preemption and occupancy. Two years later the legislature defined the improvements required for a "preference to enter by occupancy" to be a house built and land enclosed and cultivated. Finally, the Cumberland Compact of 1780 created a contractual provision for headrights for most settlers in that region.[28]

In contrast to squatters on the eastern seaboard, occupancy claimants did not premise their claims on the right to make a home for their family or the right to develop an independent competency.[29] By relying on possession, labor, sacrifices for the public good, statutes, and contracts as the basis for claims, occupancy settlers created a space in which ordinary and wealthy settlers could improve land in order to make a profit as well as to establish a competency. Both small and wealthy squatters did clear land and put in a small crop as a speculation, moving on when they found a buyer. One study of three districts in eastern Tennessee from 1790 through 1810 showed that more than half of the people on the tax lists were not there eight years later. The community validated the presumption that occupancy claims could be speculative by responding with a market for improved lands, at lower prices, of course, than for lands with legal titles. In 1796 land in the Cumberland settlement sold for two to four dollars per acre; outside the settlements, for one dollar per acre; and within Indian boundaries, for twenty-five cents per acre. By 1809, occupant claims in the French Broad area, where no land office had been opened, sold for one dollar per acre, compared to two dollars per acre charged by the United States for land sales.[30]

Landless Tennesseans and similarly situated land hunters in other western states pressured the federal government to recognize their claims. Their theory of landownership supported the Preemption Act of 1841, Thomas Hart Benton's Graduation Act of 1854, and the Homestead Act of 1862. Tennessee improvers shared an ideology about land rights with many occupancy claimants around the globe. As early as 1700, squatters in South Africa forced the British government to consider land entitlement claims of the landless. By the mid-nineteenth century, American democratic politics and campaigns to make public lands available to improvers along with pressure from settlers elsewhere informed Britain's land policies in most of its colonies. As in the United States, colonial officials were reluctant to remove squatters, and republican politicians supported the claimants and codified homestead laws. Australia was an exception—squatters there lost political support by antagonizing titled landowners of large sheepherding estates by being slow to erect fences.[31]

Although large numbers of claimants were occupancy landholders, frontier people and the local governments created a second method of landownership—North Carolina used land grants to compensate its soldiers. Men who took military warrants or grants assumed that governments rather than individuals held the right to soil in uncultivated lands. Similar to the militia service that created a sense of political entitlement as citizens, wartime sacrifices promoted an idea of an economic prerogative. Men who were compensated for the risk and sacrifices they made as soldiers felt a special entitlement to their lands. Relying on his service "to the cause of liberty (which we all now enjoy)," one Revolutionary War veteran asked the legislature for "justice" after Stokely Donelson, a wealthy speculator who engaged in massive fraud in Tennessee, forged a conveyance of his tract. He requested that the assembly issue a warrant to him for unappropriated land.[32]

Utilized by both speculators and cultivators, the third method of acquiring land was by purchase from the government or from other vendees whose chain of title originated in the government. Like military claimants, purchasers located the authority to dispose of vacant lands in the government. This theory of ownership treated land title as a commodity. Both large and more modest landowners viewed their land as a marketable property. Speculators, of course, sought to make fortunes. For many small property owners, their land represented the location of family and work. These men constructed identity as patriarchs of household farms. However, many small farmers also viewed their land as a commodity. When one farmer, then ninety years old, discovered that Stokely Donelson's fraud deprived him of his title, he complained to the legislature that he had raised a large family and wanted "my earnings."[33]

Whether a man or woman acquired land by occupancy, military warrant, or purchase, many settlers desired the benefits of landownership. Estimates vary widely as to the extent of landownership in Tennessee during the generation after Independence. Examining militia returns for Washington County in eastern Tennessee, Lucy Kennerly Gump calculated that about 54 percent of white males older than twenty-one owned land. Men and women of small property fared considerably worse in the Cumberland area. Thomas Perkins Abernathy estimated that about 13 percent of adult men were landowners there in 1787. Although many sought grants and feared tenancy, numerous westering men did not consider title crucial to their drive for prosperity. Moving beyond traditional notions that associated landownership with competency and independence, many frontier people viewed land as a locus for the production of cash crops. They entered into a variety of leasing arrangements that allowed them to create wealth without incurring the dependency of debt. Many cultivators secured favorable long-term leases, while others avoided debt by sharecropping.[34]

The movement toward establishing a uniform system of individual titles to land did not eliminate all claims to common usage of the earth. In Tennessee, as in other areas of the United States, incoming men and women acted on transatlantic beliefs about the right to public usage of the forests and rivers. Livestock in medieval Europe grazed freely on vacant land and in fields after harvest. In eighteenth-century England, ordinary men asserted their customary rights against the growing claims of authority over forests by the king, nobles, and gentry who held legal title. Foresters enforced their traditional right to hunt, fish, graze their animals, cut turf, and gather wood. In Kingswood Chase, colliers tore down turnpikes that interfered with their public use of the forest. The Ulster Irish also recognized common rights to the forest, including free pasture and the burning of wood. The immigrants from Europe brought these ancient rights with them to the eastern seaboard and trans-Appalachian west of British North America.[35]

Many Tennesseans recognized customary rights to common usage of uncultivated land. Settlers exercised their traditional rights by taking timber and sod from unclaimed forests or from tracts not used for cultivation. During the 1790s and early 1800s, trespassers ignored complaints from property owners and continued to remove natural resources. A related issue was the use of open land as public range. Because the open range lured settlers, legislators supported free-ranging stock, recognizing branding and appointing rangers to assist in locating the owners of strays. When cattle got mired and died in the salt licks, lawmakers required that owners of saltpeter works enclose their property. By 1807 the assembly placed the burden on planters to fence their smaller tracts of land if they wanted to protect it from damages caused by free-roaming cattle. Some property owners asserted countervailing rights to property. A few private landowners attempted to prohibit ranging on their lands by threatening trespass suits. In some towns citizens restricted ranging. Both Nashville and Knoxville enacted regulations prohibiting swine at large. The Nashville ordinance allowed the town sergeant to kill the offending animals. However, stock owners saw these regulations as an infringement on their customary rights. The Nashville ordinance prompted hog owners, including Sarah Robertson, who placed an extraordinarily rare signature of a woman on a petition, to object to the law as "impinging on the rights of property."[36]

In the European imagination, neither individuals nor nations could own air or ocean, but nations could claim rivers. As Vattel explained, the open sea could not be possessed because it could not be settled in a way that would prevent others from passing, but a nation that took possession of a country assumed possession of all rivers located within it. Where a river separated nations, it belonged to the nation that took first possession of it.[37] In the face of competing claims by various Native American peoples, the Spanish, and the French, the overmountain people revised this doctrine, imagining rivers as a part of an increasingly commercial and expansionist vision. The rivers and creeks that provided names for Baptist churches were the lifeblood of the trans-Appalachian West for all inhabitants. For the incoming whites, rivers watered prime farmlands and provided transportation, fish, jobs, power for mills, and access to markets. Because rivers were intricately linked to economic improvements, white thinkers portrayed the access to rivers as a common right that could not be constrained by a nation claiming ownership. Historians of the trans-Appalachian West focus on the importance of the right to navigation of the Mississippi, but white citizens did not limit their claims to river access to the right to travel on the Mississippi. In their view, all navigable rivers were "public highways." They claimed the right to access the Red River, the Holston, and numerous other rivers.[38] Transmontane thinkers articulated several intellectual bases for their claims to river access—natural rights, property rights, constitutional rights, the rights of nations, and state legislative rights.

Citizens asserted their most commonly articulated claim to navigation of the rivers as a natural right to access rivers. In 1787 the inhabitants of the Cumberland settlements contended that "every large river that passes through an empire should be considered as a general gift from heaven, which cannot be subject to any monopoly." Writing while secretary of the Southwest Territory in 1793, Daniel Smith envisioned the navigation of the Mississippi "as the light of the sun, a birth-right that cannot be alienated." The declaration by the Tennessee legislature in 1804 expressed the sentiments of most white men: "Nature has designed all rivers to be occupied as public highways, and as a right in common to the citizens of this state as well as all others."[39]

For many Tennesseans, the natural right to use nature's waterways was connected intricately to an inchoate communal right to engage in commerce. Convinced that they advanced civilization through trade, these men privileged their rights to use the rivers for commercial purposes over the claims of Native Americans and European powers to the rivers. When Native Americans controlled the rivers in 1792, Cumberland settlers complained that this action stopped immigration and increased the price of salt. Years later, Indian agent Return Meigs, in granting passports through Cherokee country to traders using river transport, characterized rivers as "canals which nature had prepared evidently for the purpose of commercial intercourse."[40] Supporters of river access noted that rivers promoted the values of a more advanced stage of civilization. As the legislative preamble to a law improving navigation of the Nolichucky River explained, the export of surpluses created a more industrious citizenry who in turn improved the wealth, commerce, and respectability of the state. From this perspective, white citizens frequently contrasted their commercial use of the river to the barbarity of Native American practices. For some, opening up the rivers brought trade and civilization to the Indians. For others, like entrepreneur Joseph McMinn, the removal of Native Americans permitted the fulfillment of greater purposes: should relocation of Native Americans west of the Mississippi take place, "we should then be ready to cultivate the fruitful of the Mobile, Mississippi and Tennessee Rivers, and enjoy without molestation all the commercial advantages thereto belonging, which appear to be assigned by Heaven as the rightful inheritance of the Sons of the West."[41]

The transformation of the natural right to access waterways into a commercial imperative created the intellectual space to envision this communal resource as a type of property right. When Spain closed the Mississippi River in the late 1780s, the government's decision reduced the value of frontier products by more than one-half. One Davidson County man called the right to access the river to be "as evident and indispensable as the rights of those who have ever owned a cow or a horse." The settlers in Franklin saw this action as equivalent to selling the frontiersmen and making them "slaves" to Spain, because Spain now controlled their access and the terms of their sales to New Orleans.[42]

Many leading men sought to give their perceived natural right to utilize the rivers more substantial intellectual moorings by creating a constitutional right, by reinterpreting the law of nations, and by promulgating legislative protections. The framers of the Tennessee Constitution took the unusual step of declaring the navigation of the Mississippi to be an inalienable right. In a unique provision possibly drafted by William Blount, the declaration of rights of the Tennessee Constitution included the right to equal participation in the free navigation of the Mississippi as an "inherent right" of its citizens that could not be conceded.[43] Including this common right not simply as a right but as an inalienable right allowed Tennesseans to assert that the federal government could not cede this right in treaty negotiations and expressed the supreme importance Tennesseans attached to river access.

Supplementing their constitutional claim to the Mississippi, westering borderers asserted a claim to navigation of rivers based on their reading of the law of nations. Vattel's law declared that the right to the navigation of a river that bounded nations went to the first in possession. The federal government chose to misinterpret Vattel to assert its right to navigate the Mississippi. Reporting to President Washington in 1792, Secretary of State Thomas Jefferson ignored the rule of earliest possession. Analogizing to the use of the ocean by all men, he maintained that the same principles applied to the inhabitants of navigable rivers. Incorrectly asserting Vattel as authority, Jefferson ignored Vattel's distinction between oceans that were generally free to all and rivers that were not. The *Knoxville Gazette* reprinted the substance of Jefferson's views several years later. Tennesseans agreed that the law of nations dictated free navigation. To promote the removal of Native American obstacles to the use of the Tombigdee and the Mobile Rivers, the publisher of the *Carthage Gazette* reminded its readers that the federal government had previously claimed the right to navigation of these rivers as sanctioned by "the law of nations."[44]

The expansionist doctrine of the common right to rivers had internal implications, as Tennesseans extended their understanding about the right to access rivers to their own usage of the waters. Upon the commencement of statehood, the Tennessee legislature articulated the state's right to protect the navigation of its rivers from obstacles to passage. In 1796 the legislature declared the Red River to be a free and open river and prohibited obstructions. Three years later, it added seven more rivers to the list. Its protective efforts continued into the next century. Because they linked river navigation to public usage and expansionism, early Tennesseans assigned a communal status to river rights. Prior to 1810, no Tennessean argued publicly that the rights to rivers should be viewed as individual rights instead of common rights. The argument was over the best use of a resource held in common. As the population grew, individuals with mills, fish traps, and other obstacles argued, sometimes successfully, that they should be permitted to hinder a navigable water. However, they always couched their request for such "privileges" in terms of the greatest public good.[45]

Assigning property rights in human beings invoked a different set of tensions than creating ownership of natural resources. During the period of Indian attacks, whites and slaves forged patronage relationships, but whites were pulled by their economic vision to imagine slaves as property. Although historians focus much attention on the importance of slave labor, masters in the frontier economy also utilized their equity in slaves to capitalize the purchase of land and to grease the wheels of commerce. Because business arrangements were very plastic in a cash-poor economy, slaves served as cash substitutes, as collateral, and as subsidies for larger enterprises in a region that vaunted an agrarian and commercial civilization. As William Blount advised his brother in 1797, "Negroes are the most valuable property in this country." Sellers of land commonly advertised that they would sell for "cash or slaves." Some men used slaves to pay their taxes. Slave owners often pledged their slaves as security on bonds or debts. Many entrepreneurs financed their businesses and dealt in land through lotteries, with slaves a frequent prize at these events.[46]

In addition to utilizing slaves as a medium of exchange, as collateral, and as a resource for capitalization, slave owners converted slave labor to property by hiring them out.[47] Whites hired slaves at least as early as 1775, when an agent of the Henderson Company leased two slaves for nine months. The new economy demanded a considerable amount of hired labor and masters profited by providing a flexible source of temporary labor. Of course, slave labor also produced great value for the farms and businesses of their owners. Although cotton had been grown for many years in both east and west Tennessee, interest quickened as peace with the Cherokees, the Louisiana Purchase, and the new gin allowed planters to develop the particular capacities of their region for cotton production. By the mid-1790s planters moved toward cotton as the major income crop.[48]

Not all market forces steered owners toward the characterization of slaves as property. The humanity of slaves intruded on this impersonal business-oriented portrayal in two ways—slaves asserted their own qualities as people, and business people assigned human roles to slaves. Although most whites imagined slaves as commodities, enslaved people had complex personalities, dispositions, and qualities that affected their marketability, giving the lie to the idea that they were only merchandise. Purchasers, of course, valued compliant slaves who worked well. A reputation for being difficult to handle or a poor worker devalued a slave's price. Bondspeople utilized their notions about patronage to create connections with their masters in order to maneuver in this terrain. Masters responded by rewarding trusted slaves with more autonomy and with better treatment. A few slaves were emancipated for good service.[49]

Slaves were not the only parties to advance the notion that they were human beings. Masters needed slaves as human agents to manage farms, mill produce, deliver and collect goods, and perform other business functions.

The repercussions of this practice—legal and otherwise—sometimes led to an erosion of white perceptions that characterized slaves as property. One arena of concern was the use of slave evidence. By law, blacks could not testify in court, except against other blacks. This rule created serious problems for business people who utilized slaves in their businesses. David Campbell's slave, Sam, incurred ferriage fees on Campbell's behalf in transporting cattle and crops on a ferry owned by Richard Waterhouse. When a dispute arose over the number of trips, Waterhouse submitted that Sam could prove the existence of the accounts. Rather than assert that Sam's testimony was inadmissible in court, Campbell agreed to pay any account Waterhouse could prove, "even by Sam or any other honest man of his color." Both Campbell and Waterhouse realized that an insistence on legal rules about the inability of blacks to take an oath would interfere significantly with their business world. By accepting the word of slaves, these businessmen recognized that enslaved people were credible human beings, not simply commodities.[50]

In spite of these countervailing market forces, most slaveholders in Tennessee declined to adopt the paternalistic style of the coastal South where sentimental masters saw their bondspeople as dependents. The Tennessean view of the slave relationship moved from patronage to one that emphasized the commercial advantages of this unique and flexible form of property. One indication of the hardening perspective is found in the bills of sale of slaves. Prior to 1793, the seller of a slave warranted only title. After that date, increasing numbers of buyers insisted on a warranty of fitness, reflecting their notion of slaves as property. Another indication was the growing sentiment during that period that owners should turn over all slave management to overseers, a practice that suggested that the interest of masters in sponsorship was weakening.[51]

The heightened importance given to slaves as property was closely linked to developing notions that connected civilization to prosperity. For many white citizens, population growth that spurred economic development nurtured civilization. The emphasis on population increase as a cause of prosperity allowed republican whites to recognize a positive value of slavery. Adam Smith believed that human beings increased according to the encouragement given the species. Where circumstances allowed families to flourish, the species grew. Because it was in the slave owner's interest to support both the parents and children, Smith contended that slaves multiplied as fast as any other class of people in America. In his view, then, the institution of slavery improved the lives of slaves. Influenced by Smith, James Priestley, named president of Cumberland College in 1809, justified slavery, "unjust and cruel as it is," because it favored the increase of humankind. Agreeing that slavery was necessary for economic advancement, other whites articulated an understanding of slavery that envisioned it to be the result of a fate beyond their control but one that was necessary to preserve an affluent standard of living. The secretary for the predominantly black Bethel Zion Presbyterian Church in Maury County described the circumstances of slavery from this perspective: "[Our black people] had been doomed to hard slavery in order to procure means to secure our education, and let us live in ease." Many slave owners simply lived with the contradiction, like the frontier farmer who owned slaves and agreed that "slavery itself is contrary to justice, consequently all laws framed for supporting it must be unjust."[52]

Not all whites accepted the conception of slaves as property. Considerable numbers of people in Tennessee opposed slavery. Many considered slavery to be wrong and blamed the British for instituting the practice. Unlike New England opponents who argued that slavery violated republican principles, most antislavery advocates west of the mountains drew on several religious or humanist objections, rather than political arguments. The strong presence of black members in many of the churches likely supported denominational opposition to slavery. Many religious leaders preached against slavery on the grounds that it was contrary to the gospel order. Methodist preachers John Roy and Peter Cartwright, Quaker minister Charles Osborn and Quaker Elihu Embree, and Presbyterian ministers Samuel Doak and Finis Ewing used their churches and meetings as platforms to oppose slavery. Itinerant preachers like Joshua Evans also traveled through the state, preaching an antislavery sentiment. Several denominations took positions that imposed at least some limitations on slavery. Some of the presiding elders and circuit ministers refused to permit slaveholders to preach, exhort, or lead the congregation in prayer. Mero District Presbyterians were part of the Transylvania Presbytery. In 1794 Transylvania ordered its slaveholder members to educate slaves younger than fifteen to prepare them for freedom. Two years later, it ordered its members to emancipate those slaves that were ready and to prepare those that were not. The Methodist General Conference of 1808 permitted each regional annual conference to determine its own position on slavery. Meeting near Liberty Hill, Tennessee, in 1808, the Western Conference decided to expel any member who speculated in slaves or who bought or sold slaves "unjustly, inhumanly, or covetously."[53]

Because of the religious influence, thinkers often framed their rationale for abolishing slavery in moral terms. These writers stressed the common humanity of all creation and the immorality of slavery. From the inception of publication in 1801, Benjamin Bradford's *Tennessee Gazette* in Nashville urged sympathy to the condition of the slaves based on humanitarian and religious concerns. Renaming his paper the *Clarion* after 1808, Bradford continued to publish sympathetic articles. The *Knoxville Gazette*, in the early 1790s, also played on humanistic sentiments about slavery. Although the moral argument appealed to the religious-minded, containing the issue of slavery in this fashion had some ideological weaknesses. Ethical exhortations invited refutation based on religious grounds, rather than republic principles. While Arthur Campbell argued that slavery was a moral evil, Colonel McDowell of Kentucky countered in 1791 that it was not, because the Christian apostle Paul supported it. Consequently, although he favored gradual emancipation, McDowell justified using slave labor to clear the forests. Caught in an imperative that associated civilization with economic plenty, most white slaveholders like McDowell refused to abandon the practice, considering it necessary to the advancement of prosperity.[54]

In a strongly republican society, economic or political arguments potentially had a more universal appeal. Some whites did advance these contentions. John Smith, a farmer in eastern Tennessee, refused to own slaves or even to accept them as collateral. A hardworking republican, he feared the idleness and disdain for labor that he associated with slavery. Quaker Thomas Embree mounted a more serious intellectual attack based on political ideology. In a letter published in the *Knoxville Gazette* in 1797, Embree argued that because slaves were human, they had the right to liberty. He proposed the formation of an antislavery society in eastern Tennessee. Although no direct evidence survives, there may have been a manumission society in Tennessee by 1809 and possibly before. In 1809 the Quarterly Meeting of the Society of Friends of Jefferson County submitted a memorial to the legislature. Led by Thomas Embree's son, Elihu Embree, ten men adverted to the natural rights of all men derived from the Creator that were trampled by slavery. The men favored "all who are injured in their rights being amply restored," but they recognized that the legislature would not abolish slavery. Relying on religious arguments as well as political ones, they petitioned for laws protecting slave families and prohibiting the further importation of slaves into the state. However, white men in the region were moving away from natural-rights theory by the 1790s. The Quaker vision of a political solution did not speak to the new concepts of rights earned by involvement in the body politic. Instead, their arguments threatened to undercut the prospects for prosperity. Not surprisingly, Elihu Embree reported that abolitionists were unpopular and their lives threatened.[55]

Activity in the legislature confirms that, while conflicted, most leading men were more concerned with regulating the conduct of slaves than moving toward emancipation. From the first meetings of the territorial legislature in 1794 through 1810, virtually every legislative session considered some legislation related to slavery. Most proposed or enacted legislation controlled slaves. To the extent that legislation protected slaves, proponents were more concerned with protecting the master's property interest in slaves than in humane treatment for slaves or in plans to emancipate slaves.[56] Several of the towns also enacted regulations concerning slavery, all geared toward slave control.[57]

Although it was limited, advocates for emancipation had some success. North Carolina's original policy toward emancipation was that the owners had the right to free their slaves. In 1777 the legislature transformed the personal decision into a political one by empowering the courts to approve manumissions only for meritorious service. In 1801 the Tennessee representatives expanded this law to authorize emancipation if "consistent with the interest and policy of the state." As elsewhere, a few Tennesseans made decisions to free their slaves. Citing concerns about "humanity and justice," some owners compromised by freeing their slaves after the labor of the slaves compensated the owner for the costs of their upbringing or purchase. Other owners permitted emancipation on the promise of the slave to pay the owner after emancipation. However, actual instances of emancipation were rare. As of 1813, masters had formally emancipated just eleven slaves in Davidson County, a county in the heart of slave country.[58] Proponents of emancipation had failed to generate a discourse that engaged wider public ideologies.

In addition to contests about the private and communal ownership of land and waters and possessory interests in human beings, the new republicans also disagreed about the extent of the accumulation of property. Faced with significant disparities of wealth, citizens had to determine how to reconcile tensions in their premises about republicanism, economic inequality, and prosperity. Both big men and commoners linked property to independence, but this connection had a different meaning to each of these groups. Men of substantial property articulated two different theories supporting the private accumulation of wealth—the right to act based on one's self-interest and the contribution that the aggregation of wealth made to the public good. Many large speculators subscribed to the belief that individuals should be free to pursue their economic interests. Aware that the legislature would soon incorporate Palmyra, William Blount schemed secretly to purchase land in the town in order to sell it in Europe. He also proposed to initiate false rumors about the Cumberland settlements in order to deflate land prices before he purchased there. The son of a moderately successful farmer in New Jersey, Richard Waterhouse exemplified a less deceptive breed of speculator who operated from similar values. Considered indolent by his father, Waterhouse left home at the age of twenty with a few personal possessions and arrived in Tennessee in 1798. By dint of hard work and shrewdness—teaching, trading, farming, boatbuilding, laboring, construction work, piloting, and selling alcohol to the Cherokees—he saved enough money to speculate in forced land sales by creditors during the first decade of the 1800s. Waterhouse believed that he was entitled to pursue his own good, as long as he acted ethically:

> I am now under no constraint, exclusive of my own happiness in this world; and, as our happiness in this life is so very dependent on virtue and the rectitude of our conduct, no rational being . . . will act eversive thereto. But he will seek after the reward of good works, by an imitation in conduct of the known attributes of the Creator.[59]

For some successful men, the assertion of self-interest and the accumulation of capital worked for the greater good. Noting that all were subject to the same laws, one newspaper correspondent argued that "whatever promotes my interest, will, in the general promote the interest of others." Hugh L. White, one of the architects of the 1807 land reform law, described the intent of the bill to be making landholders secure. This, he explained, stimulated industry and assisted individuals to become wealthy: "When the individuals of a state are rich, the state itself is rich." Advocates of this point of view lauded enterprise for its accumulation and spending of wealth.[60]

The enfranchisement of large segments of ordinary men produced a sharp dialogue about the rights of the poor in opposition to the rich. Many immigrants left Europe to find a "comfortable subsistence" in America. They wanted an "independence," which they understood as not being controlled by another. Indebtedness to rack-renting landlords or subservience to local lords or powerful forces in the marketplace, in their view, made them "slaves." These immigrants carried their fears to the United States. Seeking affordable land or lucrative tenancy arrangements, most ordinary people derided wealthy speculators. Many linked the hardships of pioneer life to "the shackles which the wealthy . . . never fail to impose on the many." They contended that the interests of speculators conflicted with the common welfare. Middling and poor men often portrayed speculators in terms that suggested that they were a threat to democracy. The *Carthage Gazette* dubbed them a "monied aristocracy."[61]

People of small property articulated a variety of concerns about the accumulation of wealth in the hands of a few men. Some advanced a labor theory of value while others feared that the rich would restrict the poor man's access to the marketplace or to politics. As was the case with occupancy claimants, many men of small property believed that value belonged to the producer. Travelers commented on the discontent among many of the ordinary farmers that the poor worked hard while the rich got richer. In 1801, 300 to 400 farmers in Sumner County, joined by some farmers and big men of Davidson County, toasted "the yeomanry of the United States—may the fruits of their industry, be enjoyed by themselves, and not appropriated for the support of those *hungry drones*, who neither toil nor spin." According to critics, speculators also inhibited the ordinary man's ability to better himself. Supporting "agrarian principles" that placed property in the hands of cultivators, these protesters saw the rich as having too much land, keeping it from purchasers and others who could use land. In addition to castigating the speculators for monopolizing land, ordinary farmers distrusted the power of the wealthy to manipulate market forces through merchant collusion that set prices unfairly. The purpose of unfair control of lands and market, these cultivators believed, was that speculators wanted to reduce the "common people" to tenants with "no will but [the speculators']."[62]

Ordinary men and women who linked leading men to aristocracy expressed a concern about the political influence that the wealthy could exert. President Jefferson's agent Return Meigs claimed that he spoke for "respectable characters" in condemning the great land companies, whose influence "insinuates itself into our election districts."[63] Suspicious of the political clout of the wealthy, middling men pressed their representatives with some success to contain the power of the rich. The Tennessee Constitution, in its declaration of rights, forbade monopolies. State representative John Phagan supported workers on a smaller scale when he voted against a bill to tax shows because the law taxed the poor man who carried the show on his back while others making significant money in shows paid nothing. Judicial reforms in 1809 aimed at creating better access to the courts for ordinary men.[64]

Related to concerns about the concentration of property in the hands of a few were disagreements about conceptualizing property rights. To poorer people, taxation constituted a taking of their property, unjustified if done for private benefit or if assessed unfairly. Restrictions on taxation protected their property rights, because the government levied taxes "to support the extravagance of the great men." Populist elements at the 1796 state constitutional convention and after fought land speculators who favored poll taxes over land taxes.[65]

The sharpest dispute about the government's role in the construction of property rights arose over the collection remedies of creditors. The wealthy in Revolutionary and post-Revolutionary America believed that proponents of debtor relief and paper money threatened their property rights by restraining their authority to collect on obligations and by devaluing currency, and many historians have uncritically accepted this view. Such fears formed the basis for drafting constitutions promoting a separation of powers that allowed the executive and judiciary to check any overreaching by the legislature and of clauses forbidding the impairment of contracts.[66] The tensions between wealthy and ordinary citizens in Tennessee came to a head during Jefferson's embargo in 1807. The embargo severely restricted specie and left farmers unable to pay their debts and taxes. Hard-pressed small landowners fought for relief from creditor foreclosures and from governmental land payments. Creditors argued that political interference in their collection efforts violated their constitutional rights to secure property by denying them due process of law and by impairing the obligations of contracts. They also insisted that governmental intervention created greater evils than those it was designed to remedy.[67]

Debtors responded with several arguments that recognized the constructed nature of the right to property. As early as 1801 farmers maintained that execution laws should guarantee that debtors receive at least two-thirds of the value of their property at forced sales. Otherwise, the creditors and government impinged on their property rights. Disputing the claims of creditors that there was one form of the constitutional right to property, debtors pointed to the ways in which property rights depended on governmental support. They disagreed that creditors wanted to restrain governmental interference in private affairs—in their view, creditors relied on it. They shrewdly observed that the government created the mechanisms by which citizens exercised their property rights and thus could change them. As one commentator noted, current law permitted the judge to stay executions of forced sales for 30 to 120 days. If the government could postpone collections for 120 days, by the same logic it could delay enforcement of judgments until the embargo ended. Furthermore, if the government could interfere with the right of producers to market their crops abroad, it certainly had the right to provide that creditors could not make use of a collection law that was of the legislature's making. Finally, debtors argued that they should not be penalized for their patriotic support of the embargo. Partially successful in their appeal, the debtors prevailed on the legislature to enact statutes postponing land payments and executions.[68]

Class tensions generated by the accumulation of wealth by a small class of speculators failed to create lasting political alliances. Although ordinary people perceived their interests to be distinct from those of large landowners, these beliefs did not always translate into class allegiances. Accepting the doctrine of private property, men and women of small property, like the rich, rejected restraints on the limitation of the profits from their exertions. Even so, their belief that landowners should hold no more property than they could cultivate had radical implications, but this potential was defused by the confusion of titles in the region. The sources clouding land titles cut across lines of wealth, uniting one set of claimants against others based on the foundation of the claim. The North Carolina legislature issued warrants on lands claimed by the Cherokees in 1783—lands that the federal government recognized as Cherokee lands two years later. The Franklin government opened its own land office in 1785, confounding North Carolina's grants and ignoring federal treaties as it disposed of Cherokee property. Numerous surveys were inaccurate, both from the incompetence of surveyors and from their inability to complete surveys because of threats from Native Americans. In several cases, surveyors fraudulently reserved huge quantities of land for speculators who sold tracts to innocent purchasers. Land office clerks kept poor records, frequently losing entries or permitting entry of multiple claimants on a single tract. Preemptive claimants established claims on lands covered by warrants or grants. John Armstrong and Stokely Donelson, among others, engaged in massive fraud by conveying titles to land that they did not own.[69]

Titles remained uncertain for a number of years while the federal and state governments disagreed about which body had the right of soil in Tennessee lands. In 1806 the parties reached an agreement that recognized Tennessee's right to convey title to most of the lands already settled and assigned the lands in western Tennessee and property subject to Cherokee claims in the Cumberland mountains to the federal government. The legislature responded with the land law in 1806, dividing the state into surveyor districts and authorizing the surveyors to determine the validity of claims. The law was so unpopular that the next assembly immediately suspended it. The land law of 1807 gave occupant claimants two years to survey and to enter their claims.[70] The ensuing battles in the legislature and the courts over contested claims extended well past 1810. The disorganized nature of the land grab from the Cherokees and the fraudulent behavior of speculators who sought prosperity created a morass of conflicting claims whose resolution had little to do with wealth, undercutting the ability of ordinary people to challenge the concept of the accumulation of land and wealth by big men.

White men and women in the Tennessee region developed an Americanized understanding of civilization by modifying European ideas and by contrasting their economy to that of the first peoples. Making prosperity central to happiness, most white people believed that through their industry they could achieve a civilized commercial economy built primarily on the sale of agricultural products and underwritten by the doctrine of private property. Crafting notions of private property proved to be laden with controversy, but the cultural logic of frontier civilization that privileged voluntary relations, merit, and entitlements did lead to prosperity for many. Keeping the drive for happiness through material improvement at the center of economic relations, numerous white citizens agreed to property rights in the environment and in human beings and accepted the growing economic inequality in their society—a toll exacted by their vision of civilization.

At peace talks after the war of 1776, Onitositah told the Virginia commissioners that he had hoped that "I should dream good, but I dreamt bad."[1] Standing on the threshold of great change for the Cherokee world, Onitositah's dream was perhaps prescient. The meeting of Cherokee, black, and white peoples in the Tennessee region in the Revolutionary and post-Revolutionary period dramatically altered the ideas and cultural premises that each group brought to this encounter. The modifications affected their relationships with each other and their ideas about intracommunal social relations, politics, and economic issues. The changes created by the meeting in the Cherokee heartlands struck the Cherokees far more forcefully than the frontier people.

In four decades, the Cherokees reconfigured how to utilize their philosophy of balance as they moved from envisioning international relations as a process of making peace by forming kinship to continuous negotiations about the meaning of a protective relationship with a much stronger treaty partner that wanted to acquire their land and to civilize their people. Male and female diplomats adapted traditional international practices of fictive kinship by including stronger demands for justice to remove encroachers, assertions of the equality of the parties, and statements of their grievances. As treaties continued to be breached after they ceded land, they developed a concept of renewal that included an enduring obligation to revisit and honor treaty commitments, even those that had been broken.

The shift from negotiations with North Carolina and Virginia to treaties with a federal partner triggered two significant intellectual moves by the Cherokees. They reassessed their kinship with local whites, casting them as friends and brothers and not as elder brothers. They also treaded the delicate ground of imagining a relationship in which the United States would offer protection but would recognize the Cherokees as equals and limit its interference in Cherokee diplomatic and internal affairs. Women spearheaded an important concession—negotiators obtained perpetual compensation for lands conveyed by the Cherokees, a covenant that implied that the Cherokee nation would endure permanently as a separate political entity. Chickamaugans asserted robust ideas about equality and autonomy, strengthening the Cherokee self-concept as a sovereign people. By the time that the Cherokees unified in 1810, their insistence on a diplomacy of kinship had influenced American officials to fashion a connection with the Cherokees that varied from the European paradigm of contractual treaties between nation states and from Great Britain's policy of absolute sovereignty over indigenous peoples. The thinking of the Cherokees contributed to Chief Justice John Marshall's articulation of Native Americans as domestic dependent nations, a holding that acknowledged a permanent relationship between the parties and recognized limited Native American sovereignty. However, Marshall fashioned the Cherokees as wards under the protection of the United States. British settlement colonies around the world adapted Marshall's doctrine to grant partial sovereignty to indigenous peoples.

Justice Marshall's recognition of Cherokee nationhood was informed in part by internal changes in Cherokee society. As the Cherokees responded to growing pressures to civilize or to relocate across the Mississippi, they embarked on a defensive nationalization project. In an ironic example of unintended consequences, federal efforts to acquire their land and settler pressure to denationalize and remove the Cherokees persuaded the Real People to imagine themselves as a nation, one in which they balanced traditional ideas and new thinking. They retained the clan system but expanded their social and political structures beyond clan connections and village chiefs. Moving away from localism in government, the Cherokees accepted a more powerful national government by conferring authority on a representative National Council—but one in which the council made decisions by the traditional methods of consensus and the acquiescence of the older chiefs and the women. The council also refused to part with land and affirmed the spiritual view that the land was owned by the Cherokees in common. In the absence of strong European powers with whom the Cherokees could create diplomatic kinships in order to offset American expansion and desiring to avoid the economic dependence of other Native Americans on one imperial power, the Cherokees sought balance and autonomy through international trade. By 1810 the Cherokees had laid the groundwork for a European-style but distinctively Cherokee nation. Unlike many first peoples, the Cherokee nation endured and continues to insist on its sovereignty and to act on principles of regeneration, holding out to the federal government that it should correct past injustices and honor its treaty commitments.

No one recorded the dreams of black borderers. With the growth of cotton plantations and the internal slave market, the African American population mushroomed. In contrast to the Cherokee emphasis on clan connections and on balance rather than hierarchy and to Tennesseans' ideas of a civilization based on consent and individual merit, African Americans drew on an African heritage that located freedom in vertical and horizontal familial relationships and on hierarchical patronage arrangements outside of kinship bonds. They were also informed by African American ideas about a black community. They responded to frontier conditions by constructing an African American relational worldview of communal life and sponsorship that embraced both black and white connections.

While the Cherokees and frontier people nationalized, bondspeople created a community whose values were detached from loyalty to the American nation or to state or local laws—reflecting an indifference or hostility that contrasted sharply to the intense negotiations among white men about how to construct nationhood and government. Many slaves worked to maintain black family and communal ties and wove a dense web of patronage connections with white masters, co-workers, and others that they used to broaden their range of choices, often disregarding slave codes that attempted to restrain their travel and gatherings. Excluded from participation in decision making in the political sphere, they conceived of white institutions and laws as second masters to manipulate in order to assert their humanity and to expand their freedom. Ignoring regulations restricting their economic activities, slaves turned their network of contacts and sponsors into a measure of freedom in the marketplace. The minuscule free black population grafted white notions about earned entitlements onto the African logic of kinship and patronage and called on white connections in order to assert their political and economic rights. By 1810 white reliance on slaves as capital, specie, and labor necessary to a civilized prosperity diminished the reach of patronage for slaves. Hardening racial categories persuaded white men to exercise their compactual political power to restrict the rights of free black people.

Shortly after his illegal attacks on several peaceful Cherokee towns in the fall of 1793, John Sevier had better dreams than Onitositah. With his political star again on the rise after the debacle of the state of Franklin, Sevier, of French Huguenot descent, dreamed that he was in an unknown country, probably France. His son, elegantly turned out in silk and satin military attire, escorted him past a tremendous number of people to meet the commander in chief in a palatial structure made of diamond or glass at the top of a high hill. As he mounted the stairs within the building, Sevier could see all the nations of the known world and many of its cities. Informed that the commander would be introduced to him later, Sevier noticed the great beauty of the palace and wondered that other nations had not built in that style.[2] Sevier's dream—set in France and featuring visions of silk, satin, and a diamond or glass palace as he climbed to the apex of the world—resonated with images of civilization and his ascending role in its governance. The doctrine of civilization that Sevier and other borderers formulated was a dynamic and pervasive concept—one that informed their ideas and cultural logic about their relationships with Native Americans, determined their understanding of black Tennesseans, and shaped their ideology about their own society, government, and economy. It was, however, a complicated and contested cluster of ideas.

During the first four decades of white settlement, land hunters in the Tennessee region refashioned European notions about civilization. They retained ideas about the superiority of civilization while largely discarding European concepts of natural rights and a harmonious social order in favor of a constructed and consensual society fueled by individual achievement. This very heady brew that privileged human agency and merit over a natural organic order while asserting the supremacy of the civilized released remarkable energies at the same time that it permitted the tragic denigration of those outside of the socially constructed civilized polity.

In international affairs, Tennesseans conjoined the ideology of civilization with an expansionist nationalism. They dismantled Native American sovereignty with the same logic that underwrote their agreement to American nationhood by creating a new classification for nations—civilized and uncivilized. Citizens in a civilized nation accepted the restraints of government, whereas savages were bloodthirsty, cruel, untrustworthy, dependent, and ungovernable. As did the Cherokees, Tennesseans encountered two intellectual challenges in embracing a federal relationship—how to conceive of their connection to the Cherokees and how to structure a nationalism that allowed them to acquire the benefits of nationhood while restraining the power of the United States. Tennessee's leading men responded to this problem by evolving a philosophy of limited federalism that allowed them to create a broad-based state role in Indian policy—one that they used to further degrade the Cherokee polity from that of an uncivilized nation to one of tenants at will. Along with other western Americans, they initiated a discourse of incompatibility and states' rights that led to the Trail of Tears.

The concept of civilization permeated the cognitive universe of the settlers in their internal relations as well as in the diplomatic realm. Unlike other British colonists who emphasized improvement, Tennessee men and women sought happiness—a condition that they believed was best achieved in the civilized state. Contrasting their social, political, and economic beliefs and practices to those of Native Americans, they complicated the European rendition of civilization by emphasizing voluntary actions and human accomplishment. These ideas about consent and agency informed their thinking about and the implicit premises of their social, political, and economic relations and supported the creation of a flourishing state by 1810.

In crafting their logic about the thick sociability that distinguished civilized societies, women intertwined families into their communities, a forum that allowed women a considerable voice in regulating morality and violence. Their contributions to the family gave rise to a belief in inchoate rights to property and custody. As men formulated social relations, they clashed over social hierarchies, democratic politics, and competitiveness over land and business relations. Many believed that they could contain disharmony by mastering their passions and by forming voluntary associations that promoted brotherhood. White men imported their premises about consent and merit into their formulation of government by embracing the idea of an explicit social compact that vested sovereignty in free men and by envisioning rights as entitlements that they earned. They created a vibrant political culture and affirmed their acquired rights in the state constitution, the ultimate social compact. As the creators of government, they assigned and limited the meaning of citizenship to others, including free black people and women. Most white men and women linked democracy and civilization to prosperity. They believed that prosperity depended on the concept of private property— a construct that promoted industry and population growth—but disagreed about how to create ownership in land, which natural resources were communal, whether slavery was justified, and whether the wealthy should accumulate large property holdings. The ideology of the landless about improvement rights later supported the Homestead Act and laws recognizing squatters' rights in various British settler colonies around the world.

Along with other white Americans and with Europeans, Tennesseans furthered a totalizing discourse about civilization—one premised on its superiority to and incompatibility with savage ways—that has profoundly shaped world history. Lacking modern theory about culture, European and American colonialists in locations around the globe pursued prosperity by acting on ideas about savagery and civilization to justify the appropriation of lands and resources, annihilation, torture, coerced labor, forced assimilation, refusal of basic rights, and destruction of the cultures of indigenous peoples. Although modified over the years and challenged on numerous fronts, some of the older tropes of the ideology of civilization still resound today. In the aftermath of the 9/11 attacks, government officials and other commentators labeled terrorists as savages and their actions as barbaric and an assault on civilization and on the civilized institutions of democracy and capitalism. They invoked old images of savages as not-quite-human, bloodthirsty, cruel, and ungovernable. The far-reaching nature of the threat posed by the perceived savagery and the implied ranking of civilization's superiority in this logic authorized civilized people to respond with war, murder, torture, and the denial of rights. The legacy of the Euro-American concept of civilization has been—and remains—both a dynamic and a troubled one.

NOTES

Abbreviations

ASP   U.S. Congress, *American State Papers: Indian Affairs*, Class II
                (Washington, D.C., 1832)

CRNC   William L. Saunders, ed., *Colonial Records of North Carolina* (Raleigh,
                1890)

Draper MSS   Draper MSS, (microfilm edition), State Historical Society of Wisconsin,
                Madison

M208   Bureau of Indian Affairs, RG 75, Records of the Cherokee Indian Agency
                in Tennessee, 1801–1835, National Archives, Washington, D.C., 1952

Papers   Sam B. Smith and Harriet Chappell Owsley, eds., *The Papers of Andrew
                Jackson, 1770–1803* (Knoxville, 1980)

SBHL   Southern Baptist Historical Library and Archives, Nashville, Tennessee

SRNC   Walter Clark, ed., *State Records of North Carolina* (New York, 1970)

Tennessee   Session Laws of American States and Territories, Tennessee State, 1796–
  Laws   1899, Redgrave Information Resources Corporation, Westport
                Connecticut

TSL   Tennessee State Library and Archives, Nashville

VSP   William P. Palmer, ed., *Calendar of Virginia State Papers and Other
                Manuscripts, 1652–1781* (Richmond, 1875)

Introduction

1. On rebellions: Richard Maxwell Brown, *The South Carolina Regulators* (Cambridge,
Mass., 1963); David P. Szatmary, *Shays' Rebellion: The Making of an Agrarian Insurrection* (Amherst, 1980); A. Roger Ekirch, "Poor Carolina": Politics and Society in Colonial North Carolina, 1729–1776 (Chapel Hill, 1981), chaps. 6 and 7; Thomas P. Slaughter, *The Whiskey Rebellion: Frontier Epilogue to the American Revolution* (New York,
1986); Terry Bouton, "A Road Closed: Rural Insurgency in Post-Independence Pennsylvania," *Journal of American History* 87 (December 2000): 855–87; Alan Taylor, *Liberty Men and Great Proprietors: The Revolutionary Settlement on the Maine Frontier,
1760–1820* (Chapel Hill, 1990). On political culture and race/ethnicity: Robert F. Berkhofer Jr., *The White Man's Indian: Images of the American Indian from Columbus to the*

Present (New York, 1978); Reginald Horsman, *Race and Manifest Destiny: The Origins of American Racial Anglo-Saxonism* (Cambridge, Mass., 1981); Andrew R. L. Cayton, *The Frontier Republic: Ideology and Politics in the Ohio Country, 1780–1825* (Kent, 1986); David Hackett Fischer, *Albion's Seed: Four British Folkways in America* (New York, 1989); Alan Taylor, *William Cooper's Town: Power and Persuasion on the Frontier of the Early American Republic* (New York, 1995); Stephen Aron, *How the West Was Lost: The Transformation of Kentucky from Daniel Boone to Henry Clay* (Baltimore, 1996); Andrew R. L. Cayton, *Frontier Indiana* (Bloomington, 1996); James Axtell, *The Indians' New South: Cultural Change in the Colonial Southeast* (Baton Rouge, 1997); Eric Hinderaker, *Elusive Empires: Constructing Colonialism in the Ohio Valley, 1673–1800* (Cambridge, 1997), 187–270; Elizabeth A. Perkins, *Border Life: Experience and Memory in the Revolutionary Ohio Valley* (Chapel Hill, 1998). On international impact: P. G. McHugh, *Aboriginal Societies and the Common Law: A History of Sovereignty, Status, and Self-Determination* (Oxford, 2004), 40–41, 47, 107–8, 117–78; John C. Weaver, *The Great Land Rush and the Making of the Modern World, 1650–1900* (Montreal, 2003), 27–28, 93–94, 135–38. Very little work has been done on the ideology of trans-Appalachian blacks. For an examination of the economic ideas of pioneer slaves, see Betty Wood, *Women's Work, Men's Work: The Informal Slave Economies of Lowcountry Georgia* (Athens, 1995), 101–21.

2. Francis Jennings, *The Ambiguous Iroquois Empire: The Covenant Chain Confederation of Indian Tribes with English Colonies from Its Beginnings to the Lancaster Treaty of 1744* (New York, 1984), 45, 161–62, 192–93; Daniel K. Richter and James H. Merrell, eds., *Beyond the Covenant Chain: The Iroquois and Their Neighbors in Indian North America, 1600–1800* (Syracuse, 1987); Richard White, *The Middle Ground: Indians, Empires, and Republics in the Great Lakes Region, 1650–1815* (Cambridge, 1991); Robert A. Williams Jr., *Linking Arms Together: American Indian Treaty Visions of Law and Peace, 1600–1800* (New York, 1997). Some intellectual/cultural historians have examined the Southeast, including Theda Perdue, *Mixed Blood Indians: Racial Construction in the Early South* (Athens, 2003), and Robbie Ethridge, *Creek Country: The Creek Indians and Their World* (Chapel Hill, 2003). The Cherokees have been the subject of some excellent intellectual, cultural, social, and legal history: John Phillip Reid, *A Law of Blood: The Primitive Law of the Cherokee Nation* (New York, 1970); Rennard Strickland, *Fire and the Spirits: Cherokee Law from Clan to Court* (Norman, 1975); John Phillip Reid, *A Better Kind of Hatchet: Law, Trade, and Diplomacy in the Cherokee Nation during the Early Years of European Contact* (University Park, 1976); William G. McLoughlin, *Cherokee Renascence in the New Republic* (Princeton, 1986); Theda Perdue, *Slavery and the Evolution of Cherokee Society, 1540–1866* (Knoxville, 1979); Tom Hatley, *The Dividing Paths: Cherokees and South Carolinians through the Era of Revolution* (New York, 1993); Theda Perdue, *Cherokee Women: Gender and Culture Change, 1700–1835* (Lincoln, 1998).

3. Each of these presidents was part of the migratory stream west. All were Carolinians who spent their adult lives in Tennessee prior to their presidency. Jackson arrived in

1788 at age twenty-one, Polk in 1806 at age eleven, and Johnson in 1826 at age seventeen. Virginia, of course, minted four of the first five Presidents, but most of them matured during the revolutionary era.

4. Nancy Shoemaker argues that Native Americans and Europeans were similar in that they sought alliances and that they had broad agreement about how to structure alliances. Shoemaker, *A Strange Likeness: Becoming Red and White in Eighteenth-Century North America* (Oxford, 2004), 83–103. While this is true of virtually all international diplomacy, the assumptions of Europeans and Native Americans about how to conduct diplomacy and the meaning attached to alliances were quite different.

5. Homi K. Bhabha, *The Location of Culture* (London, 1994).

6. Frederick Jackson Turner, "The Significance of the Frontier in American History," *Proceedings of the Forty-first Annual Meeting of the State Historical Society of Wisconsin* (Madison, 1894), 79–112; Herbert E. Bolton, *The Spanish Borderlands: A Chronicle of Old Florida and the Southwest* (New Haven, 1921); Patricia Nelson Limerick, *The Legacy of Conquest: The Unbroken Past of the American West* (New York, 1987); Richard White, "It's Your Misfortune and None of My Own": A New History of the American West (Norman, 1993); Jeremy Adelman and Stephen Aron, "From Borderlands to Borders: Empires, Nation-States, and the Peoples in Between in North American History," *American Historical Review* 104 (June 1999): 814–41; Alan Taylor, *American Colonies* (New York, 2001).

7. On savagism and civilization: Richard Beale Davis, *Intellectual Life in the Colonial South, 1585–1763* (Knoxville, 1978), 103–256; Berkhofer, *The White Man's Indian*; Horsman, *Race and Manifest Destiny*, 108–14; Francis Paul Prucha, *The Great Father: The United States Government and the American Indians* (Lincoln, 1984), 7–9, 108, 113; Roy Harvey Pearce, *Savagism and Civilization: A Study of the Indian and the American Mind* (Berkeley, 1988). On race: Axtell, *The Indians' New South*; Philip J. Deloria, *Playing Indian* (New Haven, 1998); Susan Scheckel, *The Insistence of the Indian: Race and Nationalism in Nineteenth-Century American Culture* (Princeton, 1998). On cultural intermingling: Taylor, *American Colonies*; Lucy Eldersveld Murphy, *A Gathering of Rivers: Indians, Métis, and Mining in the Western Great Lakes, 1737–1832* (Lincoln, 2000); John Mack Faragher, " 'More Motley than Mackinaw': From Ethnic Mixing to Ethnic Cleansing on the Frontier of the Lower Missouri, 1783–1833," in Andrew R. L. Cayton and Fredrika J. Teute, eds., *Contact Points: American Frontiers from the Mohawk Valleys to the Mississippi, 1750–1830* (Chapel Hill, 1998), 304–26.

8. A few scholars have considered how local whites constructed Native American sovereignty. Robert A. Williams Jr., *The American Indian in Western Legal Thought: The Discourses of Conquest* (New York, 1990), and Cynthia Cumfer, "Local Origins of National Indian Policy: Cherokee and Tennessee Ideas about Sovereignty and Nationhood, 1790–1811," *Journal of the Early Republic* 23 (2003): 21–46. Most scholars who have been concerned with the question about how whites viewed Native American nationhood have generally examined the perceptions of federal policymakers or courts. Reginald Horsman, *Expansion and American Indian Policy, 1783–1812* (Lansing,

1967); Berkhofer, *The White Man's Indian*, 134–57; Russell Lawrence Barsh and James Youngblood Henderson, *The Road: Indian Tribes and Political Liberty* (Berkeley, 1980), chap. 4; Prucha, *The Great Father*; Frances Paul Prucha, *American Indian Treaties: The History of a Political Anomaly* (Berkeley, 1994); Shoemaker, *A Strange Likeness*, 83–103.

9. White, *Middle Ground*; Alexandra Harmon, *Indians in the Making: Ethnic Relations and Indian Identities around Puget Sound* (Berkeley, 1998); James H. Merrill, *In the American Woods: Negotiations on the Pennsylvania Frontier* (New York, 1999); Daniel K. Richter, *Facing East from Indian Country: A Native History of Early America* (Cambridge, Mass., 2001); Shoemaker, *A Strange Likeness*.

10. Jennings, *The Ambiguous Iroquois Empire*, 45, 161–62, 192–93; William N. Fenton, "Structure, Continuity, and Change in the Process of Iroquois Treaty Making," in Francis Jennings et al., eds., *The History and Culture of Iroquois Diplomacy: An Interdisciplinary Guide to the Treaties of the Six Nations and Their League* (Syracuse, 1985), 3–36; Mary A. Druke, "Iroquois Treaties: Common Forms, Varying Interpretations," in Jennings, *The History and Culture of Iroquois Diplomacy*, 85–98; Mary A. Druke, "Linking Arms: The Structure of Iroquois Intertribal Diplomacy," in Richter and Merrell, *Beyond the Covenant Chain*, 29–39; Richard L. Haan, "Covenant and Consensus: Iroquois and English, 1676–1760," in Richter and Merrell, *Beyond the Covenant Chain*, 41–57; Williams, *Linking Arms Together*; Andrew R. L. Cayton, " 'Noble Actors' upon 'the Theatre of Honour': Power and Civility in the Treaty of Greenville," in Cayton and Teute, *Contact Points*, 235–69; Richard White, "The Fictions of Patriarchy: Indians and Whites in the Early Republic," in Frederick E. Hoxie, Ronald Hoffman, and Peter J. Albert, eds., *Native Americans and the Early Republic* (Charlottesville, 1999), 62–84; Merrill, *In the American Woods*; Greg O'Brien, "The Conqueror Meets the Unconquered: Negotiating Cultural Boundaries on the Post-Revolutionary Southern Frontier," *Journal of Southern History* 67 (February 2001): 39–72. For studies of the Cherokees: Gregory Evans Dowd, " 'Insidious Friends': Gift Giving and the Cherokee-British Alliance in the Seven Years' War," in Cayton and Teute, *Contact Points*, 114–50; Theda Perdue, "Cherokee Relations with the Iroquois in the Eighteenth Century," in Richter and Merrell, *Beyond the Covenant Chain*, 135–49.

11. White, *The Middle Ground*; Hatley, *The Dividing Paths*; Williams, *Linking Arms Together*; Prucha, *The Great Father*; McLoughlin, *Cherokee Renascence*; Prucha, *American Indian Treaties*.

12. I am indebted to Sabrina Gogol and Colette Gordon for this insight.

13. Scholars do document political changes in shifting native alliances, but these changes do not seem to be accompanied by underlying ideological shifts in how to construct relationships with allies. Jennings, *The Ambiguous Iroquois Empire*; Fenton, "Structure, Continuity and Change in the Process of Iroquois Treaty-Making." More recent work has begun to explore the transformation in the ideas and logic of the first peoples. White, "The Fictions of Patriarchy." Nancy Shoemaker argues that Native Americans and whites had a bedrock of shared ideas that allowed them to see their differences more sharply. Shoemaker, *A Strange Likeness*.

14. Michael Lansing, "Plains Indian Women and Interracial Marriage in the Upper Missouri Trade, 1804–1868," *Western Historical Quarterly* 31 (Winter 2000): 413–33; Gregory Evans Dowd, *A Spirited Resistance: The North American Struggle for Unity, 1745–1815* (Baltimore, 1992).

15. Bernard Bailyn and Philip D. Morgan, eds., *Strangers within the Realm: Cultural Margins of the First British Empire* (Chapel Hill, 1991); Laurent Dubois, *A Colony of Citizens: Revolution and Slave Emancipation in the French Caribbean, 1787–1804* (Chapel Hill, 2004); Jon F. Sensbach, *Rebecca's Revival: Creating Black Christianity in the Atlantic World* (Cambridge, Mass., 2005); Taylor, *American Colonies*.

16. Daniel H. Usner Jr., *Indians, Settlers, and Slaves in a Frontier Exchange Economy: The Lower Mississippi Valley before 1783* (Chapel Hill, 1992); Wilma A. Dunaway, *The First American Frontier: Transition to Capitalism in Southern Appalachia, 1700–1860* (Chapel Hill, 1996); Ira Berlin, *Many Thousands Gone: The First Two Centuries of Slavery in North America* (Cambridge, Mass., 1998), 77–92. For studies of ideologies: Cayton, *Frontier Indiana*; Murphy, *A Gathering of Rivers*.

17. Patricia Nelson Limerick, "Going West and Ending Up Global," *Western Historical Quarterly* 32 (Spring 2001): 5–24; Adelman and Aron, "From Borderlands to Borders: Empires, Nation-States, and the Peoples in Between in North American History," 814–41, and responding essays in AHR Forum, *American Historical Review* 104 (October 1999): 1221–39; Weaver, *The Great Land Rush*, 18; McHugh, *Aboriginal Society and the Common Law*, 122–23, 130–42, 159–60; Alice L. Conklin, *A Mission to Civilize: The Republican Idea of Empire in France and West Africa, 1895–1930* (Stanford, 1997).

18. Bhabha, *The Location of Culture*, 1–3, 139–70; Robert J. C. Young, *Postcolonialism: An Historical Introduction* (Oxford, 2001), 3, 25–43, 79, 202; Malini Johar Schueller and Edward Watts, "Introduction: Theorizing Early American Studies and Postcoloniality," and Laura Donaldson, "Making a Joyful Noise: William Apess and the Search for Postcolonial Method(ism)," in Schueller and Watts, eds., *Messy Beginnings: Postcoloniality and Early American Studies* (New Brunswick, 2003), 1–44. For the West: Edward Watts, " 'If Indians Can Have Treaties, Why Cannot We Have One Too?' The Whiskey Rebellion and the Colonization of the West," in Schueller and Watts, *Messy Beginnings*, 81–102.

19. Thomas Bender, "Intellectual and Cultural History," in Eric Foner, ed., *The New American History* (Philadelphia, 1997); Bernard Bailyn, *The Ideological Origins of the American Revolution* (Cambridge, Mass., 1967, 1992), v–vi; Gordon S. Wood, *The Creation of the American Republic, 1776–1787* (Chapel Hill, 1969), vii–viii. For one historian who contends that the concept of ideologies has been stretched too far, see Ralph Lerner, *The Thinking Revolutionary: Principle and Practice in the New Republic* (Ithaca, 1987).

20. Simon During, ed., *The Cultural Studies Reader* (London, 1993); Quentin Skinner, "Hermeneutics and the Role of History," *New Literary History* 7 (August 1975): 209–32; Richard Johnson, "What Is Cultural Studies Anyway?" *Social Text* 16 (Winter 1986–87): 38–80; Hayden V. White, *The Content of the Form* (Baltimore, 1990), chap. 8;

Dominick LaCapra, *Soundings in Critical Theory* (Ithaca, 1989), chap. 3; Lloyd S. Kramer, "Literature, Criticism, and Historical Imagination: The Literary Challenge of Hayden White and Dominick LaCapra," in Lynn Hunt, ed., *The New Cultural History* (Berkeley, 1989), chap. 4; John Story, *Cultural Studies and the Study of Popular Culture: Theories and Methods* (Athens, 1996); Michel Foucault, *The Archeology of Knowledge and the Discourse on Language* (New York, 1792); Janice Radway, *Reading the Romance: Women, Patriarchy and Popular Literature* (Chapel Hill, 1991); Gordon S. Wood, "Conspiracy and the Paranoid Style: Causality and Deceit in the Eighteenth Century," in Joyce Appleby et al., *Knowledge and Postmodernism in Historical Perspective* (New York, 1996), 94–104.

21. Kudos to Mary Kupiec Cayton for the post-Prince nomenclature. Mary Kupiec Cayton, book review of Daniel Walker Howe, *Making the American Self: Jonathan Edwards to Abraham Lincoln*, in *Journal of the Early Republic* 18 (Spring 1998): 143–45.

22. Clifford Geertz, *The Interpretation of Cultures: Selected Essays* (New York, 1973), 3–30, and *Local Knowledge: Further Essays in Interpretive Anthropology* (New York, 1983), 19–35; Robert Darnton, *The Great Cat Massacre and Other Episodes in French Cultural History* (New York, 1984), 75–104; Nancy Rule Goldberger, "Cultural Imperatives and Diversity in Ways of Knowing," in Nancy Golderger, Jill Tarule, Blythe Clinchy, and Mary Belenky, eds., *Knowledge, Difference, and Power: Essays Inspired by Women's Ways of Knowing* (New York, 1996), 335–71.

23. The best history of Tennessee in its early period is John R. Finger, *Tennessee Frontiers: Three Regions in Transition* (Bloomington, 2001), though my account in this section differs in some respects based on material in later chapters of this book.

24. Weaver, *The Great Land Rush*, 4, 30–45, 88–91.

25. Adelman and Aron, "From Borderlands to Borders: Empires, Nation-States, and the Peoples in Between in North American History," 814–41; Evan Haefeli, "A Note on the Use of North American Borderlands," *American Historical Review* 104 (October 1999): 1222–25.

26. The major treaty negotiations impacting the Tennessee region from 1768 through 1810 for which contemporaneous notes exist are the 1767 conference on boundary lines in *CRNC*, 7:462–71; the Treaty at Hard Labor in 1768 in *CRNC*, 7:851–55; the boundary line conference of 1770 in W. Stitt Robinson, ed., *Early American Indian Documents: Treaties and Laws, 1607–1789: Virginia Treaties, 1723–1775* (Frederick, 1983), 5:357–60; the 1770 Treaty at Lochaber in Robinson, *Virginia Treaties*, 360–71; the April 1777 peace treaty in Draper MSS, 4QQ86–148; the July 1777 Treaty of Long Island, in Archibald Henderson, "The Treaty of Long Island at Holston, July 1777," *North Carolina Historical Review* 8 (January 1931): 58–116; line talks of 1779 in "The Journal of Daniel Smith," *Tennessee Historical Magazine* 1 (March 1915): 50–52; peace talks of 1781 in Nathanael Greene Papers, Library of Congress, Washington, D.C., Ms. Div., shelf no. 13,421, reel 2, a small part of which is copied in Draper MSS, 1XX42–49; the 1785 Treaty at Dumplin Creek, in Samuel Cole Williams, *History of the Lost State of Franklin* (Johnson City, 1924), 75–76; the 1785 Treaty of Hopewell, notes at *ASP*, 38–44 and treaty at

Charles J. Kappler, comp. and ed., *Indian Affairs: Laws and Treaties* (Washington, D.C., 1904), 2:8–11; 1786 Treaty of Chota Ford, in *SRNC*, 18:696–700; the 1788–89 peace talks in *ASP*, 45–46, *SRNC*, 22:788–89, 21:534–35, and Draper MSS, 11DD84a; the 1791 Treaty of Holston, Draper MSS, 15U7–56; Treaty with the Cherokee, 1791, in Kappler, *Indian Affairs*, 2:29–33; 1792 talks with President, *ASP*, 203–6; 1792 conference at Coyatee, *ASP*, 267–269; 1793 conference at Henry's Station, *ASP*, 447–48; 1794 conference in Philadelphia, John Howard Payne Papers, Newberry Library, Chicago, and treaty at *ASP*, 543; November 1794 conference at Tellico, *ASP*, 536–538; December 1794 conference at Tellico, "Correspondence of Gen. James Robertson," *American Historical Magazine* 4 (January 1899): 82–95; 1795 peace conference, John McKee file, University of Tennessee Special Collection, Knoxville, MS-1252, 1–17; 1797 boundary line conference, in Benjamin Hawkins, *Letters of Benjamin Hawkins, 1796–1806: Collections of the Georgia Historical Society*, vol. 9 (Savannah, 1916), 160–64; 1798 Treaty, in Kappler, *Indian Affairs*, 51–55; 1801 treaty, in Hawkins, *Letters*, 359–86; 1803 treaty conference at Eustinali, April 20, 1803, M208; 1804 Treaty, Kappler, *Indian Affairs*, 73–74; 1805 Treaty, Kappler, *Indian Affairs*, 82–84; 1806 Treaty, Kappler, *Indian Affairs*, 90–92.

27. Most of this correspondence can be found in the Draper collection, the Virginia State Papers, the Colonial and State Records of North Carolina, the American State Papers, the National Archives, M208, and John Sevier's Executive Journal, in Samuel C. Williams, ed., "Executive Journal of Governor John Sevier," *East Tennessee Historical Society's Publications* (1920–35).

28. Some historians have romanticized the middle-ground relationship by narrating native-white encounters as a kind of hybridity in which each culture shared with the other. For a perceptive critique of this practice, see Daniel J. Herman, "Romance on the Middle Ground," *Journal of the Early Republic* 19 (Summer 1999): 279–91. In Tennessee, the indigenous people and settlers did influence the cognitive world of the other, but not through a mutual sharing. The Cherokees modified their society using processes of retraditionalization and transculturation, while the settlers used Cherokee ways as a foil against which to define civilization. Psychologist Nancy Goldberger defines the latter response as oppositional identity. Goldberger, "Cultural Imperatives and Diversity in Ways of Knowing," 338. Edward W. Said identifies the dynamic of oppositional identity in his work on postcolonialism. Said, *Orientalism* (New York, 1978).

29. Weaver, *The Great Land Rush*, 12, 27–28, 81–87, 91–96; John Gascoigne, *The Enlightenment and the Origins of European Australia* (Cambridge, 2002), 9, 69–71.

Chapter 1

1. No contemporaneous notes exist for the 1775 treaty. For accounts of the 1775 conference: *VSP*, 1:276–310, 315–16; Julian P. Boyd, ed., *The Papers of Thomas Jefferson, 1777–1779* (Princeton, 1950), 68–110; J. G. M. Ramsey, *The Annals of Tennessee to the*

End of the Eighteenth Century (Kingsport, 1853; repr., 1926), 116–21; William Stewart Lester, *The Transylvania Colony* (Spencer, 1935).

2. Talk of Onitositah on July 27, 1781, and talk of John Sevier, August 1, 1781, Draper MSS, 1XX47.

3. For kinship metaphors and treaty protocol among the Iroquois: Francis Jennings, *The Ambiguous Iroquois Empire: The Covenant Chain Confederation of Indian Tribes with English Colonies from Its Beginnings to the Lancaster Treaty of 1744* (New York, 1984), 45, 161–62, 192–93; William N. Fenton, "Structure, Continuity, and Change in the Process of Iroquois Treaty Making," in Francis Jennings et al., eds., *The History and Culture of Iroquois Diplomacy: An Interdisciplinary Guide to the Treaties of the Six Nations and Their League* (Syracuse, 1985), 11; Mary A. Druke, "Iroquois Treaties: Common Forms, Varying Interpretations," in Jennings et al., *History and Culture of Iroquois Diplomacy*, 85–98; Daniel K. Richter and James H. Merrell, eds., *Beyond the Covenant Chain: The Iroquois and Their Neighbors in Indian North America, 1600–1800* (Syracuse, 1987), especially the essays by Mary A. Druke, Richard L. Haan, and Theda Perdue. On Pennsylvania: James H. Merrell, *Into the American Woods: Negotiations on the Pennsylvania Frontier* (New York, 1999). On Algonquians: Richard White, "The Fictions of Patriarchy: Indians and Whites in the Early Republic," in Frederick E. Hoxie, Ronald Hoffman, and Peter J. Albert, *Native Americans and the Early Republic* (Charlottesville, 1999), 62–84. For southeastern woodland Indians generally, see Robert A. Williams Jr., *Linking Arms Together: American Indian Treaty Visions of Law and Peace, 1600–1800* (New York, 1997).

4. Robert F. Berkhofer Jr., *The White Man's Indian: Images of the American Indian from Columbus to the Present* (New York, 1978), 121–32; Francis Paul Prucha, *The Great Father: The United States Government and the American Indians* (Lincoln, 1984), 11; Robert A. Williams Jr., *The American Indian in Western Legal Thought: The Discourses of Conquest* (New York, 1990), chaps. 1, 2, 275–80; Gordon I. Bennett, "Aboriginal Title in the Common Law: A Stony Path through Feudal Doctrine," *Buffalo Law Review* 27 (Fall 1978): 617–35, at 620. On sovereignty: Nancy Shoemaker, *A Strange Likeness: Becoming Red and White in Eighteenth Century North America* (Oxford, 2004), 83–103.

5. William G. McLoughlin, *Cherokee Renascence in the New Republic* (Princeton, 1986), 4, 9, 18; James Mooney, *Myths of the Cherokee* (1900; repr., New York, 1995), 351; Tom Hatley, *The Dividing Paths: Cherokees and South Carolinians through the Era of Revolution* (New York, 1993), 32–41.

6. Theda Perdue, *Cherokee Women: Gender and Culture Change, 1700–1835* (Lincoln, 1998); James Adair, *A History of the American Indians* (New York, 1775; repr., 1968), 32, 36, 37, 81; Rennard Strickland, *Fire and Spirits: Cherokee Law from Clan to Court* (Norman, 1975), 24, 28–29.

7. John Phillip Reid, *A Better Kind of Hatchet: Law, Trade, and Diplomacy in the Cherokee Nation during the Early Years of European Contact* (University Park, 1976), 6–7; McLoughlin, *Cherokee Renascence*, 12–13; John Phillip Reid, *A Law of Blood: The Primitive Law of the Cherokee Nation* (New York, 1970), 38–39, 93–112.

8. Reid, *A Law of Blood*, 123–41; Perdue, *Cherokee Women*, 27; Rennard Strickland, *Fire and the Spirits: Cherokee Law from Clan to Court* (Norman, 1975), 44.

9. Raymond D. Fogelson, "Cherokee Notions of Power," in Raymond D. Fogelson and Richard N. Adams, eds., *The Anthropology of Power: Ethnographic Studies from Asia, Oceania, and the New World* (New York, 1977), 186; McLoughlin, *Cherokee Renascence*, 10–11; Reid, *A Better Kind of Hatchet*, 4–5; Perdue, *Cherokee Women*, 33, 53–55; Tiya Miles, *Ties that Bind: The Story of an Afro-Cherokee Family in Slavery and Freedom* (Berkeley, 2005), 102; John Haywood, *The Civil and Political History of the State of Tennessee from Its Earliest Settlement Up to the Year 1796 Including the Boundaries of the State* (Knoxville, 1823), 272–76.

10. McLoughlin, *Cherokee Renascence*, 10–11, 17; Reid, *A Law of Blood*, 67–69; Theda Perdue, "Cherokee Relations with the Iroquois in the Eighteenth Century," in Richter and Merrell, *Beyond the Covenant Chain*, 135–49. Circe Sturm describes the Cherokees as developing a confederacy after the 1730s and beginning a process of political centralization, a claim that exaggerates the level of national political organization. Circe Sturm, *Blood Politics: Race, Culture, and Identity in the Cherokee Nation of Oklahoma* (Berkeley, 2002), 39–43. Duane Champagne more accurately states that the Cherokees moved from autonomous towns to a confederation of towns with Chota as the mother city from 1752 to 1776. Duane Champagne, *Social Order and Political Change: The Constitutional Governments among the Cherokee, the Choctaw, the Chickasay, and the Creek* (Stanford, 1992), 43–87.

11. Perdue, *Cherokee Women*, 69–70, 74; William Martin to Lyman Draper, July 7, 1842, Draper MSS 3XX4; John Norton, *The Journal of Major John Norton*, ed. Carl F. Klinch and James J. Tallman (Toronto, 1816; repr., 1970), 76; Theda Perdue, *Mixed Blood Indians: Racial Construction in the Early South* (Athens, 2003), 24–25; Reverend William Richardson's report, December 29, 1758, quoted in Samuel Cole Williams, *The Dawn of Tennessee Valley and Tennessee History* (Johnson City, 1937), 221. For other native cultures where marriage is a diplomatic practice or a source of power: Alexandra Harmon, *Indians in the Making: Ethnic Relations and Indian Identities around Puget Sound* (Berkeley, 1998), 41, 62–63; Lucy Eldersveld Murphy, *A Gathering of Rivers: Indians, Métis, and Mining in the Western Great Lakes, 1737–1832* (Lincoln, 2000), 19–76; Michael Lansing, "Plains Indian Women and Interracial Marriage in the Upper Missouri Trade, 1804–1868," *Western Historical Quarterly* 31 (Winter 2000): 413–33; Susan Sleeper-Smith, "The Unpleasant Transaction on the Frontier: Challenging Female Autonomy and Authority at Michilimackinac," *Journal of the Early Republic* 25 (Fall 2005): 417–43.

12. John Heckewelder, *A Narrative of the Mission of the United Brethren among the Delaware and Mohegan Indians, from Its Commencement, in the Year 1740, to the Close of the Year 1808* (New York, 1971), 198–202; talk by Judd's Friend, in "Virginia and the Cherokees, &c: The Treaties of 1768 and 1770," *Virginia Historical Magazine* 13 (June 1906): 31–36; Reid, *A Law of Blood*, 201–7.

13. On women: Reid, *A Law of Blood*, 204; Heckewelder, *Narrative*, 198–203; Perdue,

"Cherokee Relations with the Iroquois in the Eighteenth Century," 92–94; Perdue, *Cherokee Women*, 92–94. On Nan-ye-hi: Cynthia Cumfer, "Nan-ye-hi/Nancy Ward," in Beverly Greene Bond and Sarah Wilkerson-Freeman, eds., *Tennessee Women: Challenging Boundaries, Claiming Identities* (Athens, forthcoming).

14. Talk by Attakullakulla, October 19, 1770, in W. Stitt Robinson, ed., *Early American Indian Documents: Treaties and Laws, 1607–1789; Virginia Treaties, 1723–1775* (Frederick, 1983), 5:364–65; Stuart's Account, August 25, 1776, *CRNC*, 10:764. The Cherokee had a concept of land usage by "friends" based on Cherokee courtesy that was outside of Anglo-American concepts of landownership. Onitositah in 1785 characterized the whites as living on Cherokee lands without making a legitimate purchase as "our friends." Talk of the Tassel of Chota, November 23, 1785, *ASP*, 41. In 1809 chief Selukuki Wohellengh (Turtle at Home) described the Chickasaws who lived near Muscle Shoals, an area claimed by the Cherokee, as residing there by "courtesy." Norton, *Journal*, 46. Oconostota described the Watauga and Nolachucky deeds as rental payments for the destruction of hunting. Talk by Oconostota, July 15, 1777, in "Treaty at Long Island at Holston," *North Carolina Historical Review* 8 (January 1931): 55–116, at 83. On Brown's purchase: Haywood, *History of Tennessee*, 41–43; answer by defendant, *Rugh Brown v. John McDowell*, September 1795, Allen Collection, McClung Library, Knoxville, Tennessee, CS4–23, folders box, August–September 1795; Petition of Jacob Brown, n.d., *CRNC*, 10:885–87.

15. Haywood, *History of Tennessee*, 41–44; Arthur Campbell to William Preston, June 22, 1774, Draper MSS, 3QQ41; letter from Oconostota to Col. Lewis and Preston, July 16, 1774, Draper MSS, 3QQ142.

16. The closest contemporaneous accounts include Stuart's Account, *CRNC*, 10:763–770, and a series of depositions taken from many of the white observers, *VSP*, 1:276–310, 315–16; and Boyd, *Jefferson Papers*, 68–110. For opposition: deposition of Thomas Price, in Boyd, *Jefferson Papers*, 71–76; deposition of John Reid, in Boyd, *Jefferson Papers*, 85–87; talk by Onitositah, November 23, 1785, *ASP*, 41; Brent Alan "Yanusdi" Cox, *Heart of the Eagle: Tsi-yugunsini and the Emergence of the Chickamauga Confederacy* (Milan, Tenn., 1999), 30–31.

Nathaniel Sheidley argues that the Cherokee chiefs were not deceived and did sell the lands claimed by Henderson because the chiefs used the goods received as gifts to persuade the young men not to go to war. I disagree with Sheidley's analysis for several reasons. Sheidley described similar efforts by the chiefs when they ceded land in 1770, which failed and made the young men angry. A very small cession of unwanted land in 1771 did placate the young men, but they made clear their opposition to the huge cession at Henderson's treaty prior to the alleged signing of the deeds. Furthermore, it is hard to imagine that the chiefs believed that the young hunters would be placated by fungible goods obtained at the sacrifice of half of their hunting grounds. Sheidley's belief that the Cherokees were not deceived relies on his claim that Henderson was surrounded by men with different designs—John Reid and Charles Robertson—who nevertheless supported Henderson's claim that a sale occurred. Nathaniel Sheidley,

"Hunting and the Politics of Masculinity in Cherokee Treaty-Making, 1763–1775," in Martin Daunton and Rick Halpern, eds., *Empire and Others: British Encounters with Indigenous Peoples, 1600–1850* (Philadelphia, 1999), 167–85, especially n. 4. However, Reid stated that Henderson did not read the boundaries to the chiefs prior to their signing the deeds and was not clear that the boundaries were ever read. Henderson told the Cherokees that all the deeds were the same, but he later presented deeds for several different cessions. Robertson also stated that Henderson had the Cherokees sign numerous deeds, claiming that they were all the same. Although Robertson had "different designs" from Henderson in that he was there to purchase land on behalf of the settlers at Watauga, his goal of persuading the Cherokees to cede lands was identical to Henderson's. Robertson had no interest in asserting that the Cherokees still owned the lands on which the settlers lived and thus was a biased source.

17. For studies of Tsi-yugunsini's revolt, see Colin G. Calloway, *The American Revolution in Indian Country: Crisis and Diversity in Native American Communities* (Cambridge, 1995), 189–212; Gregory Evans Dowd, *A Spirited Resistance: The North American Struggle for Unity, 1745–1815* (Baltimore, 1992), 47–64; Hatley, *The Dividing Paths*, 217–28; James Paul Pate, "The Chickamauga: A Forgotten Segment of Indian Resistance on the Southern Frontier" (Ph.D. diss., Mississippi State University, 1969), 55–149; Thomas Lawrence Connelly, "Indian Warfare on the Tennessee Frontier, 1776–1794: Strategy and Tactics," *East Tennessee Historical Society's Publications* 36 (1964): 3–22; Randolph C. Downes, "Cherokee-American Relations in the Upper Tennessee Valley, 1776–1796," *East Tennessee Historical Society's Publications* 8 (1936): 35–53; Cox, *Heart of the Eagle*.

18. Talk by Nancy Ward, July 28, 1781, Nathanael Greene Papers, Library of Congress, Ms. Div., shelf no. 13,421, reel 2, 17; Governor Patrick Henry to William Preston, January 22, 1777, Draper MSS, 4QQ77; John P. Brown, *Old Frontiers: The Story of the Cherokee Indians from Earliest Times to the Date of Their Removal to the West* (Kingsport, 1938), 162; Samuel Cole Williams, *Tennessee during the Revolutionary War* (Knoxville, 1944), 269. The treaty notes for the April 1777 meeting are found in Draper MSS, 4QQ87–148, and for the July 1777 treaty in Archibald Henderson, "The Treaty of Long Island at Holston, July 1777," *North Carolina Historical Review* 8:1 (January 1931): 55–116. For Savanukeh: William Fleming to Thomas Jefferson, January 19, 1781, Draper MSS, 11S45–48; Benjamin Harrison to Joseph Martin, August 18, 1784, Draper MSS, 1XX76.

19. Jennings, *The Ambiguous Iroquois Empire*, 45, 161–62, 192–93; Williams, *Linking Arms Together*; talk by Altahkullahkullah, October 19, 1770, in Robinson, *Virginia Treaties*, V:364–65; talk by Savanukeh, July 15, 1777, in Henderson, "Treaty of Long Island at Holston," 87–88; McLoughlin, *Cherokee Renascence*, 11–12; message from Commissioners to Tsi-yugunsini, April 24, 1777, Draper MSS, 4QQ100.

20. Talk by Onitositah, July 15, 1777, in Henderson, "Treaty of Long Island at Holston," 81 (quotation); talk by Judd's Friend, January 13, 1769, in "Virginia and the Cherokees," 31.

21. Deposition of William Farrar, taken between April 1777 and October 1778, in Boyd, *Papers of Thomas Jefferson*, 2:69; talk by Commissioners, July 21, 1777, in Henderson, "Treaty of Long Island at Holston," 113; William Christian to Governor of Virginia, July

5, 1781, Draper MSS, 10S201–05; Henry Knox to President, December 2, 1785, *ASP*, 38; talk by Savanukeh, July 15, 1777, in Henderson, "Treaty of Long Island at Holston," 79.

22. Draper MSS, 4QQ97 (Cherokee shot at April 1777 treaty); Henderson, "Treaty of Long Island at Holston," 62; William Christian to Governor of Virginia, July 5, 1781, *VSP*, 2:199; Henderson, "Treaty of Long Island at Holston," 65–66.

23. Commissioners' talk, April 21, 1777, Draper MSS, 4QQ89; Williams, *Tennessee during the Revolutionary War*, 200; talk by Savanukeh, July 15, 1777, in Henderson, "Treaty of Long Island at Holston," 82–83; Haywood, *History of Tennessee*, 254–69; *ASP*, 40; Draper MSS, 15U39; talk by Bloody Fellow, January 7, 1792, *ASP*, 203; letter from Oconostota to Col. Lewis and Preston, July 16, 1774, Draper MSS, 3QQ142; talk by Savanukeh, July 15, 1777, in Henderson, "Treaty of Long Island at Holston," 79; talk by Onitositah, April 21, 1777, Draper MSS, 4QQ94.

24. Talk by Onitositah, April 19, 1777, Draper MSS, 4QQ86; talk by Onitositah, April 19, 1777, Draper MSS, 4QQ87; talk by Onitositah, July 10, 1777, in Henderson, "Treaty of Long Island at Holston," 66–69; Scolacutta to Blount, May 25, 1794, in *Knoxville Gazette*, June 5, 1794; talk by Onitositah, July 31, 1786, *SRNC*, 18:696–97. John Phillip Reid describes the assignment of blame as one of the Cherokee devices for keeping peace in the earlier part of the century. Reid, *A Law of Blood*, 220, 222.

25. Talk by Onitositah, April 21, 1777, Draper MSS, 4QQ95; talk of Oconostota, July 2, 1777, and talk of the Mankiller of Great Hiwassee, July 13, 1777, in Henderson, "Treaty of Long Island at Holston," 62, 70.

26. White, "*The Fictions of Patriarchy*"; Reid, *A Law of Blood*, 38–41; talk of the friendly Cherokee, early 1782, Draper Mss, 11S82. Scholars tend to stress the similarities of eastern woodland Indians. Williams, *Linking Arms Together*; Shoemaker, *A Strange Likeness*.

27. Talk by Onitositah, July 17, 1777, in Henderson, "Treaty of Long Island at Holston," 91 (quotation); talk of Creek Linguister, June 29, 1791, Draper MSS, 15U37; talk by Onitositah, September 25, 1782, in Ramsey, *Annals of Tennessee*, 271. Absent from the Cherokee concept of elder brother is the deference that Nancy Shoemaker finds as part of this concept among northern Indians and suggests was present among the Cherokee. Shoemaker, *A Strange Likeness*, 119–20.

28. The doctrine of renewal was widespread among eastern woodland Indians. Williams, *Linking Arms Together*, 132–33. For discussions of this doctrine in later periods: David E. Wilkins, " 'With the Greatest Respect and Fidelity': A Cherokee Vision of the 'Trust' Doctrine," *Social Science Journal* 34 (1997): 495–510; Donald J. Pisani, "The Dilemmas of Indian Water Policy, 1887–1928," in Char Miller, ed., *Fluid Arguments: Five Centuries of Western Water Conflict* (Tucson, 2000), 88–89.

29. Reid, *A Law of Blood*, chap. 19; talks by Savanukeh, July 15, 1777 (quotation) and by Clana Nah and Theelhoona 'Koo, in Henderson, "Treaty of Long Island at Holston," 79, 114–15; talk by Onitositah, July 19, 1777, in Henderson, "Treaty of Long Island at Holston," 111; Adair, *American Indians*, 100–111; Charles Hudson, *The Southeastern Indians* (Knoxville, 1976), 365–75.

30. Reid, *A Law of Blood*, chap. 18.

31. Talk by Clanosee, April 28, 1781, Draper MSS, 1XX42; *The Oxford English Dictionary*, 2nd ed. (Oxford, 1989), s.v. "pity" and "pitying"; talk by Oconostota, October 18, 1770, in Robinson, *Virginia Treaties*, 5:L363–64; talk by the Friendly Cherokee, early 1782, Draper MSS, 11S80–83; Thomas Glass and Richard Justice to Blount, March 5, 1792, *ASP*, 263–64.

32. Onitositah's talk, July 15, 1777, in Henderson, "Treaty of Long Island at Holston," 81–82; talk by the friendly Cherokee in early 1782, Draper MSS, 11S80–83; talk by Unsuckanail, November 23, 1785, *ASP*, 41.

33. Talk by Onitositah, April 25, 1777, Draper MSS, 4QQ145–46; letter from Oconostota to Col. Lewis and Preston, July 16, 1774, Draper MSS, 3QQ142; private talks by Onitositah, April 20, 1777, Draper MSS, 4QQ89; talk by Commissioners, November 22, 1785, *ASP*, 40–41; talk by Avery, July 16, 1777, in Henderson, "Treaty of Long Island at Holston," 88–89; talk by Onitositah, July 31, 1781, Draper MSS, 1XX43; talk by Nan-ye-hi, November 23, 1785, *ASP*, 41.

34. Emmet Starr, *History of the Cherokee Indians and Their Legends and Folk Lore* (New York, 1921), 350; Virginia Commission, November 3, 1777, Draper MSS, 1XX29; William Martin to Lyman Draper, July 7, 1842, Draper MSS, 3XX4; Steiner and Schweinitz's Report, in Samuel Cole Williams, ed., *Early Travels in the Tennessee Country, 1540–1800* (Johnson City, 1928), 465–66 (James and Citico); "Brother Martin Schneider's Report of His Journey to the Upper Cherokee Towns," January 5, 1784, in Williams, *Early Travels*, 258.

35. Few scholars have explored the intellectual contributions that indigenous women made to foreign relations. For some scholarly attention to women's ideas in peacemaking, see Perdue, *Cherokee Women*, 100–101; Hatley, *The Dividing Paths*, 219–22.

36. Nathaniel Sheidley, "Unruly Men: Indians, Settlers, and the Ethos of Frontier Patriarchy in the Upper Tennessee Watershed, 1763–1815" (Ph.D. diss., Princeton University, 1999), 211–30; Hatley, *The Dividing Paths*, 211–15; McLoughlin, *Cherokee Renascence*, 92–93.

37. Draper MSS, 30S345; Williams, *Dawn of Tennessee Valley*, 403–4; Cox, *Heart of the Eagle*, 30–31. On women messengers: Governor Patrick Henry to William Preston, January 22, 1777, Draper MSS, 4QQ77; Commissioners' note, April 19, 1777, Draper MSS, 4QQ126; talk by Potclay, July 13, 1777, in Henderson, "Treaty of Long Island at Holston," 69–70; letter from commissioners to Nathanael Greene, July 21, 1781, Nathanael Greene Papers.

38. Williams, *Tennessee during the Revolutionary War*, 269; Brown, *Old Frontiers*, 162; William Springstone's deposition, January 19, 1781, Cherokee Collection, TSL, Mf. 815, box 2, folder 1, reel 1. Examples of women at conferences: Draper MSS, 4QQ85 (21 chiefs, 60 warriors, and 23 women and children attended April 1777 talks); Knox to President, December 2, 1785, *ASP*, 38 (1785 Treaty at Hopewell lists 918 chiefs, warriors, women, and children). On women's roles at treaties: Harriette Simpson Arnow, *Seedtime on the Cumberland* (Lexington, 1960), 175–76; Cox, *Heart of the Eagle*, 30–31; talk by Savanukeh, July 15, 1777, in Henderson, "Treaty of Long Island at Holston," 82–83.

39. William Springstone's deposition, January 19, 1781, Cherokee Collection, Mf. 815, box 2, folder 1, reel 1; John R. Finger, *Tennessee Frontiers: Three Regions in Transition* (Bloomington, 2001), 89; Arthur Campbell to Governor Thomas Jefferson, January 15, 1781, Draper MSS, 10S163; Samuel C. Williams, "Colonel Elijah Clarke in the Tennessee Country," *Georgia Historical Quarterly* 25 (June 1941): 151–58.

40. The 1781 treaty talks in the Nathanael Greene Papers are water-damaged and many pages are lost. The page describing who gave this talk is missing, although William Christian's response addressed to "Mothers" clearly indicates that the speaker was a woman. Talk by Nan-ye-hi, July 28, 1781, Nathanael Greene Papers. Samuel Cole Williams, a very careful historian who may have had access to more complete records, attributes the speech to Nan-ye-hi. Williams, *Tennessee during the Revolutionary War*, 201. Martin's quotation: William Martin to Lyman Draper, July 7, 1842, Draper MSS, 3XX4. For more details on Nan-ye-hi's talk: Cumfer, "Nan-ye-hi/Nancy Ward."

41. Talk by Nan-ye-hi, July 28, 1781, Nathanael Greene Papers (quotation); Campbell to Nathanael Greene, August 2, 1781, in Dennis M. Conrad et al., eds., *The Papers of General Nathanael Greene*, vol. 9 (Chapel Hill, 1997), 118–19; Williams, *Tennessee during the Revolutionary War*, 201; Message from Benjamin Harrison to friendly Cherokee, 1782, Cherokee Collection, Mf. 815, box 1, folder 7.

42. Talk by Cherokee women, July 31, 1781, Nathanael Greene Papers. The remainder of the women's talk is missing.

43. Talk by Onitossitah, November 23, 1785, *ASP*, 41; letter from Blount to Commissioners, November 28, 1785, *ASP*, 44. The quotation is the version of Ward's talk recorded by Joseph Martin who was present as one of the federal commissioners. Martin's notes can be found in Draper MSS, 14U24. The official version is found in the Talk by the War-woman of Chota, November 23, 1785, *ASP*, 41. The difference is that Martin's account uses the word "equally."

44. Talk by Katteuha to Franklin, 1787, in Samuel Hazard, ed., *Pennsylvania Archives*, ser. 1, vol. 11 (Philadelphia, 1855), 181–82; Cox, *Heart of the Eagle*, 219, 229. I want to thank Wendy St. Jean for magnanimously pointing me to Katteuha's speech.

45. Grand Talk, February 16, 1789, *SRNC*, 22:789 (quotation). On fungible goods: deposition of James Robinson, in Boyd, *Papers of Thomas Jefferson*, 2:88; talk by Onitositah, July 17, 1777, in Henderson, "Treaty of Long Island at Holston," 91.

46. Perdue, "Cherokee Relations with the Iroquois in the Eighteenth Century," in Richter and Merrell, *Beyond the Covenant Chain*, 92–94; Ramsey, *Annals of Tennessee*, 157; talk by Nan-ye-hi, July 1781, in Williams, *Tennessee during the Revolutionary War*, 200–201; talk by Katteuha to President Franklin, September 8, 1787, in Hazard, *Pennsylvania Archives*, 181.

47. Talk by Onitositah, November 26, 1785, *ASP*, 43; Treaty of Coyotee, *SRNC*, 18:696–97, 699–700; talk by Onitositah, June 12, 1787, Cherokee Collection, box 1, folder 20; talks by Oskuah and Allekieskee, September 8, 1787, *VSP*, 4:342–44.

48. Talks by Clanusek and Aukoo, July 31, 1781, Draper MSS, 1XX43; talk by Onitositah,

November 26, 1785, *ASP*, 42; talk by Tuskegatahee, November 29, 1785, *ASP*, 43; talk by chiefs, June 29, 1791, Draper MSS, 15U38.

49. Talk by Onitositah, June 12, 1787, Cherokee Collection, box 1, folder 20; talk by Onitositah to governors, September 16, 1787, *SRNC*, 20:779–80.

50. Chapter 6 describes the ancestry of the settlers in greater detail.

51. Berkhofer, *The White Man's Indian*, 120–21.

52. Ibid., 121–32; Prucha, *The Great Father*, 11; Williams, *The American Indian in Western Legal Thought*, chaps. 1, 2, 275–80; Bennett, "Aboriginal Title in the Common Law: A Stony Path through Feudal Doctrine," 617–35.

53. Francis Stephen Ruddy, *International Law in the Enlightenment: The Background of Emmerich de Vattel's "Le Droit Des Gens"* (New York, 1975), 1–57, 281–85; Roy Harvey Pearce, *Savagism and Civilization: A Study of the Indian and the American Mind* (Berkeley, 1988), 70.

54. Andrew Jackson referred to Vattel. Andrew Jackson to Nathaniel Macon, October 4, 1795, *Papers*, I. Jackson purchased a copy of Vattel's *Law of Nations* for General James Winchester in 1797. Account with Robert Campbell & Co., January 7, 1797, *Papers*, I. The Tennessee legislature relied on Vattel when it issued a remonstrance to North Carolina in 1798. *Knoxville Gazette*, February 1, 1806, 2. In an ejectment action in approximately 1805, Judge Overton cited Vattel on the law of nations. *Glasgow's Lessee v. Smith and Blackwell*, 1 Tenn. 111–30, at 128. James Priestley, president of Cumberland College in Nashville in 1809, read Vattel's *Law of Nations* in 1791 while in Kentucky. James Priestley Diary, 1787–1797, TSL, Manuscript Division, THS 367, loc. no. THS I-E-2, 1791 and January 1, 1792. The *Carthage Gazette* considered Vattel an authority. *Carthage Gazette*, August 10, 1810, 2.

55. Emmerich de Vattel, *The Law of Nations; or, Principles of the Law of Nature, Applied to the Conduct and Affairs of Nations and Sovereigns*, rev. ed. (London, 1797), bk. I, chap. I, pp. 1–4; bk. I, chap. VII, §81; Ruddy, *International Law in the Enlightenment*, 59–76, 182–85; L. C. Green and Olive P. Dickason, *The Law of Nations and the New World* (Edmonton, 1989), 73–79; Peter Sahlins, *Boundaries: The Making of France and Spain in the Pyrenees* (Berkeley, 1989) 54–59, 93–96.

56. Michael P. Zuckert, *Natural Rights and the New Republicanism* (Princeton, 1994), 252–54, 259–60; Knud Haakonssen, *Natural Law and Moral Philosophy: From Grotius to the Scottish Enlightenment* (Cambridge, 1996), 205–8; Christopher J. Berry, *Social Theory of the Scottish Enlightenment* (Edinburgh, 1997), 93–99; Berkhofer, *The White Man's Indian*, 44–49, 137–38.

57. Ruddy, *International Law in the Enlightenment*, 196–210. See Richard E. Nisbett, Incheol Choi, Kaiping Peng, and Ara Norenzayan, "Culture and Systems of Thought: Holistic versus Analytic Cognition," *Psychological Review* 108 (April 2001): 291–310, for an interesting discussion of the difference between the Chinese holistic culture that attends to the entire field and assigns causality to it and Western analytic cultures that pay attention primarily to objects and the categories to which they belong. The

Cherokees, of course, were very different from the Chinese, but the Cherokees did have a spiritual view that required them to establish a fundamental relatedness between Cherokees and strangers in order to conduct diplomatic relations.

58. Arthur Campbell to George Muter, January 16, 1781, Draper MSS, 10S171–74; letter from James Robertson, 1787, in "Correspondence of Gen. James Robertson," *American Historical Magazine* 1:1 (January 1896): 76–77.

59. Alan Taylor, *Liberty Men and Great Proprietors: The Revolutionary Settlement on the Maine Frontier, 1760–1820* (Chapel Hill, 1990), 24–29, 101–5; John Sevier to James Ore, May 12, 1798, in Samuel C. Williams, ed., "Executive Journal of Gov. John Sevier," *East Tennessee Historical Society's Publications* 4 (January 1932): 151–53. Virginians like John Sevier had been western looking since early settlement. L. Scott Philyaw, *Virginia's Western Visions: Political and Cultural Expansion on an Early American Frontier* (Knoxville, 2004).

60. James Robertson to Willie Blount, March 20, 1811, Draper MSS, 5U192; Sheidley, "Unruly Men," 128–29 (German quotation). Most historians contend that agrarian advocates overlooked Indian farmers. Pearce, *Savagism and Civilization*, 66; Stephen Aron, *How the West Was Lost: The Transformation of Kentucky from Daniel Boone to Henry Clay* (Baltimore, 1996), 65; Alan Taylor, *William Cooper's Town: Power and Persuasion on the Frontier of the Early American Republic* (New York, 1995), 38–39; Daniel H. Usner Jr., "Iroquois Livelihood and Jeffersonian Agrarianism: Reaching behind the Models and Metaphors," in Hoxie et al., *Native Americans and the Early Republic*, 200–225.

61. Ramsey, *Annals of Tennessee*, 117–22.

62. Bethabara Diary, January 9, 1775, in Adelaide L. Fries, ed., *Records of the Moravians in North Carolina* (repr., Raleigh, 1968), 2:900; talk by Onitositah, July 1777, in Williams, *Tennessee during the Revolutionary War*, 268 (quotation); talk by Daniel Smith, September 27, 1779, in "The Journal of Daniel Smith," *Tennessee Historical Magazine* 1 (March 1915): 52; commissioners' note, August 2, 1781, Nathanael Greene Papers. On civilizing missions elsewhere: Alice L. Conklin, *A Mission to Civilize: The Republican Idea of Empire in France and West Africa, 1895–1930* (Stanford, 1997); John Gascoigne, *The Enlightenment and the Origins of European Australia* (Cambridge, 2002), 8, 148–62; Luke Godwin, "The Fluid Frontier: Central Queensland 1845–63," in Lynette Russell, ed., *Colonial Frontiers: Indigenous-European Encounters in Settler Societies* (Manchester, 2001), 101–18, at 109–11; Laurent Dubois, *A Colony of Citizens: Revolution and Slave Emancipation in the French Caribbean, 1787–1804* (Chapel Hill, 2004), 176–88, 320–22. The American settlers did not originate the idea of civilization of Native Americans in the eastern woodlands. The French in the early 1700s had a policy of *francisation*: Saliha Belmessous, "Assimilation and Racialism in Seventeenth and Eighteenth-Century French Colonial Policy," *American Historical Review* 110 (April 2005): 322–49.

63. William Russell to William Preston, June 26, 1774, Draper MSS, 3QQ46; Richard Beale

Davis, *Intellectual Life in the Colonial South, 1585–1763* (Knoxville, 1978), 120; notes on Rutherford's Campaign of 1776, Draper MSS, 28S13–14 and 16–19.

64. Frances Paul Prucha, *American Indian Treaties: The History of a Political Anomaly* (Berkeley, 1994), 34–35; Haywood, *History of Tennessee*, 46–55, 488–90, 499–500; Henderson, "Treaty of Long Island at Holston," 55–116.

65. William Cocke to Anthony Bledsoe, May 27, 1776, Draper MSS, 4QQ43; Christian to Governor of Virginia, April 10, 1781, *VSP*, 2:24; Prucha, *The Great Father*, 43–50; Ramsey, *Annals of Tennessee*, 175; Haywood, *History of Tennessee*, 18, 55–56; letter from gentleman in western territory to friend in Virginia, December 20, 1784, Draper MSS, 7XX17–18; Samuel Cole Williams, *History of the Lost State of Franklin* (Johnson City, 1924), 75–76, 95–96.

66. Joseph Martin to Beverley Randolph, October 2, 1788, Brock Collection, Huntington Library, San Marino, California, BR box 6 (17); Draper MSS, 5XX17; Outlaw to Caswell, October 8, 1786, in Ramsey, *Annals of Tennessee*, 343–44; Mero to Smith, April 24, 1789, Draper MSS, 4XX51; McLoughlin, *Cherokee Renascence*, 56; Moses Price to Alexander McKee, 1793, in Philip M. Hamer, "The British in Canada and the Southern Indians, 1790–1794," *East Tennessee Historical Society's Publications* 2 (1930): 122–23.

67. Proposal by Col. Christian to Commissioners of North Carolina, July 17, 1777, in Henderson, "Treaty of Long Island at Holston," 94. On Martin: Brother Martin Schneider's Report, in Williams, *Early Travels*, 253. Martin in the 1780s stood up to a party of fifty men who came thirty miles to kill him and some Indians. After he talked and drank with the men, they departed friends. William Martin to Draper, February 13, 1843, Draper MSS, 3XX12. On Martin's advocacy for Cherokee: Martin to Governor of Virginia, February 7, 1781, Draper MSS, 11S24–26; Martin to Governor Harrison, May 3, 1782, Draper MSS, 11S26–28; Harrison to Governor Martin, November 12, 1782, Draper MSS, 10S87–90 (quotation).

68. William Christian to Governor, April 10, 1781, Draper MSS, 10S198–201; Joseph Martin to Governor Randolph, March 16, 1787, *VSP*, 4:256; Campbell to Governor Randolph, December 5, 1787, *VSP*, 4:363–64; Robertson to Alexander McGillivray?, 1788, "The Correspondence of Gen. James Robertson," *American Historical Magazine* 1:1 (January 1896): 83–84.

69. Notes, Draper MSS, 30S380–81; Thomas Hutchings to Joseph Martin, April 4, 1788, Draper MSS, 11S188–93; letter from inhabitant of French Broad, October 18, 1789, Draper MSS, 9DD53.

70. Instructions for commissioners by Governor Alexander Martin, n.d. [early 1780s], *SRNC*, 19:905–6 (quotation); David Campbell to Governor Richard Caswell, November 30, 1786, *SRNC*, 18:790–91; Arthur Campbell to Governor Harrison, July 27, 1782, Draper MSS, 11S89–92; Commentary on 1785, in Fries, *Records of the Moravians*, 5:2066; Williams, *The Lost State of Franklin*, 78; Martin to Henry, September 17, 1785, Draper MSS, 10S80–81; letter from Caswell County, Franklin, to gentleman in Washington County, Virginia, May 26, 1785, Draper MSS, 3JJ160–61; Henry to Martin,

February 4, 1785, Draper MSS, 15ZZ25–28; Joseph Martin and others to Knox, December 2, 1785, *ASP*, 38–39; letter from inhabitant of French Broad, October 18, 1789, Draper MSS, 9DD53.

71. Prucha, *The Great Father*, 43; Charles J. Kappler, comp. and ed., *Indian Affairs: Laws and Treaties* (Washington, D.C., 1904), 2:8–11; Commissioner William Blount's Protest, November 28, 1785, *ASP*, 44; Williams, *The Lost State of Franklin*, 95–101.

Chapter 2

1. Randolph C. Downes, "Cherokee-American Relations in the Upper Tennessee Valley, 1776–1796," *Tennessee Historical Society Publication* 8 (1936): 47; John P. Brown, *Old Frontiers: The Story of the Cherokee Indians from Earliest Times to the Date of Their Removal to the West, 1838* (Kingsport, 1938), 276–77; Governor Johnston to Hugh Williamson, September 22, 1788, *SRNC*, 21:484.

2. William G. McLoughlin, *Cherokee Renascence in the New Republic* (Princeton, 1986), 19–25; Brown, *Old Frontiers*, 137–441; James Paul Pate, "The Chickamauga: A Forgotten Segment of Indian Resistance on the Southern Frontier" (Ph.D. diss., Mississippi State University, 1969); R. S. Cotterill, *The Southern Indians: The Story of the Civilized Tribes before Removal* (Norman, 1954), 37–110; Colin G. Calloway, *The American Revolution in Indian Country: Crisis and Diversity in Native American Communities* (Cambridge, 1995), 189–212; Tom Hatley, *The Dividing Paths: Cherokees and South Carolinians through the Era of Revolution* (New York, 1993); John R. Finger, "Tennessee Indian History: Creativity and Power," *Tennessee Historical Quarterly* 54 (Winter 1995): 286–305; Rennard Strickland, *Fire and the Spirits: Cherokee Law from Clan to Court* (Norman, 1975), 48; Theda Perdue, *Cherokee Women: Gender and Culture Change, 1700–1835* (Lincoln, 1998), 97–98.

3. Eric Hinderaker, *Elusive Empires: Constructing Colonialism in the Ohio Valley, 1673–1800* (Cambridge, 1997), 236–44; Thomas P. Slaughter, *The Whiskey Rebellion: Frontier Epilogue to the American Revolution* (New York, 1986); Homi K. Bhabha, *The Location of Culture* (London, 1994), 139–70; Malini Johar Schueller and Edward Watts, "Introduction: Theorizing Early American Studies and Postcoloniality," in Malini Johar Schueller and Edward Watts, eds., *Messy Beginnings: Postcoloniality and Early American Studies* (New Brunswick, 2003), 14–16; Peter Sahlins, *Boundaries: The Making of France and Spain in the Pyrenees* (Berkeley, 1989), 7–9, 103–32, 198–237.

4. Deposition of Robert Dews, January 21, 1777, *SRNC*, 22:997; Brent Alan "Yanusdi" Cox, *Heart of the Eagle: Tsi-yugunsini and the Emergence of the Chickamauga Confederacy* (Milan, Tenn., 1999), 137–38; McLoughlin, *Cherokee Renascence*, 57.

5. Hatley, *The Dividing Paths*, 226–28; McLoughlin, *Cherokee Renascence*, 20–22; Pate, "The Chickamauga: A Forgotten Segment of Indian Resistance on the Southern Frontier"; Downes, "Cherokee-American Relations"; Gregory Evans Dowd, *A Spirited Resistance: The North American Struggle for Unity, 1745–1815* (Baltimore, 1992), 105, 109–

13. For Tsi-yugunsini's speech: Samuel Cole Williams, *Dawn of Tennessee Valley and Tennessee History* (Johnson City, 1937), 407.

6. The economic ideas of the Chickamaugans are discussed in greater detail in Chapter 4.

7. Brown, *Old Frontiers*; Hatley, *The Dividing Paths*; Pate, "The Chickamauga," 122.

8. Tsi-yugunsini to commissioners, June 8, 1777, in Archibald Henderson, "The Treaty of Long Island at Holston, July 1777," *North Carolina Historical Review* 8 (January 1931): 64–65; talk by Onitositah, July 27, 1781, Draper MSS, 1XX47; Nathanael Greene Papers, Library of Congress, Washington, D.C., Ms. Div., shelf no. 13,421, reel 2; Isaac Shelby to Arthur Campbell, December 29, 1781, in *VSP*, 2:679; Joseph Martin to Arthur Campbell, July 28, 1782, *VSP*, 3:243; accounting for treaty held July 9, 1783, at Long Island, Draper MSS, 1XX55; Donelson and Martin to Governor Harrison, December 16, 1783, *VSP*, 3:548; Martin to Governor Martin, January 25, 1784, *SRNC*, 17:11–13; various letters to Martin, Draper MSS, 12S18–23.

9. John Sevier to Alexander Martin, March 22, 1785, *SRNC*, 22:640–42; Charles J. Kappler, comp. and ed., *Indian Affairs: Laws and Treaties* (Washington, D.C., 1904), 2:8–11; talk by Newota, November 29, 1785, *ASP*, 43; Draper MSS, 30S507–9.

10. Talk by Scolacutta, March 24, 1787, *VSP*, 4:262; J. G. M. Ramsey, *The Annals of Tennessee to the End of the Eighteenth Century* (Johnson City, 1853; repr., 1926), 519; Alexander McGillivray to James Robertson, December 1, 1788, Draper MSS, 31S78–80.

11. McLoughlin, *Cherokee Renascence*, 25–32; talk from the Kenneteag, November 20, 1788, *ASP*, 46; talk from Headmen and Warriors, November 1, 1788, *ASP*, 47.

12. Brown, *Old Frontiers*, 295; talk from the headmen and warriors, November 1, 1788, *ASP*, 47–48.

13. Talk from the headmen and warriors, November 20, 1788, *ASP*, 45–46; Grand Talk, February 16, 1789, *SRNC*, 22:788–89; General Meeting at Turkeys Town, March 10, 1789, *SRNC*, 21:534–35; Kunoskeskie to Governor, October 17, 1789, Draper MSS, 11DD84a; talk from headmen and warriors, November 20, 1788, *ASP*, 46; General Meeting at Turkeys Town, March 10, 1789, *SRNC*, 21:534–35.

14. Reginald Horsman, *Expansion and American Indian Policy, 1783–1812* (Lansing, 1967), 57. The United States' civilization policy is the predecessor to the European colonialist ideology of civilization that claimed that civilization would benefit the colonized. Robert J. C. Young, *Postcolonialism: An Historical Introduction* (Oxford, 2001), 4–5.

15. William H. Masterson, *William Blount* (Baton Rouge, 1954); letter from Blount to Commissioners, November 28, 1785, *ASP*, 44; note in Benjamin Hawkins, *Letters of Benjamin Hawkins, 1796–1806: Collections of the Georgia Historical Society*, vol. 9 (Savannah, 1916), 250.

16. Knox's instructions to Blount have disappeared, but the secretary of war voiced his concern to the president that the governor's idea of a boundary prior to the treaty was materially different from the one in his instructions. Knox to President, March 10, 1791, in Clarence Edwin Carter, ed., *The Territorial Papers of the United States: The Territory South of the River Ohio, 1790–1796*, vol. 4 (Washington, D.C., 1936), 50–52.

On negotiations: Draper MSS, 15U10–19, 37–38; talk of Nentooyah, January 7, 1792, *ASP*, 204–5.

17. Draper MSS, 1XX76; letter from Joseph Martin, September 19, 1785, Draper MSS, 12S36–38; Brown, *Old Frontiers*, 295, 309; Draper MSS, 15U40; Journal of the Grand Cherokee National Council, June 26, 1792, *ASP*, 271; McLoughlin, *Cherokee Renascence*, 25–32.

18. The American State Papers contain no treaty notes about the Treaty at Holston. Virtually all historians have relied on the very abbreviated account Nentooyah gave of the conference at his meeting with the secretary of war a few months later and found in *ASP*, 203–6. The Draper papers contain the much more extensive recordings made by Daniel Smith in Draper MSS, 15U1–56.

19. Draper MSS, 15U11, 40–43; talk by Nentooyah, January 5, 1792, *ASP*, 203.

20. Draper MSS, 15U39; talk by Blount, June 26, 1791, Draper MSS, 15U39; James Mooney, *Myths of the Cherokee* (New York, 1995), 281–83, 453; John Norton, *The Journal of Major John Norton*, ed. Carl F. Klinch and James J. Tallman (Toronto, 1816; repr., 1970), 114–15; William N. Fenton, *The Iroquois Eagle Dance: An Offshoot of the Calumet Dance* (Syracuse, 1991), 200–201; Ramsey, *Annals of Tennessee*, 555–56.

21. Talk by Chulcoah, June 29, 1791, Draper MSS, 15U37.

22. Report of Steiner and Schweinitz, in Samuel Cole Williams, ed., *Early Travels in the Tennessee Country, 1540–1800* (Johnson City, 1928), 496.

23. Talk by Clanosee, April 28, 1781, Draper MSS, 1XX42; talk by Commissioners, April 21, 1777, Draper MSS, 4QQ91 (quotation).

24. Talk by Attakullakulla, October 19, 1770, in W. Stitt Robinson, ed., *Early American Indian Documents: Treaties and Laws, 1607–1789; Virginia Treaties, 1723–1775* (Frederick, 1983), 5:364–65; talk by Clanosee, April 28, 1781, Draper MSS, 1XX42; talk by Aukoo, July 31, 1781, Draper MSS, 1XX43; talk by Onitositah, September 25, 1782, in Ramsey, *Annals of Tennessee*, 271 (quotation).

25. Talk by Attahkullahkullah, October 19, 1770, in Robinson, *Virginia Treaties*, 5:364; talk by Oostope'teh, July 13, 1777, in Henderson, "Treaty of Long Island at Holston," 70.

26. Talk by chiefs, June 28, 1791, Draper MSS, 15U43, 45.

27. Talk by Blount, June 28, 1791, Draper MSS, 15U46.

28. Talk by chiefs, June 28, 1791, Draper MSS, 15U43 (quote).

29. Questions by Watts, June 28, 1791, Draper MSS, 15U10–11.

30. Talk by Judd's Friend, June 1, 1767, *CRNC*, 7:466; talk by Altahkullahkullah, October 19, 1770, in Robinson, *Virginia Treaties*, 5:365; talk by Onitositah, July 17, 1777, in Henderson, "Treaty of Long Island at Holston"; talk by Blount, June 29, 1791, Draper MSS, 15U12 (quotation).

31. Talk by Scolacutta, July 2, 1791, Draper MSS, 15U21–23.

32. Talk by Nentooyah, January 7, 1792, *ASP*, 204; talk by Onitositah, November 26, 1785, *ASP*, 42; talk by Watts, June 29, 1791, Draper MSS, 15U13; Hawkins, *Letters*, April 25, 1797, 160; Grand Talk by Cherokee Chiefs, February 16, 1789, *CRNC*, 22:789.

33. Treaty with the Cherokee, 1791, in Kappler, *Indian Affairs*, 2:29–33; talks on June 28 and

39 and July 1, 1791, Draper MSS, 15U13, 18, 37–38; talk of Nentooyah, January 7, 1792, *ASP*, 203–4; George Welbank to Alexander McKee, January 16, 1793, in Philip M. Hamer, "The British in Canada and the Southern Indians, 1790–1794," *East Tennessee Historical Society's Publications* 2 (1930): 15–118. The chiefs' statements to the British may have been dissembling, although the silence in Smith's treaty notes about the capitulation is very odd. In addition, when the United States ran the boundary line in 1797, the chiefs again raised the claim that the lines were to be the same as the ones at Hopewell in 1785. Hawkins, *Letters*, April 25, 1797, 160–61. On the other hand, it seems unlikely that the chiefs would expect to be paid if they had ceded no lands, unless they believed that the annuities were compensation for lands unjustly seized in the past.

34. Talk by Secretary of War, January 11, 1792, *ASP*, 205; George Welbank to Alexander McKee, April 12, 1794, in Hamer, "The British in Canada and the Southeastern Indians, 1790–1794," 129–32; Brown, *Old Frontiers*, 338–441; Norton, *Journal*, 39; Doublehead to Blount, October 20, 1794, *ASP*, 532.

35. Talk by Kenneteag, June 29, 1792, *ASP*, 272–73; talk by Cherokee at Philadelphia conference, June 11, 1794, John Howard Payne Papers, Newberry Library, Chicago, vol. 7, parts 1, 4; Report of James Carey to Blount, March 19, 1793, *ASP*, 437; Blount to Knox, March 20, 1793, *ASP*, 436–37; Pickering to Blount, March 23, 1795, in Carter, *Territorial Papers*, 4:386–93; Horsman, *Expansion and American Indian Policy*, 80. The federal government's refusal to support land speculators like Blount cost the Federalists the support of much of Tennessee's elite. Kristofer Ray, "Land Speculation, Popular Democracy, and Political Transformation on the Tennessee Frontier, 1780–1800," *Tennessee Historical Quarterly* 54 (2002): 160–81.

36. Emmerich de Vattel, *The Law of Nations; or, Principles of the Law of Nature, Applied to the Conduct and Affairs of Nations and Sovereigns*, rev. ed. (London, 1797), bk. I, chap. 1, §§5–10, 2–4, and chap. 16, §§93–96.

37. Many students of the trans-Appalachian West have overlooked the contentious development of nationalism among the settlers in this region. Malcolm J. Rohrbough, *The Trans-Appalachian Frontier: People, Societies, and Institutions, 1775–1850* (New York, 1978); R. Douglas Hurt, *The Ohio Frontier: Crucible of the Old Northwest, 1720–1830* (Bloomington, 1996); Stephen Aron, *How the West Was Lost: The Transformation of Kentucky from Daniel Boone to Henry Clay* (Baltimore, 1996). For scholars who recognize a difficult adjustment to federal authority in Ohio: Andrew R. L. Cayton, *The Frontier Republic: Ideology and Politics in the Ohio Country, 1780–1825* (Kent, 1986), 33–50; Hinderaker, *Elusive Empires*, 187–270.

38. Joseph Martin to Patrick Henry, November 21, 1786, Draper MSS, 12S63; Arthur Campbell to Joseph Martin, December 9, 1780, Draper MSS, 1XX40; Proclamation by Governor Samuel Johnston, July 29, 1788, *SRNC*, 21:487–88; Knox to Blount, March 31, 1792, *ASP*, 250–21; Blount to John Gray Blount, October 22, 1793, in Alice Barnwell Keith, William H. Masterson, and David T. Morgan, eds., *The John Gray Blount Papers* (Raleigh, 1952), 2:314–15; Blount to Knox, March 20, 1793, *ASP*, 436–37; Knox to Blount, May 14, 1793, *ASP*, 429–30.

39. Scholars have identified approximately a dozen rebellions in the backcountry areas of the eastern seaboard states of British North America in the late eighteenth century. Activated by a number of causes, these insurrections had in common a homestead ethic that recognized the right to possess a farm without crushing economic debt and without fear of violence. Richard Maxwell Brown, "Back Country Rebellion and the Homestead Ethic," in Richard Maxwell Brown and Don E. Fehrenbacher, eds., *Tradition, Conflict, and Modernization* (New York, 1977), 73–99. Tennessee historians have overlooked the fact that the militia invasions fit the profile of backcountry rebellions. For challenges to metropole authority elsewhere: Sahlins, *Boundaries*, 128–31; John C. Weaver, *The Great Land Rush and the Making of the Modern World, 1650–1900* (Montreal, 2003), 162–77; John Gascoigne, *The Enlightenment and the Origins of European Australia* (Cambridge, 2002), 155.

40. On attacks: *Knoxville Gazette*, June 15, 1793, 3; July 27, 1793, 3; August 27, 1793, 3; September 14, 1793, 3; Sevier to Blount, October 25, 1793, in Cora Bales Sevier and Nancy S. Madden, *Sevier Family History* (Washington, D.C., 1961), 114–15; *Knoxville Gazette*, November 23, 1793, 3; January 16, 1794, 3; Roulstone to Sevier, March 27, 1794, Draper MSS, 11DD116; *Knoxville Gazette*, June 5, 1794, 2; Knox to Blount, July 26, 1794, *ASP*, 634; *Knoxville Gazette*, September 26, 1794, 3.

41. Examples: Blount to Knox, January 14, 1793, *ASP*, 431–33; Blount to John Gray Blount, July 2, 1794, Keith et al., *John Gray Blount Papers*, 2:414–15. Most historians of Tennessee, relying largely on Blount's official correspondence, have assumed that Governor Blount opposed the attacks on the Cherokee or, at most, silently approved. On historians who exonerate Blount: John Haywood, *The Civil and Political History of the State of Tennessee from Its Earliest Settlement Up to the Year 1796 Including the Boundaries of the State* (Knoxville, 1823), 285–97, 311–19; Brown, *Old Frontiers*, 417–33; Thomas Perkins Abernathy, *From Frontier to Plantation in Tennessee: A Study in Frontier Democracy* (University, 1967), 128–32. The best account of Blount's involvement is by Walter T. Durham although it fails to include the eyewitness accounts from the Draper reports. Walter T. Durham, *Before Tennessee: The Southwest Territory, 1790–1796* (Piney Flats, 1990), 177–82.

42. Knox to Blount, November 26, 1792, Carter, *Territorial Papers*, 4:220–26; Knox to Blount, July 26, 1794, *ASP*, 634.

43. Notes by Weakley, Draper MSS, 32S372–74; note, John Haywood Papers, TSL, THS 448, loc. III-D-4, folder 4; note, Draper Mss, 5XX19; Val Sevier to John Sevier, August 9, 1794, Draper MSS, 11DD118; notes by Weakley, Draper MSS, 32S372–74; notes about Kidwell and Combs, Draper MSS, 32S257–71.

44. Abishai Thomas to John Gray Blount, October 26, 1794, Keith et al., *John Gray Blount Papers*, 2:447–48; Blount to Robertson, September 9, 1794, in "Correspondence of Gen. James Robertson," *American Historical Magazine* 3 (October 1898): 357; Blount to Knox, October 2, 1794, *ASP*, 633–34; Blount to Robertson, September 9, 1794, "Correspondence of Gen. James Robertson," *American Historical Magazine* 3 (October 1898): 357; Robertson to Blount, October 23, 1794, "Correspondence of Gen. James Robert-

son," *American Historical Magazine* 3 (October 1898): 363; Blount to Knox, October 24, 1794, *ASP*, 529; Knox to Blount, December 29, 1794, *ASP*, 634–35.

45. Letter from William Cocke, *Knoxville Gazette*, October 6, 1792, 2; letter from Arthur Campbell dated May 13, 1788, to *Virginia Independent Chronicle* of June 1788, Draper MSS, 9DD48. On historians: Francis Paul Prucha, *The Great Father: The United States Government and the American Indians* (Lincoln, 1984), 46, 51; Richard White, *The Middle Ground: Indians, Empires, and Republics in the Great Lakes Region, 1650–1815* (Cambridge, 1991), chaps. 10 and 11; Russell Lawrence Barsh and James Youngblood Henderson, *The Road: Indian Tribes and Political Liberty* (Berkeley, 1980), 33–35; Robert A. Williams Jr., *The American Indian in Western Legal Thought: The Discourses of Conquest* (New York, 1990).

46. Letter from William Cocke, *Knoxville Gazette*, December 29, 1792, 1; letter from "A Citizen, of the Frontiers of the South-West Territory," *Knoxville Gazette*, June 1, 1793, 3; unsigned letter, *Knoxville Gazette*, August 13, 1793, 2.

47. *Knoxville Gazette*, June 1, 1793, 2; *Knoxville Gazette*, December 31, 1791, 3; letter from "Observer," *Knoxville Gazette*, November 3, 1792, 2; letter from "X," *Knoxville Gazette*, April 20, 1793, 4.

48. Congressional Committee Resolutions of February 19, 1794, *ASP*, 475–76; Robert V. Remini, *Andrew Jackson and the Course of American Empire, 1767–1821* (New York, 1977), 94–98; Cocke to Robertson, February 18, 1797, "Correspondence of Gen. James Robertson," *American Historical Magazine* 4 (October 1899): 337–38.

49. Letter from Andrew Rights, *Knoxville Gazette*, January 30, 1797, 3; unsigned letter, *Knoxville Gazette*, March 6, 1797, 1; *Knoxville Gazette*, December 31, 1791, 3; *Knoxville Gazette*, May 8, 1795; H. H. Brackenridge, "Thoughts on the Present Indian War," *Knoxville Gazette*, May 5, 1792, 4; letter from Frontier People of the State of Tennessee dated February 19, 1797, *Knoxville Gazette*, March 6, 1797, 1; letters from David Campbell, *Knoxville Gazette*, March 6, 1797, 1; March 13, 1797, 1.

50. Letter from inhabitant of French Broad, August 20, 1788, Draper MSS, 9DD50; Major King and Daniel Carmichael's report, June 12, 1793, *ASP*, 459; letter from a Fellow Sufferer, *Knoxville Gazette*, June 15, 1793, 3; letter from P.Q., *Knoxville Gazette*, July 13, 1793, 1; letter from LM, *Knoxville Gazette*, February 27, 1794, 1; charge to Grand Jury at Hamilton by Judge Campbell, *Knoxville Gazette*, November 1, 1794, 3; letter from LM, *Knoxville Gazette*, February 27, 1794, 1; charge to Grand Jury by Judge McNairy, *Knoxville Gazette*, May 2, 1796, 2.

51. Daniel Smith, *A Short Description of the Tennessee Government [by Daniel Smith]-1793* (Spartanburg, 1974), 24–26; Haywood, *History of Tennessee*, 468–70; A Fellow Citizen, *Knoxville Gazette*, April 6, 1793, 1, 4.

52. Letter from a Citizen of the Frontiers of the South-West Territory, *Knoxville Gazette*, June 1, 1793, 3; petition by Thomas Dillon to the General Assembly of North Carolina, *Tennessee Gazette*, March 14, 1804, 1.

53. Although historians chronicle long-range changes in the doctrine of savagery, they tend to simplify a complex picture and fail to explore many of the cultural and intellec-

tual currents that produced these changes. Roy Harvey Pearce, *Savagism and Civilization: A Study of the Indian and the American Mind* (Berkeley, 1988); Reginald Horsman, *Race and Manifest Destiny: The Origins of American Racial Anglo-Saxonism* (Cambridge, Mass., 1981), 103–15; Robert F. Berkhofer Jr., *The White Man's Indian: Images of the American Indian from Columbus to the Present* (New York, 1978), 29, 38–44.

54. Brother Martin Schneider's Report, Williams, *Early Travels*, 253, 265; letter from "X," *Knoxville Gazette*, April 20, 1793, 4; Blount to James Robertson, "Correspondence of Gen. James Robertson," *American Historical Magazine* 3 (July 1898): 288–90; Governor Alexander Martin of North Carolina to Governor Harrison, November 21, 1782, *VSP*, 3:376 (quotation).

55. Blount to Nentooyah, September 13, 1792, *ASP*, 281–82; Blount to Knox, "A Return of persons killed, wounded, and taken prisoners, from Mero District, since the 1st of January, 1791," *ASP*, 329–31; *Knoxville Gazette*, December 19, 1793, 2–3; December 19, 1793, 3; July 13, 1793, 2; talk by Colonel Campbell, March 3, 1787, *VSP*, 4:249–50.

56. 1775 letter, *CRNC*, 9:1219–20; resolution of House, May 14, 1782, *CRNC*, 16:1551; talk by Bever of Chickamauga, *VSP*, 3:571; Scolacutta to Blount, May 25, 1794, in *Knoxville Gazette*, June 5, 1794; Blount to Knox, November 8, 1792, *ASP*, 325–27; Knox to Blount, June 26, 1793, *ASP*, 430 (Knox quotation).

57. Gordon S. Wood, *The Radicalism of the American Revolution* (New York, 1992); Sean Wilentz, *Chants Democratic: New York City and the Rise of the American Working Class, 1788–1850* (New York, 1984).

58. Letter from gentlemen in western country to friend in Philadelphia, December 22, 1791, Draper MSS, 4JJ237–39; letter from William Blount to Secretary of War Knox, January 14, 1793, *ASP*, 431–33; Blount to Knox, March 20, 1793, *ASP*, 436–37; William Blount to John Gray Blount, September 19, 1793, Keith et al., *John Gray Blount Papers*, 2:314–15; charge to Grand Jury at Hamilton by Judge Anderson, *Knoxville Gazette*, November 1, 1794, 2–3.

59. Haywood, *History of Tennessee*, 43–44; Ramsey, *Annals of Tennessee*, 274; Blount to Secretary of War, September 11, 1792, in Carter, *Territorial Papers*, 2:167–68; Haywood, *History of Tennessee*, 46–48, 97–99, 457–58; Brother Martin Schneider's Report, in Williams, *Early Travels* 254; *Knoxville Gazette*, June 1, 1793, 2; *Tennessee Gazette*, August 24, 1803, 1; *Tennessee Gazette*, May 18, 1803, 1; June 29, 1803, 3; March 28, 1807, 4; *Knoxville Gazette*, October 20, 1792, 2; November 3, 1792, 2; July 3, 1795, 3; Brother Martin Schneider's Report, in Williams, *Early Travels*, 255–57; report of Steiner and Schweinitz, in Williams, *Early Travels*, 486.

60. *Knoxville Gazette*, March 24, 1792, 3; May 5, 1792, 2; April 20, 1793, 2–3; July 13, 1793, 2; June 5, 1794, 2; July 17, 1795, 3; July 31, 1794, 2–3.

61. Louis-Philippe, *Diary of My Travels in America: Louis-Philippe, King of France, 1830–1848*, trans. Stephen Becker (New York, 1976), 75; Smith to Knox, October 27, 1792, in Carter, *Territorial Papers*, 3:198–99; Haywood, *History of Tennessee*, 268–69, 332; Blount to Knox, November 8, 1792, *ASP*, 325–27; Ramsey, *Annals of Tennessee*, 641 (quotation).

62. Private letter, *Knoxville Gazette*, June 5, 1793, 3; letter from John McKee to Governor Blount, *Knoxville Gazette*, June 15, 1794, 3; Ramsey, *Annals of Tennessee*, 622.

63. Pearce, *Savagism and Civilization*, 5, 53, 66–67; Perdue, *Cherokee Women*, 17–23.

64. *Knoxville Gazette*, June 15, 1793, 3 (quotation). A Memorial from the Mero District asking the president for the right to retaliate against the "invaders" expressed similar sentiments, when it alleged that treaties were slender ties on "barbarian people" unless accompanied by coercion or fear. *Knoxville Gazette*, August 13, 1793, 2–3. So did a young Andrew Jackson, who asked: "[W]hy do we attempt to Treat with Savage Tribe that will neither adhere to Treaties, nor the law of nations?" Remini, *Andrew Jackson*, 70–71.

65. See chapters 6–8 for a more detailed discussion about white views on civilization.

Chapter 3

1. *Knoxville Gazette*, June 16, 1792, 3 (Clinch Mountain, four balls); *Knoxville Gazette*, September 24, 1792, 3 (Little River, two balls); December 7, 1793, 2 (Wells Station, three balls); October 20, 1792, 3 (Station Camp, seven balls); letter from General Robertson to Governor Blount, August 22, 1793, *ASP*, 467 (south of Tennessee River, four balls); *Knoxville Gazette*, January 16, 1794, 3 (Nashville on December 30, 1793, one ball); January 30, 1794, 3 (Clinch, seven balls); Wells Station (one ball); March 13, 1794, 2 (Mero District, one ball); April 10, 1794, 2 (Crooked Creek, one ball); December 13, 1794, 3 (Beaver Dam Creek, eight balls).

2. Letter from Oconostotee, *Knoxville Gazette*, August 1, 1796, 4.

3. Andrew R. L. Cayton explores some of these dynamics in a very astute comparison of Ohio and Tennessee. Cayton, " 'Separate Interests' and the Nation-State: The Washington Administration and the Origins of Regionalism in the Trans-Appalachian West," *Journal of American History* 79 (June 1992): 39–67.

4. P. G. McHugh, *Aboriginal Societies and the Common Law: A History of Sovereignty, Status, and Self-Determination* (Oxford, 2004), 117–78.

5. John C. Weaver, *The Great Land Rush and the Making of the Modern World, 1650–1900* (Montreal, 2003), 81–87; John Gascoigne, *The Enlightenment and the Origins of European Australia* (Cambridge, 2002), 71, 151–52, 155–64; Julie Evans et al., *Equal Subjects, Unequal Rights: Indigenous Peoples in British Settler Colonies, 1830–1910* (Manchester, 2003), 49–53.

6. William G. McLoughlin, *Cherokee Renascence in the New Republic* (Princeton, 1986), 42–48.

7. Council minutes, March 18, 1803, M208; council at Willstown, September 19, 1806, M208. See chapter 4 for a more extensive discussion of Cherokee politics.

8. Historians generally conclude that women's influence in diplomacy and councils declined in the latter part of the eighteenth century. Theda Perdue, *Cherokee Women: Gender and Culture Change, 1700–1835* (Lincoln, 1998), 103–8; McLoughlin, *Cherokee Renascence*, 398. However, women remained involved in diplomacy through at least 1810.

9. Thomas Nuttall, *A Journal of Travels into the Arkansas Territory during the Year 1819* (Norman, 1980), 145 (quotation by Nuttall); David Henley to John Chisholm, October 29, 1796, David Henley Papers, TSL, Mf. 625; David Henley Waste Book, April 19, 1797, March 28 and May 17, 1798, McClung Library, Knoxville, Tennessee, CS 6-2; Freeman Survey Notes of 1802, August 21, 1802, M208; Samuel Riley to Meigs, March 22, 1808, M208; *Carthage Gazette*, January 23, 1809, 2; Sevier to Robertson, May 20, 1808, "Correspondence of Gen. James Robertson," *American Historical Magazine* 5 (July 1900): 255–56 (quotation).

10. McLoughlin, *Cherokee Renascence*, 56–57.

11. Scholars have devoted little attention to the ideas underlying the construction by indigenous nations of their relationship with the United States, focusing on the decline in Native American power after 1794. Richard White, *The Middle Ground: Indians, Empires, and Republics in the Great Lakes Region, 1650–1815* (Cambridge, 1991), chap. 11; Frances Paul Prucha, *The Great Father: The United States Government and the American Indians* (Lincoln, 1984); Eric Hinderaker, *Elusive Empires: Constructing Colonialism in the Ohio Valley, 1673–1800* (Cambridge, 1997), 189. Notable exceptions are Robert A. Williams Jr., *Linking Arms Together: American Indian Treaty Visions of Law and Peace, 1600–1800* (New York, 1997); David E. Wilkins, "'With the Greatest Respect and Fidelity': A Cherokee Vision of the 'Trust' Doctrine," *Social Science Journal* 34 (1997): 495–510; Cynthia Cumfer, "Local Origins of National Indian Policy: Cherokee and Tennessean Ideas about Sovereignty and Nationhood, 1790–1811," *Journal of the Early Republic* 23 (2003): 21–46; Nancy Shoemaker, *A Strange Likeness: Becoming Red and White in Eighteenth-Century North America* (Oxford, 2004), 86–103.

12. Treaty with the Cherokee, 1791, in Charles J. Kappler, comp. and ed., *Indian Affairs: Laws and Treaties* (Washington, D.C., 1904), 2:29–33.

13. Perdue, *Cherokee Women*, 13; Gordon Wood, *The Radicalism of the American Revolution* (New York, 1992); Frances Paul Prucha, *American Indian Treaties: The History of a Political Anomaly* (Berkeley, 1994), 16–19.

14. Letter from Oconostotee, May 15, 1796, *Knoxville Gazette*, August 1, 1796, 4; talks by Hawkins, April 27, 1797, in Benjamin Hawkins, *Letters of Benjamin Hawkins, 1796–1806: Collections of the Georgia Historical Society*, vol. 9 (Savannah, 1916), 161; talks by chiefs, April 25, 1797, in Hawkins, *Letters*, 160–61.

15. Robert A. Williams Jr. introduced the concept of the doctrine of regeneration among eastern woodland Indians. Treaty partners were under a constitutional obligation to continually renew the bonds that ensured their mutual survival. Williams, *Linking Arms Together*, 110–12. I agree with and expand here on Williams's insight.

16. Talk by Chuquilatague, September 5, 1801, in Hawkins, *Letters*, 380–81.

17. Talk by Secretary of War, June 12, 1794, John Howard Payne Papers, Newberry Library, Chicago, vol. 7, part 1; John Norton, *The Journal of Major John Norton*, ed. Carl F. Klinch and James J. Tallman (Toronto, 1816; repr., 1970), 124 (quotation).

18. Perdue, *Cherokee Women*, 115–32; Meigs to Hawkins, February 13, 1805, M208.

19. Address to President by National Council, April 11, 1810, in Norton, *Journal*, 156; address of the chiefs to Thomas Jefferson, President, December 21, 1808, M208; Dearborn to Meigs, March 16, 1803, M208.

20. Council at Eustenanlee, March 4, 1804, M208; talk by Selukuki Wohellengh, April 20, 1803, M208; Hawkins, *Letters*, April 25, 1797, 160–61; minutes respecting Long Island at Holston, June 11, 1802, M208.

21. Council at Eustenanlee, March 4, 1804, M208; talk by Selukuki Wohellengh, April 20, 1803, M208; talk by Chuquilatague, September 5, 1801, and letter from commissioners to Henry Dearborn, September 6, 1801, in Hawkins, *Letters*, 380–83; Norton, *Journal*, 124.

22. McLoughlin, *Cherokee Renascence*, 87–88, 101–6; Selukuki Wohellengh to Meigs, October 1, 1809, M208. On removals in 1800s: Meigs to Sevier, December 27, 1803, M208; Meigs to Dearborn, February 17, 1804, M208; Sampson Williams to Meigs, April 2, 1805, M208; Lt. Thomas Vaughn to A. B. Armstead, April 4, 1808, M208; Meigs to John Smith, June 12, 1809, M208; Meigs to Eustis, May 10, 1810, M208; Colonel Alexander Smith to George Sevier, February 11, 1811, THS Miscellaneous, TSL, Mf. 1080, reel 15, box 23, folder 44. On McDonald: Norton, *Journal*, 59.

23. Muscle Shoals chiefs to Meigs, March 23, 1804, M208 (quotation); Dearborn to Meigs, June 21, 1804, M208; address of chiefs to President, December 1808, M208.

24. Hawkins, *Letters*, December 1 and 2, 1796, 20–22; Perdue, *Cherokee Women*, 115–17.

25. Chiefs to President, December 1808, M208; talk by James Wilkinson, September 4, 1801, Hawkins, *Letters*, 377. Richard White describes how the northern Indians used similar language about fatherhood and pity but lost control of the language of patriarchy in 1794 when whites relied on images of Indians as children in the infancy of civilization. Richard White, "The Fictions of Patriarchy: Indians and Whites in the Early Republic," in Frederick E. Hoxie, Ronald Hoffman, and Peter J. Albert, eds., *Native Americans and the Early Republic* (Charlottesville, 1999), 62–84, at 81–82. The Cherokees responded to this challenge by invoking the language of rights.

26. Talk by chiefs, June 28, 1791, Draper MSS, 15U45; Hawkins, *Letters*, April 27, 1797, 163–64; chiefs to President, February 18, 1808, M208.

27. Chiefs to President, February 18, 1808, M208; Jobber's Son to chiefs, November 20, 1801, M208.

28. Wilcomb E. Washburn, *Red Man's Land/White Man's Law: The Past and Present Status of the American Indian* (Norman, 1995), 57; Meigs to Roan, January 30, 1802, M208.

29. Perdue, *Cherokee Women*, 13; Joyce Appleby, *Inheriting the Revolution: The First Generation of Americans* (Cambridge, Mass., 2000), 27; McLoughlin, *Cherokee Renascence*, 72.

30. Reginald Horsman, *Expansion and American Indian Policy, 1783–1812* (Lansing, 1967), 53–58.

31. Hawkins, *Letters*, August 10, 1801, 363; Hawkins to Meigs, September 15, 1801, M208; Meigs to Daniel Smith, March 6, 1805, M208 (quotation). On federal government: Washburn, *Red Man's Land/White Man's Law*, 57.

32. Perdue, *Cherokee Women*, 41–47, 56; Norton, *Journal*, 50, 55; Hawkins, *Letters*, April 26 and 27, 1797, 160–61.

33. Meigs to Levin Lovely, April 7, 1802, M208; Meigs to Lewis Lovely, July 19, 1802, M208; letter from Meigs, June 10, 1806, M208; Meigs to Lewis Lovely, February 9, 1802, M208; McLoughlin, *Cherokee Renascence*, 87–88, 101–6; Meigs to Dearborn, November 1, 1802, M208; Eustis to Meigs, May 23, 1810, M208.

34. Council minutes, March 18, 1803, M208; Council at Willstown to Meigs, September 19, 1806, M208; National Council to Meigs, September 27, 1809, M208; Chiefs to Meigs, April 11, 1810, M208.

35. The Glass and Dick Justice to Sevier, February 19, 1804, in Cora Bales Sevier and Nancy S. Madden, *Sevier Family History* (Washington, D.C., 1961), 156; talk from The Nephew and other chiefs, March 20, 1801, M208.

36. Letter from Chuquilatague to Governor Blount, in *Knoxville Gazette*, November 1, 1794; Chuquilatague to Samuel Miller, February 26, 1803, M208; Dearborn to Meigs, July 10, 1801, M208; McLoughlin, *Cherokee Renascence*, 72–77.

37. Sevier to legislature, April 8, 1809, in Robert H. White, ed., *Messages of the Governors of Tennessee* (Nashville, 1952), 267–69; McNary to Butler, April 18, 1801, M208; James Lyon and Richard Burke, June 25, 1810, M208.

38. Most scholars assume that the federal government exercised an unchallenged exclusive domain over Indian diplomacy. Horsman, *Expansion and American Indian Policy*, 115–18, 124–28; Russell Lawrence Barsh and James Youngblood, *The Road: Indian Tribes and Political Liberty* (Berkeley, 1980), 33–34; Prucha, *American Indian Treaties*, 38, 67, 88–112. Some scholars document the existence of state Indian policies but offer little comment on the conflict between these efforts and federal preemption. Charles M. Hudson, *The Catawba Nation* (Athens, 1976), 63–64; J. David Lehman, "The End of the Iroquois Mystique: The Oneida Land Cession Treaties of the 1780s," *William and Mary Quarterly* 47 (October 1990): 523–47, at 547. An important exception is the work by Tim Alan Garrison, including *The Legal Ideology of Removal: The Southern Judiciary and the Sovereignty of Native American Nations* (Athens, 2002).

39. Letter from inhabitant of French Broad, October 18, 1789, Draper MSS, 9DD53; Sevier to Secretary of War, July 20, 1796, in Samuel C. Williams, ed., "Executive Journal of Governor John Sevier," *East Tennessee Historical Society's Publications* 1 (1929): 111–14. Postcolonialists warn that national identity is very unstable in postcolonial settings, particularly in borderland regions. Homi K. Bhabha, *The Location of Culture* (London, 1994), 139–70; Thongchai Winichakul, *Siam Mapped: A History of the Geo-Body of a Nation* (Honolulu, 1994), 113–39.

40. *Glasgow's Lessee v. Smith and Blackwell*, 1 Tenn. 111–30; David Campbell to Benjamin Hawkins, August 13, 1797, Penelope Allen Papers, Chattanooga/Hamilton County Library, Chattanooga, Tennessee, Acc. 268, box 10, folder 1; Petition of sundry inhabitants, February 22, 1811, Commission on Public Lands—Petitions, RG 233, National Archives, Washington, D.C., HR 11A-F8.3; Benjamin Blackburn to Meigs, April 29, 1802, M208.

41. Hawkins, *Letters*, April 15, 1797, 153–54; letter from Joseph Flower, March 3, 1808, David Henley Papers; Journal of Thomas Taylor, January 1798, Draper MSS, 16U141–44; David Henley Waste Book, September 8, 1798, September 21, 1798; Daniel Bradley, Committee on Claims, RG 233, National Archives, HR 11A-C2.1; Petition of David [*sic*] Bradley of Connecticut, June 12, 1809, Committee on Claims, RG 233, National Archives, HR 11A-F1.1.

42. *Journal of the Senate and House*, October 20, 1797 (Kingsport, 1933); Sevier to Samuel Handly, March 1, 1798, "Executive Journal of Governor John Sevier," *East Tennessee Historical Society's Publications* 3 (January 1931): 156; John Tealsford and others to Sevier, Military Elections, 1796–1862, TSL, RG 131, reel 1, box 1, folder 32; Sevier to Ore, May 12, 1798, in White, *Messages of the Governors*, 57–58; remonstrance of legislature, December 4, 1799, in White, *Messages of the Governors*, 33–35; Sevier to Thomas Butler, February 17, 1798, in "Executive Journal of Governor John Sevier," *East Tennessee Historical Society's Publications* 3 (January 1931): 172; Sevier to Butler, February 19, 1798, in "Executive Journal of Governor John Sevier," *East Tennessee Historical Society's Publications* 3 (January 1931): 177; Sevier to inhabitants of Powell's Valley, February 17, 1797, in "Executive Journal of Governor John Sevier," *East Tennessee Society's Historical Publications* 1 (1929): 135; letter from Joseph Flower, March 3, 1808, David Henley Papers; J. G. M. Ramsey, *The Annals of Tennessee to the End of the Eighteenth Century* (Johnson City, 1853; repr., 1926), 686; Joseph Anderson's report, n.d. [approximately September 1803], in White, *Messages of the Governors*, 142–48.

43. Sevier to chiefs, April 2, 1796, in "Executive Journal of Governor John Sevier," *East Tennessee Historical Society's Publications* 1 (1929): 101–2; Sevier to chiefs, July 7, 1796, in "Executive Journal of Governor John Sevier," *East Tennessee Historical Society's Publications* 1 (1929): 110–11; Sevier to Little Turkey, August 25, 1796, in "Executive Journal of Governor John Sevier," *East Tennessee Historical Society's Publications* 1 (1929): 119; Sevier to Sampson Williams, January 11, 1797, in "Executive Journal of Governor John Sevier," *East Tennessee Historical Society's Publications* 1 (1929): 124; Journal of the House of Representatives of Tennessee, October 30, 1801, TSL; Sevier to Robertson, April 8, 1805, in "Correspondence of Gen. James Robertson," *American Historical Magazine* 5 (April 1900): 169–70.

44. Tennessee Laws, 1799, 3rd General Assembly, 1st session, Chapter X, 188–89; McLoughlin, *Cherokee Renascence*, 92–108; Tennessee Laws, 1807, chapter XXXIX, 270–71; An Act to Regulate Trade and Intercourse with the Indian Tribes, and to Preserve Peace on the Frontiers, March 30, 1802, §12 at 2 *Statutes at Large* 139 (Boston, 1845); Sevier to congressional representatives, December 8, 1807, John Sevier Papers, McClung Library, CS 5–2 (Sevier quotation); Dearborn to Meigs, March 26, 1808, M208; *ASP*, 754; *Carthage Gazette*, January 12, 1810; Dearborn to Meigs, November 21, 1803, M208.

45. William Blount to John Gray Blount, July 29, 1794, in Alice Barnwell Keith, William H. Masterson, and David T. Morgan, eds., *The John Gray Blount Papers* (Raleigh, 1952), 2:420–21; Governor Archibald Roane to Henry McKinney, April 28, 1802, TSL, Cher-

okee Collection; Citizens of Battle Creek to Meigs, October 19, 1809, M208; Meigs to Wear, September 21, 1802, M208; Wear to Meigs, September 27, 1802, M208.

46. Journal of William L. Brown, January 1, 1805–May 12, 1807, Topp Papers, TSL, Mf. 173; James Norman Smith Memoirs, 1807–1810, TSL, Mf. 157; Jane Henry Thomas Memoirs, 1804–1810, TSL, Ms. 1164, box 2; Norton, *Journal*, 29, 30, 31; report of Steiner and Schweinitz, in Samuel Cole Williams, ed., *Early Travels in the Tennessee Country, 1540–1800* (Johnson City, 1928), 458–59; *Tennessee Gazette*, August 21, 1805; Sevier to Gideon Blackburn, February 10, 1807, in Sevier and Madden, *Sevier Family History*, 163–64; private thoughts of John Steele, 1797, in H. M. Wagstaff, ed., *The Papers of John Steele* (Raleigh, 1924), 2:773; Draper MSS, 14DD15.

47. John Sevier to John Steele, May 8, 1798, "Executive Journal of Governor John Sevier," *East Tennessee Historical Society's Publications* 4 (January 1932): 149; Sevier to Anderson, April 5, 1798, in "Executive Journal of Governor John Sevier," *East Tennessee Historical Society's Publications* 4 (January 1932): 138–67, quotation at 138.

48. Gascoigne, *The Enlightenment and the Origins of European Australia*, 8, 12–13, 148–72; Alice L. Conklin, *A Mission to Civilize: The Republican Idea of Empire in France and West Africa, 1895–1930* (Stanford, 1997).

49. Ramsey, *Annals of Tennessee*, 641 (Blount quotation), 660–61 (Joint Committee quotation); General Assembly of Tennessee to William Blount, 1796, in Clarence Edwin Carter, ed., *The Territorial Papers of the United States: The Territory South of the River Ohio, 1790–1796*, vol. 4 (Washington, D.C., 1936), 423; letter from Campbell dated May 10, 1797, *Knoxville Gazette*, June 12, 1797, 1.

50. Sevier to John Steele, May 8, 1798, in "Executive Journal of Governor John Sevier," *East Tennessee Historical Society's Publications* 4 (January 1932): 149; 1796 remonstrance to Congress, in White, *Messages of the Governors*, 22–24. Stuart Banner notes the change in white belief from that of Indian ownership of land to one of occupancy among eastern lawyers and the federal government, a change that he locates in the early nineteenth century. He suggests that one cause of the change was the creation of preemption rights that holders reinterpreted as fee simple rights. Banner, *How the Indians Lost Their Land: Law and Power on the Frontier* (Cambridge, Mass., 2005), 150–90. I argue that the theory of occupancy arose in the 1790s. Settlers and the western state governments, not eastern lawyers or the United States, created this doctrine as part of the intellectual reconceptualization in which they degraded indigenous nationhood.

51. "Memorial of the Legislature of the State of Tennessee praying the extinguishing of Indian claims to lands within the limits of the State," November 25, 1803, Select Committee, National Archives, HR 8A-F5.5; McLoughlin, *Cherokee Renascence*, 49, 56; Ramsey, *Annals of Tennessee*, 641.

52. Message of governor to legislature, October 15, 1809, in White, *Messages of the Governors*, 285–87; Willie Blount to Andrew Jackson, December 28, 1809, in David T. Morgan, ed., *John Gray Blount Papers* (Raleigh, 1982), 4:112–14.

53. *The Cherokee Nation v. The State of Georgia*, 30 U.S. 1 (1831); *Worcester v. The State of*

Georgia, 31 U.S. 515, 550–56 (1832); McHugh, *Aboriginal Societies and the Common Law*, 117–77. Nancy Shoemaker positions Marshall's dilemma in *Johnson v. McIntosh* (1823) and the Cherokee cases as one in which he struggled with the concept of a nation within a nation and makes the very interesting observation that Native Americans had experience with this concept. Shoemaker, *A Strange Likeness*, 101–2. Marshall found this issue important in the earlier case of *Johnson v. McIntosh* (1823), where he held that the Indians had been conquered by Europeans and the sales of land by the Kaskaskias and Illinois Indians to private parties were not valid, but he did not articulate this as a concern in the Cherokee cases other than to note in *Cherokee Nation* that the Cherokees were not a foreign nation since they were located within the United States. In *Worcester*, Marshall nonetheless held that the Cherokees were a separate nation with rights to their lands. Unlike in *Johnson*, Marshall's concern in the Cherokee cases was to decide the meaning and extent of Cherokee sovereignty in relationship to the federal and state governments. The significant reason for the difference in some of the language about sovereignty in *Johnson* and the Cherokee cases was that, in *Johnson*, Marshall was dealing with a factual situation in which the Indians sold land to private individuals, neither party in the case was Native American, and there were no treaties pertinent to the sale between the United States and the Indians. In the Cherokee cases, Marshall's thinking was shaped in significant part by the posture of the case that did call on him to decide Native American sovereignty in relation to the United States and by the relationship embedded in the treaties and other facts of the case, a familial relationship that included Cherokee ideas.

54. Some legal scholars contend that the idea of trust supervision of Native Americans originated in Spain in 1532 with Franciscus de Vitoria, who proposed that Spain could govern Indians for the benefit of the Indians. In a few cases, the Crown or colonial officials appointed trustees to supervise Indian lands. Robert N. Clinton, Carole E. Goldberg, and Rebecca Tsosie, eds., *American Indian Law: Native Nations and the Federal System, Cases and Materials*, rev. 4th ed. (Newark, 2005), 72–75. While this may be true, Marshall did not cite any of these sources as authority.

55. Emmerich de Vattel, *The Law of Nations; or, Principles of the Law of Nature, Applied to the Conduct and Affairs of Nations and Sovereigns*, rev. ed. (London, 1797), bk. I, chap. I, §5, 6; chap. XVI, §192–99.

56. Susan Scheckel, *The Insistence of the Indian: Race and Nationalism in Nineteenth-Century American Culture* (Princeton, 1998), 4–7; Clinton et al., *American Indian Law*, 72, 219–414, 589–96.

57. Gascoigne, *The Enlightenment and the Origins of European Australia*, 163–64; McHugh, *Aboriginal Societies and the Common Law*, 117–78; John Hookey, "Settlement and Sovereignty," in Peter Hanks and Bryan Keon-Cohen, eds., *Aborigines and the Law: Essays in Memory of Elizabeth Eggleston* (Sydney, 1984), 1–18, at 4–6.

Chapter 4

1. *Knoxville Gazette*, June 15, 1793, 2; Tom Hatley, *The Dividing Paths: Cherokees and South Carolinians through the Era of Revolution* (New York, 1993), 161–63; Arthur Campbell to Governor, January 15, 1781, Draper MSS, 10S165.

2. Homi K. Bhabha, *The Location of Culture* (London, 1994), 1–2; Robert J. C. Young, *Postcolonialism: An Historical Introduction* (Oxford, 2001), 201–2; Silva Spitta, *Between Two Waters: Narratives of Transculturation in Latin America* (Houston, 1995), 1–12; Laura Donaldson, "Making a Joyful Noise: William Apess and the Search for Postcolonial Method(ism)," in Malini Johar Schueller and Edward Kunoskeskie, eds., *Messy Beginnings: Postcoloniality and Early American Studies* (New Brunswick, 2003), 40–41.

3. William G. McLoughlin, *Cherokee Renascence in the New Republic* (Princeton, 1986), 19–205; Colin G. Calloway, *The American Revolution in Indian Country: Crisis and Diversity in Native American Communities* (Cambridge, 1995), 189–212; Gregory Evans Dowd, *A Spirited Resistance: The North American Struggle for Unity, 1745–1815* (Baltimore, 1992), 47–64; Hatley, *The Dividing Paths*, 217–28; James Paul Pate, "The Chickamauga: A Forgotten Segment of Indian Resistance on the Southern Frontier" (Ph.D. diss., Mississippi State University, 1969), 55–149; Rennard Strickland, *Fire and Spirits: Cherokee Law from Clan to Court* (Norman, 1975), 48–49; Brent Alan "Yanusdi" Cox, *Heart of the Eagle: Tsi-yugunsini and the Emergence of the Chickamauga Confederacy* (Milan, Tenn., 1999); John P. Brown, *Old Frontiers: The Story of the Cherokee Indians from Earliest Times to the Date of Their Removal to the West* (Kingsport, 1938), 137–256; John R. Finger, "Tennessee Indian History: Creativity and Power," *Tennessee Historical Quarterly* 54 (Winter 1995): 286–305; R. S. Cotterill, *The Southern Indians: The Story of the Civilized Tribes before Removal* (Norman, 1954), 37–110. Anthony F. C. Wallace states that the Upper Towns were unified and the Chickamaugans were ruled by war councils, rather than a tribal council. Anthony F. C. Wallace, *Jefferson and the Indians: The Tragic Fate of the First Americans* (Cambridge, Mass., 1999), 301–2.

4. See chapter 2 for a discussion of the Chickamaugan military goals.

5. William McLoughlin recognized the nationalization process that the Cherokees undertook but saw it as part of their acceptance of the civilization program. McLoughlin, *Cherokee Renascence*, xvii.

6. Partha Chatterjee describes how anticolonial nationalists, unlike European nationalists, turned to the domain of their country's distinctive cultural identity to imagine the postcolonial nation into being. Partha Chatterjee, *The Nation and Its Fragments: Colonial and Postcolonial Histories* (Princeton, 1993), 5–10.

7. On blaming: talk by Onitositah, July 31, 1786, *SRCN*, 18:696–97; Patrick Henry to Richard Caswell, January 8, 1779, *SRNC*, 14:243–46. On mythmaking: Draper MSS, 5XX52. Tennesseans were participants in a national reimagining of Native Americans as tragic heroes. Susan Scheckel, *The Insistence of the Indian: Race and Nationalism in Nineteenth Century American Culture* (Princeton, 1998), 8–9.

8. McLoughlin, *Cherokee Renascence*, 58–59; Finger, "Tennessee Indian History: Creativ-

ity and Power," 286–305, at 301; Tiya Miles, *Ties that Bind: The Story of an Afro-Cherokee Family in Slavery and Freedom* (Berkeley, 2005), 71; Dowd, *A Spirited Resistance*, 160–61; Nathaniel Sheidley, "Unruly Men: Indians, Settlers, and the Ethos of Frontier Patriarchy in the Upper Tennessee Watershed, 1763–1815" (Ph.D. diss., Princeton University, 1999), 265–97. All historians seem to agree that the Lower Town's acceptance of civilization represented a major break from the past, although they assign different reasons, with McLoughlin, Finger, and Miles pointing to the influence of the *métis*, and Dowd and Sheidley noting the wealth and plunder accumulated by the chiefs. I argue that the Lower Town's interest in economic expansion was a continuation of earlier beliefs.

9. Talk by Chulcoah, June 29, 1791, Treaty of Holston, Draper MSS, 15U37–38; talk by Onitositah, July 17, 1777, in Archibald Henderson, "The Treaty of Long Island at Holston, July 1777," *North Carolina Historical Review* 8 (January 1931): 91; John Norton, *The Journal of Major John Norton*, ed. Carl F. Klinch and James J. Tallman (Toronto, 1816; repr., 1970), 81; talk by chiefs, April 11, 1810, M208 (quotation); talk by Attakullahkullah, October 19, 1770, Journal of Treaty of Lochaber, in W. Stitt Robinson, ed., *Early American Indian Documents: Treaties and Laws, 1607–1789; Virginia Treaties, 1723–1775* (Frederick, 1983), 5:364–65; talk by Onitositah, September 25, 1782, in J. G. M. Ramsey, *The Annals of Tennessee to the End of the Eighteenth Century* (Johnson City, 1853; repr., 1926), 271; talk by Onitositah, November 23, 1785, Treaty of Hopewell, *ASP*, 41.

10. Talk by Onitositah, November 26, 1785, *ASP*, 42.

11. Talk by Scolacutta, July 2, 1791, Draper MSS, 15U21–23; talk by Onitositah, 1777, in Samuel Cole Williams, *Tennessee during the Revolutionary War* (Knoxville, 1944), 268 (quotation).

12. Cynthia Cumfer, "Nan-ye-hi/Nancy Ward," in Beverly Bond and Sarah Wilkerson-Freeman, eds., *Tennessee Women: Challenging Boundaries, Claiming Identities* (Athens, forthcoming).

13. Joseph Martin to Governor Caswell, May 11, 1786, *SRNC*, 18:604–6; George Welbank to Alexander McKee, April 12, 1791, in Philip Hamer, "The British in Canada and the Southern Indians, 1790–1794," *East Tennessee Historical Society's Publications* 2 (1930): 112–13; Brown, *Old Frontiers*, 262, 281–84; Ramsey, *Annals of Tennessee*, 518–19; Draper MSS, 31S29, 33; talk by Newota, November 29, 1785, *ASP*, 43; Treaty of Holston, Draper MSS, 15U7–46; Blount to Henry Knox, March 20, 1792, *ASP*.

14. Pate, "The Chickamauga," 99, 158; Brown's captivity, Draper MSS, 5XX52; Louis-Philippe, *Diary of My Travels in America: Louis-Philippe, King of France, 1830–1848*, trans. Stephen Becker (New York, 1976), April 30, 1797, p. 77; Draper MSS, 5XX41. Chapter 1 described instances of women warning traders.

15. Letter from a Tiptonite, Draper MSS, 9DD53; Red Bird's information, September 15, 1792, *ASP*, 282.

16. Calloway, *The American Revolution in Indian Country*, 190–91, 201; Hatley, *Dividing Paths*, 217–28.

17. Brown, *Old Frontiers*, 164, 353; Cox, *Heart of the Eagle*, 204–5; Arthur Campbell to

Governor, January 15, 1781, Draper MSS, 10S167; letter from Tuskegethee, June 12, 1787, Cherokee Collection, TSL, Ms. 1787, box 1, folder 27.

18. Draper MSS, 5XX41; Carey's report, November 3, 1792, *ASP*, 328; Norton, *Journal*, 39; narrative of Joseph Brown, in Ramsey, *Annals of Tennessee*, 510–13; Draper MSS, 32S299–300.

19. Talk by The Raven, July 16, 1777, in Henderson, "Treaty of Long Island at Holston," 87.

20. William Christian to Joseph Martin, July 8, 1778, Draper MSS, 1XX36; Carolyn Thomas Foreman, *Indian Women Chiefs* (Muskogee, 1954), 78; Draper MSS, 3JJ208–10; talk by Scolacutta, October 6, 1788, Draper MSS, 12S207–11; Joseph Martin to Henry Knox, January 15, 1789, *ASP*, 46–47; *Knoxville Gazette*, May 5, 1792, 2–3.

21. Commissioners to Richard Henry Lee, December 2, 1785, *ASP*, 38; letter from inhabitant of French Broad, October 18, 1789, Draper MSS, 9DD53.

22. Onitositah to Governor of Virginia, March 16, 1784, Cherokee Collection, Mf. 815; Ramsey, *Annals of Tennessee*, 274; John Haywood, *The Civil and Political History of the State of Tennessee from Its Earliest Settlement Up to the Year 1796 Including the Boundaries of the State* (Knoxville, 1823), 97–99, 452–53, 457–58; Blount to Secretary of War, September 11, 1792, Clarence Edwin Carter, ed., *The Territorial Papers of the United States: The Territory South of the River Ohio, 1790–1796*, vol. 4 (Washington, D.C., 1936), 167–68.

23. Talk by Scolacutta, October 6, 1788, Draper MSS, 12S207-1; letter from inhabitant of French Broad, October 18, 1789, Draper MSS, 9DD53 (quotation).

24. Account of Henry Stuart, August 25, 1776, *CRNC*, 10:764.

25. John Sevier to Alexander Martin, March 22, 1785, *SRNC*, 22:640–42 (quotation); McGillivray to Joseph Martin, April 11, 1788, Cherokee Collection, Mf. 815, reel 1, box 1, folder 14; Draper MSS, 30S486–88; deposition of Daniel Thornbury, April 10, 1792, *ASP*, 275–75.

26. Talk by Chulcoah, June 28, 1791, Draper MSS, 15U9 (quotation); Draper MSS, 12S24–26; Joseph Martin to Governor of Virginia, March 26, 1785, *VSP*, 4:22; James Bolls to David Henley, June 18, 1801, David Henley Papers, TSL, Mf. 625; report on the petition of Alexander Scott, December 20, 1810, Select Committee, National Archives, Washington, D.C., HR 11A-C9.4; report by Blount to Knox, *ASP*, 329–31; deposition of Daniel Thornbury, April 10, 1792, *ASP*, 274.

27. Martin's letter, July 10, 1788, in Stephen B. Weeks, "General Joseph Martin and the War of the Revolution in the West," *American Historical Association Annual Report*, 1893 (Washington, D.C., 1894), 401–77, at 462; McGillivray to Joseph Martin, April 11, 1788, Cherokee Collection, Mf. 815, reel 1, box 1, folder 14; talk by Kaiateh, July 18, 1785, Draper MSS, 12S31–32; Joseph Martin to Governor Caswell, May 11, 1786, *SRNC*, 18:604–6; Joseph Martin to Governor Caswell, September 19, 1785, *SRNC*, 17:521–22; Joseph Brown captivity narrative, in Ramsey, *Annals of Tennessee*, 514.

28. Draper MSS, 30S479–83; Joseph Martin to Henry Knox, July 10, 1788, in Weeks, "General Joseph Martin and the War of the Revolution in the West," 401–77, at 462; Martin to General Russell, August 29, 1785, Cherokee Collection, Mf. 815, box 1, folder 17.

29. Brown, *Old Frontiers*, 217–19, 342; Pate, "The Chickamauga," 159; Joseph Brown's captivity narrative, in Ramsey, *Annals of Tennessee*, 514.

30. Governor Beverley Randolph to George Washington, November 27, 1790, Draper MSS, 10S117–18; note by Blount, September 13, 1792, in Cora Bales Sevier and Nancy S. Madden, *Sevier Family History* (Washington, D.C., 1961), 112; Draper MSS, 30S486–88; talk by The Nephew, May 20, 1795, John McKee file, University of Tennessee Special Collection, Knoxville, MS-1252 (quotation).

31. Hatley, *Dividing Paths*, 225; narrative of Joseph Brown, in Ramsey, *Annals of Tennessee*, 510–13.

32. Blount to Knox, November 8, 1792, *ASP*, 325–27; talk by Tuskegethee, June 12, 1787, Cherokee Collection, Ms. 1787, folder 27; Brown, *Old Frontiers*, 270; Cox, *Heart of the Eagle*, 191; talk by Nentooyah, January 7, 1792, *ASP*, 204.

33. Norton, *Journal*, 63–64, 70, 114–15; William G. McLoughlin, *Cherokees and Missionaries, 1789–1839* (New Haven, 1984), 1–81; Cumfer, "Nan-ye-hi/Nancy Ward."

34. Theda Perdue, *Cherokee Women: Gender and Culture Change, 1700–1835* (Lincoln, 1998), 104, 139–40; Cox, *Heart of the Eagle*, 201; Strickland, *Fire and the Spirits*, 58–60, 96–98, 104. For other evidence that clan law survived the new governmental law, see Theda Perdue, "Clan and Court: Another Look at the Early Cherokee Republic," *American Indian Quarterly* 24 (2000): 562–69.

35. William Lovely to Meigs, June 1, 1803, M208; J. Blacke to Meigs, December 19, 1803, M208; McLoughlin, *Cherokee Renascence*, 31, 170–71.

36. Several historians have examined the Cherokee understanding of race primarily with reference to how Indians saw themselves in relation to Europeans. William G. McLoughlin and Walter H. Conser, " 'The First Man Was Red'—Cherokee Responses to the Debate over Indian Origins, 1760–1860," *American Quarterly* 41 (June 1989): 243–64; Nancy Shoemaker, "How Indians Got to Be Red," *American Historical Review* 102 (June 1997): 624–44. Nancy Shoemaker describes how skin color came to be the body marker of race and how Indians manipulated this marker for diplomatic ends. Shoemaker, *A Strange Likeness: Becoming Red and White in Eighteenth-Century North America* (Oxford, 2004), 125–40. Nancy Shoemaker and Circe Sturm argue that by the late eighteenth century, the Cherokees had internalized some ideas of race as fundamental to their own identity, citing as evidence statements by Cherokees claiming that God made them the first possessors of the land, to which they were thus entitled. Shoemaker, *A Strange Likeness*, 137; Sturm, *Blood Politics: Race, Culture, and Identity in the Cherokee Nation of Oklahoma* (Berkeley, 2002), 47. However, the Cherokees made these statements not to assert a claim to ownership based on race but on first possession.

　　Scholars have also considered how southern Indians viewed *métis*. Theda Perdue points out that the Cherokees used racial categories to see blacks as inferior but did not use race as a classification to distinguish between native-white *métis* and full-blooded Cherokees and other southern Indians in internal affairs until long after removal. Perdue, *Slavery and the Evolution of Cherokee Society, 1540–1866* (Knoxville, 1979), 48; *Mixed Blood Indians: Racial Construction in the Early South* (Athens, 2003),

90–94; and "Race and Culture: Writing the Ethnohistory of the Early South," *Eth-nohistory* 51 (2004): 701–723. Examining primarily Indians' views about African Americans, other scholars have argued that race played a major role in southern Indian affairs much earlier, a point with which Perdue agrees. Claudio Saunt et al., "Rethinking Race and Culture in the Early South," *Ethnohistory* 53 (2006): 399–405; Theda Perdue, "A Reply to Saunt, et al." *Ethnohistory* 53 (2006): 407. The Cherokee did use a vocabulary of color to distinguish between Native Americans and people of African and American ancestry but I am arguing that, in this early period, they used these categories loosely to articulate differences of status or culture, not inherent racial characteristics.

37. Perdue, *Slavery*, 12, 16, 23–42; Hatley, *Dividing Paths*, 196 (quotation); J. Seagrove to William Blount, February 10, 1794, "Correspondence of Gen. James Robertson," *American Historical Magazine* 3 (July 1898): 284–85; Louise-Philippe, *Diary*, April 30, 179; John McDonald to Meigs, April 20, 1809, M208; Benjamin Hawkins, *Letters of Benjamin Hawkins, 1796–1806: Collections of the Georgia Historical Society*, vol. 9 (Savannah, 1916), January 16, 1805, 447.

38. Perdue, "Clan and Court"; Draper MSS, 32S140–80; Draper MSS, 29S95–96; Brown, *Old Frontiers*, 212; Ross to Meigs, June 14, 1803, M208; Lovely to Meigs, May 15, 1803, M208; Atawgwatihih to Meigs, March 6, 1805, M208; McLoughlin, *Cherokee Renascence*, 339.

39. For different views on the origins of the categories of red and white: McLoughlin and Conser, " 'The First Man Was Red'—Cherokee Responses to the Debate over Indian Origins, 1760–1860"; Shoemaker, "How Indians Got to Be Red."

40. Talk by Scolacutta, July 2, 1791, Draper MSS, 15U21–22; talk by Badger's Speaker The Nephew, July 2, 1791, Draper MSS, 15U21; Carrie C. Deming and Laura E. Lattrell, comp., "Marriage Notices Appearing in Knoxville Newspapers, 1791–1813," *East Tennessee Historical Society's Publications* 11 (1939): 116–20; report of Steiner and Schweinitz, in Samuel Cole Williams, ed., *Early Travels in the Tennessee Country 1540–1800* (Johnson City, 1928), 486; Norton, *Journal*, 41–42, 51.

41. Perdue, *Cherokee Women*, 53–54; Brown, *Old Frontiers*, 331.

42. Information to Mrs. Meigs by John Westpoint, end of 1805, M208; Nicholas Byers to Meigs, August 28, 1805, M208; William Lovely to Meigs, March 17, 1803, M208; Adam Rothman, *Slave Country: American Expansion and the Origins of the Deep South* (Cambridge, Mass., 2005), 60.

43. Claim by Bartlet Robbins against Vann, October 25, 1808, M208; Jonathan Lowry to Meigs, May 18, 1808, M208 (quotation).

44. Norton, *Journal*, 76, 78; Meigs to Secretary of War, October 7, 1801, M208; Two Killer and others to Meigs, January 8, 1808, M208; quotation in Strickland, *Fire and the Spirits*, 59.

45. Talk by Nentooyah, December 31, 1794, in "Correspondence of Gen. James Robertson," *American Historical Magazine* 4 (January 1899): 85; report of Steiner and Schweinitz, 1799, in Williams, *Early Travels*, 474.

46. McLoughlin, *Cherokee Renascence*, 58–60; conference at Eustinale, April 20, 1803, M208; talk from the Upper District, March 20, 1801, M208; Kanetetoka and others to Meigs, May 2, 1802, M208.

47. Springplace Diary, June 23, 1803, Moravian Mission among the Indians, Library of Congress, Washington, D.C., Ms. Div., reel 193, folder 3; Meigs to Dearborn, February 5, 1803, M208; Sevier to Robertson, May 20, 1808, in "Correspondence of Gen. James Robertson," *American Historical Magazine* 5:3 (July 1900): 255–56. See chapter 3 for more discussion on the role of women in diplomacy after 1794.

48. Meigs to William Lovely, February 9, 1802, M208; Chuquilatague to Meigs, November 20, 1802, M208. On northern annuity chiefs: Richard White, *The Middle Ground: Indians, Empires, and Republics in the Great Lakes Region, 1650–1815* (Cambridge, 1991), 469–523.

49. David Henley's Waste Book, March 28, April 10, April 26, May 17, and May 24, 1798, McClung Library, Knoxville, Tennessee, CS 6–2.

50. McLoughlin, *Cherokee Renascence*, 139–41.

51. Meigs to Dearborn, March 31, 1802, M208; Meigs to Dearborn, June 27, 1802, M208; Charles Hicks to Meigs, March 31, 1805, M208; Jonathan Lowry to Meigs, October 20, 1808, M208; Meigs to Dearborn, October 25, 1803, M208; Atawgwatihih, Uwenahi, and Selukuki Wohellengh to Meigs, March 23, 1805, M208; Meigs to Daniel Smith, April 26, 1805, M208; Meigs to Daniel Smith, May 21, 1805, M208; address to Cherokee Council by Meigs, April 2, 1806, M208; notes of Speech by Meigs to Cherokee, n.d. [found at end of 1806], M208; McLoughlin, *Cherokee Renascence*, 126.

52. Atawgwatihih to Meigs, May 6, 1807, M208; Captain A. B. Armisteads to Meigs, August 9, 1807, M208; L. C. Hall to Addison Armstead, August 8, 1807, M208; Joseph Phillips to Meigs, August 15, 1807, M208. As in the Northwest, the United States attempted to control the Cherokees through annuity chiefs but, unlike the Northwest Indians, the Cherokees successfully assumed control of their government. White, *The Middle Ground*, 469–523.

53. McLoughlin, *Cherokee Renascence*, 119–24; William G. McLoughlin, "Thomas Jefferson and the Beginning of Cherokee Nationalism, 1806–1809," *William and Mary Quarterly* 32 (October 1975): 547–80; *Clarion*, November 15, 1808, 3 (quotation).

54. Norton, *Journal*, 133.

55. Raymond D. Fogelson, "Cherokee Notions of Power," in Raymond D. Fogelson and Richard N. Adams, eds., *The Anthropology of Power: Ethnographic Studies from Asia, Oceania, and the New World* (New York, 1977), 186; National Council to Meigs, September 27, 1809, M208; Norton, *Journal*, 73.

56. Report of Steiner and Schweinitz, 1799, in Williams, *Early Travels*, 468; McLoughlin, *Cherokee Renascence*, 56–57, 94, 106–7, 129–37, 143–67, 170–71; Norton, *Journal*, 151 (quotation). William McLoughlin contends that there was considerable hostility between the Cherokees who moved and those who remained in the East and that the new Cherokee identity required that, to be Cherokee, one had to remain in the East. McLoughlin, *Cherokee Renascence*, 128–45. This assumes that the political decision to

retain ownership of the lands in those who remained dictated social opprobrium toward those who left. Contemporaneous sources state that this was not the case.

57. Chiefs to Meigs, April 11, 1810, M208; National Council to Meigs, April 9, 1810, M208.

58. Meigs to Eustis, July 20, 1810, M208; talk by Chuquilatague, June 12, 1794, John Howard Payne Papers, Newberry Library, Chicago, vol. 7, part 1; Norton, *Journals*, 126.

59. Hawkins, *Letters*, November 26, 28, 1798; Norton, *Journal*, 36, 46, 70–71, 125; Louis-Philippe, *Diary*, April 30, 1797, p. 82; report of Steiner and Schweinitz, 1799, in Williams, *Early Travels*, 469–71, 489–90; "Journal of Governor John Sevier," November 14, 1798, *Tennessee Historical Magazine* 5 (January 1920); Meigs to Cherokee chiefs, March 27, 1810, M208; Meigs to Cherokee chiefs, March 27, 1810, M208; Foreman, *Indian Women Chiefs*, 78; claim by Bartlet Robbins against Vann, October 25, 1808, M208; Perdue, *Cherokee Women*, 118–20.

60. James Norman Smith Memoirs, 1807–1810, TSL, Mf. 157, p. 85; talk by John McKee, May 20, 1795, John McKee Papers, University of Tennessee Special Collection, MS-1252; Richard Thomas book, August 16, 1798, in Hawkins, *Letters*, 497; Meigs to Eustis, December 1, 1809, M208; Norton, *Journal*, 38, 61–62, 66; Silas Dinsmoor to Meigs, January 27, 1803, M208; Meigs to Sampson Williams, July 29, 1803.

61. James Iwrin to Andrew Jackson, January 25, 1805, *Papers*, II; James Ore to John Sevier, May 31, 1798, in "Executive Journal of Governor John Sevier," *East Tennessee Historical Society's Publications* 4 (January 1932); McLoughlin, *Cherokee Renascence*, 71, 73, 85, 124–25, 137, 151; Louis-Philippe, *Diary*, April 30, 1797; Norton, *Journal*, 54–55; William Stanley to Return Meigs, January 3, 1802, M208.

62. John Hurst to Meigs, November 22, 1806, M208; William Small to Meigs, June 17, 1809, M208; James Ore to Meigs, October 2, 1809, M208; Meigs to Henry Dearborn, February 9, 1801, M208; Meigs to William Lovely, June 8, 1804, M208; McLoughlin, *Cherokee Renascence*, 55.

63. McLoughlin, *Cherokee Renascence*, 107; Meigs to Dearborn, March 21, 1802, M208; report of Steiner and Schweinitz, November 10, 1799, in Williams, *Early Travels*, 470; Meigs to Israel Wheeler, November 22, 1801, M208; Chuquilatague to Meigs, June 24, 1803, M208; Meigs to Secretary of War, February 5, 1803, M208; Resolutions of deputation of Cherokee, January 4, 1806, M208; Enola and Atawgwatihih to Meigs, April 7, 1806, M208; Meigs to Dearborn, July 11, 1808, M208; Council at Willstown, September 19, 1806, M208.

Chapter 5

1. Joanna Tipton to Sinking Creek Baptist Church, May 16, 1807, Stickley Collection, TSL, Mf. 1198, box 20, folder 3. The letter is somewhat garbled. My account represents the most likely reconstruction of events.

2. Very little scholarship focuses on the beliefs and cultural logic of slaves or free blacks on the trans-Appalachian frontier. In his monumental work on slavery, Ira Berlin classified Tennessee as part of the Upper South, but his study of the region emphasized

Maryland, North Carolina, and Virginia, where the dynamics of slavery were very different. Ira Berlin, *Many Thousands Gone: The First Two Centuries of Slavery in North America* (London, 1998), 256–89; Ira Berlin, *Generations of Captivity: A History of African-American Slaves* (Cambridge, Mass., 2003), 159–244; Adam Rothman, *Slave Country: American Expansion and the Origins of the Deep South* (Cambridge, Mass., 2005), 36–70. For studies focused largely on white experience of slavery on the frontier: Betty Wood, *Slavery in Colonial Georgia, 1730–1775* (Athens, 1984); Julia Floyd Smith, *Slavery and Rice Culture in Low Country Georgia, 1750–1860* (Knoxville, 1985). Free blacks on the trans-Appalachian frontier are almost unstudied. For a rare exception, see Anita S. Goodstein, "Black History on the Nashville Frontier, 1780–1810," *Tennessee Historical Quarterly* 38 (Winter 1979): 401–20. The works on free blacks in slave states include some examination of their cognitive universe. Brenda Stevenson, *Life in Black and White: Family and Community in the Slave South* (New York, 1996). More has been written about free black thinking in the north: Gary Nash, *Forging Freedom: The Formation of Philadelphia's Black Community, 1720–1840* (Cambridge, Mass., 1988); Robert J. Swan, "John Teasman: African-American Educator and the Emergence of Community in Early Black New York City, 1787–1815," *Journal of the Early Republic* 12 (Fall 1992): 331–56.

3. On frontiers: Peter Wood, *The Black Majority: Negroes in Colonial South Carolina from 1670 through the Stono Rebellion* (New York, 1974), 95–130; Daniel H. Usner Jr., *Indians, Settlers, and Slaves in a Frontier Exchange Economy: The Lower Mississippi Valley before 1783* (Chapel Hill, 1992), 54–56, 136–41; Peter Kolchin, *American Slavery, 1619–1877* (New York, 1993), chap. 1; Jane Landers, *Black Society in Spanish Florida* (Urbana, 1999); Berlin, *Many Thousands Gone*, 29–46, 64–71; Berlin, *Generations of Captivity*, 136–38. The period of relative freedom for slaves varied greatly. It lasted about a century in Louisiana, either because a slave and Native American revolt in the 1720s or neglect by the French metropole destroyed the developing plantation economy. Berlin, *Generations of Captivity*, 42, 88–96 (revolt); Usner, *Indians, Settlers, and Slaves in a Frontier Exchange Economy*, 79–80 (neglect). Slaves in Florida experienced looser regulation for centuries because of Spain's defensive policy of luring slaves from the British colonies. Landers, *Black Society in Spanish Florida*. The period was only a couple of decades for South Carolina creoles, many of whom were shipped from Caribbean plantations. Berlin, *Many Thousands Gone*, 64–71. On Africa: John Thornton, *Africa and Africans in the Making of the Atlantic World, 1400–1680* (Cambridge, 1992), 206–34; Sylvia R. Frey, *Water from a Rock: Black Resistance in a Revolutionary Age* (Princeton, 1991), chap. 9.

4. Eugene D. Genovese, *Roll, Jordan, Roll: The World the Slaves Made* (New York, 1972); James Oakes, *The Ruling Race: A History of American Slaveholders* (New York, 1982, 1983); Stephen Aron, *How the West Was Lost: The Transformation of Kentucky from Daniel Boone to Henry Clay* (Baltimore, 1996), 143–48, 164–66; Philip D. Morgan, *Slave Counterpoint: Black Culture in the Eighteenth-Century Chesapeake and Lowcountry* (Chapel Hill, 1998), 257–300; Berlin, *Generations of Captivity*, 51–96.

5. George P. Rawick, *From Sundown to Sunup: The Making of the Black Community* (Westport, 1972); Herbert G. Gutman, *The Black Family in Slavery and Freedom, 1750–1925* (New York, 1976); Lawrence W. Levine, *Black Culture and Black Consciousness* (New York, 1977); Thomas L. Webber, *Deep Like the Rivers: Education in the Slave Quarter Community, 1831–1865* (New York, 1978); Jacqueline Jones, *Labor of Love, Labor of Sorrow: Black Women, Work, and the Family from Slavery to the Present* (New York, 1985); Stevenson, *Life in Black and White*. On religious beliefs: Mechal Sobel, *The World They Made Together: Black and White Values in Eighteenth-Century Virginia* (Princeton, 1987); Frey, *Water from a Rock*, chap. 9; Robert Olwell, *Masters, Slaves, and Subjects: The Culture of Power in the South Carolina Low Country* (Ithaca, 1998), 103–40.

6. Jon F. Sensbach, *Rebecca's Revival: Creating Black Christianity in the Atlantic World* (Cambridge, Mass., 2005); Laurent Dubois, *A Colony of Citizens: Revolution and Slave Emancipation in the French Caribbean, 1787–1804* (Chapel Hill, 2004); Landis, *Black Society in Spanish Florida*; Berlin, *Many Thousands Gone*.

7. Postcolonial writers describe how subaltern and plural narratives of community can exist with and challenge the universalistic narrative of nationalism. Partha Chatterjee, *The Nation and Its Fragments: Colonial and Postcolonial Histories* (Princeton, 1993); Gayatri Chakravorty Spivak, *A Critique of Postcolonial Reason: Toward a History of the Vanishing Present* (Cambridge, Mass., 1999).

8. Very little work has been done on how slaves viewed white governance. Sylvia R. Frey notes that the revolutionary ideology inspired slaves to escape and to plan insurrections. Frey, *Water from a Rock*, 49–64. William Wiecek describes the impact of republican ideology on slaves in the post-Revolutionary period. Wiecek, *The Sources of Antislavery Constitutionalism in America, 1760–1848* (Ithaca, 1977), 40–61.

9. Historians have explored slave attitudes, values, and ethics about work and the economy in other regions. Ira Berlin and Philip D. Morgan, eds., *Cultivation and Culture: Labor and the Shaping of Slave Life in the Americas* (Charlottesville, 1993); Betty Wood, *Women's Work, Men's Work: The Informal Slave Economies of Lowcountry Georgia* (Athens, 1995).

10. Thornton, *Africa and Africans in the Making of the Atlantic World*, 183–234; Frey, *Water from a Rock*, 27–28; Suzanne Miers and Igor Kopytoff, eds., *Slavery in Africa: Historical and Anthropological Perspectives* (Madison, 1977), 17–18; Parker Shipton, "Legalism and Loyalism: European, African, and Human Rights," in Bartholomew Dean and Jerome M. Levi, eds., *At the Risk of Being Heard: Identity, Indigenous Rights, and Postcolonial States* (Ann Arbor, 2003), 46, 65; Ira Berlin, Steven F. Miller, and Leslie S. Rowland, "Afro-American Families in the Transition from Slavery to Freedom," *Radical History Review* 42 (1988): 88–121, at 89; John S. Mbiti, *African Religions and Philosophy* (Garden City, 1970), 135–36; Sobel, *The World They Made Together*, 9, 18–20, 26–33, 71–74, 174–75.

11. Miers and Kopytoff, *Slavery in Africa*, 19–21, 24–25, 39; Morgan, *Slave Counterpoint*, 611; Paul E. Lovejoy, *Transformations in Slavery: A History of Slavery in Africa*, 2nd ed. (Cambridge, 2000), 13–14; Thornton, *Africa and Africans in the Making of the Atlantic World*, 129–303, chap. 8; Sobel, *The World They Made Together*, 52, 180.

12. Genovese, *Roll, Jordan, Roll*; Berlin, *Generations of Captivity*, 63–64; Rothman, *Slave Country*, 20; Morgan, *Slave Counterpoint*, 257–300; Kenneth S. Greenberg, *Masters and Statesmen: The Political Culture of American Slavery* (Baltimore, 1985).

13. Genovese, *Roll, Jordan, Roll*; Berlin, *Many Thousands Gone*, 37–46, 109–41, 256–89; Kolchin, *American Slavery,* chap. 1; Kathleen M. Brown, *Good Wives, Nasty Wenches, and Anxious Patriarchs: Gender, Race, and Power in Colonial Virginia* (Chapel Hill, 1996); Sobel, *The World They Made Together*, 202–9.

14. There has been relatively little study of slavery during the pioneer period in the trans-Appalachian region. Ira Berlin's otherwise masterful synthesis subsumes Tennessee into the Upper South and discusses slavery throughout the region as part of the "Revolutionary Generation." Berlin, *Many Thousands Gone*, 256–89. This approach overlooks the impact that frontier conditions had on slavery in the transmontane areas during the post-Revolutionary period.

15. James Smith's account, 1766–67, in Samuel Cole Williams, *Early Travels in the Tennessee Country, 1540–1800* (Johnson City, 1928), 204–7; letter from Joseph Martin dated May 9, 1769, Draper MSS, 3XX4; William Christian to brother, December 5, 1778, Draper MSS 2U52.

16. William K. Boyd, "Some North Carolina Tracts of the Eighteenth Century," *North Carolina Historical Review* 3 (1926): 591–648, at 616; Lucy Kennerly Gump, "Possessions and Patterns of Living in Washington County: The 20 Years before Tennessee Statehood, 1777–1796" (master's thesis, East Tennessee State University, 1989), 136–37; Nathaniel Sheidley, "Unruly Men: Indians, Settlers, and the Ethos of Frontier Patriarchy in the Upper Tennessee Watershed, 1763–1815" (Ph.D. diss., Princeton University, 1999), 117–21.

17. Hugh Williamson to John Gray Blount, November 25, 1792, and William Blount to John Gray Blount, July 29, 1794, in Alice Barnwell Keith, ed., *The John Gray Blount Papers*, vol. 2 (Raleigh, 1959), 218–19, 420–21; John Chisholm to Isaac Shelby, January 24, 1795, Draper MSS 11DD53; Robert E. Corlew, *Tennessee: A Short History*, 2nd ed. (Knoxville, 1980), 212; Harriette Simpson Arnow, *Flowering of the Cumberland* (New York, 1963), 94. The population data in this and the remainder of this chapter were derived from the following sources: U.S. Census, 1790, *Return of the Whole Number of Persons within the Several Districts of the United States* (Philadelphia, 1791); 1795 Census Schedule for Territory of the United States of America South of the River Ohio, in Clarence Edwin Carter, ed., *The Territorial Papers of the United States: The Territory South of the River Ohio, 1790–1796*, vol. 4 (Washington, D.C., 1936), 405; 1800 Schedule of the Inhabitants in the State of Tennessee, *Tennessee Gazette*, November 11, 1801, 2; U.S. Census, 1810 (Early American Imprints, 2nd series, no. 24084); 1810 census schedules for Rutherford and Grainger counties, National Archives and Records Service, *Federal Population Censuses, 1790–1890* (Washington, D.C., 1971). Except for these schedules, all of the census schedules from 1790 to 1810 for the Southwest Territory and the state of Tennessee have been lost.

18. Three of the seventy-eight advertisements for escaped Tennessee slaves in the Ten-

nessee papers from the inception of publication in 1791 until 1811 described African-born slaves or slaves with broken English. *Knoxville Gazette*, March 27, 1795, and August 6, 1806; *Clarion*, July 27, 1810, 4. On beliefs: Edwin M. Gardner Memoirs, Diaries, TSL, Mn. 1225, loc. no. II-H-4, box 3, pp. 8–9; Kolchin, *American Slavery*, 41.

19. Harriet C. Owsley, ed., "Travel through the Indian Country in the Early 1800's: The Memoirs of Martha Philips Martin," *Tennessee Historical Quarterly* 21 (March 1962): 66–81, at 66; James Norman Smith Memoirs, TSL, Mf. 157, p. 64; Edwin M. Gardner Memoirs, p. 6.

20. Washington County Court Clerk Minute Books, TSL, roll 129, vol. 1, February 1779, pp. 64, 69, 75–76; Draper MSS, 30S156, 246–48; Jonathan D. Martin, *Divided Mastery: Slave Hiring in the American South* (Cambridge, Mass., 2004), 44–56; "Journal of Governor John Sevier," October 18, 1795, October 2, 1795, in *Tennessee Historical Magazine* 5 (October 1919); *Margaret Brown v. William Henry*, Knox County Court of Pleas and Quarter Sessions, Knox County Archives, Knoxville, Tennessee, box 1, docket #107/123; Goodstein, "Black History on the Nashville Frontier, 1780–1810," 404.

21. Robert King to Andrew Jackson, October 23, 1793, *Papers*, I; *Knoxville Gazette*, October 28, 1801, 3; Goodstein, "Black History on the Nashville Frontier, 1780–1810," 409; Rules and Regulations of Knoxville, February 12, 1802, Knoxville City Council Minute Book, 1801–1834A, Article 2, Knox County Archives; Records of the Board of Commissioners for Nashville, April 7, 1802, TSL, THS Miscellaneous Files, Mf. 678, reel 6, box 11, N-19.

22. John Bezis-Selfa, "A Tale of Two Ironworks: Slavery, Free Labor, Work, and Resistance in the Early Republic," *William and Mary Quarterly* 56 (October 1999): 677–700; Samuel C. Williams, "Early Iron Works in the Tennessee Country," *Tennessee Historical Quarterly* 6 (March 1947): 39–46; deposition of Ellias Kapper, June 2, 1800, Stanley Horn Collection, TSL, loc. III-F-1, box 1, folder 14; *Clarion*, October 5, 1810, 4; December 28, 1810, p. 4; *Carthage Gazette*, June 29, 1810; *Clarion*, June 18 and 23, 1809.

23. Records of the Board of Commissioners for Nashville, April 7, 1802; petition from Nashville, Legislative Petitions 1799, TSL, [1-2-1799]; Goodstein, "Black History on the Nashville Frontier, 1780–1810," 406, 409, 411.

24. Bethel Communities Zion Church, TSL, THS Miscellaneous Files, Mf. 678, reel 7, box 12, P-109; Mill Creek Baptist, November 15, 1800, SBHL, Mf. 3337; Zion Presbyterian Church, 1805–1812, TSL, Mf. 125; Goodstein, "Black History on the Nashville Frontier, 1780–1810," 416–17.

25. "Historical Sketch of Church," Mill Creek Baptist Church and February 14, 1801; Mill Creek Baptist, January 17, 1801.

26. Theda Perdue, *Slavery and the Evolution of Cherokee Society, 1540–1866* (Knoxville, 1979); John Norton, *The Journal of Major John Norton*, ed. Carl F. Klinch and James J. Tallman (Toronto, 1816; repr., 1970), 45; *Knoxville Gazette*, October 6, 1792 (Cherokee); James Vann to Return Meigs, November 15, 1802, M208; Memoirs of William Hall, Diaries, TSL, Ms. 891, loc. II-H-2, box 1, pp. 3–20.

27. Historians find that slaves had white allies and trading partners who provided assis-

tance in other locations. John Hope Franklin and Loren Schweninger, *Runaway Slaves: Rebels on the Plantation* (New York, 1999), 30–33; John Campbell, "As 'A Kind of Freeman'?: Slaves' Market-Related Activities in the South Carolina Up Country, 1800–1860," in Berlin and Morgan, *Cultivation and Culture*, 251–52. On defense: Draper MSS, 30S246–48; Joseph Bishop, *The Life of Joseph Bishop* (Spartanburg, 1974), 34–36. Historians are beginning to comment on the use of slaves as capital. Martin, *Divided Mastery*, 18–19. There has been less recognition of their importance as collateral and specie.

28. James Ross, *Life and Times of Elder Reuben Ross* (Philadelphia, 1882), 189–90; Goodstein, "Black History on the Nashville Frontier, 1780–1810," 406, 409; Account Book, Demoss Family Papers, TSL, Mn. 90–145, loc. IX-D-1, box 1, folder 2; Martin Dickenson Diary, April 9, 1797, Diaries, TSL, Mn. 78–88.

29. Andrew Jackson to Eliza Donelson, June 28, 1801, Papers of Andrew J. Donelson, TSL, Mf. 403, reel 10, container 20; Ledger Book for lumber mill, 1806, Demoss Family Papers, loc. IX-D-1, box 1, folder 7; Andrew Jackson to John Overton, November 30, 1799, *Papers*, I (quotation); Draper MSS, 6XX50.

30. Mill Creek Baptist Church, February 11, 1801.

31. Billie G. Smith, "Black Women Who Stole Themselves," in Carla Gardina Pestana and Sharon V. Salinger, eds., *Inequality in Early America* (Hanover, 1999), 134–59.

32. James Mulhorn to John Overton, April 15, 1802, TSL, Murdock Collection, Overton Papers, box 4, folder 17 (Bob); William Blount to Daniel Smith, May 13, 1795, in "Papers of General Daniel Smith," *American Historical Magazine* 6 (July 1901): 213–35, at 229–30.

33. John Irwin to John Coffee, May 29, 1801, Dyas Collection, John Coffee Papers, TSL, box 7, folder 9.

34. Robert King to Andrew Jackson, October 23, 1793, *Papers*, I; *Tennessee Gazette*, May 16, 1807; petition by William Nodding, Legislative Petitions, 1803 [38-1-1803]; "Free Sam," Jill Knight Garrett Collection, TSL, Mf. 1196, roll 4, box 13, folder 1.

35. Draper MSS, 32S211, 308; bond, September 30, 1790, Paul Fink Collection, McClung Library, Knoxville, Tennessee, 1781–1796, box 1, "1790" folder.

36. Joanna Tipton to Sinking Creek Baptist Church, May 16, 1807, Stickley Collection. On role of gossip, see chapter 6.

37. Ross, *Elder Reuben Ross*, 189; Red River Baptist Church, October 15 and December 17, 1803, SBHL, Mf. 289.

38. Robin W. Winks, Larry Garn, Jane H. Pease, William H. Pease, and Tilden G. Edelstein, eds., *Four Fugitive Slave Narratives* (Menlo Park, 1969), 232–33; Olwell, *Masters, Slaves, and Subjects*, 103–40.

39. Tennessee Baptist Association, October 1792 and August 1793, SBHL, Mf. 836; Big Pigeon Baptist, December 8, 1792, and January 12, 1793, McClung Library, MCC 62319; Red River Baptist, September 19, 1801, and January 15, 1802; Red River Baptist, May 3, 1806–May 15, 1807; Mill Creek Baptist, May and June 1810.

40. Spring Creek Baptist Church, July 1806, TSL, Mf. 764; Red River Baptist, February 20, 1808; February 15, 1809. At the Dumplin Creek Baptist Church, membership figures

show that 4 of the 8 black members (50 percent) in 1797 were eventually excommunicated while 39 of the 256 whites (15 percent) met this fate. Dumplin Creek Baptist, July 30, 1797, SBHL, Mf. 2049. The Mill Creek Baptist Church was wracked with disputes involving its black members, especially from 1801 to 1806.

41. On Methodists and Presbyterians, see chapter 8. On Baptists: Ross, *Reuben Ross*, 136–37; Albert W. Wardin Jr., *Tennessee Baptists: A Comprehensive History, 1779–1999* (Brentwood, 1999), 81; Sobel, *The World They Made Together*, 194–95.

42. Thornton, *Africa and Africans in the Making of the Atlantic World*, chap. 9; Mt. Oliver Baptist, April 25, 1801, October 1809, Church Records, TSL, Mf. 511, vol. I; Mill Creek Baptist, November 15, 1800, May 16, 1801–November 5, 1806; February 15, 1807.

43. Tennessee Laws, 1806, 6th General Assembly, 2nd session, Chapter XXXII; Rules and Regulations of Knoxville, February 12, 1802; Rules and Regulations of Nashville, April 7, 1802, Records of the Board of Commissioners for the Town of Nashville, TSL, THS Miscellaneous Files, Mf. 678, box 11, N-19; Tennessee Laws, 1809, 7th General Assembly, 2nd session, Chapter LI.

44. *Knoxville Gazette*, November 7, 1796; *Tennessee Gazette*, December 18, 1802; July 26, 1806, 1; John Kennedy to Return Meigs, December 25, 1807, M208.

45. Dubois, *A Colony of Citizens*, 110, 221–48; Caleb Perry Patterson, *The Negro in Tennessee, 1790–1865* (New York, 1922), 35–36; Draper MSS, 30S384, 458–67; *Tennessee Gazette*, August 4, 1802, 2. From the time of publication of the first Tennessee newspaper in 1791 through 1810, the extant copies of Tennessee papers contained seventy-eight escaped slave advertisements for Tennessee slaves. These figures are drawn from those advertisements.

46. Petition, Legislative Petitions, 1801 [20-1-1801] (Renfroe); Tennessee Laws, 1804, 5th General Assembly, 2nd session, Chapter XXIX (Thomas); Walter T. Durham, *Before Tennessee: The Southwest Territory, 1790–1796* (Piney Flats, 1990), 222 (Nelly).

47. Patterson, *The Negro in Tennessee*, 54; *Tennessee Gazette*, June 22, 1803, 2; *Knoxville Gazette*, October 28, 1801, 3; *Phillip Parchment v. Sampson Williams*, July 1800 session, Sumner County Lawsuits, Sumner County Archives, Gallatin, Tennessee, roll 5048, case #1822; *Knoxville Gazette*, August 4, 1802, 4; *Samuel Cowan v. Patty Chisholm*, Superior Court, Knox County Archives, Hamilton District, March term 1800, docket #1065/533; *Tennessee Gazette*, March 28, 1807, 4.

48. *Anne Smith v. Samuel Smith*, Superior Court, Knox County Archives, Hamilton District, docket #117; deposition of James Robertson, 1800, Stanley Horn Collection, TSL, box 1, folder 14.

49. Scholars have uncovered a dynamic slave economy in the frontier, as well as more developed regions. Usner, *Indians, Settlers, and Slaves in a Frontier Exchange Economy*; Berlin and Morgan, *Cultivation and Culture*, 26–44; Joseph P. Reidy, "Obligation and Right: Patterns of Labor, Subsistence, and Exchange in the Cotton Belt of Georgia, 1790–1860," in Berlin and Morgan, *Cultivation and Culture*, 138–54; Campbell, "As 'A Kind of Freeman'?: Slaves' Market-Related Activities in the South Carolina Up Country, 1800–1860," 243–74; Wood, *Women's Work, Men's Work*.

50. Thomas Anburey, *Travels through the Interior Parts of America* (1789; repr., New York, 1969), 331–34; Berlin, *Many Thousands Gone*, 136–37; Boyd, "Some North Carolina Tracts of the Eighteenth Century," 616. Historians have not studied the structure of slave labor in Tennessee.

51. Berlin, *Many Thousands Gone*, 33; Patterson, *The Negro in Tennessee*, 67; Draper MSS, 5XX50; Tennessee Laws, 1803, 5th General Assembly, 1st session, Chapter XLVII; Aron, *How the West Was Lost*, 144–45; William Blount to John Gray Blount, August 9, 1787, in Alice Barnwell Keith, ed., *John Gray Blount Papers* (Raleigh, 1952), 1:331; *Clarion*, November 1, 1808; Williams, "Early Iron Works in the Tennessee Country," 39–46; letter of David Ross, April 30, 1812, in Charles R. Dew, "David Ross and the Oxford Iron Works," *William and Mary Quarterly* 31 (April 1974): 189–224, quotation at 211–12. The description of Ross's system is based on his Virginia foundry, one he lauded. There is no reason to suppose that he did not implement the same structure in Tennessee.

52. Journal of William L. Brown, January 16, February 22, 1805, and January 17, 1805, Topp Papers, TSL, reel 1, box 2, folder 1; account book, February 6, 1807, James Winchester Papers, TSL, Mf. 794, reel 1, box 1, folder 2; Goodstein, "Black History on the Nashville Frontier, 1780–1810," 414; Martin Dickenson Diary, August 4, 1797; *Tennessee Gazette*, October 19, 1810, 4.

53. Patterson, *The Negro in Tennessee*, 12–20, 46–49; Tennessee Laws, 1799, 3rd General Assembly, 1st session, Chapter XXVIII; records of the Board of Commissioners for Nashville, April 7, 1802, and March 11, 1803; *Knoxville Gazette*, February 11, 1801; *Tennessee Gazette*, August 31, 1803; Nashville market regulations, *Tennessee Gazette*, July 3, 1805, 1; *Tennessee Gazette*, April 18, 1807, 3.

54. *Clarion*, June 23, 1809, 3; Agreement between William Faith and John Gordon and Andrew Jackson, March 10, 1793, Small Collections—John Cocke Papers, TSL, Mn. 67–71, loc. V-J-3. Jonathan Martin describes owners' fears about injuries to their slaves and slaves' running away but does not comment on the bargaining power that slaves obtained because of owners' concerns about their slaves' reputations as runaways. Martin, *Divided Mastery*, 54, 72–103.

55. John Hope Franklin, "Slaves Virtually Free in Ante-Bellum North Carolina," *Journal of Negro History* 28 (July 1943): 284–310; Richard B. Morris, "The Measure of Bondage in the Slave States," *Mississippi Valley Historical Review* 41 (September 1954): 219–40; Sarah S. Hughes, "Slaves for Hire: The Allocation of Black Labor in Elizabeth City County, Virginia, 1782 to 1810," *William and Mary Quarterly* 35 (April 1978): 260–86; Clement Eaton, "Slave-Hiring in the Upper South: A Step toward Freedom," *Mississippi Valley Historical Review* 46 (March 1960): 663–78; Olwell, *Masters, Slaves, and Subjects*, 160–64; Berlin and Morgan, *Cultivation and Culture*, 34; Wood, *Women's Work, Men's Work*, chap. 5.

56. Ilai Metcalfe Account Book, March 24, 1800, University of Tennessee Special Collection, Knoxville, MS-603, p. 26; Earle's claim, October 24, 1808, M208; Journal of John Sevier, August 23, 1797, *Tennessee Historical Magazine*, 5.

57. Scholars do not discuss this type of self-hire in other regions, so it is unclear how widespread this practice was. Sam's example shows that it was known in the East. However, the extensiveness of its practice in Tennessee may have been a response to Tennessee's frontier conditions.

58. *Knoxville Gazette*, May 2, 1796, 4; *York v. Isaac Pierce*, Court of Pleas and Quarter Sessions, 1803–1808, Sumner County Archives, p. 1; petition from Nashville, Legislative Petitions, 1799, [1-2-1799]; Goodstein, "Black History on the Nashville Frontier, 1780–1810," 418; account book, 1795, *Papers*, I, app. IV.

59. Petition from Nashville, Legislative Petitions, 1799, [1-2-1799]; Tennessee Laws, 1801, 4th General Assembly, 1st session, Chapter LXXVI; Records of the Board of Commissioners for Nashville, April 7, 1802.

60. Petition from Davidson County, Legislative Petitions, 1801, [20-1-1801]; Martin Dickenson Diary, April 9 and August 4, 1797; Andrew Jackson to John Hutchings, April 7, 1806, *Papers*, II; *Tennessee Gazette*, May 16, 1807, 2; Patterson, *The Negro in Tennessee*, 36.

61. *Clarion*, July 26, 1808, 2; *Tennessee Gazette*, May 3, 1806, 4; John Kennedy to Return Meigs, December 25, 1807, M208. John Hope Franklin and Loren Schweninger discuss the Mustapha/Howe team as "one of the strangest episodes," but this occurrence may have been more common than Franklin and Schweninger suggest. Franklin and Schweninger, *Runaway Slaves*, 31–32.

62. In eleven of the seventy-eight Tennessee runaway advertisements from 1791 until 1811, the owners described skills or businesses of the slave. *Knoxville Gazette*, February 2, 1798; October 31, 1803; *Tennessee Gazette*, February 18, 1801; June 6, 1804; October 26, 1805; *Clarion*, November 1, 1808; December 13, 1808; January 12, 1810; February 9, 1810; June 22, 1810.

63. *Papers*, I, app. IV; *Clarion*, February 9, 1810, 3.

64. Greenberg, *Masters and Statesmen*. See chapter 8 for a discussion of white ideology about slaves.

65. There has been relatively little written about free blacks in frontier regions. For a limited look: Ira Berlin, *Slaves without Masters: The Free Negro in the Antebellum South* (New York, 1974), 28–29, 46, 62–70, 79–84, 91–107, 154.

66. U.S. Census data. These figures are actually for all free persons who were not white and so may include some Indians or other nonwhites living in the settlements. Ira Berlin has noted that census figures undercount the number of free blacks. He suggests that the census underestimated the number of southern free blacks by at least 20 percent. Berlin, *Slaves without Masters*, 174.

67. Philip D. Morgan, *Slave Counterpoint: Black Culture in the Eighteenth-Century Chesapeake and Lowcountry* (Chapel Hill, 1998), 485–96.

68. U.S. Census; 1810 census schedules for Rutherford and Grainger counties; Goodstein, "Black History on the Nashville Frontier, 1780–1810."

69. Jane Thomas Memoir, Diaries, TSL, loc. II-H-4, Mn. 1164, box 2, p. 10; *Carthage Gazette*, March 16, 1810, 3; *Tennessee Gazette*, February 22, 1804, 2; *Carthage Gazette*, September 21, 1810, 3; John Redd, "Reminiscences of West Virginia," *Virginia Magazine*

of History and Biography 6 (April 1899): 337–46; Edward Michael McCormack, *Slavery on the Tennessee Frontier* (n.p., 1977), 20.

70. Berlin, *Generations of Captivity*, 136–38; petition, Legislative Petitions, 1803, [35-1-1803]; petition, Legislative Petitions, 1806 [17-1-1806]; Goodstein, "Black History on the Nashville Frontier, 1780–1810," 406; *Tennessee Gazette*, June 29, 1803, 2 (fire); *Tennessee Gazette*, February 1, 1806, 4.

71. *Tennessee Gazette*, March 31, 1802, 2; August 22, 1804, 2.

72. Scholars have documented the attraction of the gospel of a common humanity for African Americans in the post-Revolutionary period. Frey, *Water from a Rock*, chap. 8; Nash, *Forging Freedom*, 111–13, 190–211, 230.

73. Petition by Gideon Blackburn, Legislative Petitions, 1806, [18-1-1806]; Union Presbytery, October 28, 1806; February 12, 1807; April 20, 1807; October 22, 1807; September 19, 1808; September 5, 1809; April 2, 1801, TSL, Mf. 545; Mill Creek Baptist Church, October 1807.

74. Petition, December 1787, SRNC, 22:705, 713.

75. Draper MSS, 32S345; Patterson, *The Negro in Tennessee, 1790–1865*, 167–68; Goodstein, "Black History on the Nashville Frontier, 1780–1810," 418; Journal of the Senate, August 3, 1804, TSL, Records of the States of the United States, Senate Journals, Mf. Tenn. A.1a, reel 1, 1794–1812; Rejected Bills, RG 60, TSL, box 6, folder 38; Tennessee Laws, 1805, Chapter XXV; *James Gowan v. Isaac Baker*, Tennessee Records of Sumner County, County Court Minutes, vol. V, 1804–1805 (Works Progress Administration transcriber, 1936); 643–44; Washington County Clerk Minute Books, TSL, roll 129, vol. 2, February 1790, p. 329. The understanding of political entitlement by white men is discussed in chapter 7.

76. Scholars have focused their efforts on free blacks and the economy mainly on urban blacks in the North and the border cities of the South. These historians emphasize the race-based constraints on free blacks but have done little exploration of black ideas about economic relations. Leon Litwak, *North of Slavery: The Negro in the Free States, 1790–1860* (Chicago, 1961), 153–86; Berlin, *Slaves without Masters*, 217–49; Nash, *Forging Freedom*, 74, 210–11, 238.

77. 1802 account, *Papers*, I:267; *Tennessee Gazette*, August 22, 1804, 2; Union Presbytery, April 20, 1807, vol. I; Arnow, *Flowering of the Cumberland*, 93.

78. Petition, Legislative Petitions, 1803, [35-1-1803]; Journal of the Senate, April 5, 1809; September 19, 1809; November 8, 1809.

Chapter 6

1. Depositions of Polly Boley and John Boley in *State v. William Small*, September 5, 1797, Superior Court, Knox County Archives, Knoxville, Tennessee, Hamilton District, #338.

2. Gregory H. Nobles, "Breaking into the Back Country: New Approaches to the Early American Frontier, 1750–1800," *William and Mary Quarterly* 46 (1989): 641–70, at 652;

Malcolm J. Rohrbough, *The Trans-Appalachian Frontier: People, Societies, and Institutions, 1775–1850* (New York, 1978), chaps. 1, 6; Richard R. Beeman, *The Evolution of the Southern Backcountry: A Case Study of Lunenburg County, Virginia, 1746–1832* (Philadelphia, 1984), 8–9, 97–119. David Hackett Fischer does study the cultural practices of British backcountry people, tracing their folkways to their British roots. Fischer, *Albion's Seed: Four British Folkways in America* (New York, 1989), 662–68, 759–65. On religion and war: Stephen Aron, *How the West Was Lost: The Transformation of Kentucky from Daniel Boone to Henry Clay* (Baltimore, 1996), 170–91; Beeman, *The Evolution of the Southern Backcountry*, 97–119; Nobles, "Breaking into the Backcountry," 652–54; Elizabeth A. Perkins, *Border Life: Experience and Memory in the Revolutionary Ohio Valley* (Chapel Hill, 1998), 81–115. Much of the best work on pioneer families concerns families after 1820. Joan E. Cashin, *A Family Venture: Men and Women on the Southern Frontier* (New York, 1991) (after 1820); John Mack Faragher, *Women and Men on the Overland Trail* (New Haven, 1979) (covers 1842–75).

3. For several decades, historians of women and gender focused much of their efforts on debating and refining the trope of separate spheres. Barbara Welter, "The Cult of True Womanhood: 1820–1860," *American Quarterly* 18 (Summer 1966): 151–74; Nancy F. Cott, *The Bonds of Womanhood: "Woman's Sphere" in New England, 1780–1835* (New Haven, 1977). By the 1980s, historians exploring the cognitive worlds of working-class women, African American women, and southern white women in the antebellum years, for different reasons, found the metaphor of separate spheres inapplicable to the lives and mental worlds of these women. Christine Stansell, *City of Women: Sex and Class in New York, 1789–1860* (New York, 1982; repr., 1986); Deborah Gray White, *"Ar'N't I a Woman?": Female Slaves in the Plantation South* (New York, 1987); Stephanie McCurry, *Masters of Small Worlds: Yeoman Households, Gender Relations, and the Political Culture of the Antebellum South Carolina Law Country* (New York, 1995). Studying benevolent activities by women, other historians challenged the belief that the cult of true womanhood rendered women submissive and relegated them to the home. Lori D. Ginzberg, *Women and the Work of Benevolence: Morality, Politics, and Class in the Nineteenth-Century United States* (New Haven, 1990). More recent work is interested in the ways in which men and women interacted, the more direct roles women played in politics or business, and how gender intersects with other relations of power, such as race and class. Kathleen M. Brown, *Good Wives, Nasty Wenches, and Anxious Patriarchs: Gender, Race, and Power in Colonial Virginia* (Chapel Hill, 1996); Catherine Allgor, *Parlor Politics: In Which the Ladies of Washington Help Build a City and a Government* (Charlottesville, 2000).

4. In contrast to studies of white women in the North that suggest that women occupied a separate sphere of domesticity, some historians argue that southern men, as head of the household, made the family decisions and controlled family life. Nobles, "Breaking into the Backcountry," 650–51; Aron, *How the West Was Lost*, 69, 155–56; Cashin, *A Family Venture*; John Mack Faragher, *Women and Men on the Overland Trail* (New Haven, 1979), chap. 3; Fischer, *Albion's Seed*, 675–80. Other work suggests that women

in frontier conditions had some public voice, at least in matters of defense related to the family. Perkins, *Border Life*, 142–46; Harriette Simpson Arnow, *Flowering of the Cumberland* (New York, 1963), 73–74. I argue that women in Tennessee assumed a much stronger role and weaved webs of connection based on their assumptions about civilized life.

5. James Moore, "The Two Systems of Frances Hutcheson: On the Origins of the Scottish Enlightenment," in M. A. Stewart, ed., *Studies in the Philosophy of the Scottish Enlightenment* (Oxford, 1990), 37–59; Christopher J. Berry, *Social Theory of the Scottish Enlightenment* (Edinburgh, 1997), 23–51, 93–99. On Tennessee: Neal O'Steen, "Pioneer Education in the Tennessee Country," *Tennessee Historical Quarterly* 35 (Summer 1976): 199–219; Gary Wills, *Inventing America: Jefferson's Declaration of Independence* (New York, 1978), 175–80. Some historians question Wills's conclusions about the extent of the Scottish influence on Jefferson's Declaration, but many find valuable his description of the early influence of Scottish thinkers on the founding fathers in the United States. Richard B. Sher and Jeffrey R. Smitten, eds., *Scotland and America in the Age of the Enlightenment* (Edinburgh, 1990), 11–12.

6. Anthony F. C. Wallace, *Jefferson and the Indians: The Tragic Fate of the First Americans* (Cambridge, Mass., 1999), 95; J. G. A. Pocock, *The Machiavellian Moment: Florentine Political Thought and the Atlantic Republican Tradition* (Princeton, 1975), chaps. 14 and 15; Michael P. Zuckert, *Natural Rights and the New Republicanism* (Princeton, 1994), 150–83.

7. Letter from Gentleman in Cumberland, *Knoxville Gazette*, June 15, 1793, 3; *Knoxville Gazette*, March 23, 1793, 4; *Knoxville Gazette*, April 7, 1792, 3; *Knoxville Gazette*, May 19, 1792, 4 (quotation); letter from Eliza Campbell, *Knoxville Gazette*, July 31, 1795; John Rhea to constituents, February 13, 1805, TSL, THS Miscellaneous Files, reel 7, box 13, R103.

8. *Washington Advertiser*, February 1, 1804, 4; "Journal of Governor John Sevier," December 11, 1796, in *Tennessee Historical Magazine* 5 (October 1919) (quotation); John McIver Diary, June 15, 1805, and August 22, 1805, TSL, Mf. 1061; Arnow, *Flowering of the Cumberland*, 400. For a similar response in Kentucky, see Perkins, *Border Life*, 81–115.

9. C. F. Volney, *The Ruins; or, Meditation on the Revolutions of Empires: and The Law of Nature* (New York, 1890), 180, 183. The book was advertised for sale by the *Tennessee Gazette*, December 25, 1802, and July 13, 1803. On happiness: *Tennessee Gazette*, September 16, 1801, 4; John Donelson to Johnny, September 4, 1785, Papers of Andrew J. Donelson, TSL, Mf. 403, reel 10, container 20, "Copies, Transcriptions, 1785–1829" (quotation).

10. Draper MSS, 10NN13 (1774); Draper MSS, 30S246–48 (1780); Richard Green Waterhouse Diary, July 30–August 4, 1798, University of Tennessee Special Collection, Knoxville, MS-918; Arthur Campbell to William Preston, September 4, 1774, Draper MSS, 3QQ94; Draper MSS, 3XX4; J. G. M. Ramsey, *The Annals of Tennessee to the End of the Eighteenth Century* (Johnson City, 1853; repr., 1926), 369–70. On settlers in Ohio and

Kentucky: Andrew R. L. Cayton, *The Frontier Republic: Ideology and Politics in the Ohio Country, 1780–1825* (Kent, 1986), 1–4; Perkins, *Border Life*, 41–79.

11. "Journal of Governor John Sevier," July 21 and 22, 1795; November 14, 1795, in *Tennessee Historical Magazine* 5 (October 1919); August 9, 1798, in *Tennessee Historical Magazine* 5 (January 1920); December 16, 1808, in *Tennessee Historical Magazine* 6 (April 1920); James Ross, *Life and Times of Elder Reuben Ross* (Philadelphia, 1882), 169–70; Lucy Kennerly Gump, "Possessions and Patterns of Living in Washington County: The 20 Years before Tennessee Statehood, 1777–1796" (master's thesis, East Tennessee State University, 1989), 134; Martin Dickenson Diary, April 3, 1797, TSL, Ms. 78–88, VI-F-3, box 5.

12. Mary Beth Norton, *Founding Mothers and Fathers: Gendered Power and the Forming of American Society* (New York, 1996), especially chap. 1; Arnow, *Flowering of the Cumberland*, 49–50; Robert V. Remini, *Andrew Jackson and the Course of American Empire, 1767–1821* (New York, 1977), 161; *Hooper's Administratrix v. Hooper*, 1 Tenn 146–47, (November 1805); Draper MSS, 32S320–21.

13. John Knibb Winn Papers, TSL, Mn. 333, I-E-3, folder 6; Washington County Clerk Minute Books, vol. 1, February 1783, 192; November 1788, 343; February 1789, 361; July 1790, 440; *Journal of the House* (Knoxville, 1808), October 23, 1807; September 28, 1809; Robert Morris to John Overton, April 1, 1798, John Overton Papers, TSL, Mf. 748, folder 24; Thomas Ware, *Sketches of the Life and Travels of Reverend Thomas Ware* (New York, 1842), 133; Arnow, *Flowering of the Cumberland*, 52–54. Bigamous relationships were common throughout America. Hendrik Hartog, *Man and Wife in America: A History* (London, 2000), 87–92.

14. Nathaniel Sheidley, "Unruly Men: Indians, Settlers, and the Ethos of Frontier Patriarchy in the Upper Tennessee Watershed, 1763–1815" (Ph.D. diss., Princeton University, 1999), 156–70; Draper MSS, 3XX4; Carolyn Thomas Foreman, *Indian Women Chiefs* (Muskogee, 1954), 74; Cora Bales Sevier and Nancy S. Madden, *Sevier Family History* (Washington, D.C. 1961), 225, 230; Tennessee Laws, 1812, Chapter XLIX; deposition of Pleasant Miller, Legislative Petitions, 1799, TSL, [37-2-1799]; Brent Alan "Yanusdi" Cox, *Heart of the Eagle: Dragging Canoe and the Emergence of the Chickamauga Confederacy* (Milan, Tenn., 1999), 193–95.

15. Letter from "The People," *Knoxville Gazette*, May 19, 1992, 3; letter from "One of the People," *Knoxville Gazette*, June 16, 1792, 2; *Knoxville Gazette*, May 8, 1797.

16. Historians contend that backcountry women submitted to a patriarchal order. E. Estyn Evans, "The Scotch-Irish: Their Cultural Adaptation and Heritage in the American Old West," in E. R. R. Green, *Essays in Scotch-Irish History* (Belfast, 1992), 76; Fischer, *Albion's Seed*, 675–80. On law and custom: Hartog, *Man and Wife in America*, 115–22, 136–58.

17. Draper MSS, 32S140–80; *Knoxville Gazette*, December 29, 1792, 2; Draper MSS, 30S256–57; John W. Gray, ed., *The Life of Joseph Bishop*, (Spartanburg, 1974), 65; Draper MSS, 32S318; Mrs. A. E. Richmond Memoirs, Diaries, TSL, Ms. 210, loc. VI-F-3, box 5; Draper MSS, 3XX18.

18. *Knoxville Gazette*, November 19, 1791, 2; Draper MSS, 30S246–48; Draper MSS, 32S202–3; letter from John Kirk to John Watts, October 17, 1788, in Samuel Cole Williams, *History of the Lost State of Franklin* (Johnson City, 1924), 208; letter from inhabitant of French Broad, October 18, 1789, Draper MSS, 9DD53.

19. Arnow, *Flowering of the Cumberland*, 31–34, 75; Remini, *Andrew Jackson*, 68–69 (quotation); Edwin M. Gardner Memoirs, II-H-4, box 3.

20. Ramsey, *Annals of Tennessee*, 578; Samuel Cole Williams, *Tennessee during the Revolutionary War* (Knoxville, 1944), 10; *Knoxville Gazette*, December 19, 1793, 1. The economic aspects of women's work in the home are discussed more fully in chapter 8.

21. *Knoxville Gazette*, December 29, 1792, 2; letter from Dr. Thomas Watkins, *Tennessee Gazette*, May 23, 1807, 1–3; Mary Bradley to Rachel Henderson, November 29, 1806, William Henderson Papers, Sumner County Archives, Gallatin, Tennessee, MSC 88-12, box 9.

22. Deposition of John Allen Smith Carrington, June 2, 1795, Allen Smith Carrington Deposition, University of Tennessee Special Collection, MS-1826 (Martin); Draper MSS, 5XX 43 (Handly); William Brown Journal, January 14, 1807, Topp Papers, TSL, Mf. 173, reel 1, box 2, folder 1.

23. On gossip: Max Gluckman, "Gossip and Scandal," *Current Anthropology* 4 (June 1963): 307–16; Jorg R. Bergmann, *Discreet Indiscretions: The Social Organization of Gossip* (New York, 1993). Postcolonialists recognize the use of gossip as a subaltern strategy. Homi K. Bhabha, *The Location of Culture* (London, 1994), 200. On honor: Kenneth S. Greenberg, *Masters and Statesmen: The Political Culture of American Slavery* (Baltimore, 1985); Steven M. Stowe, *Intimacy and Power in the Old South: Ritual in the Lives of the Planters* (Baltimore, 1987).

24. Slander cases were one of the categories of cases state attorney Andrew Jackson prosecuted most frequently during his tenure. James W. Ely Jr., "The Legal Practice of Andrew Jackson," *Tennessee Historical Quarterly* 38 (Winter 1979): 421–35, at 428. On morality: Instrument by Gasper Fault, January 19, 1793, Minutes of Knox County Court of Pleas and Quarter Sessions, Knox County Archives, Knoxville, Tennessee, Book "O"; *Elizabeth Looney v. Agness Gray*, Paul Fink Collection, McClung Library, Knoxville, Tennessee, CS 11-3, box 1, "1790" folder; Washington District Court, August 1791, Paul Fink Collection, box 1, "1791" folder; *Susanah Baker v. Robert Nelson*, May 1790, Minutes of Mero District Superior Court of Law and Equity, Davidson County Archives, Nashville, Tennessee, Book A, 21. On men: Paul Fink Collection, box 1, "1789" and "1795," folder 2. On church: Big Pigeon Baptist Church, April 11, 1795, McClung Library, MCC 62319; Dandridge Baptist Church, June 1795, SBHL, Mf. 2050.

25. John Montgomery to William Preston, October 2, 1774, Draper MSS, 3QQ110; William Preston to Daniel Smith, October 7, 1774, Draper 4XX44; James Robertson to William Preston, September 1, 1774, Draper MSS, 3QQ88; Thomas Hutchings to Joseph Martin, April 4, 1788, Draper MSS, 12S188–93; J. W. Casey Diary, Diaries, TSL, Mf. 45; John Lipscomb Diary, June 30, 1784, Diaries, TSL, Mf. 1375.

26. Evans, "The Scotch-Irish," 69–86; Samuel Cole Williams, *William Tatham, Wataugan*

(Johnson City, 1947), 15; Ross, *Elder Reuben Ross*, 114; Sheidley, "Unruly Men," 186–90; Larry H. Whiteaker and W. Calvin Dickinson, *Tennessee: State of the Nation* (New York, 1998), 9–16.

27. See chapter 7 for a discussion of this transition.

28. U.S. Census, 1790, *Return of the Whole Number of Persons within the Several Districts of the United States* (Philadelphia, 1791); 1795 Census Schedule for Territory of the United States of America South of the River Ohio, in Clarence Edwin Carter, ed., *The Territorial Papers of the United States: The Territory South of the River Ohio, 1790–1796*, vol. 4 (Washington, D.C., 1936), 405; 1800 Schedule of the Inhabitants in the State of Tennessee, *Tennessee Gazette*, November 11, 1801, 2; U.S. Census, 1810 (Early American Imprints, 2nd series, no. 24084); William H. Masterson, *William Blount* (Baton Rouge, 1954), 181–82. The movement toward refinement in Tennessee was part of a broader national trend. Richard L. Bushman, *The Refinement of America: Persons, Houses, Cities* (New York, 1992).

29. Tennessee Laws, 1805, 6th General Assembly, 1st session, Chapter II; letter from R. G. Foster, *Clarion*, October 6, 1809, 3.

30. *Tennessee Gazette*, September 16, 1801, 4; *Washington Advertiser*, February 15, 1804, 4; *Knoxville Gazette*, April 24, 1795, 1; Joseph Anderson to Andrew Jackson, December 3, 1795, *Papers*, I.

31. *Tennessee Gazette*, November 2, 1803, 4 (quotation); *Tennessee Gazette*, September 16, 1801, 4. Historians in the last two decades have developed a significant literature about the concept of the republican mother. Linda K. Kerber, *Women of the Republic: Intellect and Ideology in Revolutionary America* (New York, 1980); Mary Beth Norton, *Liberty's Daughters: The Revolutionary Experience of American Women, 1750–1800* (Boston, 1980), 228–94.

32. *Knoxville Gazette*, April 24, 1795, 1; *Washington Advertiser*, February 15, 1804, 4; *Tennessee Gazette*, October 24, 1804, 3; February 25, 1800, 3; *Knoxville Gazette*, November 21, 1796, 2; *Tennessee Gazette*, July 29, 1801, 4; February 9, 1803, 4.

33. *Tennessee Gazette*, February 29, 1804, 4; October 24, 1804, 4; May 13, 1801, 1.

34. *Tennessee Gazette*, April 13, 1803, 4; May 16, 1804, 4; July 28, 1803; *Knoxville Gazette*, July 18, 1796, 3; *Carthage Gazette*, July 6, 1810; *Tennessee Gazette*, May 20, 1801 (quotation).

35. *Tennessee Gazette*, December 28, 1805, 4; February 3, 1802, 4; *Knoxville Gazette*, August 15, 1804, 3; *Carthage Gazette*, September 1, 1809.

36. Rachel Henderson to Paulina Henderson, September 1, 1815, William Henderson Papers; G. M. Deaderick to Andrew Jackson, April 25, 1807, *Papers*, II; *Carthage Gazette*, November 12, 1810, 4; *Knoxville Gazette*, January 19, 1796, 2; *Tennessee Gazette*, November 9, 1801, 2; Legislative Petitions, 1799, [10-2-1799].

37. *Knoxville Gazette*, November 21, 1796, 2; *Tennessee Gazette*, September 8, 1802, 4; July 29, 1801, 4; February 9, 1803, 4; Richard Green Waterhouse Diary, pp. 159, 189.

38. William Blount to John Gray Blount, September 22, 1790, in Alice Barnwell Keith, ed., *The John Gray Blount Papers*, vol. 2 (Raleigh, 1959), 120–21; Stockely Donelson to Andrew Jackson, January 15, 1802, *Papers*, I. Historians have generally emphasized

women's powerlessness in the decision to move. Aron, *How the West Was Lost*, 69. For a later period, see Cashin, *A Family Venture*; Faragher, *Women and Men on the Overland Trail*.

39. Clarence Edwin Carter, ed., *The Territorial Papers of the United States: The Territory South of the River Ohio, 1790–1796*, vol. 4 (Washington, D.C. 1936), 268; Arnow, *Flowering of the Cumberland*, 41–42. John Sevier's journal reflects that his wife spent days away from home without him. For examples: "Journal of Governor John Sevier," August 20 and October 6, 1794, and January 23, 1795, *Tennessee Historical Magazine* 5 (October 1919): 170.

40. *Knoxville Gazette*, May 6, 1801, 3. I reviewed a compilation of wills in Wilson County from 1802 to 1810 and identified thirty estates in which the decedent had a surviving wife. In five cases (17 percent), the wife was the sole administrator of her husband's estate; in fifteen cases (50 percent), the wife was a joint administrator with a male executor; in ten cases (33 percent), the wife was not an administrator. Thomas E. Partlow, *The People of Wilson County, Tennessee, 1800–1899* (Easley, S.C., 1983), 1–8. The role of women as partners with men is described in more detail in chapter 8.

41. I reviewed the extant issues of the *Knoxville Gazette*, *Knoxville Register*, *Tennessee Gazette*, *Carthage Gazette*, the *Clarion*, and the *Washington Advertiser*.

42. *Knoxville Gazette*, March 10, 1792, 3; *Elizabeth Kerns v. Nicholas Kerns*, Superior Court, Knox County Archives, Hamilton District, 1802, docket #804/677; *Carthage Gazette*, January 12, 1810, 4.

43. House and Senate Journals, TSL, 1797–1809; Tennessee Laws, 1797–1809.

44. The varying analyses of divorce laws by historians do not explain why Tennessee's laws were so permissive. Richard H. Chused, *Private Acts in Public Places: A Social History of Divorce in the Formative Era of American Family Law* (Philadelphia, 1994); Lawrence B. Goodheart, Neil Hanks, and Elizabeth Johnson, " 'An Act for the Relief of Females . . .': Divorce and the Changing Legal Status of Women in Tennessee, 1796–1860, Part I," *Tennessee Historical Quarterly* 44 (Fall 1985): 318–39, at 320–21; Norma Basch, *Framing American Divorce: From the Revolutionary Generation to the Victorian* (Berkeley, 1999), 23–24, 48–49. The westering emphasis on contract and consent persuaded many women and men in Tennessee to see marriage and divorce as contractual matters and to permit divorce when the contract was dissolved.

45. Tennessee Laws, 1799, 3rd General Assembly, 1st session, Chapter XIX; Tennessee Laws, 1807, 7th General Assembly, 1st session, Chapter XCVII; Tennessee Laws, 1809, 8th General Assembly, 1st session, Chapter LXLVIII; letter from R. C. Foster, *Clarion*, October 6, 1809, 3.

46. *Tennessee Gazette*, June 8, 1803, 2; Richard Green Waterhouse Diary, December 1807, 196–97; William Blount to John Gray Blount, March 28, 1795, Keith et al., *John Gray Blount Papers*, II; Ware, *Life of Reverend Thomas Ware*, 134.

47. Hartog, *Man and Wife in America*, 115–22, 194–95; *Kerns v. Kerns*; *Henry v. Henry*, Knox County Archives; *Clarion*, October 19, 1810, 1. Legal theorist Martha Minow describes a rights consciousness created by women without political power whose

world is strongly relational. In her view, authority without autonomy creates an expectation of rights that depend not on autonomy but on relationship. Martha Minow, " 'Forming Underneath Everything That Grows': Toward a History of Family Law," *Wisconsin Law Review* 4 (1985): 819–98. White women in Tennessee developed a similar sense of entitlement based on their connection with their children and on their contribution to the marital property.

48. Petition on behalf of Rebecca Barker, Legislative Petitions, 1809, [31-1-1809]; *Reed v. Reed*, Knox County Archives; *Carthage Gazette*, March 6, 1809; Big Pigeon Baptist, January 2, 1796–September 1799.

49. Washington County Clerk Minute Books, February 1782, TSL, roll 129, vol. 1, p. 156; Records of Smith County Minute Book, June 14, 1804, and September 11, 1804, TSL, WPA typescript, 77, 80 (quotation); "Granny White," *Clarion*, July 26, 1808, 4.

50. *Tennessee Gazette*, April 18, 1807, 3; *Agness v. Alexander Torbett*, Paul Fink Collection, box 20, folder 5; Washington County Clerk Minute Books, March 1799, vol. I, 156 and 185; Samuel Martin to Return Meigs, July 21, 1809, M208.

51. Bennett Smith to Andrew Jackson, May 1, 1810, *Papers*, II; *Brewar v. Weakley*, September 1807, 2 Tenn 489–91 (quotation).

52. *Elizabeth Looney v. Agness Gray*, Paul Fink Collection, box 1, "1790" folder (bastardy); *Papers*, II, n. 2 on p. 251.

53. Letter from William Purnell, *Clarion*, December 21, 1810, 3; Donelson Caffery to Andrew Jackson, July 20, 1810, and Isabella Vinson to Andrew Jackson, September 10, 1810, *Papers*, II.

54. Religious life in the early republic has been the source of considerable study. Scholars dispute whether dissenting religions contributed to the development of democratic or republican sensibilities. Nathan O. Hatch, *The Democratization of American Christianity* (New Haven, 1989); Jon Butler, *Awash in a Sea of Faith: Christianizing the American People* (Cambridge, Mass., 1990), chap. 9. Some point to cultural resistance to evangelism. Christine Leigh Heyrman, *Southern Cross: The Beginnings of the Bible Belt* (New York, 1997). Historians remark on the large numbers of women in church life. Heyrman, *Southern Cross*, chap. 4.

55. Herman A. Norton, *Religion in Tennessee, 1777–1945* (Knoxville, 1981), 16, 28. Examples of majority of female founders: Zion Presbyterian Church, in September 1, 1811, TSL, Mf. 125; Wilson Creek Primitive Baptist Church, October 13, 1804, TSL, Mf. 90; Ross, *Elder Reuben Ross*, 120–21; Sinking Creek Baptist Church, August 17, 1797, SBHL, Mf. 1918.

56. Red River Baptist, July 25, 1791, January 25, 1794, 1803, membership list, November 13, 1807, June 16, 1810, SBHL, Mf. 289; Wilson Creek Primitive Baptist, October 13, 1804; June 18, 1808; Mill Creek Baptist, August 1808, SBHL, Mf. 3337; Ross, *Elder Reuben Ross*, 120–21, 125–27; Lorenzo Dow, *Lorenzo Dow's Journal*, 3rd ed. (Wheeling, 1848), 407–18.

57. Sinking Creek Baptist, n.d.; *Carthage Gazette*, January 30, 1809, 2; Big Spring Primitive Baptist, March 1805–January 1807, Claiborne County Records, 1795–1948, TSL, Mf. 557.

58. Circular letter of the Tennessee Baptist Association, August 1811, Holston Record Book, SBHL, Mf. 836; Zion Presbyterian Church, 1810; Dandridge Baptist, August 1787, June 1803; July 1809; Turnbull Primitive Baptist Church, June 13, 1807, TSL, Mf. 164; Union Presbytery, December 9, 1999, TSL, Mf. 545; Mt. Olivet Baptists, May 1810, Church Records, TSL, Mf. 511. Bertram Wyatt Brown and Christina Leigh Heyrman have described the convergence of and dissonance between evangelism and the white southern culture. Bertram Wyatt Brown, "Religion and the 'Civilizing Process' in the Early American South, 1600–1860," in Mark A. Noll, ed., *Religion and American Politics: From the Colonial Period to the 1980s* (New York, 1990), 172–95; Heyrman, *Southern Cross*, 237–52. I argue that the efforts of churches to change white male culture were in significant part a response to the concerns of religious women.

59. *Tennessee Gazette*, March 7, 1804, 4; March 2, 1805, 2, 4; June 6, 1804, 4; *Carthage Gazette*, October 13, 1809.

60. *Clarion*, November 16, 1810, 3; letter from Aristides, *Tennessee Gazette*, March 20, 1805, 2, 4; James Robertson to Andrew Jackson, February 1, 1806, Thomas Matthews Collection, TSL, Mn. 174, 184, location I-F-3, box 3, folder 1 (quotation); Martin Dickenson Diary, pp. 57–66.

61. Historians have developed a significant literature on the importance of honor to southern white men. Jack K. Williams, *Dueling in the Old South: Vignettes of Social History* (College Station, 1980); Greenberg, *Masters and Statesmen*; Stowe, *Intimacy and Power in the Old South*. The code of honor extended to national politics. Joanne B. Freeman, *Affairs of Honor: National Politics in the New Republic* (New Haven, 2001). Scholars have not yet fully explored the tensions between the code of honor and the cultural logic of refinement. Richard L. Bushman commented on the resistance to refined norms within the gentry class among religious and republican members who feared its emphasis on luxury. Bushman, *The Refinement of America*, 186–97. I point here to a different concern—one in which resistance to the genteel morality is based not on concerns about luxury but on a desire to retain character rather than accomplishment as the defining quality of gentility.

62. Memorandum of Duel by Andrew Jackson, July 28, 1805, *Papers*, II; deposition of John Sevier, Washington County Court, Paul Fink Collection, box 1, "1793" folder; Rhys Isaac, *The Transformation of Virginia, 1740–1790* (New York, 1982), 77–78.

63. Greenberg, *Masters and Statesmen*; James Oakes, *The Ruling Race: A History of American Slaveholders* (New York, 1982, 1983); Aron, *How the West Was Lost*.

64. Linda Ann Thompson, "A Study of Two Early-Nineteenth Century Houses in Sumner County, Tennessee: Cragmont and Wynnewood" (master's thesis, Vanderbilt University, 1977), 21, 29–56; James Robertson to David Henley, April 21, 1800, Stanley Horn Collection, TSL, Mf. 1115, box 2, folder 14; Winchester Petition, December 10, 1805, National Archives, Washington, D.C., RG 233, HR 9A-F1.1.

65. *Knoxville Register*, August 14, 1798, 1; *Clarion*, January 19, 1808, 2; *Tennessee Gazette*, November 9, 1801, 2; November 30, 1805, 1; May 31, 1806, 2; December 13, 1806, 2–3; James Grant to Robert Houston, November 24, 1795, Robert Houston Papers, Mc-

Clung Library, CS11-3, folder 7; *Tennessee Gazette*, February 25, 1800, 4; August 14, 1805, 3; April 10, 1805, 3; May 17, 1806, 2.

66. Joseph C. Strong Journal, March 1816, University of Tennessee Special Collection, MS-1032; Mt. Olivet Baptist Church, October 22, 1805; Dandridge Baptist, October 1806; Gump, "Washington County," 217; Bishop, *The Life of Joseph Bishop*, 44–46 (hunter), 47–52, 67–80.

67. Chapter 7 discusses the changing political culture and chapter 8 explores economic conflicts.

68. Charles Albert Snodgrass, *The History of Freemasonry in Tennessee, 1789–1943* (Chattanooga, 1944), 22–29; *Tennessee Gazette*, September 23, 1801 (quotation); Draper MSS, 5XX52; Andrew Jackson to G. W. Campbell, January 15, 1807, Andrew Jackson Papers, TSL, Mf. 809.

69. *Tennessee Gazette*, February 11, 1801, 3; speech by president of Nashville Mechanical Society, *Tennessee Gazette*, July 20, 1803, 2; oration, *Clarion*, July 19, 1808, 2.

70. Arthur Campbell to Col. Oliver Spencer, November 30, 1789, Draper MSS, 9DD54; Draper MSS, 30S485–86; Mt. Olivet Baptist Church, June 23, 1804.

71. *Knoxville Gazette*, March 13, 1794, 1; petition from Grainger County, TSL, Legislative Petitions 1799, roll 1, [16-1-1799]; petition of Adam Pick, TSL, Legislative Petitions 1805, roll 3 [2-1-1805]; Richard Green Waterhouse Diary, 65; letter from Paul Cunningham, March 3, 1796, Correspondence by Author, TSL, Ms. 82–41 (quotation).

Chapter 7

1. Letter from "A Friend of the People," *Carthage Gazette*, February 1809, 3.

2. David Waldstreicher, *In the Midst of Perpetual Fetes: The Making of American Nationalism* (Chapel Hill, 1997). Scholars disagree about the extent of democratization of the West, with more recent accounts emphasizing the importance of elites in political affairs. Stephen Aron, *How the West Was Lost: The Transformation of Kentucky from Daniel Boone to Henry Clay* (Baltimore, 1996); Kristofer Ray, "Land Speculation, Popular Democracy, and Political Transformation on the Tennessee Frontier, 1780–1800," *Tennessee Historical Quarterly* 54 (2002): 160–81.

3. Edmund S. Morgan, *American Slavery, American Freedom: The Ordeal of Colonial Virginia* (New York, 1975); Richard Beeman, *The Evolution of the Southern Backcountry*, chap. 3; James Oakes, *The Ruling Race: A History of American Slaveholders* (New York, 1982, 1983), chap. 5; Stephanie McCurry, *Masters of Small Worlds: Yeoman Households, Gender Relations, and the Political Culture of the Antebellum South Carolina Law Country* (New York, 1995). Scholars do recognize political activity in the backcountry rebellions in the late eighteenth century. Richard Maxwell Brown, *The South Carolina Regulators* (Cambridge, Mass., 1963); David P. Szatmary, *Shays' Rebellion: The Making of an Agrarian Insurrection* (Amherst, 1980); A. Roger Ekirch, "Poor Carolina": Politics and Society in Colonial North Carolina, 1729–1776 (Chapel Hill, 1981), chaps. 6 and 7; Thomas P. Slaughter, *The Whiskey Rebellion: Frontier Epilogue to the American Revolu-*

tion (New York, 1986); Terry Bouton, "A Road Closed: Rural Insurgency in Post-Independence Pennsylvania," *Journal of American History* 87 (December 2000): 855–87; Alan Taylor, *Liberty Men and Great Proprietors: The Revolutionary Settlement on the Maine Frontier, 1760–1820* (Chapel Hill, 1990). The southerners' implicit Faustian bargain with wealthy slave owners was reminiscent of the assumption by northern workers of an identity of whiteness as a psychological payoff while northern capitalists exploited their labor. David R. Roediger, *The Wages of Whiteness: Race and the Making of the American Working Class* (London, 1991).

4. Frederick Jackson Turner enshrined the frontier as the locus for democracy. In his robust account, the wilderness strips frontiersmen of civilization until the pioneers slowly transform the wilderness. The frontier produces individualism and a resistance to authority, and individualism promoted democracy. Frederick Jackson Turner, *Annual Report of the American Historical Association for the Year 1893* (Washington, D.C., 1894). Turner's argument has been challenged on many fronts. Patricia Limerick Nelson, *The Legacy of Conquest: The Unbroken Past of the American West* (New York, 1987). Although I agree with Turner that the white men and, to a lesser degree, free black men in Tennessee created a more democratic society than the ones that they left, I disagree with both his reasoning and his emphasis on individualism, and I also complicate his analysis by considering the local meaning of and restrictions on democracy. On another frontier where democracy came more slowly: John Gascoigne, *The Enlightenment and the Origins of European Australia* (Cambridge, 2002).

5. Militias are a somewhat neglected area of scholarship. Military historians have studied them primarily to contrast them with standing armies and to assess their efficiency. Jerry Cooper, *The Militia and the National Guard in America since Colonial Times: A Research Guide* (Westport, 1993). There is very little scholarship on the contribution that militia service made to the development of political ideologies. For four exceptions: Steven Rosswurm, *Arms, Country, and Class: The Philadelphia Militia and "Lower Sort" during the American Revolution, 1775–1783* (New Brunswick, 1987); Elizabeth A. Perkins, *Border Life: Experience and Memory in the Revolutionary Ohio Valley* (Chapel Hill, 1998), 124, 130–32; Albert H. Tillson Jr. "The Militia and Popular Political Culture in the Upper Valley of Virginia, 1740–1775," *Virginia Magazine of History and Biography* 94 (July 1986): 285–306; Laurence Dubois, *A Colony of Citizens: Revolution and Slave Emancipation in the French Caribbean, 1787–1804* (Chapel Hill, 2004), 221–48.

6. Knud Haakonssen, *Natural Law and Moral Philosophy: From Grotius to the Scottish Enlightenment* (Cambridge, 1996), 5–8; Michael P. Zuckert, *Natural Rights and the New Republicanism* (Princeton, 1994), 216–46.

7. Haakonssen, *Natural Law and Moral Philosophy*, 15–62; Christopher J. Berry, *Social Theory of the Scottish Enlightenment* (Edinburgh, 1997), 106–7; J. G. A. Pocock, *The Machiavellian Moment: Florentine Political Thought and the Atlantic Republican Tradition* (Princeton, 1975) and *The Ancient Constitution and the Feudal Law: A Study of English Historical Thought in the Seventeenth Century* (Cambridge, 1957); Zuckert, *Natural Rights and the New Republicanism*.

8. Kerby A. Miller, *Emigrants and Exiles: Ireland and the Irish Exodus to North America* (New York, 1985), 157, 161–66; S. J. Connolly, "Ulster Presbyterians: Religion, Culture, and Politics, 1660–1850," in H. Tyler Blethen and Curtis W. Wood Jr., eds., *Ulster and North America: Transatlantic Perspectives on the Scotch-Irish* (Tuscaloosa, 1997), 33–34.

9. A. G. Roeber, *Palatines, Liberty, and Property: German Lutherans in Colonial British America* (Baltimore, 1993), especially 19–20, 63, 120, 320–23; Aaron Spencer Fogleman, *Hopeful Journeys: German Immigration, Settlement, and Political Culture in Colonial America, 1717–1775* (Philadelphia, 1996), 4–9, 36–65.

10. Eric Richards, "Scotland and the Uses of the Atlantic Empire," in Bernard Bailyn and Philip D. Morgan, eds., *Strangers within the Realm: Cultural Margins of the First British Empire* (Chapel Hill, 1991), 94–95, 108–9; Richard B. Sher and Jeffrey R. Smitten, eds., *Scotland and America in the Age of the Enlightenment* (Edinburgh, 1990), 11–12; Berry, *Social Theory of the Scottish Enlightenment*, 23–51, 93–99; Gary Wills, *Inventing America: Jefferson's Declaration of Independence* (New York, 1978), 184–90. See chapter 6 for details on the spread of the Scottish Enlightenment tradition in the colonies and Tennessee.

11. Gordon Wood, *The Creation of the American Republic, 1776–1787* (Chapel Hill, 1969); Pocock, *The Machiavellian Moment*; Joyce Appleby, *Liberalism and Republicanism in the Historical Imagination* (Cambridge, Mass., 1992); John Phillip Reid, *Constitutional History of the American Revolution: The Authority of Rights* (Madison, 1986); Wills, *Inventing America*; Michael Zuckert, "Natural Rights in the American Revolution: The American Amalgam," in Jeffrey N. Wasserstrom, Lynn Hunt, and Marily B. Young, eds., *Human Rights and Revolution* (Lanham, 2000), 59–76.

12. John R. Finger, *Tennessee Frontiers: Three Regions in Transition* (Bloomington, 2001), 153–55; Beeman, *The Evolution of the Southern Backcountry*, 88–96; Ekirch, *Poor Carolina*; J. W. M. Breazeale, *Life as It Is or the World of Things in General* (Knoxville, 1812), 101 (quotation).

13. Gascoigne, *The Enlightenment and the Origins of European Australia*, 35–66.

14. David Campbell to Committee, November 2, 1790, Draper MSS, 11DD89.

15. Harriette Simpson Arnow, *Flowering of the Cumberland* (New York, 1963), 156–64.

16. Letter from William Cocke, June 25, 1775, Draper MSS, 26CC71–72; John Lipscomb Journal, June 29, 1784, and August 12, 1784, TSL, THS Miscellaneous Files, 1742–1859, Mf. 1080, reel 13, box 20, folder 41; Memoirs of William Hall, Diaries, TSL, Ms. 891, loc. II-H-2, box 1, p. 6.

17. Petition from Washington District, August 22, 1776, *CRNC*, 10:708–11; petition from Committee and Journal, August 22, 1776, *CRNC*, 10:702–3, 708–11.

18. Cumberland Compact and minutes of the Cumberland court, July 1, 1783, in *Three Pioneer Documents: Donelson's Journal, Cumberland Compact, Minutes of Cumberland Court* (Nashville, 1964), 39; Samuel Cole Williams, *History of the Lost State of Franklin* (Johnson City, 1924).

19. J. G. M. Ramsey, *The Annals of Tennessee to the End of the Eighteenth Century* (Johnson City, 1853; repr., 1926), 434–37; Proceedings, January 12, 1789, *SRNC*, 22:722–25;

Draper MSS, 32S353–56; Memorandum of October 29, 1793, THS Miscellaneous Files, Mf. 678, box 10, reel 6, M-57; petition on behalf of Thomas Peyton, Legislative Petitions 1801, TSL, roll 1, [21-1-1801].

20. Upper Station militia list, circa 1774, Draper MSS, 5XX2; Memoirs of William Hall, Diaries, TSL, Ms. 891, loc. II-H-2, box 1, pp. 13, 18; Cooper, *The Militia and the National Guard in America*, 15; E. Milton Wheeler, "Development and Organization of the North Carolina Militia," *North Carolina Historical Review* 16 (July 1964): 307–23; Tennessee Historical Commission, Cumberland Compact, in *Three Pioneer Documents*, 15, 17; William Martin to Lyman Draper, May 13, 1843, Draper MSS, 3XX18; Sara Bradford Saunders, *Salt of the Earth* (n.p., n.d.), 126–27.

21. Doack to Preston, September 22, 1774, Draper MSS, 3QQ101; Draper MSS, 10NN24–26; Draper MSS, 30S370; Joseph Martin to Arthur Campbell, April 22, 1781, Draper MSS, 10S182–85; James Robertson to William Preston, July 5, 1774, Draper MSS, 3QQ55; Draper 32S257–71; Draper MSS, 1S49–53; William Christian to William Preston, June 22, 1774, Draper MSS, 3QQ42–43.

22. Draper MSS, 30S209–10; Draper MSS, 3XX4 (quotation); Draper MSS, 5U31–32; Governor Martin to Brigadier General McDowell, July 23, 1782, *SRNC*, 16:697–98; *William Shillern v. Nicholas Hawkins*, Washington County Clerk Minute Books, TSL, roll 129, Court of Equity, March 1801, pp. 218–19.

23. William Christian to William Preston, July 9, 1774, Draper MSS, 3QQ60; William Preston to Daniel Smith, March 7, 1782, Draper MSS, 4XX49; Washington County Clerk Minute Books, May 1780, pp. 92, 112; July 1790, pp. 443–44; meeting of representatives of several militia companies, June 2, 1786, Draper MSS, 5XX18; William Christian to Arthur Campbell, February 19, 1782, Draper MSS, 9DD32.

24. Ekirch, *Poor Carolina*, chap. 3; Beeman, *The Evolution of the Southern Backcountry*, 43–51; William Christian to Daniel Smith, March 31, 1781, Draper MSS, 16DD20; William Russell to William Fleming, March 24, 1788, Draper MSS, 2U148; Samuel Cole Williams, *William Tatham, Wataugan* (Johnson City, 1947), 15. On election culture generally: Rhys Isaac, *The Transformation of Virginia, 1740–1790* (New York, 1982), 110–14, 251–55, 319–20.

25. Ramsey, *Annals of Tennessee*, 435; letter from one of Tipton's party, August 20, 1788, Draper MSS, 9DD50; petition from Watauga, *CRNC*, 10:709; Cumberland Compact, in *Three Pioneer Tennessee Documents*, 16; Proceedings, *SRNC*, 22:722.

26. Knud Haakonssen, "Natural Law and Moral Realism: The Scottish Synthesis," in M. A. Stewart, ed., *Studies in the Philosophy of the Scottish Enlightenment* (Oxford, 1990), 61–85; Wood, *The Creation of the American Republic*, 344–89; Cumberland Compact, in *Three Pioneer Tennessee Documents*; Captain Martin Armstrong to Brigadier General Sumner, February 26, 1782, *SRNC* 16:524–26; Legislative Petitions 1809, [24-1-1809].

27. Journal of the House, December 22, 1789, *SRNC*, 21:429–30; Minutes of Mero District Superior Court of Law and Equity, Davidson County Archives, Nashville, Tennessee, Book A, May 1789, p. 9; Washington County Clerk Minute Books, May 1781, p. 133; report by Committee of Privileges and Elections, November 23, 1787, in *American*

Historical Magazine 1 (July 1896): 298–300; Richard Caswell to John Sevier, February 23, 1787, in Cora Bales Sevier and Nancy S. Madden, *Sevier Family History* (Washington, D.C., 1961), 71–72.

28. "The Provisional Constitution of Frankland," *American Historical Magazine* 1:1 (January 1896): 48–63, quotations on 52–53. Examples of clauses about virtue in other state constitutions: Virginia's of 1776, Bill of Rights, §15; Pennsylvania's of 1776, §45; Vermont's of 1777, Chapter I, §XIV.

29. Clarence Edwin Carter, ed., *The Territorial Papers of the United States: The Territory South of the River Ohio, 1790–1796*, vol. 4 (Washington, D.C., 1936), 24–25; Robert E. Corlew, *Tennessee: A Short History*, 2nd ed. (Knoxville, 1980), 88.

30. Ray, "Land Speculation, Popular Democracy, and Political Transformation on the Tennessee Frontier, 1780–1800"; Carter, *Territorial Papers*, 4:328–29; *Journal of the Proceedings of a Convention, began and held at Knoxville, on January 11, 1796* (Knoxville, 1796), 10–12; Tennessee Constitution, Article I, §§1–3, 7; Article III, §1.

31. Inaugural address, March 30, 1796, in Robert H. White, ed., *Messages of the Governors of Tennessee, 1796–1821* (Nashville, 1952), 1:3; letter from Aristides, *Tennessee Gazette*, September 28, 1803, 1; *Knoxville Gazette*, November 1, 1794, 2–3; May 2, 1796, 2, 3; Charge by Judge Innes to Grand Jury, *Tennessee Gazette*, November 18, 1801, 1; *Tennessee Gazette*, July 17, 1805 (toast).

32. Scholars contended southerners favored limited government. Oakes, *The Ruling Race*, chap. 5; Kenneth S. Greenberg, *Masters and Statesmen: The Political Culture of American Slavery* (Baltimore, 1985), chap. 5.

33. Charge to the Grand Jury, *Knoxville Gazette*, December 31, 1791, 3; letter from "the Reviewers," *Knoxville Gazette*, March 10, 1792, 2; *Tennessee Gazette*, July 10, 1805, 3.

34. *Carthage Gazette*, February 9, 1809; *Knoxville Gazette*, August 4, 1802, 3; *Tennessee Gazette*, August 4, 1802, 2; petitions from Greene County, Legislative Petitions, [9-1-1799], [1-1-1803]; *Knoxville Register*, August 28, 1798; *Carthage Gazette*, September 10, 1808; February 5, 1809.

35. Letter from James Winchester, February 3, 1793, Draper MSS, 4JJ348; Journal of Council of Safety, July 22, 1776, *SRNC* 10:702–3; petition of the inhabitants of the Western Country, December 1787, *SRNC* 22:705–14; memorial of inhabitants south of French Broad to Congress, September 12, 1794, in Ramsey, *Annals of Tennessee*, 631.

36. The records on the petitions are extensive. The Tennessee State Library and Archives has 298 petitions with 15,597 signatures on microfilm for the period from December 1798 through 1810. Legislative Petitions, 1798–1810, TSL, rolls 1–3. However, the records on microfilm are not complete. The Journals of the House and Senate throughout that period frequently refer to petitions not on microfilm. Petitions for the year 1804 are completely missing, and all but three for 1805 are also missing. In addition, the overwhelming response to the Land Law of 1806 is missing. Governor Sevier received 14 petitions with more than 2,000 signatures from the District of Washington alone requesting its repeal. Petitions came in from virtually every county of the state. *Tennessee Gazette*, November 15, 1806, 3.

37. My calculations are rough, but suggest that about 16 percent of the men older than sixteen signed a petition each election cycle. Some men signed more than one petition, which I assume is offset (probably more than offset) by the missing petitions. The two years for which I have the best population and petition data are 1799 and 1803. In 1800 population data indicate that there were about 22,199 men over the age of sixteen. This means that about 17.4 percent of them signed a petition in 1799. In 1803 there were about 27,439 men older than sixteen, and 4,427, or 16 percent, signed a petition. U.S. Census, 1790, *Return of the Whole Number of Persons within the Several Districts of the United States* (Philadelphia, 1791); *Tennessee Gazette*, November 11, 1801, 2 (1800 census).

38. Petition of January 29, 1808, in Barnes Collection, University of Tennessee Special Collection, Knoxville, Rhea County Court Papers, 1785–1810, MS-19, box 1–3, 1808; minutes of Knox County Court of Pleas and Quarter Sessions, November 6, 1793, Knox County Archives, Knoxville, Tennessee, Book No. "O," 89.

39. Simon P. Newman, *Parades and the Politics of the Street: Festive Culture in the Early American Republic* (Philadelphia, 1997); Waldstreicher, *In the Midst of Perpetual Fetes*. Simon P. Newman suggests that the large-scale festivals and parades were less common in the rural south. Newman, *Parades and the Politics of the Street*, 188. However, Tennesseans seem to have celebrated with the same vigor exhibited by their rural northern counterparts.

40. *Tennessee Gazette*, May 20, 1801; October 4, 1806, 2–3; *Carthage Gazette*, March 22, 1808, 2; *Clarion*, May 19, 1809, 3; *Knoxville Gazette*, July 13, 1793, 2; July 17, 1795, 2 (quotation); *Tennessee Gazette*, May 20, 1801, 3; July 8, 1801, 2 (500 attended); *Clarion*, July 12, 1808, 3 (500–1,000 of all ranks).

41. For examples: *Knoxville Gazette*, July 13, 1793, 2 (government); July 13, 1793 (leading men); *Tennessee Gazette*, July 8, 1801, 2 (mechanics); July 10, 1805, 3 (militia); *Clarion*, July 12 and 19, 1808 (Farmer's Society); July 13, 1810, 3 (ordinary citizens).

42. For examples: *Knoxville Gazette*, July 17, 1795, 2 (government); *Clarion*, May 19, 1809, 3 (leading men); *Tennessee Gazette*, July 20, 1803, 2 (mechanics); *Clarion*, July 13, 1810, 2 (militia); *Tennessee Gazette*, July 13, 1803, 2 (ordinary citizens).

43. Newman, *Parades and the Politics of the Street*, 30–31; Waldstreicher, *In the Midst of Perpetual Fetes*, 219–24; *Tennessee Gazette*, August 21, 1805; *Knoxville Gazette*, July 17, 1795, 2; *Clarion*, July 13, 1810, 2.

44. Tennessee Laws, 1798, 2nd General Assembly, 2nd session, Chapter I; petitions, Legislative Petitions, [35-2-1799], [16-2-1806]; *Carthage Gazette*, June 15, 1809; Tennessee Constitution, Article VII; Military Elections, 1796–1862, TSL, reel 1, box 1, folder 4; Tennessee Election Returns, TSL, RG 87, roll 1; Legislative Petitions, 1809, [24-1-1809].

45. Washington County Clerk Minute Books, July 1790, p. 426; John Tealsford and others to John Sevier, November 6, 1797, Military Elections, 1796–1862, reel 1, box 1, folder 32; Legislative Petitions, [24-2-1801], [57-1-1803-1], [3-1-1806]; *Carthage Gazette*, May 25, 1810; deposition of Benjamin Weaver, October 2, 1809, Rejected Bills, TSL, RG 60, box 9, folder 4; deposition of Noah Bennett, Legislative Petitions, 1809, [16-2-1809-12]; Rejected Bills, box 1, folder 27 (1799) and box 9, folder 4 (1809).

46. Alan Taylor "'The Art of Hook & Snivey': Political Culture in Upstate New York during the 1790s," *Journal of American History* 79 (March 1993): 1371–96; letter from Isaac Clark, February 17, 1807, in *Tennessee Gazette*, March 28, 1807, 3; *Tennessee Gazette*, January 17, 1807, 4; Samuel Spencer to John Sevier, February 24, 1790, Draper MSS, 16DD28.

47. William Claiborne to Andrew Jackson, July 20, 1797, *Papers*, I; *Knoxville Gazette*, July 18, 1796, 2 (toast).

48. Letter from S. Williams, *Carthage Gazette*, June 8, 1809, 3; letter from Thomas Harris, *Carthage Gazette*, April 10, 1809, 3; *Clarion*, July 16, 1809, 1–2.

49. Haakonssen, *Natural Law and Moral Philosophy*, 5–8, 15–62; Berry, *Social Theory of the Scottish Enlightenment*, 106–7; Zuckert, *Natural Rights and the New Republicanism*; Pocock, *The Ancient Constitution and the Feudal Law*, 30–55; Reid, *Constitutional History of the American Revolution*.

50. *Knoxville Gazette*, May 19, 1792, 4.

51. Private thoughts of John Steele, in H. M. Wagstaff, ed., *The Papers of John Steele* (Raleigh, 1924), 2:773. For a more extensive discussion of prosperity, abolitionism, and civilization, see chapter 8.

52. John D. Barnhart, "The Tennessee Constitution of 1796: A Product of the Old West," *Journal of Southern History* 9 (November 1943): 532–48; Pennsylvania Constitution, 1790, Article IX, §1; Tennessee Constitution, 1796, Article XI, §1; §§3.

53. Many historians and legal scholars of the federal constitution assume that all constitutional rights are individual rights. Robert Allen Rutland, *The Birth of the Bill of Rights, 1776–1791* (Chapel Hill, 1955); David Thelen, ed., *The Constitution and American Life* (Ithaca, 1987). Following federal scholars, many historians who have studied state constitutional rights tend to assume that these rights are individual rights. Bernard Schwartz, *The Great Rights of Mankind: A History of the American Bill of Rights* (New York, 1977), 67–85; Willi Paul Adams, *The First American Constitutions: Republican Ideology and the Making of the State Constitutions in the Revolutionary Era* (Chapel Hill, 1980), 144–47. Some writers discount state constitutions that do not follow the federal model by describing them as bloated or sloppy, believing that they reflect the concerns of interest groups. Lawrence Friedman, *A History of American Law* (New York, 1985), 117–22. Even John J. Dinan, who rejects that view, seems to accept that rights in state constitutions prior to the Civil War, like the federal constitution, were negative rights designed to limit the scope of governmental action. John J. Dinan, *The American State Constitutional Tradition* (Lawrence, 2006), 3–5, 184–221.

However, state constitutions often assumed a different concept of rights than the federal constitution. Their declarations of rights sought to ensure the citizen's right to a free government, not merely to recognize rights in individuals existing apart from government. Consequently, rights in state constitutions articulated principles about the structure of government by defining and circumscribing governmental authority and by stimulating community cohesion and citizen virtue. All state constitutions of the period with declarations of rights had mixtures of public rights that supported and limited government. The state constitutions can be found in Francis Newton Thorpe, comp. and ed., *The Federal and State Colonial Charters, and Other Organic Laws* (Washington, D.C., 1909). Recently, a few legal scholars have argued that the broader statements of public principles in state bills of rights point to a different view of constitutionalism than the liberal view of individual rights. Donald S. Lutz contends that delegates designed these early declarations as a statement of fundamental values to the legislature and to the citizenry. Donald S. Lutz, "Political Participation in Eighteenth-Century America," in Paul Finkelman and Stephen E. Gottlieb, *Toward a Usable Past: Liberty under State Constitutions* (Athens, 1991), 19–49, and "The Pedigree of the Bill of Rights," in Ronald Hoffman and Peter J. Albert, *The Bill of Rights: Government Proscribed* (Charlottesville, 1997), 42–76. G. Alan Tarr argues that the state constitutions reflected a republican view of government, stating political principles that placed faith in majoritarian rule to secure rights and to ensure a republican form of government. G. Alan Tarr, *Understanding State Constitutions* (Princeton, 1998), 76–81. In the case of Tennessee, I agree with Tarr that the framers intended that the declarations act to ensure a republican government but argue that wealthy and poorer men had different ideas about what this meant.

54. On public rights: Tennessee Constitution, Article XI, §§2, 5, 9, 17 (partial), 23, 24, 29, 30, 32. On individual rights: Tennessee Constitution, Article XI, §§3, 4, 6–22, 25–28. On Pennsylvania constitution: Pennsylvania Constitution of 1790, Article IX, §11.

55. Tennessee Constitution, Article X, §§29, 31, 32.

56. Bernard Bailyn, *The Ideological Origins of the American Revolution* (Cambridge, Mass., 1992), 18–21, 55–93; William Blount to John Gray Blount, January 13, 1787, in Alice Barnwell Keith, ed., *The John Gray Blount Papers* (Raleigh, 1952), 1:235–37; *Journal of the Convention*, 11, 24, 25, 31, 33.

57. Tennessee Constitution, Article X, §4 (emphasis added).

58. Scholars of the federal constitution have been fascinated with the potential of the federal clause. They raise this in a debate about the "unwritten constitution"—that is, whether the written document captures the entire American constitution or whether the United States has a judicially enforceable unwritten constitution that prevails over contrary legislation or that includes unenumerated rights. The legal community intensified this debate in the 1960s in response to Justice Goldberg's concurring opinion in *Griswold v. Connecticut*, 381 U.S. 479 (1965), in which Justice Goldberg located a right to marital privacy squarely within the Ninth Amendment. Historians have joined the fray in an effort to determine how the framers regarded the unwritten Constitution in the founding period. Suzanna Sherry, "The Founders' Unwritten Constitution," *University of Chicago Law Review* 54 (Fall 1987): 1127–77; Thomas C. Grey, "The Original Understanding and the Unwritten Constitution," in Neil L. York, ed., *Toward a More Perfect Union: Six Essays on the Constitution* (Provo, 1988), 145–73. The concept of a right to privacy tickled a lot of legal fancy, and the outpouring of law review articles on this subject is amazing. See, for example, Lyman Rhoades and Rodney R. Patula, "The Ninth Amendment: A Survey of Theory and Practice in the

Federal Courts since Griswold v. Connecticut," *Denver Law Journal* 50 (1973): 153; Russell L. Caplan, "The History and Meaning of the Ninth Amendment," *Virginia Law Review* 69 (1983): 223–68; Randy E. Barnett, ed., "Symposium on Interpreting the Ninth Amendment," *Chicago-Kent Law Review* 64 (1988): 35–270; Jeb Rubenfeld, "The Right to Privacy," *Harvard Law Review* 102 (1989): 737–807. Even state constitutionalists, a small club, got into the act. Note, "Unenumerated Rights Clauses in State Constitutions," *Texas Law Review* 63 (1985): 1321–38. This interesting article incorrectly suggests that the first such state clauses appeared in the Maine and Alabama constitutions in 1819 (note, 1322, n. 6). Operating from a liberal paradigm that sees nondelegated rights as individual rights, legal scholars and historians fail to consider whether the nondelegated rights include common or public rights.

59. Legislative Petitions, 1799, [8-1-1799-5a]. Other examples: Legislative Petitions, 1799, [3-2-1799]; [5-2-1799]; [3-1-1799]; letter from Andrew W. Rights, *Knoxville Gazette*, February 17, 1797, 3.

60. Petition from Knoxville, Legislative Petitions 1799, [7-1-1799]; Tennessee Laws, 1809, 8th General Assembly, 1st session, Chapter XXXIX; Tennessee Laws, 1801, 4th General Assembly, 1st session, Chapter XXXII; Tennessee Laws, 1803, 5th General Assembly, 1st session, Chapter XLVII; *Journal of the Senate* (Knoxville, 1809), October 12, 1809.

61. Historians of women have long noted the role that women played in advancing morality in the North after the Revolution. Nancy F. Cott, *The Bonds of Womanhood: "Woman's Sphere" in New England, 1780–1835* (New Haven, 1977), 126–59. But it was several decades before northern women carried their private concerns into the legislative arena. Paula Baker, "The Domestication of Politics: Women and American Political Society, 1780–1920," *American Historical Review* 89 (June 1984): 620–47. Most historians believe that southern women's involvement in promoting legislation began later in the South after the Civil War. Drew Gilpin Faust, *Mothers of Invention: Women of the Slaveholding South in the American Civil War* (Chapel Hill, 1996), 247–54. Tennessee women did not follow this trajectory.

62. James R. Gilmore, *John Sevier as a Commonwealth Builder* (New York, 1887), 64–68; "Journal of Governor John Sevier," *Tennessee Historical Magazine* 5 (October 1919); minutes, July 8, 1795, *Journal of the Proceedings of the Legislative Council of the Territory of the United States of America, South of the River Ohio, Begun and Held at Knoxville, the 29th Day of June, 1795* (Knoxville, 1795); petition from Maury County, Legislative Petitions 1809, [12-2-1809].

63. Circular letter, August 1807, Tennessee Baptist Holston Record Book, SBHL, Mf. 836 (quotation); James H. Kettner, *The Development of American Citizenship, 1608–1870* (Chapel Hill, 1978); Tennessee Constitution, Article V, §11; Article VII; Article XI; Legislative Petitions, 1799–1803, TSL, reels 1 and 2.

64. Tennessee Constitution, Article I, §7; Article II, §§2, 3; Article 3, §1; Article VII; *Journal of the Convention*, 25.

65. *Tennessee Gazette*, April 13, 1803, 4; *Journal of the Convention*, p. 25; Washington County Trustee Tax Books, 1778–1846, TSL, roll 639: 1778, pp. 4–12; 1779, pp. 4, 16, 31;

1781, pp. 20, 26, 34; *Ruth Brown v. William Whitson*, Court of Equity, Washington County Clerk Minute Books, September 1802; *Journal of the Senate* (Knoxville, [1807?], September 13, 1806.

66. *Tennessee Gazette*, March 31, 1802, 2; *James Gowan v. Isaac Baker*, County Court Minutes, Sumner County Archives, Gallatin, Tennessee, Tennessee Records of Sumner County, vol. 5, 1804–1805 (WPA, 1936), 643–44 (Gowan); County Court Minutes, Tennessee Records of Sumner County, vol. 4, 1801–1804 (WPA, 1936), p. 469 (Sumner County tax).

67. Tennessee Constitution, Article III, §1; 2nd General Assembly, 2nd session, 1798, Chapter I (militia service).

68. Petition, August 4, 1803; Legislative Petitions, 1803, [35-1-1803]; Tennessee Laws, 1803, 5th General Assembly, 1st session, Chapter LII; bill on Moses Brown, Rejected Bills, box 6, folder 38; Tennessee Laws, 1805, 6th General Assembly, 1st session, Chapter XXV.

69. Tennessee Laws, 1796, 1st General Assembly, 2nd session, Chapter II; Records of the Board of Commissioners, July 5, 1802, THS Miscellaneous Files, Mf. 678, reel 6, box 11, N-19; Knoxville City Council Minute Book, April 9, 1802, Knox County Archives, Minute Book A; Records of Smith County Minute Book, 1799–1800, March 16, 1801, TSL, WPA typescript, 16; Tennessee Laws, 1799, 3rd General Assembly, 1st session, Chapter XXVIII; Journal of the Senate, August 3, 1804; Tennessee Laws, 1806, 6th General Assembly, 2nd session, Chapter XXXII; David Brion Davis, *The Problem of Slavery in Western Culture* (Ithaca, 1966), 118–21.

Chapter 8

1. Robert H. White, ed., *Messages of the Governors of Tennessee, 1796–1821* (Nashville, 1952), 1:3; "Journal of John Sevier," *Tennessee Historical Magazine* 5 (October 1919): 183–93; *Tennessee Gazette*, February 25, 1800, 3, and September 15, 1802, 1–2, publishing extract from Boyd's letter of December 1800.

2. For a summary of the literature on the northern and southern viewpoints: Gregory H. Nobles, "Breaking into the Back Country: New Approaches to the Early American Frontier, 1750–1800," *William and Mary Quarterly* 46 (1989): 641–70, at 654–62. On the South: Malcolm J. Rohrbough, *The Trans-Appalachian Frontier: People, Societies, and Institutions 1775–1850* (New York, 1978), chap. 2; A. Roger Ekirch, "Poor Carolina": Politics and Society in Colonial North Carolina, 1729–1776 (Chapel Hill, 1981), chaps. 1 and 2; Richard R. Beeman, *The Evolution of the Southern Backcountry: A Case Study of Lunenburg County, Virginia, 1746–1832* (Philadelphia, 1984), 61–80; Stephen Aron, *How the West Was Lost: The Transformation of Kentucky from Daniel Boone to Henry Clay* (Baltimore, 1996), 124–49. Historians of early Tennessee have focused their study of economic relations almost exclusively on speculators. James R. Gilmore, *John Sevier as a Commonwealth Builder* (New York, 1887); A. P. Whitaker, "The Muscle Shoals Speculation, 1783–1789," *Mississippi Valley Historical Review* (June 1926): 365–86; William H. Masterson, *William Blount* (Baton Rouge, 1954), and "The Land Specula-

tor and the West—The Role of William Blount," *East Tennessee Historical Society's Publications* 27 (1955): 3–8; Thomas Perkins Abernathy, *From Frontier to Plantation in Tennessee: A Study in Frontier Democracy* (University, 1967); Kristofer Ray, "Land Speculation, Popular Democracy, and Political Transformation on the Tennessee Frontier, 1780–1800," *Tennessee Historical Quarterly* 54 (2002): 160–81. Scholars have not studied the ideas about the economy of ordinary white Tennesseans in this period.

3. John C. Weaver, *The Great Land Rush and the Making of the Modern World, 1650–1900* (Montreal, 2003), 264–65, 294–95; Alan Taylor, *Liberty Men and Great Proprietors: The Revolutionary Settlement on the Maine Frontier, 1760–1820* (Chapel Hill, 1990).

4. John Gascoigne, *The Enlightenment and the Origins of European Australia* (Cambridge, 2002); Christopher J. Berry, *Social Theory of the Scottish Enlightenment* (Edinburgh, 1997), 93–99; J. G. A. Pocock, *The Machiavellian Moment: Florentine Political Thought and the Atlantic Republican Tradition* (Princeton, 1975), chaps. 13 and 14; Michael P. Zuckert, *Natural Rights and the New Republicanism* (Princeton, 1994), 247–88.

5. Neal O'Steen, "Pioneer Education in the Tennessee Country," *Tennessee Historical Quarterly* 35 (Summer 1976): 199–219, at 215; Harriette Simpson Arnow, *Flowering of the Cumberland* (New York, 1963), 157, 160; William Cocke to Anthony Bledsoe, May 27, 1776, Draper MSS, 4QQ43; *Tennessee Gazette*, February 18, 1801, p. 2 (quotation).

6. *House Journal of the Second General Assembley of the State of Tennessee*, transcribed by R. L. C. White (Nashville, 1903), September 30, 1797 (quotation); letter from Nashville dated November 5, 1785, in Draper MSS, 3JJ235–36; accounting records, 1802–1804, Dyas Collection, John Coffee Papers, TSL, Mf. 814, reel 1, box 3, folder 6; *Carthage Gazette*, April 3, 1809.

7. Letter by Eliza Campbell, *Knoxville Gazette*, July 31, 1795, 3; *Tennessee Gazette*, February 18, 1801, 2 (quotation).

8. John Augustus Williams, *Life of Elder John Smith* (Cincinnati, 1870), 19; *William Doherty v. Lydia Doherty*, September 23, 1800, Superior Court files, Knox County Archives, Knoxville, Tennessee, Hamilton District; William Polk to Sarah Polk, July 9, 1811, Leonidas Polk Papers, TSL, Mf. 381; Sallie Smith to Daniel Smith, July 20, 1793, in "Rock Castle," *American Historical Magazine* 5 (October 1900): 293; Articles of Agreement, September 24, 1806, Rhea County Files, University of Tennessee Special Collection, Knoxville, MS-19, group III, box I, folder 1; Robert V. Remini, *Andrew Jackson and the Course of American Empire, 1767–1821* (New York, 1977), 68–69, 133; William N. Chambers, "Thomas Hart Benton," *Tennessee Historical Quarterly* 8 (December 1949): 291–331.

9. James Ross, *Life and Times of Elder Reuben Ross* (Philadelphia, 1882), 183–85, 188; Andrew Stuffern Account Book, December 6, 1809, University of Tennessee Special Collection, MS-1524; Lucy Kennerly Gump, "Possessions and Patterns of Living in Washington County: The 20 Years before Tennessee Statehood, 1777–1796" (master's thesis, East Tennessee State University, 1989), 131, 172–73; Tench Coxe, digester, *A Statement of the Arts and Manufactures of the United States of America, for the Year 1810*

(Philadelphia, 1814), 137–39; bill to establish inspection of butter, 1801, Rejected Bills, TSL, RG 60, box 5, folder 23.

10. Gump, "Washington County," 221; account book for Hunter's Hill, December 19 and 23, 1804, and account book for Clover Bottom, December 19, 1805, Ladies Hermitage Association Collection, Andrew Jackson Papers, TSL, Mf. 1099, reel 1, box 1, folder 28, and reel 2, box 1, folder 34; Coxe, *Arts and Manufactures of the United States for 1810,* 137, 140.

11. James Norman Smith Memoirs, 1807, TSL, Mf. 157, p. 82; John Thompson Diary, June 19, 1804, University of Tennessee Special Collection, MS-1271; travel diary, March 17 and 22, 1805, November 27, 1810, Draper 5XX29; Washington County Clerk Minute Books, TSL, roll 129, vol. 1, May 1789, p. 404; *Knoxville Register,* August 14, 1798, 1; *Knoxville Gazette,* October 14, 1801, 1; *Tennessee Gazette,* April 24, 1805, 3; *Clarion,* December 13, 1808, 3.

12. *Tennessee Gazette,* October 5, 1810, 4; John Coffee to Andrew Jackson, May 14, 1810, *Papers,* II; Ilai Metcalfe Account Book, October 22, 1813, University of Tennessee Special Collection, MS-603, p. 37; *Clarion,* July 21, 1809, 4; January 19, 1810, 1; Dr. R. L. C. White, "The Great Seal of the State of Tennessee," *American Historical Magazine* 6 (July 1901): 195–212, at 209; *Journal of the Senate* (Knoxville, [1807?]), September 13, 1806; *Carthage Gazette* January 23, 1809, 1; *Clarion,* July 12, 1808, 1; December 1, 1809, 3.

13. Letter from Eliza Campbell, *Knoxville Gazette,* July 31, 1795, 3.

14. Mill Creek Baptist Church, June 15, 1804, SBHC, Mf. 3337; Wilson Creek Primitive Baptist Church, May 16, 1807, TSL, Mf. 90; Williams, *Elder John Smith,* 16; Red River Baptist Church, July 16, 1808, SBHL, Mf. 289; Turnbull Primitive Baptist Church, June 11, 1808, and December 9, 1808, TSL, Mf. 164.

15. Historians disagree about how white men viewed the role of government in economic matters in the early republic. Historians writing in the liberal tradition stressed the freedom of the marketplace from government regulation. James W. Ely Jr., *The Guardian of Every Other Right: A Constitutional History of Property Rights* (New York, 1992). Jonathan R. T. Hughes contended that the government has always regulated the market, not from a comprehensive plan, but in response to political forces, resulting in haphazardous controls that create serious problems. Jonathan R. T. Hughes, *The Governmental Habit: Economic Controls from Colonial Times to the Present* (New York, 1977). Agreeing that the government has been deeply involved in economic regulation, William J. Novak argues that regulations articulate and achieve a vision of public welfare. William J. Novak, *The People's Welfare: Law and Regulation in Nineteenth Century America* (Chapel Hill, 1996). Frontier historians also differ. Some characterize the settlers as preferring a marketplace free from governmental regulation. Eric Hinderaker, *Elusive Empires: Constructing Colonialism in the Ohio Valley, 1673–1800* (Cambridge, 1997), 250–54; David Hackett Fischer, *Albion's Seed: Four British Folkways in America* (New York, 1989), 765–76. Malcolm J. Rohrbough describes the early period as characterized by little government, with government asserting increasing control over economic matters after 1795. Rohrbough, *The Trans-Appalachian Frontier.* In

Kentucky, Stephen Aron found an elite eager for governmental involvement to the detriment of the poor man. Aron, *How the West Was Lost*.

16. Legislative message, December 5, 1798, White, *Messages of the Governors*, 45–47; Petition from Davidson County, Legislative Petitions 1803, TSL, [23-1-1803]; Washington County Clerk Minute Books, November 1778, p. 54; minutes, April 7, 1802, Records for Nashville, THS Miscellaneous Files, TSL, Mf. 678, reel 6, box 11, N-19, pp. 6–9; Tennessee Laws, 1805, 6th General Assembly, 1st session, Chapter XXX.

17. Petition, Legislative Petitions, 1799, [25-1-1799]; petition from Sumner and Davidson counties, Legislative Petitions, 1799, [8-2-1799]; petition from Davidson county, Legislative Petitions, 1799, [11-2-99]; petition of Miller and Whitney, Legislative Petitions, 1803, [28-1-1803]; Journal of the Senate, March 31, 1796; petition of Samuel Doak, Legislative Petitions, 1803, [60-1-1803]; Trimble's resolution, Journal of the House, November 16, 1807.

18. Berry, *Social Theory of the Scottish Enlightenment*, 93–99; petition from the Citizens of Elk River, Legislative Petitions, 1806, [10-2-1806]; Emmerich de Vattel, *The Law of Nations; or, Principles of the Law of Nature, Applied to the Conduct and Affairs of Nations and Sovereigns*, rev. ed. (London, 1797), bk. I, chap. I, pp. 1–4; bk. I, chap. VII, §81; unsigned letter, *Knoxville Gazette*, March 6, 1797, 1 (quotation); Tennessee Constitution, Article XI, §32; Paul H. Bergeron, Stephen V. Ash, and Jeannette Keith, *Tennesseans and Their History* (Knoxville, 1999), 76.

19. Historians have described claims by squatters in other backcountry locations. Andrew R. L. Cayton, *The Frontier Republic: Ideology and Politics in the Ohio Country, 1780–1825* (Kent, 1986), 1–11; Hinderaker, *Elusive Empires*, 238–41; Taylor, *Liberty Men and Great Proprietors*, 101–5; Aron, *How the West Was Lost*, 65–69. There has been no study of landless settlers or of their ideology in Tennessee.

20. James G. Leyburn, *The Scotch-Irish: A Social History* (Chapel Hill, 1962), 192–94.

21. Warren R. Hofstra, " 'The Extension of His Majesties Dominion': The Virginia Backcountry and the Reconfiguration of Imperial Frontiers," *Journal of American History* 84 (March 1998): 1281–1312; Leyburn, *The Scotch-Irish*, 200–205; Kerby A. Miller, *Emigrants and Exiles: Ireland and the Irish Exodus to North America* (New York, 1985), 163–64; Aron, *How the West Was Lost*, 64–89; Hinderaker, *Elusive Empires*, 236–41.

22. Draper MSS, 3XX4; William Johnson to Joseph Martin, July 12, 1785, Draper MSS, 1XX8; talk by The Raven, July 15, 1777, in Archibald Henderson, "Treaty of Long Island at Holston," *North Carolina Historical Review* 8 (January 1931): 55–116; J. G. M. Ramsey, *The Annals of Tennessee to the End of the Eighteenth Century* (Johnson City, 1853; repr., 1926), 369–72; *Knoxville Gazette*, November 5, 1791, 2 (quotation); report to the Secretary of State by Blount, November 8, 1791, in Clarence Edwin Carter, ed., *The Territorial Papers of the United States: The Territory South of the River Ohio, 1790–1796*, vol. 4 (Washington, D.C., 1936), 4.2:85–100.

23. Circular to Intruders on westside of Cumberland Mountains, February 15, 1804, M208; Return Meigs to Henry Dearborn, February 17, 1804, M208. Journal of the House, April 19, 1796; Journal of the House, September 12, 1806; petition by citizens of

Bledsoe County, Legislative Petitions, [26-2-1809]. The extant section of the book for the Fifth District contains 453 surveys based on lands held by certificate, entries, warrants, and preemption. The 210 preemption claims covered 27,059.5 acres. Tennessee Fifth District Surveyors Book, 1807–1810, University of Tennessee Special Collection, MS-1673. On Cumberland: report of land commissioners, Journal of the Senate, October 12, 1807; Intruders, May 27, 1809, M208.

24. *George Martin v. Andrew English*, September 1793, Washington County Clerk Minute Books, Court of Equity, vol. 2, p. 492; preemption claim, March 23, 1784, TSL, THS Miscellaneous Collection, reel 2, box 2, C-181; *Smith v. Kain*, 1 Tenn. 573–75 (November 1812).

25. James Robertson to Willie Blount, March 20, 1811, Draper MSS, 5U192; *William Blevins v. John Shelby*, September 1794, Washington County Clerks Minute Book, Court of Equity, vol. 1, 204–5; preemption claims, January 20, 1783, in "Records of the Cumberland Association," *American Historical Magazine* 7 (July 1902): 254; petition from Elk River, Legislative Petitions, 1806, [10-2-1806]; unsigned letter, *Knoxville Gazette*, March 6, 1797, 1 (quotation); *Smith v. Kain*, 1 Tenn 573–75 (November 1812); petition of people south of French Broad, Legislative Petitions, 1809, [36-2-1809].

26. *Barnet's Lessee v. Russel and others*, 2 Tenn 424–32, at 430 (Superior Court of Law and Equity: November 1808) (quotation). Courts created the doctrine *Communis error facit jus* because "what was at first illegal is presumed, when repeated many times, to have acquired the force of usage: and then it would be wrong to depart from it." Henry Campbell Black, *Black's Law Dictionary*, rev. 4th ed. (Minneapolis, 1968).

27. North Carolina Act of 1782, THS Miscellaneous Files, box 22-10; Tennessee Constitution, 1796, Article XI, §31; Tennessee Laws, 1798, 2nd General Assembly, 2nd session, Chapter XXIV. Most historians who study public lands and preemption tend to overlook the role that state legislation played in validating preemption claims. Payton Jackson Treat, *The National Land System, 1785–1820* (New York, 1940); Malcolm J. Rohrbough, *The Land Office Business: The Settlement and Administration of American Public Lands, 1789–1837* (New York, 1968), 1–49, 200–201.

28. John D. Cushing, comp., *The First Laws of the State of North Carolina* (Wilmington, 1984), Chapter VI, 1779; Chapter III, 1783; Chapter LII, 1783; Chapter XIV, 1784; Tennessee Constitution, Article XI, §31; Tennessee Laws, 1798, 2nd General Assembly, 2nd session, Chapter XXIV, §4; Cumberland Compact, May 1, 1780, in *Three Pioneer Documents: Donelson's Journal, Cumberland Compact, Minutes of Cumberland Court* (Nashville, 1964), 12.

29. Historians have generally treated the ethos of the squatters as a homestead ethic. Most scholars picture small claimants seeking sufficient land on which to establish an independent and autonomous household free from the burdens of landlords or creditors rather than to realize a financial benefit. Richard Maxwell Brown, "Back Country Rebellion and the Homestead Ethic in America, 1740–1799," in Richard Maxwell Brown and Don E. Fehrenbacher, eds., *Tradition, Conflict, and Modernization* (New York, 1977), 73–99; Taylor, *Liberty Men and Great Proprietors*, 6–7. One exception is

Stephen Aron, who explores the ways in which large and small speculators exploited Kentucky's preemption laws for economic gain. Aron, *How the West Was Lost*, 71–81.

30. David C. Hsiung, *Two Worlds in the Tennessee Mountains: Exploring the Origins of Appalachian Stereotypes* (Lexington, 1995), 110; Thomas Dillon to James McHenry, May 22, 1796 [typographical error shows date as 1776], in "Letters of Jefferson, etc.," *Virginia Magazine of History and Biography* 12 (January 1905): 259–64 (Cumberland prices); memorial, Legislative Petitions, 1809, [14-2-1809] (French Broad prices).

31. Treat, *The National Land System*, 389; Weaver, *The Great Land Rush*, 27–28, 79–81, 93–94, 112, 178–79, 264–65; Gascoigne, *The Enlightenment and the Origins of European Australia*, 36–37, 64–65, 70; Julie Evans et al., *Equal Subjects, Unequal Rights: Indigenous Peoples in British Settler Colonies, 1830–1910* (Manchester, 2003), 21–22 (Canada).

32. Grant, March 7, 1796, Rogers Papers, University of Tennessee Special Collection, MS-738, "1784–1824" folder; petition by A. Pinkly, Legislative Petitions, 1807, [22-1-1807] (quotation).

33. Petitions, Legislative Petitions, 1806, [14-1-1806] and 1807, [22-1-1807] (quotation).

34. Gump, "Washington County," 53–56; Abernathy, *From Frontier to Plantation*, 209; John W. Gray, ed., *The Life of Joseph Bishop* (Spartanburg, 1974), 24–164; Green County Court, February term 1788, Paul Fink Collection, McClung Library, Knoxville, Tennessee, CS11-3, box 1, "1788" folder; Agreement between Andrew Jackson and James Pearson and William Pit Bowers, February 19, 1796, *Papers*, I.

35. Jesús F. de la Teja, "Only Fit for Raising Stock," in Char Miller, ed., *Fluid Arguments: Five Centuries of Western Water Conflict* (Tucson, 2000), 6; E. P. Thompson, *Whigs and Hunters: The Origin of the Black Act* (New York, 1975); John Brewer and John Styles, eds., *An Ungovernable People: The English and Their Law in the Seventeenth and Eighteenth Centuries* (London, 1980); E. Estyn Evans, "Cultural Relics of the Ulster-Scots in the Old West of North America," *Ulster Folklife* 11 (1965): 33–37; Vermont Constitution of 1793, II, §40; Aron, *How the West Was Lost*, 102–23.

36. Notices, *Knoxville Gazette*, January 30, 1797, 3; *Tennessee Gazette*, August 8, 1804, 3; January 17, 1807, 1; Tennessee Laws, 3rd General Assembly, 1st session, 1799, Chapter LII; Tennessee Laws, 1807, 7th General Assembly, 1st session, Chapter LXXX; Tennessee Laws, 1797, 2nd General Assembly, 1st session, Chapter XLVI; Tennessee Laws, 1807, 7th General Assembly, 1st session, Chapter VIII; *Tennessee Gazette*, January 17, 1807, 1; Rules and Regulations, April 7, 1802, Records of the Board of Commissioners for Nashville; Rules and Regulations, February 12, 1802, §5, Knoxville City Council Minute Book, 1801–1834A, Knox County Archives; petition from Nashville, Legislative Petitions 1803, [47-1-1803].

37. Vattel, *The Law of Nations*, bk. I, chap. XXIII, §§266, 279–88.

38. Tennessee Laws, 1804, 5th General Assembly, 2nd session, Chapter XXII (public highways); Tennessee Laws, 1796, 1st General Assembly, 1st session, Chapter XXIII; *Knoxville Gazette*, July 17, 1794, 2; Tennessee Laws, 1801, 4th General Assembly, 1st session, Chapter LXX.

39. Letter from Zespedes, an inhabitant of Davidson County, to Benjamin Hawkins, 1787,

in D. C. Corbitt and Roberta Corbitt, trans. and eds., "Papers from the Spanish Archives, Relating to Tennessee and the Old Southwest, 1783–1800," *East Tennessee Historical Society's Publications* 13 (1941): 118–121 (quotation); Smith, "A Short Description of the Tennassee Government," in Daniel Smith and Willie Blount, *Tennessee Beginnings, combining A Short Description of the Tennessee Government [by Daniel Smith]—1793—and A Catechetical Exposition of the Constitution of the State of Tennessee, by Willie Blount, 1803* (Spartanburg, 1974), 22–26.

40. Petition of Tennessee County to James Robertson, February 1, 1792, in "Correspondence of Gen. James Robertson," *American Historical Magazine* 1 (July 1896): 284–85; Meigs to Benjamin Hawkins, February 25, 1810, M208, reel 5 (quotation).

41. Tennessee Laws, 1801, 4th General Assembly, 1st session, Chapter LXIX; David M. Neirs to Chimmoby Creek chiefs, March 23, 1809, M208; James McIntosh to Meigs, January 22, 1810, M208; Joseph McMinn to James Robertson, June 10, 1804, in "Correspondence of Gen. James Robertson," *American Historical Magazine* 5 (January 1900): 74.

42. Letter from Zespedes to Benjamin Hawkins, circa 1787, in "Papers from the Spanish Archives," 119–20; letter from gentleman at Falls of Ohio, December 4, 1786, *VSP*, 4:242–43.

43. Masterson, *William Blount*, 290; Tennessee Constitution, Article XI, §29.

44. Vattel, *Law of Nations*, bk. I, chap. XXII, §266; chap. XXIII, §§266, 279–88; report to the President by Jefferson, March 18, 1792, *ASP*, 2:253–54; James Innes to Isaac Shelby, July 3, 1795, *Knoxville Gazette*, June 19, 1795, 1, 4; July 3, 1795, 1, 4; *Carthage Gazette*, March 16, 1810, 2, 3.

45. Tennessee Laws, 1796, 1st General Assembly, 1st session, Chapter XXIII; 1799, Chapter XXXV; 1801, Chapter LXX; 1805, Chapter LVIII; 1807, Chapter XXXIII; 1807, Chapter LXXVI; 1809, Chapter XXI; petitions, Legislative Petitions, 1803, [22-1-1803] and [30-1-1803].

46. Daniel Smith to William Preston, March 22, 1774, Draper MSS, 3QQ15; John Salter to John Gray Blount, September 2, 1800, and William Blount to John Gray Blount, November 7, 1797 (quotation), in William H. Masterson, ed., *The John Gray Blount Papers* (Raleigh, 1965), 3:174–86; *Knoxville Gazette*, January 23, 1795, 1; Thomas Houghton's tax list of 1779, Washington County Trustee Tax Books, TSL, roll 639, 30; Washington County Clerk Minute Books, May 1783, pp. 215–16; *James Anderson v. Jacob Anderson*, Execution Docket, 1807–1813, White County Archives, Sparta, Tennessee, #34; *Carthage Gazette*, August 17, 1809.

47. Chapter 5 discusses the practice of hiring slaves out.

48. 1775 contract, Draper MSS, 6XX109; *Knoxville Gazette*, July 9, 1806, 2; receipt from W. Winston to Andrew Jackson, December 30, 1803, *Papers*, I; Hsiung, *Two Worlds in the Tennessee Mountains*, 88.

49. William Blount to Daniel Smith, May 13, 1795, in "Papers of Gen. Daniel Smith," *American Historical Magazine* 6 (July 1901): 229–30; William Carvin to John Coffee, July 10, 1801, Dyas Collection, John Coffee Papers, box 5, folder 9; petition of William

Calvert, August 9, 1804 and petition by William Nodding, November 8, 1804, to Court of Pleas and Quarter Sessions, Washington County Legal Documents, 1786–1804, University of Tennessee Special Collection, MS-152.

50. Session law, August 1794, Records of the States of the United States, TSL, Tennessee, B.2, reel 1, 1790–1809, chap. 1, §32; Richard Waterhouse to David Campbell, September 24, 1809, Penelope Allen Papers, Chattanooga/Hamilton County Library, Chattanooga, Tennessee, Acc. 268, box 10, folder 1; David Campbell to Richard Waterhouse, October 2, 1809, Penelope Allen Papers.

51. *George Gillespie v. Armstead Blevins and Dillon Blevins*, Washington County Court, Paul Fink Collection, box 1, "1794" folder; bill of sale for Joseph, March 8, 1809, Michael Campbell Papers, TSL, Mn. 82-74, loc. I-A-2; Mark Mitchell to Andrew Jackson, November 21, 1795, *Papers*, I; *Clarion*, October 26, 1810, 1.

52. Second Inaugural Address, September 22, 1797, White, *Messages of the Governors*, 24; James Priestly Diary, n.d., after 1789 entry, TSL, Diaries, THS Mn. 367, loc. THS I-E-2; Bethel Zion Presbyterian Church journal entry, 1809, quoted in speech by A. W. Putnam, TSL, THS Miscellaneous, Mf. 678 (first quotation); John Norton, *The Journal of Major John Norton*, ed. Carl F. Klinch and James J. Tallman (Toronto, 1816; repr., 1970), 28 (second quotation).

53. *Knoxville Gazette*, October 23, 1795, 1–2; *Tennessee Gazette*, October 7, 1801, 4; Caleb Perry Patterson, *The Negro in Tennessee, 1790–1865* (New York, 1922), 108–9, 180–85; Larry Anthony Wise Jr. "'A Sufficient Competence to Make Them Independent': Attitudes towards Authority, Improvement and Independence in the Carolina-Virginia Backcountry, 1760–1800" (Ph.D. diss., University of Tennessee, Knoxville, 1997), 111–12; Walter T. Durham, *Before Tennessee: The Southwest Territory, 1790–1796* (Piney Flats, 1990), 243. On New England opponents of slavery: William M. Wiecek, *The Sources of Antislavery Constitutionalism in America, 1760–1848* (Ithaca, 1977), 20–61.

54. *Tennessee Gazette*, October 28, 1801, 4, and "Fine Feelings of an African," August 4, 1802, 4; *Clarion*, May 31, 1808, 3; *Knoxville Gazette*, December 17, 1791, 2; McDowell to Campbell, June 22, 1791, Draper MSS, 9DD61; William Blount to John Gray Blount, November 7, 1797, Masterson, *John Gray Blount Papers*, 3: 174–86.

55. Williams, *Elder John Smith*, 14–15; *Knoxville Gazette*, January 23, 1797, 4; Patterson, *The Negro in Tennessee*, 80, 186; Memorial from Quarterly Meeting, Legislative Petitions, 1809, [3-1-1809]. Chapter 7 describes why white men rejected natural rights.

56. For examples: Session law, August 1794, Records of the States of the United States, Tennessee, B.2, reel 1, 1790–1809, chap. 1, §32; Journal of Legislative Council, July 7, 1795; Tennessee Laws, 1799, 3rd General Assembly, 1st session, Chapters IX and XXVIII; Tennessee Laws, 1806, 6th General Assembly, 2nd session, Chapter XXXII.

57. Knoxville Rules and Regulations, February 12, 1802, Article 2 and minutes, April 9, 1802, Knoxville City Council Minute Book, 1801–1834A; Nashville Rules and Regulations, Records of the Board of Commissioners, April 7, 1802, §4, and minutes of March 11, 1803, THS Miscellaneous Files; regulations of Nashville Board, June 7, 1805,

in Patterson, *The Negro in Tennessee*, 48; Tennessee Laws, 1809, 7th General Assembly, 2nd session, Chapter LII.

58. Patterson, *The Negro in Tennessee*, 153; Tennessee Laws, 1801, 4th General Assembly, 1st session, Chapter XXVII, November 13, 1801; Journal of the House, June 30, 1795; Journal of the Senate, September 28, 1801; Tennessee Laws, 1804, 5th General Assembly, 2nd session, Chapter XXIX; petition by William Calvert, August 9, 1804, and petition by William Nodding, November 8, 1804, to the Washington County Court of Pleas and Quarter Sessions, Washington County Legal Documents, 1786–1804; Anita S. Goodstein, "Black History on the Nashville Frontier, 1780–1810," *Tennessee Historical Quarterly* 38 (Winter 1979): 401–20, at 409.

59. William Blount to John Gray Blount, April 20, 1795, in Alice Barnwell Keith, ed., *John Gray Blount Papers* (Raleigh, 1959), 2:534–35; William Blount to John Gray Blount, November 7, 1797, in Masterson, *John Gray Blount Papers*, 3:174–81; Richard Green Waterhouse Diary, February 1798, p. 67, University of Tennessee Special Collection, MS-918.

60. Letter from A Subscriber, *Clarion*, July 19, 1808, supplement; *Clarion*, October 25, 1808, 3; letter to constituents by James White, July 30, 1817, , TSL, THS Miscellaneous, Mf. 1080, box 23, folder 22, pp. 2–3.

61. Miller, *Emigrants and Exiles*, 156–62; J. W. M. Breazeale, *Life as It Is or the World of Things in General* (Knoxville, 1812), 101 (quotation); *Carthage Gazette*, February 1809, 2 (quotation).

62. Stephen Becker, trans., *Diary of My Travels in America: Louis-Philippe, King of France, 1830–1848* (New York, 1976), 112, 116–17; *Tennessee Gazette*, May 20, 1801, 3 (toast); *Knoxville Gazette*, November 5, 1791, 2; E. P. Gaines to James Gaines, September 3, 1802, Howard-Smith Collection, McClung Library, CS 11–3, box 2; *Carthage Gazette*, February 1809, 3; *Tennessee Gazette*, November 9, 1810, 2.

63. Letter from Washington County, Virginia, December 15, 1784, Draper MSS, 7XX17–18 (Franklin); Return Meigs to William Eustis, October 15, 1810, M208 (quotation).

64. Tennessee Constitution, Article XI, §23; Journal of the House, October 16, 1809; *Carthage Gazette*, March 6, 1809, 2; May 11, 1809, 2.

65. "The Provisional Constitution of Frankland," *American Historical Magazine* 1:1 (January 1896): 48–63, at 52–53 (quotation); Wallace McClure, "The Development of the Tennessee Constitution," *Tennessee Historical Magazine* 1 (December 1915): 292–314; letter from James Harvy, *Clarion*, October 15, 1810, 2.

66. Many scholars accept creditor arguments that their version of the right to property defined property rights, and consequently they portray debtor revolts as threats to secure property rather than recognizing in them the promotion of an alternative version of property rights. Forrest McDonald, *Novus Ordo Seclorum: The Intellectual Origins of the Constitution* (Lawrence, 1985), 152–57, 173–77; Willi Paul Adams, *The First American Constitutions: Republican Ideology and the Making of the State Constitutions in the Revolutionary Era* (Chapel Hill, 1980), 189–217; Ely, *The Guardian of Every Other Right*.

67. *Carthage Gazette*, February 1809; *Clarion*, July 5, 1808, 2; letter from correspondent, February 21, 1809, 3; petition from Knox County, Legislative Petitions 1809, [8-1-1809].

68. Petitions from Greene County, Legislative Petitions 1801, [24-1-1801], [24-1-1801-2]; letter from "A Friend of the People," *Carthage Gazette*, February 6, 1809, 2–3; March 6, 1809, 2; petitions from inhabitants south of French Broad, Legislative Petitions, 1809, [23-1-1809], [32-2-1809]; Tennessee Laws, 1809, 7th General Assembly, 2nd session, Chapter II.

69. Protest by William Blount, November 28, 1785, *ASP*, 44; Petition, Legislative Petitions, 1809, [1-2-1809], [25-2-1809]; petition of John Bullard, Legislative Petitions, 1809, [15-1-1809]; petition, Legislative Petition, 1806, [13-1-1806]; petition, Legislative Petitions, 1809, [29-2-1809]; petition, Legislative Petitions, 1809, [14-1-1809], [34-1-1809], [10-2-1809]; petition, Legislative Petitions, 1809, [19-2-1809]; petition, Legislative Petitions, 1809, [17-1-1809].

70. Treat, *The National Land System, 1785–1820*, 347–52; Tennessee Laws, 1806, 6th General Assembly, 2nd session, Chapter I; 1807, 7th General Assembly, 1st session, Chapters I and II.

Conclusion

1. Talk by Onitositah, April 23, 1777, Draper MSS, 4QQ98.

2. "Journal of John Sevier," January 14, 1794, *Tennessee Historical Magazine* 5 (October 1919): 167.

121; and women, 27–30, 49, 85, 107–8, 117–18, 121–23. *See also* Chickamaugans; Commerce: and Cherokees; Diplomacy; Lower Towns; Upper Towns

Chesterfield, Lord, 183

Chickamauga Creek, 10, 29

Chickamaugans, 9–11, 29, 103, 106–7, 111–12; agreement with Upper Towns, 103–6; autonomy, 108–11; captives, 70–71; forfeiture of property to, 109–10; and international trade, 54, 108–11; and peace efforts, 54, 63–4; resistance, 53–55, 63, 108; and slaves, 53, 54, 70, 109; and women, 106–7. *See also* Commerce: and Cherokees; Diplomacy; Lower Towns

Chickasaws, 8, 11, 53, 96, 110, 250 (n. 43)

Chilhowie, 51

Chisholm, James, 119

Chisholm, John, 130, 160

Chisholm, Mrs., 192

Choctaws, 11

Choosing a master, 141–42

Chota, 26, 39, 40, 59, 103

Christian, William, 48, 54, 187

Christianity, 18, 78, 102, 190, 212; and African Americans, 127, 129, 132, 134, 136–38, 149, 151; and civilization of Native Americans, 45, 69, 94, 112; support for slavery, 224; and white women, 166, 172. *See also* Churches

Chulcoah, 57–58, 105, 109, 117

Chuquilatague, 64, 82, 84, 106, 117–19, 121–23

Churches: of African Americans, 125, 129–38, 149–51; of Euro-Americans, 163, 169–72, 177, 201, 210, 223. *See also* Christianity

Citico, 35

Civic humanism, 181, 190, 207

Civilization: and economy, 207, 210; as restriction on rights, 202–4; and slav-ery, 222–23; and sociability, 157–59; as source of rights, 197–98; stages of, 157–58, 207; women's view of, 166. *See also* Diplomacy

Civils, Jack, 114

Claiborne, William, 2, 176, 196

Clans. *See* Cherokees: clans

Clarion (newspaper), 164, 224

Clarksville, 137

Cleveland, Benjamin, 161

Cleveland, Mrs., 161

Clinch Mountain, 77

Clinch River, 91, 211

Cloth manufacture: of Cherokees, 85, 108, 121, 123, 161; of white women and slaves, 208, 209

Cocke, William, 68, 190

Coercion. *See* Diplomacy—Cherokee: coercion of

Colby, Major, 48

Cold Water, 110, 176

Colonialism, 3, 4, 6–9, 14

Combs, Philip, 67

Commerce: and African Americans, 131–32, 152; and Cherokees, 35, 43, 49, 54, 110–11, 121–22; and Euro-Americans, 69, 157–58, 206–10, 218–22. *See also* Economy; Traders

Communis error facit jus, 214

Congress, 176, 184–85, 190; and Cherokee affairs, 10, 39–40, 46, 49, 55–57, 64–65, 68, 87, 91–95, 198

Conjurer, 25, 112

Consent: Cherokees, 104, 117. *See also* Euro-Americans: and consent

Constitution. *See* Tennessee Constitution; United States Constitution

Coosowothee, 56

Corn: and African Americans, 134, 136, 143; and Cherokees, 25, 107–9, 121; and Euro-Americans, 72, 159

Corn rights, 212

Natural rights. *See* Government: and natural rights doctrines
Nelly (free black), 141, 144
Nentooyah, 55–57, 63, 105, 106, 117
Neo-European settler colonies, 6, 45, 79
The Nephew, 111, 117
New Orleans, La., 10, 47, 110, 122, 150, 219
Newota, 55, 105
Newspapers, 72, 89, 93, 156, 158, 164, 167, 193, 194, 226. See also *Carthage Gazette*; *Clarion*; *Knoxville Gazette*; *Tennessee Gazette*
New Zealand, 8, 9, 65, 96, 98
Nickajack, 55, 64, 66–68, 111, 114
Nodding, William, 135
Nolichucky River, 219
North Carolina, 9–10, 25–65, 83–96, 109, 126–51, 159–69, 176, 183–216, 225, 229
Northern Indians, 31–32, 46, 53, 80, 102, 117–18, 248 (n. 27)

Oconostota, 23, 28–29, 34, 39, 57, 106
Ocunna, 56
Old Tassel. *See* Onitositah
Onitositah, 23, 106, 231; death, 51; dream, 231; and peace conferences, 29, 32, 35, 38–41, 45, 54, 62, 79; views, 45, 60, 83, 104
Ookoousdi, 55, 105
Oostope'the, 60
Ore, James, 66–67, 92
Osborn, Charles, 223
Oskuah, 40, 51, 57
Ostenaco, 106
Outlaw, Alexander, 47
Overhill Cherokees, 8–10, 25, 30, 36, 46
Overton, John, 90, 134–35, 170

Paine, Thomas, 183
Palmyra, 225
Parker, Mrs., 170
Passions. *See* Euro-Americans: and passions

Paternalism: toward African Americans, 126–29, 133–35, 222; toward Cherokees, 89, 97
Patriarchy: in relation to African Americans, 126–29, 133; in relation to Cherokees, 32, 73, 112; in relation to Euro-Americans, 156–59, 216
Patronage, 125–54 passim, 220–22
Peace conferences: 1788–89 talks, 39, 55–56. *See also* Diplomacy—Cherokee: peace chiefs; Treaties
Pearce, Isaac, 145
Pensacola, Fla., 110, 122
Phagan, John, 227
Philadelphia, Pa., 57, 58, 63, 66, 67, 80, 115, 190, 208
Phillips, Judith, 155, 169, 170
Pick, Adam, 177
Pickering, Timothy, 64
Pinckney Treaty, 11
Pity, 34, 40, 85–86
Polk, James, 2
Poll (slave), 150
Population statistics: for Cherokees, 11, 30, 113; for free blacks, 148–49, 152; for slaves, 130, 132; for Tennesseans, 93, 164
Postcolonialism, 6, 8, 52, 90, 101–3, 126
Powell Valley, 91, 129
Powers, John, 150
Preemption, 67; and land rights, 192, 199, 212–15, 229
Preemption Act of 1841, 215
Presbyterians, 132, 137, 151, 157, 171, 223
Price, Thomas, 36
Priestley, James, 222
Prince, Caesar, 132, 145, 147
Private property, 43, 206–7, 210–11, 229–30
Proclamation of 1763, 3, 9, 27, 42
Proclamation of 1783, 49
Proclamation of 1788, 55